From Fireplace to Cookstove

From Fireplace to Cookstove

TECHNOLOGY AND THE DOMESTIC IDEAL IN AMERICA

PRISCILLA J. BREWER

Syracuse University Press

Library of Congress Cataloging-in-Publication Data

Brewer, Priscilla J.
    From firepalce to cookstove : technology and the domestic ideal in America /
    Priscilla J. Brewer. — 1st ed.
        p.   cm.
    Includes bibliographical references and index.
    ISBN 0-8156-0650-8 (alk. paper)
        1. Stoves—Social aspects—United States. 2. Stoves—United States—History.
I. Title

GT425.U5 B74 2000
392.3'7—dc21

                                                        00-029705

to Ruth and Jack
with thanks,
and in loving memory of Grove

Priscilla J. Brewer is associate professor of American studies at the University of South Florida. She is the author of *Shaker Communities, Shaker Lives* and has published frequently on popular and material culture in journals such as *Journal of American Culture, Signs,* and *Winterthur Portfolio.*

Contents

Illustrations

Illustrations

Illustrations

Preface

WHY STUDY THE COOKSTOVE? Because it is one of the most significant yet least understood artifacts in American history. Although the story of industrialization in American manufacturing and transportation is familiar, the impact of technological change on the home has received far less attention from scholars.[1] Yet if we are to understand the everyday life of the past, it is important to comprehend the process of adjustment to new technologies, particularly those technologies that became so integral a part of Americans' lives that they have been overlooked. This book examines one of these transformations—the shift from the fireplace to the wood- or coal-burning cookstove.

In 1948, Siegfried Giedion pointed out that in the nineteenth century "the cast-iron stove and range were identified with America much as the automobile was later."[2] Ruth Schwartz Cowan suggested more recently that as the "first mass-produced appliance intended for use in people's homes,"[3] "the cast-iron cooking stove could well serve as the single most important domestic symbol of the nineteenth century."[4] Mary Stranahan Pattison, an early-twentieth-century champion of "domestic engineering," would have agreed, for she asserted in 1915 that the kitchen stove, as "the pivot around which a people . . . live," was "an instrument of international importance[,] the one having the greatest influence over . . . family health and . . . peace."[5]

If Giedion, Cowan, and Pattison are right, then why has the cookstove received so little attention?[6] Largely because historians have traditionally considered public events, typically involving men, more important than those within the household, centering around women. Divisions between scholarly fields and disciplines have also played a role in reducing the significance of the cookstove. Historians of technology have only recently become interested in women's history; the reverse has also been true. Moreover, the interpretation of artifacts has been more the province of anthropologists than historians.

But much of the answer lies in the stove itself. Unlike locomotives, steam engines, and power looms, eighteenth- and nineteenth-century stoves are unfamiliar and rarely seen, even in museums. This absence isn't surprising. Stoves did much of the dirty work of American households; they wore out (sometimes distressingly quickly) and were discarded. Perhaps if stoves had been associated with fun—if they could have been raced or used for family vacations, like the automobiles to which Giedion compared them—"classic" models such as the James saddlebags and the Stanley rotary would be as well known as the Model T and the Corvette. But, despite manufacturers' efforts to the contrary, cookstoves were far from glamorous. They were also so much a part of everyday life that few Americans took the time to record their interactions with them.

As a result, examining the shift from fireplace to cookstove has proven challenging. Cowan has argued that an explanation of the dispersion of stoves in America "requires attention not just to the history of the artifact itself but also to economic history (the price of fuels), demographic history (growth of cities, westward expansion), and industrial history (alterations in iron production)."[7] I would add that the story cannot be told without equal attention to family and women's history (especially the ideology of domesticity), social history (the impact of immigration and changes in the household labor market), and popular culture. Thus, the sources for this study are varied; they include patent records, manufacturers' and dealers' sales records and advertisements, probate inventories, census schedules, diaries, private correspondence, personal reminiscences, popular art and fiction, architecture guides, domestic advice literature, and cookbooks. All quotations from these materials appear with their original spelling and punctuation.

My goal is to explore the changing meaning of the cookstove as a cultural symbol. This book also examines household heating systems because the tasks and tools of cooking and heating were necessarily linked before the widespread adoption of central heating. Moreover, the cookstove must be compared to the kitchen fireplace that preceded it, as well as to the gas, oil, and electric stoves that replaced it. My regional focus is the northern states because stove manufacturing and dispersion began there.

Attitudes toward the cookstove have changed dramatically over time. In the early national period, Americans accustomed to the drafty and inefficient fireplace hailed it as a marvel of convenience and fuel economy—tangible proof of the ability of inventors and manufacturers to improve the quality of life. In the middle of the nineteenth century, however, social critics such as Harriet Beecher Stowe and Nathaniel Hawthorne suggested that the stove had contributed to the breakdown of the family, and they pleaded for a return to the fireplace. Mistresses and servants struggled over the control of cookstoves, as did husbands and wives. Reformers who campaigned to remove housework from the home regarded the cookstove as a symbol of women's enslavement, but women who had learned to master the frequently balky appliance often viewed it as an emblem of their domestic skill.

In the early twentieth century, the cookstove assumed a new role as the embodiment of tradition at the time that it was being superseded by gas, oil, and electric models. This reconstruction flowered again beginning in the 1970s, when a fuel crisis and concern for the environment reawakened interest in wood stoves. Then, in the late 1990s as the Y2K situation loomed, the cookstove ironically became a bulwark against dependence on technological networks. These reinterpretations of the cookstove have been rooted in important debates about the role of women, the meaning of home, the impact of industrialization, the definition of social class, and the development of a consumer economy. The cookstove has always been about more than cooking.

Priscilla J. Brewer
Tampa, Florida
January 2000

Acknowledgments

I DEDICATE THIS BOOK to fellow University of South Florida (USF) faculty members Ruth Banes and Jack Moore, colleagues whom I am also fortunate to have as friends. I know they won't mind sharing the page with Grove, who was there at the beginning.

My parents were also there from the start. They helped prune an unwieldy early version of the manuscript and provided assistance with translations of materials in French. Their emotional (and financial!) support has been crucial throughout the many years it has taken to bring this project to completion.

This book began life as a doctoral dissertation. Pat Malone, my thesis director, as well as Mari Jo Buhle and Rich Meckel, my readers, provided a judicious blend of guidance and freedom to help me navigate that stage of the project. I also received invaluable moral support from many other people at Brown University, especially Rheta Martin, Carter Jones Meyer, and Sandy Norman.

My understanding of what it was like for women to adjust to the cookstove has been considerably enhanced by Cheryl Anderson, Marcia Byrom Hartwell, Kim Norman, and Sandy Norman, who taught me much about the intricacies of open-hearth and brick-oven cooking. I am also very grateful to Frank G. White and J. Ritchie Garrison for sharing with me aspects of their own research on stoves. Jack Larkin of Old Sturbridge Village read the revised manuscript thoughtfully and carefully. This book owes a great deal to his comments and suggestions.

Robert Alexander, Ruth Banes, David Bealmear, Dan Belgrad, Hallie Bond, Amy Bowers, Barbara Chomko, Ann Jerome Croce, Paul Jerome Croce, Cathy Davidson, Jim D'Emilio, Larry Gross, Duncan Hay, Margaret Hindle Hazen, Robert M. Hazen, Patricia Hills, Karen Lamoree, Paula Lee, Jack Moore, Sandy Norman, Jane Nylander, Sheila Tagliarini, June Sprigg Tooley, and David Williams generously provided research leads, helped locate and obtain illustrations, responded to questions, read portions of the manuscript, or gave me house room on research trips. Holly Simpson Walker, who worked as my graduate research assis-

Acknowledgments

tant for one semester, turned up a great deal of material I might otherwise have
overlooked. Paul Camp, of USF's Special Collections, kindly took a number of
photographs for me.

I am grateful to the staffs of the following libraries and archives for their
assistance during my research: American Antiquarian Society, Worcester, Mass.;
Barnstable County Courthouse, Barnstable, Mass.; City Archives, Providence, R.I.;
Historic Deerfield Library, Deerfield, Mass.; National Museum of American History, Washington, D.C.; New York Historical Society, New York, N.Y.; and Old
Sturbridge Village, Sturbridge, Mass. I would also like to thank the interlibrary
loan staff at the Rockefeller Library at Brown University and the Tampa campus
library at the University of South Florida.

Permission to quote from manuscripts in their custody has kindly been granted
by the following institutions and individuals: American Antiquarian Society,
Worcester, Mass.; Baker Library, Harvard Business School, Boston, Mass.; Harriet
Beecher Stowe Center, Hartford, Conn.; Historic Deerfield Library, Deerfield,
Mass.; New York Historical Society, New York, N.Y.; Museum of American Textile
History, Lowell, Mass.; Western Reserve Historical Society, Cleveland, Ohio; and
Mrs. Nina Taylor, Cranberry Lake, N.Y..

Permission to reproduce images of items in their collections has kindly been
granted by the following institutions and individuals: Albany Institute of History
and Art, Albany, N.Y.; American Antiquarian Society, Worcester, Mass.; American
Philosophical Society, Philadelphia, Penn.; Ashmolean Museum, Oxford, England; Bredius Museum, The Hague, Netherlands; Donald Carpentier, Eastfield
Village, E. Nassau, N.Y.; Chicago Historical Society, Chicago, Ill. Howard Godel,
Godel & Co., New York, N.Y.; Robert Hazen and Margaret Hindle Hazen, Wash-
ington, D.C.; Henry Ford Museum and Greenfield Village, Dearborn, Mich.; His-
toric Hudson Valley, Tarrytown, N.Y.; Historical Society of York County, York,
Penn.; Kitchens by Design, Bangor, Maine; Memorial Hall Museum, Deerfield,
Mass.; Mercer Museum, Bucks County Historical Society, Doylestown, Penn.;
Musèe Condè, Chantilly, France; Museum of Fine Arts, Boston, Mass.; National
Gallery of Art, London, England; National Gallery of Art, Washington, D.C.;
New York Historical Society, New York, N.Y.; New York Public Library, New
York, N.Y.; Ohio Historical Society, Columbus, Ohio; Old Dartmouth Historical
Society, New Bedford, Mass.; Old Sturbridge Village, Sturbridge, Mass.; Parrish
Art Museum, Southampton, N.Y.; Rensselaer County Historical Society, Troy,
N.Y.; Rhode Island Historical Society, Providence, R.I.; Society for the Preserva-
tion of New England Antiquities, Boston, Mass.; Spruance Library, Bucks County
Historical Society, Doylestown, Penn.; Staatliche Kunstsammlungen, Dresden,
Germany; Storey Publications, Pownal, Vt.; Toledo Museum of Art, Toledo, Ohio;

and the Winterthur Museum, Winterthur, Del. I would particularly like to thank Georgia Barnhill of the American Antiquarian Society and Scott DeHaven of the American Philosophical Society for their efforts in helping me track down elusive illustrations.

I was fortunate to receive timely financial support for this project from the American Antiquarian Society, the Woodrow Wilson National Fellowship Foundation, and the University of South Florida Division of Sponsored Research. Publication costs were underwritten by a grant from the University of South Florida Publications Council.

I am grateful, too, for the patience, professionalism, and editorial skill of the staff at Syracuse University Press. Without them, this book would not be.

From Fireplace to Cookstove

1

"Good Living for Those That Love Good Fires"

THE AMERICAN PREDILECTION for conspicuous consumption may well have begun with firewood. In the seventeenth century, most Englishmen and women came to the "new world" hoping to improve their standard of living, drawn by abundant natural resources that promised both profit and a level of comfort rare in Europe. The typical household in colonial New England consumed up to forty cords of wood annually, an amount unimaginable in timber-starved England.[1] Thus, the domestic hearth symbolized both the opportunity to build a better life and the hard work necessary to realize that dream.

Fire also exemplified life's unpredictability. It could escape at any time, destroying property and lives, yet the colonists could not survive long American winters without it. Fire was a weapon, too, utilized by both Native Americans and Europeans, and its devastation was typically interpreted by English victims as divine judgment. To devout Puritans especially, "fire . . . connoted future punishment for earthly sin and confirmed folk beliefs in subterranean explosions, demons, and exhalations."[2] Thus, the fires that destroyed their towns, those that forged their tools, and even those on their own hearths prefigured the hellfire that seventeenth-century Anglo-Americans dreaded and reminded them that they did not control their own destinies.

During the early eighteenth century, however, these fears diminished, altering attitudes toward fire. Many colonists came to believe that they could, if not save their own souls, at least prepare themselves for the work of God's grace. New ideas about individual rights percolated through society and were reflected in a more individualistic material culture.[3] Anglo-Americans became especially interested in temporal comfort, including that provided by the domestic fireplace. They were, however, slow to seek improvements in cooking techniques and equipment.

Of course, at the beginning of English settlement, no one could know what lay ahead, but most settlers hoped that America's abundance would assure them a better life. Wood and its by-products, in chronically short supply in the mother country, attracted a great deal of attention. England was becoming a world power, and new, secure sources of forest products were crucial. Richard Hakluyt, an early colonization advocate, assured Queen Elizabeth I in 1584 that America would provide "plentie of excellent trees for mastes, of goodly timber to . . . make good navies."[4] Thirty-nine years later, King James I announced delightedly, "We shall be able to furnish ourselves out of our own territories with many of those commodities that now we are beholding to our neighbors for." Pitch, masts, and "other timber of all sorts" were high on his list.[5]

America's vast forests enticed the English because they had been experiencing a steadily worsening timber shortage for centuries.[6] As a result, the price of firewood had doubled between 1540 and 1570, and had tripled again by the 1630s.[7] In 1623, village leaders in Sudbury complained that the wood-hungry local brewing industry had driven the price of firewood so high that the "poorer sort" could not afford to heat their homes in winter. Increasing numbers of them were driven to steal wood from "the common hedges, or fences, or gates, or stiles" or to "cut wood . . . growing on other men's ground, without lawful leave," acts that typically landed them in the local house of correction.[8] In this context, it is easy to understand the appeal of a place where wood was free to all in return for the labor necessary to prepare it for use.

Even so, the English were overwhelmed by the luxuriance of the American environment. John Brereton, who spent part of the summer of 1602 on Martha's Vineyard, reported a land "full of high timbered oaks . . . cedars straight and tall, beech, elm, holly, [and] walnut trees in abundance."[9] Later in the seventeenth century, John Holme exulted, "Here's store of timber trees of the best sort, / Both for our use and also to transport; / Cedar, Beech, Maple, and Black Walnut fine / The Ash, Oak, Hickory, and sweet scented Pine; / With such abundance a more, both great and small, / That scarcely any man can name them all."[10]

Such reports did much to encourage English migration. While sailing off Cape Ann, Massachusetts, in 1629, Francis Higginson saw "hill and dale and every island full of gay woods and high trees." "For wood," he decided, "there is no better in the world." The sight made him eager to begin life in the "paradise of New England." Higginson had heard that in winter "the earth is commonly covered with snow, which is accompanied with sharp biting frosts, something more sharp than is in old England," but he was not worried. "We have plenty of fire to warm us," he noted, "a great deal cheaper than . . . in London." "All Europe is not able to afford . . . so great fires as New-England," he boasted. "A poor servant here . . . may . . . give more wood for . . . fire . . . than many noblemen in England." Surely, he concluded, "here is good living for those that love good fires."[11] Higginson had stumbled onto something that has become an enduring part of the American dream—the expectation that the average American would live more comfortably than the average person anywhere else in the world.

As it turned out, dream and reality did not wholly coincide. The English had erroneously assumed that New England, at the same latitude as southern France, would have a similar climate.[12] One disillusioned Massachusetts settler complained in the 1630s that "the air of the country is sharp, the rocks many, the trees innumerable, the grass little, the winter cold, the summer hot, the gnats in summer biting, [and] the wolves at midnight howling."[13] In particular, the length and harshness of New England winters proved a surprise. John Winthrop remarked tersely in 1634 that "our winters are sharp and long."[14] During the winter of 1641–42, parts of Massachusetts Bay actually froze "so as horses and carts went over."[15]

Some settlers and investors began to wonder if a profitable colony could be established in such a place. Could familiar English crops be grown successfully? Would cattle require expensive shelter and feed during the coldest months? William Wood, author of an early promotional tract, tried to convince readers that New England winters did not pose an insuperable problem. "It may be objected that it is too cold a Countrey for our English men, who have been accustomed to a warmer Climate," he acknowledged, but he claimed that America's "peircing cold" was actually healthier than the "raw winters of England." He also pointed out that "there is Wood good store . . . to build warm houses, and make good fires."[16]

Staying warm in winter was not the only reason to fell trees. The "new world's" alien forests made colonists nervous because they provided hiding places for potential enemies. In 1662, Michael Wigglesworth called America's native inhabitants "hellish fiends" who haunted the mysterious "dark and dismal western woods / (The Devil's den)."[17] Mather Byles echoed this view, complaining that "savage Nations howl'd in ev'ry wood."[18] What better reason could there be for clearing woodland? David Cressy has observed that the ex post facto designation of precontact New England as a "howling wilderness" was merely a "Puritan conceit" intended to magnify the accomplishment of taming it,[19] but the idea certainly proved convenient.

The colonists' perplexity over Native American land use reinforced their determination to impose a European order on the landscape. How, they wondered, could a people who did not enclose their territory be considered "civilized"? After all, as Karen Ordahl Kupperman has noted, "early modern English people believed that human beings are responsible for the environment, and that this responsibility entails taking an active role in perfecting and shaping it. Raw, unfinished nature was not beautiful."[20] Realizing the "new world's" potential and obeying the biblical imperative to "replenish and subdue" the earth required that America be "improved," which would entail, among other things, the felling of innumerable trees.

One of the first tasks was to prepare land for cultivation. Once the clearings acquired from Native Americans were utilized, a way had to be found to plant crops elsewhere. Clear-cutting timber was both time-consuming and unnecessary. The English quickly learned, as John Smith explained in 1631, how to "spoile the woods": "cut a notch in the barke a hand broade round about the tree, which pull off and the tree will sprout no more."[21] Later, dying trees were cut down for fencing or fuel and, eventually, the fields were cleared of stumps. Solid timber-framed houses replaced earlier temporary shelters. Even the climate appeared to be moderating, as the harsh weather of the early seventeenth century was succeeded by more temperate conditions.[22]

The climate was about to change, however. In the 1680s and 1690s, New England experienced a return of the Little Ice Age that periodically gripped much of the northern hemisphere between 1550 and 1700.[23] The winter of 1680–81 was the coldest in forty years. Four years later, Boston harbor froze solid.[24] The weather was so severe that it interfered with the private devotions of the elect. In February 1697, Cotton Mather noted in his diary that even in a "Warm Room, on a great Fire, the Juices forced out . . . of short Billets of Wood . . . froze." "It was impossible," he concluded, "to serve the Lord, without such Distraction, as was inconvenient."[25]

This climatic shift was especially disturbing because it closely followed a series of natural disasters, including a 1676 fire in Boston that destroyed some fifty homes. The sense of crisis was heightened by Metacom's War in 1675–76, during which fifty-two New England settlements were attacked and twelve destroyed.[26] The return of bitter winter weather was seen as one more divine judgment to punish New Englanders for their failure to live up to their ancestors' spiritual standards. Winter was no longer a challenge easily mastered by thrifty, hardy folk, but had become, instead, a serious drain on physical and moral resources.

In this atmosphere, New Englanders exhibited a growing preoccupation with fire's destructive potential. Everyone knew, of course, about the eternal flames of hell, vividly portrayed in numerous works of medieval European art and literature. An early-fifteenth-century book of hours, for example, depicts hell as an infernal forge fanned by enormous bellows operated by eager assistants.[27] The devil lies on a gridiron, and mountains in the background serve as boilers for those of the damned who are not to be grilled—both symbolic references to the kitchen fireplace.

Seventeenth-century Americans were heirs of this tradition. Thomas Shepard, a prominent Massachusetts minister, made an explicit connection between domestic and demonic fire, reminding members of his flock that they could not "endure the torments of a little kitchen fire on the tip of thy finger." "How," he asked, "wilt thou bear the fury of this infinite, endless, consuming fire . . . throughout all eternity?"[28] In the early eighteenth century, Jonathan Edwards invoked a similar image, telling listeners that a horrible perpetual punishment awaited those of "God's visible people . . . who lived under the means of grace" but ignored the need for salvation. "The wrath of God burns against them," he railed. "Their damnation does not slumber; the pit is prepared, . . . the flames do now rage and glow."[29]

A humble hearth fire could also cause extensive damage and send a pointed message to a backsliding Christian. In 1631, when two houses in Boston burned to the ground, Deputy Governor Thomas Dudley concluded that God had intended "to exercise us with corrections."[30] But there was also a pedestrian cause of such destruction. House fires were common in the early years of settlement when wattle-and-daub chimneys and thatched roofs were the norm. After the 1631 fires, these construction techniques were outlawed, an order that "was readily assented unto, for that divers other houses have been burned since our arrival, (the fire always beginning in the wooden chimneys)."[31]

Injuries from domestic fires were also a daily concern. Toddlers learning to walk in homes heated by unprotected hearths were especially at risk. In 1699, Cotton Mather's daughter Hannah fell into her father's study fire and was badly burned. Although she recovered, Mather, in true Puritan fashion, interpreted the accident as a judgment from God for his own sin, noting in his diary, "The Friday following, I sett apart for the Exercises of a secret Fast . . . under this rebuke of Heaven." His meditations gave him a clear understanding of God's intent. "The Fire that hath wounded the Child," he concluded, "hath added a strong Fire & Force to the zeal of my Prayer."[32]

Mather's simultaneously positive and negative reaction to this tragedy was common in his day. Expressing similar ambivalence about fire, poet Anne Bradstreet acknowledged its usefulness in cooking food, warming "shrinking limbs" in winter, and shaping tools from iron, but she worried about its unpredictability. She called fire a "most impatient element" and knew that it could turn against those who tried to master it. Fire could quickly change "stately seats of mighty kings" into "confus'd heaps of ashes," and the final conflagration was yet to come. "The rich I oft make poore," Bradstreet's personified Fire boasted, "the strong I maime, / Not sparing life when I can take the same; / And in a word, the World I shall consume, / And all therein at that great day of doome."[33]

This emphasis on the negative aspects of fire moderated after the turn of the century as new scientific and philosophical ideas encouraged a more optimistic, individualistic view of the world. John Locke had explained in 1689 that "all men are naturally in . . . a state of perfect freedom to order their actions and dispose of their possessions and persons as they think fit, within the bounds of the law of nature, without asking leave . . . of any other man."[34] As Lawrence Stone has observed, this revolutionary concept inspired "growing confidence in man's capacity to master the environment and turn it to his use and benefit," producing a "reorientation towards the pursuit of pleasure in this world rather than postponement of gratification until the next."[35] In the domestic sphere, comfort rather than survival became the goal.[36] As a result, the focus on fire as divine retribution dwindled and a more earthy, cheerful characterization of it emerged.

Early-eighteenth-century Americans remembered the hopeful attitude of those who had promoted colonization and chose to "love" rather than fear "good fires." They modified fire's symbolic meaning to emphasize its positive features, drawing on a countervailing medieval tradition. Gruesome renditions of the fires of hell were common in fifteenth- and sixteenth-century art and literature, but so were portrayals of biblical figures clustered intimately around glowing hearths.[37] According to Carra Ferguson O'Meara, the domestic fireplace and its accessories were often used in religious art to remind believers of the good news of Christianity, conveying "a theological and liturgical message concerning the nature of Christ's sacrifice on the Cross and the daily reenactment of this sacrifice in the Eucharist."[38]

Medieval artists also understood that everyday folk enjoyed fires. In the early-fifteenth-century painting *February* (illus. 1.1), the Limbourg brothers captured both the hardship of working outdoors to care for livestock and gather firewood, and the welcome refuge of the domestic hearth. The lady of the house decorously lifts her skirt to warm her legs, while a man and woman, possibly servants, expose themselves to the fire less modestly. Although barely visible, the fireplace dominates the scene. It is easy to imagine how grateful the man making his way toward the house, huddled under a cloak and surrounded by his own frozen breath, will be to enter and warm himself.

Though fearful of fire, Anglo-Americans were also heirs of this more optimistic tradition. Even in the late seventeenth century, when they had emphasized fire's destructive power, they had also celebrated the domestic fireplace. Anne Bradstreet, for example, knew that the remedies for winter were "warm cloaths, ful diet, and good fires."[39] As Daniel Russell pointed out in his 1671

1.1. Pol, Jean, and Herman de Limbourg, *February, Très Riches Heures du duc de Berry,* c. 1413–16. Courtesy of Musée Condé, Chantilly, France; photograph courtesy of Photographie Giraudon, Paris.

description of November, a hearth fire could be a cozy refuge: "Exit Autumnus: Winter now draws neare, / Armed with Frost i' th' Van, with Snow i' th' Rere; / Whose freezing Forces cause men to retire, / For help to th' Fortress of a well-made Fire."[40]

After 1700, Americans increasingly focused on the positive aspects of fire. In 1701, for example, Cotton Mather wrote *Christianus Per Ignem*, "Meditations fetch'd out of the Fire, by a Christian in a Cold Season, sitting before it."[41] Mather's friend Nicholas Noyes responded with a poem in which the domestic fire and its accouterments became symbols of piety: "The Brass, the Iron Doggs and Tongs, / And Bellows that have leather Lungs / Fire, Wood, Brands, Ashes, Coals, and Smoke, / Do all to Godliness provoke!"[42] Edward Taylor, a minister in Westfield, Massachusetts, also saw lessons in homely fire scenes. In reflecting on the meaning of Galatians 3:16, he decided: "Thy Altars Fire burns not to ashes down / This Offering. But it doth roast it here. / This is thy Roast meate cooked up sweet, brown, / Upon thy table set for Souls good cheer."[43]

Taylor's metaphor suggests that he spent substantial time in the kitchen; heated retreats for study were rare in his day. Surviving winters in homes heated by few fireplaces created occasionally inconvenient intimacy. One cold day in March 1631, Thomas Dudley sat down to write the Countess of Lincoln. He apologized for the letter's "rude" appearance, explaining that he had no place to work other "than by the fireside . . . to which my family must have . . . resort, though they break good manners and make me sometimes forget what I would say, and say what I would not."[44]

Dudley's letter and Taylor's "meditation" provide valuable hints about the day-to-day experience of living with fire, but other literary sources are largely silent on the subject. To understand how Anglo-Americans in the northern colonies used fire in the seventeenth and early eighteenth centuries, it is necessary to look elsewhere—into their homes. The most notable exterior feature of New England houses in this period was a massive chimney, which after 1640 was typically built of brick. Chimneys had become common in England only during the second half of the sixteenth century,[45] so it is not surprising that design was crude. Fireplaces were huge—up to three and a half feet deep, five feet high, and ten feet wide. Because of their large size, straight rear walls, unsplayed sides, and lack of dampers, they were also extremely inefficient, creating an insatiable demand for firewood.[46]

As a result, houses were small, cold, and uncomfortable, at least by modern standards. The average household had five to seven members,[47] but homes typically contained few rooms, most unheated. The 102 Essex, Middlesex, and Suffolk County, Massachusetts, households inventoried room by room between

1636 and 1661, for example, averaged 4.2 "living" rooms,[48] but only twenty-three had two fireplaces, and just eight had three or more. Not surprisingly, there was a close correlation between income and extra warmth; all of the families whose homes had three or more fireplaces were substantially wealthier than their neighbors.[49] In the countryside, multiple fireplaces were even more rare; only five of the fifty-two room-by-room inventories recorded in rural Suffolk County, Massachusetts, between 1674 and 1725 list fireplace tools in two or more rooms.[50]

Although cumulative statistics provide valuable insight into the use of fire in early Anglo-American homes, individual inventories make it possible to examine the phenomenon in more detail. The inventories of three late-seventeenth-century households in Roxbury, Massachusetts, just outside Boston, suggest the range of experience common in the period.

When Benjamin Childe died in 1678, he left property valued at £506.19.0, near the median for rural Suffolk County in the last quarter of the century.[51] His house had three rooms, only one of which had a fireplace. Childe and his wife likely slept downstairs in the unheated "parlor," protected from cold only by their curtained bedstead. Other members of the household were even less fortunate; they slept upstairs on "beds" (mattresses) placed directly on the floor. Not surprisingly, daily life in this household centered around the only heated room — the "kitchin," a space that served many purposes. It contained an "old table," doubtless used for both work and dining, as well as two chairs. The "woolen wheel" suggests the time devoted to spinning yarn, the churn indicates butter manufacture, and the "powdering tub" hints at pickling meat.

The chief activity in the Childe kitchen, however, was the preparation of everyday food. Cooking was simple in the seventeenth century, as a list of supplies recommended for early settlers attests. In the 1630s, John Josselyn suggested that a family planning migration to New England take one "great copper kettle," two smaller kettles, an iron pot, two frying pans, two skillets, a gridiron, and a spit.[52] More than forty years later, Mrs. Childe made do with fewer implements and probably prepared most meals in a single pot. Stews and pottages were easy to assemble and tend, and they minimized clean-up.[53] Family members also enjoyed roasts from time to time (the inventory includes an "old Spit"), and some of their food was fried, as the "old frying pan" suggests. Baking was the other common method of food preparation. Some seventeenth-century kitchen fireplaces had domed ovens built into the rear wall, but Mrs. Childe apparently did without, baking instead in a covered iron pot set on the hearth and surrounded with coals.[54] The Childes' kitchen was also outfitted with two sets of trammels, ratcheted devices used to suspend pots at various heights over the fire, thus making it possible to control cooking temperature.

Whereas the Childe inventory documents a "middle-class" standard of living, the inventory of Lieutenant Philip Curtice's property illustrates the lifestyle of a family nearer the bottom of the social order.[55] At his death in 1675, Curtice owned real estate worth £175. His two-room house was furnished with little more than the bare necessities. The "chamber," an unheated upstairs room, contained a bedstead, a cupboard, and several storage chests. The catch-all "lower room," where Curtice and his wife may well have slept, also served for eating, cooking, and other household tasks. Here, Mrs. Curtice prepared meals using a "brass pott brass kettle two brass scillits . . . [and] one Iron pott" at a fireplace outfitted with "Tramels cobirons [andirons] tongs and fire shovels." Despite the disparity between their husband's estates, Mrs. Curtice's and Mrs. Childe's kitchens were not substantially different, a function of the modest level of investment in culinary equipment common in the seventeenth century.

Even wealthy families had few ways to reduce the burdens of food preparation. John Bowles, a "gentleman" who died in 1691 leaving an estate worth £1,509.1.6,[56] had a number of luxuries elsewhere in his house, but his family made do with relatively simple kitchen implements. His "mansion house" was far larger and more ostentatiously furnished than either the Childe or the Curtice home. The contents of the "parlour," in particular, reveal how progressive the family was; there was no bed.[57] Instead, Bowles and his family enjoyed the comfort of nineteen chairs (an enormous number for a late-seventeenth-century household), as well as a table covered with a "turkey work" carpet, a chest of drawers, a looking glass, and—crucial to the family's comfort in cold weather— a fireplace. The home also had a "hall," but it bore little resemblance to the multipurpose, work-oriented rooms that went by that name earlier in the century. This "hall" was more like a dining room, although common usage of that term was far in the future. It contained a "great table," a small table, two "old plain great chairs," eight stools, a cupboard, and, like the "parlour," a fireplace.

The sleeping accommodations in this household also indicate a higher than average standard of living. Bowles and his wife almost certainly used the "parlour chamber" (as distinguished from the downstairs "parlour"), with its impressive "down bed and bolster, . . . green serge silk fringed Curtains & Vallains with the bedstead & cord." The room's windows had curtains as well, and there was only one bed, indicating both an income and privacy level rare at the time. Despite Bowles's wealth, however, the "parlour chamber" was unheated, whereas the "hall chamber" was equipped with a fireplace. Why would a man of such means have gone without heat in his bedroom but chosen to heat another sleeping room? The contents of the "hall chamber" suggest the likely answer. In addition to a bed, this room was furnished with a small table covered with a carpet and a "library" valued at £35. The room evidently doubled as Bowles's study and would need to be warmer in winter than his bedroom, where he could escape the cold behind bed curtains and under heavy covers.

The last of the main rooms in the Bowles home was the "kitchen," probably a lean-to added to the back of the house, an increasingly common arrangement that isolated the dirtier, more difficult housework from spaces devoted to family gatherings and entertaining.[58] Here, Mrs. Bowles (or her servants) worked with three brass kettles, seven skillets, three "pottage pots," and an iron pot. The household also had several specialized kitchen tools, including three spits and a roasting "jack," the latter a clockwork mechanism that, when wound, turned meat automatically as it cooked.[59]

1.2. Adriaen van Ostade, *Tavern Interior*, 1674. Courtesy of Staatliche Kunstsammlungen, Dresden, Germany.

The York Hotels, Kept In 1800.
No Better, And good Cooks Can be found no where
to prepare Victuals for the table, As these Taverns.
See the names—Mrs. Abraham Miller, mrs. Polly waltemyer.
mrs. Gosler, mrs. Laub, mrs. Upp. mrs. Kimel, mrs. baltzers Spangler.
mrs. George Hay, mrs. Beard. and mrs. Eichelberger. not far
from town. the two last names.
old Style Cooking,

the Bake oven, backing
Bread.
Smokeing Saus
and ballo·

the had plenty of raw materials, to Cook them, Beef. veal. lam. Mutton.
Pork, and fish. oysters. Poultry. Eggs. Butter, Cheese, milk and honey.
And all kind of vegetables—and fruit. See mrs. Oftersh in 1804. She
Could take every—bbone out of A Chicken, for the table it was good to Carve,
for the Customers at her tavern.

After-frying the Sausage—
the potatos put in the pan.

Little Sally.

Mrs. Lottman Frying Sweetpotatos and give to Lewis Miller,
some of them the first I ever tasted the where good Eating.
It was in her tavern South George Street. 1799.

1.3. Lewis Miller, "Mrs. Lottman Frying Sweet Potatos," n.d. In *Lewis Miller: Sketches and Chronicles* (York, Penn.: Historical Society of York County, 1966), 24. Courtesy of the Historical Society of York County, York, Penn.

1.4. Pieter Gerritsz van Roestraeten, *Woman Frying Pancakes*, 1678.
Courtesy of Bredius Museum, The Hague, Netherlands.

Despite these advantages, however, Mrs. Bowles was only marginally better off than Mrs. Childe and Mrs. Curtice. Seventeenth-century cooking techniques placed substantial demands on women. Careful attention was necessary to monitor the cooking process, yet too frequent removal of oven doors or pot lids let valuable heat escape. A woman had to know which woods would burn slowly and steadily, and which would produce a quick, intense heat. Regulating temperature was tricky, requiring periodic adjustment of the height of cooking vessels over the fire. Moving heavy pots and pans on or off the fire was also difficult and dangerous.

To make matters worse, kitchen fireplaces were often actually part of the room. To adjust a pot hanging over the fire, a woman had to stoop and literally enter the fireplace. The portrayal of a late seventeenth-century Dutch tavern interior in illustration 1.2 demonstrates how awkward this procedure was. One of the pieces of cooking equipment scattered on the floor to the right of the hearth provides another important clue to the rigors of preparing meals in such circumstances: the frying pan is equipped with a long handle to keep the cook further from the fire. Using such an implement required stooping, however, as the depiction of a York, Pennsylvania, tavern-keeper's wife reveals (illus. 1.3).

Simmering and broiling were also physically challenging because they were done on the hearth floor; a woman had to squat or kneel unless she had a small stool handy. A 1678 Dutch painting (illus. 1.4) shows a woman sitting hunched over her hearth frying pancakes. Her work is complicated by the fact that she is also trying to keep an eye on her two children, one a toddler who could easily tip something over or burn himself by touching something hot.[60] Furthermore, the size of the fireplace would make it very easy for a burning log, an ember, or even a spark to escape and set ablaze something or someone in the room.

Seventeenth- and early-eighteenth-century kitchens in the northern colonies resembled those depicted by Dutch genre artists. These images make it possible for a modern observer to understand some of the challenges of cooking under such conditions, but the bitter cold these women and their families had to endure every winter is more difficult to appreciate. During the next half century, a number of Americans tried to improve the design and efficiency of domestic heating systems. Some of their alterations made cooking marginally easier, but the enhancement of personal comfort and the improvement of fuel economy were much higher priorities.

2

"So Much of the Comfort
of Our Lives Depends on Fire"

EIGHTEENTH-CENTURY Americans were proud of what they had accomplished and looked ahead to even greater achievements. They took seriously the biblical injunction to "be fruitful and multiply," doubling their numbers every twenty years.[1] The economy developed nearly as rapidly; the per capita gross national product of Britain's North American colonies increased twice as fast as that of the mother country after 1750. By the 1770s, the standard of living for average Americans may well have been the highest attained up to that time.[2]

In 1782, Frenchman J. Hector St. John de Crèvecoeur, who had stayed in the colonies after his homeland's defeat in the Seven Years War, explained the difference between Europeans and Americans. "The American is a new man, who acts upon new principles," he asserted. Freed from economic dependence by the availability of cheap land, these "new men" enjoyed an "easy, decent maintenance."[3] Echoing Crèvecoeur, Jack Greene has concluded that the "central orientation" of life in late-eighteenth-century America was the "achievement of . . . a state in which a man and his family . . . could live 'at ease' rather than in anxiety."[4] Control of the domestic environment and the pursuit of comfort, equated for the first time with physical well-being,[5] were crucial to this endeavor. Motivated by these goals, as well as by rising wood prices, increasing numbers of Americans decided to experiment with improved heating and cooking technology.

Modifying the household climate was a formidable challenge, however. Large fireplaces were still the norm. Built according to English custom, their straight side and rear walls made them simple to construct but inefficient to operate. Benjamin Franklin noted in 1744 that their generous size provided "good Room for the Cook to move" and corners for people to warm themselves, but he admitted that they failed miserably when it came to heating a room. Even if people huddled close to the fire, "the cold Air so nips [their] Backs and Heels . . . that they have no Comfort," he reported, concluding: "'Tis next to impossible to warm a Room with such a Fire-place."[6] Franklin's comments are revealing. Earlier generations of Americans, he knew, had "never thought of warming Rooms to sit in; all they purpos'd was to have a Place to make a Fire in, by which they might warm themselves when acold."[7] Franklin and his contemporaries demanded more. They wanted not only to get warm, but to stay warm.

One solution, pursued in both Europe and America, was to improve fireplace and chimney design. In the 1620s, Frenchman Louis Savot had determined that narrowing fireplaces reduced the amount of air entering from the sides,[8] but it was not until the eighteenth century that much progress was made. In 1713, another Frenchman, Nicholas Gauger, published *La méchanique de feu,* a work quickly translated and reprinted in England. Gauger recommended that fireplaces be lined with iron plates and equipped with raised hearths. Air in cavities in the brickwork below and behind was heated by exposure to the plates and expelled into the room, diminishing drafts.[9] These fireplaces were expensive and difficult to install, however, and most of the heat rising from the fire itself was lost,[10] but Gauger had correctly realized that the key to improving fireplace function lay in manipulating the movement of heated and unheated air. Gradually, masons and builders recognized that changing the shape of chimneys and fireplaces would reduce smoke and drafts. Beginning in the early eighteenth century, European hearths were narrowed and deepened, mantels lowered, and chimney shafts curved to keep smoke from descending into the room.[11]

These improvements appeared unevenly in America, especially in kitchens. In 1744, Franklin observed that the "large open [kitchen] Fire-places used in the Days of our Fathers" were still typical.[12] Henry Kauffman has likewise claimed that "there seems to have been little deviation in kitchen fireplaces until the cast-iron stove displaced them."[13] Both men exaggerate somewhat. There were, in fact, several significant alterations in the design of some American kitchen hearths during the eighteenth century. The first was the addition of a channel in the middle of the rear fireplace wall to facilitate the upward movement of smoke;[14] the second was the introduction of the fireback, a cast-iron plate set against the back wall to increase heat output. In the most modern kitchens, fireplace side walls were slanted, another change that improved radiation.[15]

Other modifications indicate an embryonic concern with convenience. Brick ovens were increasingly built to the side of the fireplace, instead of into the rear wall, and were equipped with separate flues. Moving the oven to one side made it possible to reduce both the height and width of the fireplace.[16] This change improved fuel efficiency, but the major gain was in safety; cooks no longer had to lean over a hot fire in order to access their ovens. The other noteworthy innovation in eighteenth-century kitchens was the crane—a horizontal iron bar supported by a bracket mounted on the side wall of the fireplace. Beginning in the 1720s, the crane began to replace the lugpole that had previously been used to hang cooking vessels over the fire.[17] A crane made a cook's job easier and safer by making it possible for her to adjust the heat under a pot simply by swinging the crane closer to or farther from the fire. She could also check more readily on the progress of dishes being cooked and no longer had to lean directly into the fireplace to hang or remove a cooking vessel.

Except for these improvements, however, American cooking fireplaces changed little until they were superseded by the cookstove. The techniques and tools used to prepare food changed even less. Women continued to hoist heavy cast-iron pots over the fire, and much cooking still took place on the hearth itself, which necessitated much stooping or crouching. Eighteenth-century Americans were apparently unconcerned about these conditions, however, placing little emphasis on the acquisition of more or better cooking tools. Between 1700 and 1775, the level of investment in cooking equipment in rural Suffolk County, Massachusetts, actually declined from 1.0 to 0.4 percent of estate value.[18]

Most Americans in this period were more interested in making the rest of their homes comfortable than in upgrading their kitchens. This focus is evident in the increasing popularity and changing design of nonkitchen fireplaces. As the eighteenth century progressed, the side walls of these fireplaces were curved or splayed to direct more heat into the room, and their height was lowered to limit the amount of air escaping up the chimney.[19] By the time Franklin published *An Account of the New Invented Pennsylvanian Fire-Places* (1744), these advances had become widespread. "Most . . . old-fashion'd Chimneys," he observed, "have been, of late, Years, reduc'd . . . by building Jambs within them, narrowing the Hearth, and making a low Arch."[20]

Masons and builders worked to improve fireplace appearance as well. Although kitchen hearths remained plain and functional, fireplaces elsewhere in the house exemplified a growing consciousness of Georgian aesthetics. Especially in parlors, fireplace walls were enhanced by moldings, mantel shelves, raised paneling, and even painted landscapes. By the middle of the eighteenth century, it was common for nonkitchen fireplaces to be framed entirely by decorative trim.[21]

Sophisticated appearance went hand in hand with increased comfort. Although some families continued to manage with a single fireplace for both heating and cooking, those who could afford it preferred to have more than one warm room during cold weather. Nearly three-quarters of the room-by-room household inventories recorded in rural Suffolk County, Massachusetts, between

1725 and 1775 list andirons and related equipment in at least two rooms.[22] By the eve of the Revolution, northerners of substantial means considered a fireplace necessary for nearly every room. When Roxbury, Massachusetts, merchant Aaron Davis Jr. died in 1774, for example, assessors found that six of the eight principal rooms in his imposing "Mansion House" were heated by fireplaces.[23] In winter, members of his household could thus enjoy a level of personal comfort unimaginable in the previous century. The Davises and others like them had achieved the goal described by Franklin thirty years before: they could do more than huddle by a fireplace to get warm; they could sit in a room and stay warm.

Continental Europeans chose a different way to increase domestic warmth, one that, for a variety of reasons, the English and Anglo-Americans were slow to emulate. Beginning in the fifteenth century, several types of stoves, a technology pioneered by the Germans, were introduced in northern Germany, France, Holland, and Scandinavia.[24] In the mid–fifteenth century, French traveler Gilles le Bouvier reported, "For the cold . . . [Germans] have stoves that heat in such a way that they are warm in their rooms, and in winter craftsmen do their work and keep their wives and children there and it takes very little wood to heat them."[25] This "stove" was probably not a freestanding device but a room (also called a "stove") warmed by a tile or earthenware "oven" built into one wall. Such "stoves" were in use in France by the early sixteenth century and elicited similar praise. Erasmus noted approvingly in 1527 that "in the stove you take off your boots, . . . change your shirt, . . . hang up your clothes . . . near the fire and . . . draw near to dry yourself."[26]

Life in such a "stove" was communal, as shown in a 1524 German woodcut (illus. 2.1). In this rowdy scene, only a few people are working; in fact, the most popular activity is the pursuit of the opposite sex. There is an island of comparative calm to the right, however, where three men gather around a tile stove, one dozing against a wooden tub, another playing a musical instrument, and a third warming himself, just as Erasmus described. A garment hangs over a drying rack suspended from the ceiling, another indication of the stove's humble but important role.

In the sixteenth and seventeenth centuries, such "stoves" became common in northern European public buildings,[27] and some families were incorporating them into their homes as well. In the arrangement depicted in Johann Comenius's *Orbis Sensualium Pictus* (illus. 2.2), a tile "oven" protrudes from the wall of the "stove," a room "beautified with an arched Roof and wainscoted Walls," and furnished with an elaborate table and seating furniture. The adjoining room, which would also benefit from the heat of the "oven," holds two beds. A family living in such a house could thus eat, work, visit, and sleep in reasonable comfort.[28]

Inhabitants of Holland and Scandinavia relied on a different kind of "stove," one made of cast iron, with either five or six plates. Five-plate or "jamb" stoves extended into an adjacent room through the back wall of a fireplace, typically in the kitchen (illus. 2.3). Six-plate stoves were freestanding, radiating heat from all sides, and could be set up anywhere in a room for maximum effect.

Stoves such as these made an important but often overlooked difference in the way northern Europeans conducted their lives. In Dutch artist Willem Duyster's early-seventeenth-century depiction of a backgammon game (illus. 2.4), for example, the stove is almost an afterthought. It stands, barely visible, on the right edge of the painting, yet, without it, the players would be far less at ease. A 1658 etching by Rembrandt (illus. 2.5) conveys a similar feeling. The stove portrayed here has obviously warmed this room to at least a minimally comfortable temperature because the half-dressed woman seems in no hurry to put on more

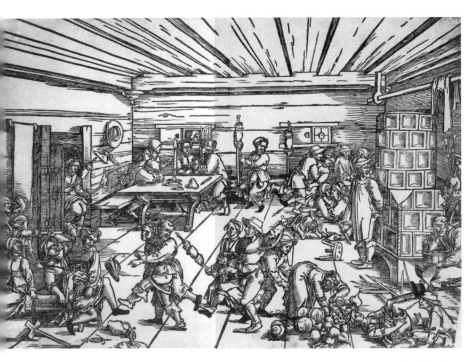

2.1. Barthel Beham, *The Spinning Chamber,* 1524. Woodcut. Courtesy of Ashmolean Museum, Oxford, England.

LXXV.
The Stove with the Bed-Room.

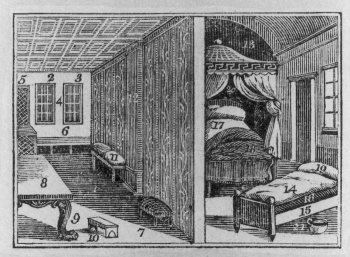

Hypocaustum cum Dormitorio.

The Stove, 1.
is beautified
with an arched Roof, 2.
and wainscoted Walls; 3.
   It is enlightened
with Windows; 4.
   It is heated
with an Oven. 5.
   Its Utensils are
Benches, 6.
Stools, 7.
Tables, 8.
with Tressels, 9.
Footstools, 10.
and Cushions. 11.

Hypocaustum, 1.
ornatur
Laqueari, 2.
& *tabulatis Parietibus;* 3.
   Illuminatur
Fenestris; 4.
   Calefit
Fornace. 5.
   Ejus Utensilia sunt
Scamna, 6
Sellæ, 7.
Mensæ, 8.
cum *Fulcris,* 9.
ac *Scabellis,* 10.
& *Culcitris.* 11.

2.2. "The Stove with the Bed-Room." In Johann Amos Comenius, *Orbis Sensualium Pictus* (1658; reprint, New York: 1810), 108. Courtesy of the American Antiquarian Society, Worcester, Mass.

STOVE
ROOM

KITCHEN

58. *Five Plate Jamb Stove in position*

A. The End Plate   E. Stoke-hole
B. Side Plate   F. Flue
C. Stone Leg   G. Kitchen Fireplace
D. Postament   H. Chimney
              I. Lintel Beam

2.3. Five-plate jamb stove in position. Henry C. Mercer et al., *The Bible in Iron: Pictured Stoves and Stoveplates of the Pennsylvania Germans* (Doylestown, Penn: Bucks County Historical Society, 1961), Pl. 58. Collection of the Spruance Library of the Bucks County Historical Society, Doylestown, Penn.

clothes. These views of mundane activities demonstrate how stoves, depending on where they were used, could facilitate both privacy and comfort.

The English were aware of the revolution in domestic heating technology under way across the Channel but were reluctant to abandon the open fireplace. English travelers gave continental stoves mixed reviews. Fynes Moryson, who visited Germany in the 1610s, commented: "When my selfe first entred into one of them, the unwonted heate . . . made my head dull and heavy." He was also disturbed that his hosts "not only . . . receive Gentlemen into these stoves, but even . . . permit rammish clownes to stand by the oven till their wet clothes be dried, and themselves sweat." He was even more shocked that they allowed young children to "sit upon their close stooles, and ease themselves within this close and hot stove." Overwhelmed, Moryson concluded that "these ill smells, never purged by the admitting of any fresh ayre, should dull the braine, and almost choke the spirits."[29] Peter Mundy, an Englishman who visited Germany twenty-five years later, agreed. Stoves were, he declared, "noisome att First to those thatt are nott accustomed, and I thincke unwholesome att last."[30]

These reservations aside, Moryson and Mundy also found much to like about stoves. Moryson commented on their fuel economy and admitted that "after I

2.4. Willem Duyster, *Two Men Playing Tric-Trac, with a Woman Scoring*, c. 1599–1635. Courtesy of the National Gallery of Art, London, England.

2.5. Rembrandt Harmensz van Rijn (Dutch 1606–1669), *Woman Sitting by a Stove,* 1658. Etching, burin, and dry point, 7th state; 22.8×18.7 cm (8¹⁵⁄₁₆×7⅜ in.). Harvey D. Parker Collection. Courtesy of the Museum of Fine Arts, Boston, Mass.

had used them, custome became another nature, for I never injoyed my health in any place better than there."[31] Mundy was even more impressed, calling the stove "commonly the best Furnished room in the house, where the Master therof, his wiffe and children (as allsoe strangers) doe sitt, converse, write, [and] passe away their tyme." He thought the tile-decorated "oven" a "pretty little structure" and concluded that stoves were both "commodious and proffitable . . . for by that Meanes a little woode will suffice to Make Fire to warme a great Company, all participating alike, one Not hindering the other." This was not the case, he remarked ruefully, "att our Chimney Fires."[32]

Despite these advantages, Mundy's countrymen were not eager to adopt stoves. Lawrence Wright argued that love of open fires was part of the English national character. "The closed stove has always been more popular in . . . Northern Europe," he asserted. "The English have seldom thought the economy [of closed stoves] worth the sacrifice of the cheerful flicker . . . of a fire."[33] Wright may have been on to something; an anonymous Elizabethan commentator claimed that his countrymen were wary of "fyre secret felt but not scene."[34] It is more likely, however, that the comparatively moderate winters characteristic of the British Isles explain why the English were slow to accept closed stoves.

In America, however, the harsh climate convinced some English colonists to experiment with the new technology. Those who chose to do so preferred the portable iron stove of northwestern Europe to the built-in tile "oven" and "stove" room of Germany. In 1647, Robert Child informed John Winthrop Jr. that the new ironworks in Saugus and Braintree, Massachusetts, had had a good year. "We have cast some tuns of pots," he reported, "likewise mortars, stoves, [and] skillets."[35] John Howland, a resident of Plymouth Colony, may have been a customer; archaeological evidence has revealed that his house, built in 1638 and burned before 1691, was equipped with a "Dutch" stove (likely a five-plate model).[36]

Boston judge Samuel Sewall also experienced the comfort of a stove. He used his multipurpose "Stove-room" as a place to entertain guests and as an office, noting in his diary in February 1706 that he had seen a petitioner there. In January 1702, Sewall's wife hosted a dinner there for her "Midwife and Women." Sewall attended and commented with satisfaction: "Comfortable . . . a good fire in the Stove warm'd the Room." Sewall's son and daughter-in-law, who lived in outlying Roxbury, also enjoyed the benefits of a stove. After Sewall visited them in December 1702, he noted that they had dined "in their Chamber, where their Stove is."[37]

High prices as well as custom kept Howland's and Sewall's neighbors from following their example, however. In the late 1720s, five-plate stoves cost between £3 and £5 at one Pennsylvania furnace;[38] transportation would have added a substantial amount to the retail price. It is not surprising, therefore, that the few stoves in use in New England were found in the homes of the well-to-do. They are listed in only two of the seventy-four room-by-room household inventories recorded in rural Suffolk County, Massachusetts, before 1760. In both cases, however, they demonstrate the growing importance of physical comfort to Anglo-Americans with substantial incomes.

At his death in 1732, the "late Honble. Col. Wm. Tailer Esqr of Dorchester" left an estate worth £9,366.19.3, more than seven times the median for the period.[39] Tailer's home contained ten principal rooms, making it much larger and more expensive to heat than usual. Five of these rooms had open hearths, but in one of them, the kitchen, appraisers also found "1 Dutch Stove." Why would a man as wealthy as Tailer install a stove in a room already outfitted with a fireplace? The likely explanation is that it was a jamb stove. If so, it would have been fed from the kitchen and used the kitchen flue, but would have warmed an adjacent room, perhaps the "Counting House" where Tailer did business. Tailer's decision to use a stove in his home's work areas but to heat family gathering places with open fires was a choice many nineteenth-century Americans would also make.

Jacob Williams, a Roxbury "Mariner," made a stove a more integral part of his daily life. When he died in 1737, he left an estate valued at £937.1.0.[40] Although only a tenth as wealthy as Tailer, Williams shared many of his aspirations. The furnishings in his "Great Chamber" were especially sophisticated. Here, probate assessors found a £26 bed, a "dressing glass," a table, six chairs, a tea table, and a "Case of Drawers." Completing the room's furnishings was "1 Stove," the least-valuable item in the room, but the one that would have contributed the most to Williams's comfort in cold weather.

Despite the example of men such as Tailer and Williams, most Anglo-Americans in the northern colonies chose not to buy stoves in this period, even if they had the means. Although Henry Mercer exaggerated when he claimed that stoves were "never heard of among the English . . . in New England,"[41] Josephine Peirce's contention that "it seems . . . logical that stoves were one of the first comforts" they obtained is vastly overstated. Her own research provides weak support for such a conclusion, showing evidence of stove use in only four New England homes between 1640 and 1750, and just three instances of stoves being manufactured or advertised in the region.[42] Peirce argued that "stoves were commonly used, and so were mentioned only for some special purpose,"[43] but her assertion fails to account for the overwhelming absence of stoves in probate inventories. It is very unlikely that stoves could have been widely used in the region without being listed in these records.

Europeans elsewhere in North America did not share New Englanders' lack of interest in stoves. Five- and six-plate models were common in both Pennsylvania

German and French Canadian homes. In 1734, David Seibt, recently settled in Germantown, Pennsylvania, wrote his brother in Silesia to suggest that he bring a five-plate stove with him to America because "they are dear here." Seibt was not sure where he could find one, but commented that "the people of the Palatinate generally bring theirs with them and I think they buy them in Rotterdam."[44] Such advice evidently had an impact. Recalling life in Pennsylvania's German communities in the mid–eighteenth century, John Watson noted that "every house was warmed in winter by 'jamb stoves.'"[45] When Swedish naturalist Peter Kalm visited Quebec in the late 1740s, he found that farmhouses there also had "iron stoves in one of the rooms and fireplaces in the rest."[46]

When Americans began manufacturing stoves, they understandably concentrated their efforts in regions where the inhabitants favored the technology. Kalm reported that the Trois Rivieres ironworks in Quebec produced stoves in addition to bar iron, cannons, kettles, and mortars.[47] Pennsylvania iron plantations also emphasized the production of pig iron, as well as hollowware and agricultural implements, but they, too, were casting stove plates as early as the 1720s.[48] Outside of these areas, however, stove manufacturing was rare, especially in the first half of the eighteenth century, presumably due to weak demand.

Some Anglo-Americans, such as Benjamin Franklin, worried that stoves undermined health. He complained in 1744 that the occupants of rooms heated by jamb stoves were "oblig'd to breathe the same unchang'd Air . . . mix'd with the Breath and Perspiration from one another's Bodies which is very disagreeable to those who have not become accustomed to it." Six-plate stoves were somewhat better, he thought, because their position closer to the center of the room facilitated air circulation. Moreover, with this type of stove, "the Air is gradually changed by the Stove-Door's being in the Room, thro' which part of it is continually passing, and that makes these Stoves wholesomer . . . than the German [i.e., jamb] stoves." But even six-plate stoves did not meet with Franklin's wholehearted approval: "There is no sight of the Fire, which is in itself a pleasant thing." He was also afraid that people would forget to add wood to a stove if they could not see the fire, and he thought that air circulation in rooms heated by six-plate stoves was not as good as it should be. "For these reasons," he concluded, "the Holland [i.e., six-plate] Stove has not obtain'd much among the English (who love the Sight of the Fire)."[49] Kalm agreed with Franklin's parenthetical statement; commenting on colonial lifestyles in the late 1740s, he remarked that "Englishmen liked to see the fire burn instead of confining it in a stove."[50]

Franklin and Kalm may have overlooked another explanation for Anglo-American reluctance to use stoves—nativism. During the colonial period, between 65,000 and 100,000 Germans came to America. At independence, nearly a quarter of a million Americans, almost 9 percent of the population, claimed

German ancestry.[51] In Pennsylvania, in particular, English resentment ran high, and settlers such as Archibald Kennedy predicted colony leaders would one day regret encouraging so many Germans to make their home there. "Most of them [are] old Soldiers, who hardly know what the word LIBERTY means," he explained in 1751.[52] Franklin was equally worried. "This will in a few years become a German Colony," he complained the same year, reporting that some English families, "made uneasy by the Disagreeableness of disonant Manners," were moving away. He approved of the Germans' "industry and frugality," and conceded they were "excellent husbandmen and contribute greatly to the improvement of a Country," but he concluded that "there can be no cordial Affection or Unity between the Two Nations," and fumed, "Why should the Palatine Boors be suffered to swarm into our Settlements? Why should Pennsylvania, founded by the English, become a colony of Aliens, who will . . . Germanize us instead of our Anglifying them?"[53]

Even German physician Johann Schoepf, who visited America in the 1770s and 1780s, voiced similar sentiments. He agreed that Germans were justly known for their "industry and economy," but was disappointed that they did not "use their gains for allowable pleasures," noting disdainfully that "In their houses, they live thriftily, often badly," with minimal furnishings—a table, two or three benches, a few books, and a "great 4-cornered stove." In contrast, the English made an effort "to live seemly, in a well-furnished house, in every way as comports with a gentleman."[54] Schoepf evidently equated stoves with "thrifty" subsistence rather than genteel "pleasures." Even if Americans of English ancestry did not entirely agree with this point of view, it is possible that they considered the adoption of closed stoves a sign of "Germanization."

Whatever its causes, the Anglo-American predilection for the open hearth was not without cost. Even though improvements in design and construction had made fireplaces somewhat more efficient, their proliferation in American homes substantially increased the demand for firewood. Nevertheless, Americans practiced "not the least economy" with regard to wood. Schoepf thought he knew how this attitude had developed. Since the beginning of settlement, he explained, "wood has been everywhere in the way."[55] Driven by the need to clear land, Americans actually considered themselves "plagued" by their "troublesome" forests.[56] Because the "new world" was resource rich but labor poor, saving time was more important than conserving materials, but European visitors had difficulty grasping this basic fact of American life. When Kalm visited the middle colonies in the 1740s, he was shocked at how much lumber was used to build the zig-zag split rail fences common in the region.[57] Schoepf likewise remarked that American fencing showed "more care . . . to avoid trouble than to save wood."[58]

Although fencing undeniably consumed a vast number of trees, it was not the primary cause of deforestation in America. William Cronon has estimated that in 1800 New Englanders burned eighteen times more wood in their homes than they cut for lumber; a typical family used between twenty and forty cords of firewood a year.[59] The observations of eighteenth-century travelers bear out Cronon's findings. Kalm reported that "an incredible amount of wood is . . . squandered in this country for fuel; day and night all winter, . . . in all rooms, a fire is kept going."[60] Schoepf worried that Americans' extravagance would not "leave for their grandchildren a bit of wood over which to hang the tea-kettle."[61]

It would be many years before Americans took these concerns to heart, despite the fact that timber shortages had begun to affect long-settled areas as early as the seventeenth century. The Boston peninsula was stripped of trees by 1637, necessitating the importation of wood from Cape Ann.[62] By 1689, officials in Malden, Massachusetts, had forbidden cutting for fuel any tree less than a foot in diameter. In 1713, leaders in Waterbury, Connecticut, banned burning over woodland (a technique used to increase the amount of grazing land) for seven years in order to give young trees a chance to grow.[63]

The problem grew more acute as the eighteenth century progressed. In 1744, Benjamin Franklin reported that "WOOD, our common Fewel, which within these 100 Years might be had at every Man's Door, must now be fetch'd near 100 Miles to some Towns."[64] Six years later, West Indian merchant James Birket heard New Hampshire settlers complaining that lumber was "far to fetch out of the Country."[65]

As wood became scarcer and had to be transported from further away, prices rose, especially in cities. An anonymous visitor to Boston observed in 1740 that fuel was "one of the most expensive articles of housekeeping."[66] Franklin concurred that firewood "makes a very considerable Article in the Expence of Families."[67] In the late 1740s, Kalm heard "everybody" in Philadelphia griping that fuel "had risen to a price many times as much as it had been." Every year, suppliers' efforts to take advantage of the arrival of winter exacerbated the situation. Kalm noted in the fall of 1748 that the price of a cord of hickory was 18s. By the next year, it had climbed to 22s, and after a December cold spell, the price rose as high as 27s. Despite this rapid inflation, he reported that wood was still so scarce that "one had to hurry and take it lest it be snapped up by someone else."[68]

Hoping to improve fuel economy but leery of closed stoves, Franklin developed an ingenious compromise between the stove and the fireplace. In 1744, he described the benefits of his "New Invented Pennsylvanian Fire-Place[s]," proclaiming "Their ADVANTAGES above every other METHOD of WARMING

ROOMS." "As . . . so much of the Comfort and Conveniency of our Lives . . . depends on . . . FIRE," he argued, "any new Proposal for Saving . . . Wood, and . . . augmenting the Benefit of FIRE . . . may . . . be thought worth Consideration."[69] Although his invention came to be called the "Franklin stove," it was not, in fact, a stove at all. Schoepf described it as "a sort of iron affair, half stove, half fire-place . . . a longish rectangular apparatus made of cast-iron plates . . . [which] stands off from the wall the front being open, in every respect a detached movable fire-place."[70] The Franklin stove utilized descending flues to minimize smoke and a honeycomb of chambers (called an "air box") to warm air before directing it into the room (illus. 2.6). Combining the principles of conduction, radiation, and convection, it was an important advance in domestic heating.[71]

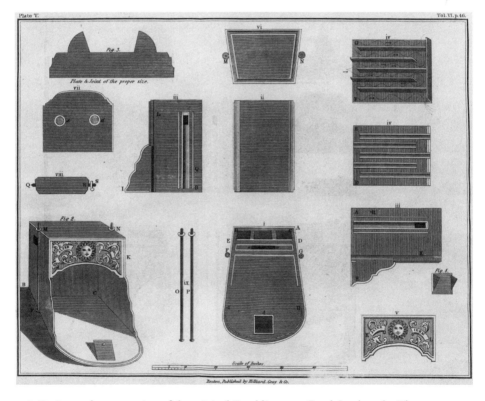

2.6. Design and construction of the original Franklin stove. Jared Sparks, ed., *The Works of Benjamin Franklin,* 10 vols. (Boston: Hilliard, Gray, 1836–40), 6:opposite 46. Courtesy of the American Philosophical Society, Philadelphia, Penn.

Franklin's pamphlet included directions for the construction, installation, and use of these "Machines." He also devoted considerable attention to their advantages over the "common Fire-Place": "Your whole Room [will be] equally warmed," he promised, "so that People need not croud . . . round the Fire." Moreover, cold drafts would be eliminated—no more fear of "being scorcht before and . . . froze behind." Franklin further pledged that the device would decrease "Cold[s,] Coughs, Catarrhs, Tooth-Achs, Fevers, Pleurisies and many other Diseases." Most important, it would save fuel as it enhanced personal comfort. He reported that his "common Room" was twice as warm using a quarter of the wood he had formerly consumed; some users claimed fuel savings as high as five-sixths.[72] Schoepf agreed that the Franklin stove was efficient, commenting that it "warm[ed] a room at less expense of fuel than is possible with the wall fire-place." He also appreciated the fact that the "comfortable sight of the open fire" was retained.[73] Franklin felt the same way, reassuring potential purchasers that they would not lose "the pleasant sight . . . of the Fire."[74]

The New Pennsylvanian Fire-Place was also versatile. Franklin explained that it could be used to "boil the Tea-Kettle, warm the Flat-Irons, heat Heaters, [and] keep warm a Dish of Victuals."[75] Kalm, to whom Franklin loaned one of his inventions, was even more creative. He made hot chocolate on the stove top and noted that "it proved possible, by suspending a cord . . . in front of the fire-box, to roast meat . . . attached to it and turned." Kalm was adapting a culinary technique long in use in kitchens equipped with open fireplaces, but the results surprised him. The meat, he found, "was roasted better and quicker than in a regular kitchen fireplace."[76]

Kalm thus became the first documented person in America to use the new technology of domestic heating to prepare a meal. His contemporaries did not share his interest in using stoves for cooking, however. What they valued was warmth in winter. In pursuit of this goal, Franklin turned down an offer from the governor of Pennsylvania for exclusive rights to his "stove," saying, "We should be glad of an Opportunity to serve others by any Invention of ours."[77] Instead, he gave a prototype to Robert Grace, proprietor of the Warwick Furnace, who began production by 1741. First advertised in the *Pennsylvania Gazette* on 3 December of that year, the Franklin stoves were evidently a success in the Philadelphia area, even though they sold for the substantial sum of five pounds. Six weeks later the paper announced the arrival of a new shipment.[78]

Retailers in Boston, New York, Newport (Rhode Island), and Yorktown (Virginia) took note and entered into agreements to sell Grace's products,[79] but high transportation costs made this arrangement impractical. Franklin's brother Peter, who offered Franklin stoves for sale in Newport, sold only two in twenty years, probably because he charged £27.10.0.[80] The more cost-effective strategy was to use the specifications and engravings in Franklin's pamphlet to produce the "stoves" closer to local markets, a practice increasingly common after 1745.[81]

Although they were undeniably fuel efficient, Franklin stoves did not please everyone. Consumers in rural areas with easy access to woodlots thought them too expensive. Critics worried that bricking up chimneys to attach Franklin stoves would discourage sweeping and thus increase the risk of chimney fires.[82] Franklin stoves were also complicated to manufacture and operate, and could be dangerous if improperly installed. In 1747, for example, members of the Pierpont household of Boston nearly lost their lives in a house fire "occasioned by the Heat of the Iron Hearth on one of the Newly invented Fire-places."[83]

For these reasons, by the mid-1760s Franklin's invention had been superseded by other "Franklin stoves," simpler cast-iron fireplaces that did not have descending flues or air boxes and resembled the original in name only.[84] In 1765, while living in London, Franklin asked his friend Hugh Roberts to obtain "2 Pensylvania Fire Places cast when Robert Grace's Moulds were good," but Roberts was unable to comply. Authentic Franklin stoves, he discovered, were "much out of use." "Many have been laid aside," he reported; "some parts of the plates have been apply'd for Backs or hearths of Chimneys . . . [but] I have not found . . . one Compleat."[85] Franklin's "half stove, half fire-place" was thus only partly successful. "Englishmen," Kalm explained, "were not accustomed to this [and] they liked open fires better . . . [whereas] the Germans preferred their . . . stoves."[86]

The fuel crisis that had inspired Franklin to develop his stove worsened as the century progressed. During the 1750s and 1760s, fuel prices continued to climb, partly due to inflation during the Seven Years War. The firewood price index in Philadelphia nearly doubled between 1754 and 1764. Prices dropped somewhat in the next decade but rose again during the Revolutionary War—a trend that was especially hard on the poor, who could not afford to buy wood in bulk when prices were low. Using a conservative estimate of firewood consumption (4.88 cords per year), Billy G. Smith has determined that a poor family in mid-eighteenth-century Philadelphia spent a minimum of £5.11.10 each year for fuel. At that price, a laborer had to work nearly thirty days to pay for his family's annual firewood needs.[87] Gary Nash suggests an even higher level of fuel consumption, estimating that the average American "laboring-class" family in the late eighteenth century used between five and ten cords of firewood per year. According to his calculations, a 10s increase in the cost of firewood was equivalent to three to six weeks' earnings.[88]

Under these conditions, wood theft became a problem. In January 1760, the *Pennsylvania Gazette* reported, "Help! Help! Help! Wood at Three Pounds Ten Shillings a Cord, a Price never heard of! . . . The Widow hears a noise in her yard, rises from her Bed . . . sees a Thief, and asks him what he is doing; he answers, I must have Wood." This thief was not alone; according to the *Gazette,* "perhaps two Hundred families have not a stick to burn."[89]

The plight of these individuals did not go unnoticed. Smith discovered that the "problem evoked numerous charity drives to supply wood to the . . . poor, as well as recurrent demands to regulate the amount charged by carters and boatmen for carrying firewood."[90] But philanthropy and price controls were not the answer; the solution lay in the adoption of fuel-efficient heating devices. Although Anglo-Americans continued to prefer open fireplaces, by the middle of the eighteenth century they could no longer deny that changes were needed. Increasingly, though perhaps unwillingly, they began to think about using closed stoves.

British mercantile policy may have retarded the development of colonial stove manufacturing, however. As American iron output increased during the first half of the century, iron interests in the mother country looked on with growing concern. Aiming to reduce competition from colonial finished goods while assuring continued imports of American pig iron, Parliament passed the Iron Act in 1750, which halted all duties on colonial pig iron imported to England but prohibited the erection of any new slitting mills, plating forges, or blister steel furnaces in the colonies. The results of this legislation were not entirely satisfactory. Although colonial exports of pig iron did increase slightly in proportion to England's total imports, colonial legislatures and entrepreneurs repeatedly violated the provisions directed at suppressing the manufacture of finished goods. Pennsylvania, New Jersey, and Maryland even went so far as to grant land, bounties, and tax exemptions to anyone willing to set up a new ironworks.[91]

Despite British regulation, American production of pig iron, wrought iron, and castings increased significantly, from 1,500 tons in 1700 to 30,000 tons in 1775.[92] The average weekly output of colonial furnaces rose from between fifteen and twenty tons in the 1720s to between twenty-five and forty tons by the 1780s, an expansion made possible by an accumulation of skills, larger furnaces, and the substitution of blowing tubs for bellows to regulate their blast. Product quality improved as well, as ironmasters learned the benefit of mixing iron recovered from cinder banks with the ore.[93]

The continuing growth of the iron industry increased pressure on America's forests, however. Because they had a voracious appetite for the wood needed to produce charcoal, furnaces were usually located some distance from settled regions. A typical New Jersey iron plantation included approximately twenty thousand acres of woodland, one thousand of which were cleared for coaling each year. The trees cut from an acre of forest yielded about twenty-five cords of wood, which in turn produced roughly forty bushels of charcoal. In 1783, Pennsylvania's Oley Furnace consumed 840 bushels of charcoal every twenty-four hours it was in blast, with a daily output of slightly more than two tons of iron. Thus, the production of every ton of iron required cutting approximately ten and a half acres of forest.[94]

The iron industry's growing consumption of wood exacerbated America's developing fuel crisis, thereby stimulating further interest in the development of fuel-efficient stoves, one of the industry's new products. Stove manufacturers recognized this connection and worked hard to make stoves acceptable to Anglo-American consumers. Before 1750, most American stove plates were decorated with traditional German images, usually biblical scenes intended to impart a religious lesson.[95] Thereafter, English words began to replace their German equivalents in inscriptions, and instead of morality tales such as "The Wheel of Fortune" or "Cain and Abel," stove plates sprouted flower pots, sheaves of wheat, and eight-pointed stars. Henry Mercer, writing in the twentieth century, was puzzled that mid-eighteenth-century Pennsylvania stove manufacturers abandoned "more interesting picture designs" in favor of what he considered "a very peculiar conventionalized floral pattern"; he concluded that the new images were signs of "decadence." "The carving [of the molds] is better," he conceded, "but the religious spirit, previously universal, occasionally yields to worldliness."[96] Mercer overlooked an obvious explanation for the change in stove design: floral patterns accompanied by stars, sheaves of wheat, and other naturalistic motifs harmonized well with fashionable Anglo-American interiors.

In the 1760s, American iron manufacturers also diversified their product line by introducing the first stove designed, in part, for cooking. The new ten-plate stove had six exterior plates and a four-plate oven around which smoke passed before exiting into the stove pipe (illus. 2.7). Although ten-plate stoves did not permit cooking in direct contact with the fire, their ovens were far more fuel-efficient, easier to use, and less messy than bake kettles. They were small, however—six inches high, ten inches wide, and eighteen inches deep in a small stove[97]—which meant that women either had to bake more often or continue to use their brick ovens. Mercer correctly pointed out that the ten-plate stove was for many years "an auxiliary to the open fire,"[98] but it was nevertheless an important precursor of the full-function cookstove.

Unimpressed by these innovations, Anglo-Americans remained hesitant about adopting stoves. Although these eighteenth-century models were undeniably more fuel-efficient than fireplaces, they were far from perfect. Stove plates were cast flat in open sand molds, which made them prone to cracking.[99] Any decoration had to be laboriously carved into the plate mold and then pressed into the

2.7. Late-eighteenth-century ten-plate stove, Hopewell Furnace, Penn. Collection of the Mercer Museum of the Bucks County Historical Society, Doylestown, Penn.

sand, a process that made fine design difficult. Stove doors had to be hand forged from thinner metal, so they wore out frequently.[100] Marketing was also a problem. It was cost prohibitive to transport stoves weighing at least 250 pounds each over long distances,[101] so furnaces had to attract most of their customers from a small area.

Despite these obstacles, stoves did become more widely available as the eighteenth century progressed. One of the earliest stove ads to appear outside Pennsylvania, published in the *Boston Gazette* in October 1723, announced the sale "at a reasonable price" of "a very good and large Holland stove," probably a six-plate model. In the next thirty years, "large Dutch stoves" were advertised at least twice more in the same city,[102] but the rarity of such records suggests that few Bostonians were interested in the new technology. Even in the middle colonies, where German immigrants had introduced stoves early in the century, domestic usage among Anglo-Americans was still unusual. In Chester County, Pennsylvania, and New Castle County, Delaware, for example, stoves are listed in only two of the 127 estate inventories recorded in the 1750s.[103]

Limited consumer acceptance made it inadvisable for entrepreneurs to specialize in stove production. In the late 1760s, the New York Air Furnace manufactured "Pots, Kettles, skillets, . . . chimney backs, . . . forge and fullers plates, hatters basons, forge hammers & anvils, sugar house boilers . . . [and] pye pans," in addition to "round and square stoves."[104] Retailers had to be equally flexible. In 1761, John and Isaac Shoemaker, who operated a general store in Cheltenham Township, Pennsylvania, offered "iron stoves, pots, kettles and skillets, [and] bake plates" in addition to their other stock.[105] Nineteen years later, William Sitgreaves of Philadelphia advertised the importation of an impressive list of luxury items including porcelain, fabric, "ivory combs," and "English playing cards." At the end of the list, he mentioned that he also had "two or three iron stoves" available.[106]

Despite the rarity of domestic stove use before 1760, Americans were increasingly willing to employ the new technology outside their homes. Stoves made particular sense on sailing vessels, where storage space for firewood was at a premium and the risk of fire aboard was high. A 1759 advertisement in the *Boston Evening Post* informed readers of the availability of "a handsome new iron stove, with a brass front, suitable for a Ship's Cabin."[107] Farther to the south, New York City tinplate workers Elias Bonnell and Robert Farris placed an ad in the *New York Gazette* to let potential customers know that they had begun to sell "ship and shop stoves." In 1767, proprietors of the "New York Air Furnace" likewise emphasized the fact that their stoves were suitable for use on ships.[108]

Stoves were also considered appropriate for public buildings. After arriving in Pennsylvania in 1750, Henry Steigel (better known for his work in the glass industry) began manufacturing cylindrical "cannon" stoves assembled from curved plates cast in flask molds, an expensive technique not yet in common use. Despite their cost, cannon stoves achieved some success; they were installed in both Christ Church and the Friends Meetinghouse in Philadelphia by 1752.[109] Twelve years later, Michael Hillegas advertised in the *Pennsylvania Gazette* that he sold "STOVES of various Sorts . . . among which are the admired Cannon Stoves, proved to be so well adapted for Meeting-houses, and all publick Places, Stores [and] Shops."[110]

Box stoves also became more common in public buildings in these years. In 1772, Hillegas was paid £27.16.11 for "two Stoves and Pipes" he had installed in the Pennsylvania State House. Four years later, General Phillip Schuyler, concerned about the approach of winter, asked the New York State Convention to supply his army with fifty six-plate stoves "of the largest size in common use." It is not clear whether the members of the Convention complied, but they were certainly aware of the benefits of closed stoves, having just requested to buy or borrow the stove used in the Presbyterian Church in Albany.[111]

Convention members' enthusiasm for the new technology was not shared by all of their countrymen. After all, stoves were still expensive. In the early 1770s, a "big" six-plate stove purchased directly from the Elizabeth Furnace in Lancaster County, Pennsylvania, cost £5, and a "big" ten-plate stove cost £5.10.[112] Retail prices were higher in cities; in the next decade, large six- and ten-plate stoves sold in Philadelphia for £6 and £10 respectively,[113] the equivalent of between twenty and fifty days' work for a laborer.[114] Thus, stoves remained out of the reach of most families.

Nevertheless, closed stoves were beginning to be utilized in American homes, at least in the middle colonies. A sample of probate inventories from 1774 collected by Alice Hanson Jones indicates that 37.1 percent of decedents in three Pennsylvania counties had owned stoves.[115] Significantly, stove ownership was not strongly associated with wealth, and urban dwellers, who were experiencing the pinch of rising fuel costs, were only marginally more likely to own stoves than rural residents.[116]

Individual inventories in this sample provide other clues about the growing domestic use of stoves. For one thing, cost remained an obstacle. Although Philadelphia shopkeeper Lawrence Opman carried stoves as part of his stock, he did not use them to heat his own home.[117] John Durham, a farmer in Northampton County, did have a stove in his home, but at £4 it was by far the most valuable item he owned.[118]

Even when price was not an issue, stove owners did not always make a full commitment to the new technology. Samuel Neave, who left an estate worth more than £11,000, heated his back parlor with "an Iron Stove ornamented," but in his front parlor assessors found "large Chimney Dogs with brass fluted Columns."[119] Although utility ruled in the room Neave and his family used most, hospitality dictated that guests be welcomed by an open fire.

Outside of Pennsylvania, far fewer Americans had adopted stoves. These appliances are listed in just 3.0 percent of the New England and New York inventories and 1.9 percent of the Maryland, Virginia, North Carolina, and South Carolina inventories in Jones's sample.[120] But even in these regions, trendsetters were beginning to use the new technology. When Janet Schaw arrived at the home of a Brunswick, North Carolina, merchant in the winter of 1775, for example, she was delighted to be welcomed into the hall "which . . . had a cheerful look, to which a large . . . stove . . . not a little contributed."[121] As fuel costs continued to rise in subsequent decades, more Americans would share Schaw's experience.

There was a clear connection between the availability of affordable fuel and the decision to acquire a stove. In 1777, for example, firewood shortages during the British occupation of Philadelphia convinced local merchant Henry Drinker that the time had come to invest in the new technology. His wife Elizabeth noted in her diary in November, "We had a stove put up in the back Parlor; this Morning Wood is so very scarce, that unless things mend there is no likelyhood of a Supply, and we have no more than 4 or 5 Cord." Oak, she complained, was selling for between 17s and 20s a cord.[122] In the mid-1780s, Johann Schoepf also observed the effect of rising fuel costs, noting that "iron or tin-plate draught-stoves . . . are used more and more by English families (as a result of the increasing dearness of wood)."[123] This trend was to strengthen as the new nation's fuel crisis continued to worsen.

3

"The Art of Economizing Fuel"

T HEIR VICTORY OVER Great Britain in the Revolutionary War strengthened Americans' belief that God had particularly blessed the new United States.[1] After 1790, exports boomed, lifting the nation's standard of living to a new high.[2] German visitor Johann Schoepf reported that "luxury prevails here" but quickly added that Americans were both industrious and thrifty. What they sought, he explained, was "largely restricted to the luxury of the body."[3] Confident that "Columbian science" could "redress the ravage of [the] encroaching clime,"[4] Americans demonstrated growing interest in improved heating and cooking devices. The nation's industrial pioneers played a crucial role in satisfying this demand, refining manufacturing techniques and expanding output. Inventors such as Benjamin Franklin, Charles Willson Peale, and Benjamin Thompson (Count Rumford) experimented with and wrote about new fireplace and stove designs, heightening public awareness. By the 1790s, domestic heating had become a subject "upon which every gentleman was expected to be knowledgeable."[5]

But fashion was not the principal reason growing numbers of Americans were considering modifying their fireplaces or installing stoves. Obtaining affordable firewood in sufficient quantity continued to be a problem in long-settled parts of the country, especially northern urban areas. Tench Coxe, assistant to Alexander Hamilton in the Treasury Department, observed in 1794 that "wood and timber are very much decreased in the principal part of New-England and in New-Jersey."[6] The same year, Connecticut clergyman Timothy Dwight told his countrymen to "Look round, and see your wood's decay'd, / Your fuel scarce, your timber fled." He advised woodlot owners to exercise greater care in managing these resources and pleaded with them to begin reforestation. Otherwise, he predicted, "winter's blast / Will soon the frozen skies o'ercast; / And, pinch'd, your children crowding nigher, / [Will] hang shivering o'er the scanty fire."[7] Despite Dwight's eloquence, few Americans appear to have acted on his recommendations. Twenty years later, Revolutionary War general Benjamin Lincoln reiterated Dwight's proposals, explaining that "our . . . trees are greatly reduced, and quite gone in many parts . . . not only from the demand of timber and planks, but from scarcity of other fuel."[8]

Even if all Americans had rushed to plant acorns and tend seedlings, it would have been many years before they could have alleviated the conditions that worried Dwight and Lincoln. In many areas, the problem was acute, so fuel prices continued to rise. Billy G. Smith has calculated that the firewood price index in Philadelphia increased 50 percent between 1783 and 1800.[9] Circumstances were much the same in other urban areas. In 1794, English visitor Thomas Cooper reported that "firing in the great towns [is] very dear, a chord of hickory . . . selling . . . in winter, at 7 dollars."[10]

The situation continued to deteriorate after the turn of the century. During a trip to Rhode Island, Englishman Charles Janson heard rural residents complaining about the high cost of firewood. "Wood is almost their only fuel," he observed. "Though the country is abundantly furnished . . . yet consumption renders it daily more difficult to be procured." Several "masters of families" he met claimed they spent up to $400 a year on fuel.[11] Conditions in cities were even worse. During the severe winter of 1804–5, Philadelphia merchant Thomas Cope noted in his diary that oak was selling for $12 a cord, and he had heard that the price in New York had reached the "enormous rate" of $48.[12]

Fuel shortages and high prices were especially hard on those with limited incomes because they were unable to buy and store large quantities of wood when prices were low. In January 1809, Thomas Robbins, a minister in East Windsor, Connecticut, commented in his diary that "poor people in this quarter suffer considerably for the want of wood."[13] In February 1815, after noting that the respective prices per cord of pine, oak, and hickory had reached $10, $15, and $18, Cope likewise observed that this was a "severe time on the poor."[14]

Philanthropists had proven unable to solve the problem, so the American Philosophical Society tried another approach, offering a $60 prize in 1796 "for the best construction or improvement of stoves." The "principal end," contest organizers explained, was "the benefit of the poorer class of people, especially . . . such as live . . . where fuel is dear."[15]

This competition attracted only four entries, but other efforts to improve domestic heating systems were under way. Between 1790, when the nation's patent system was inaugurated, and 1815, thirty-three patents were issued for improved fireplaces and chimneys. The pace of invention accelerated after the turn of the century; all but two of these devices were patented after 1799. Many of their inventors lived in Pennsylvania, where stove use was common, but interest in improved heating technology was beginning to spread to other parts of the country. More than half of these ideas originated in New York and New England, and several had roots in the upper South. Although many of these inventors lived in cities such as Philadelphia, Boston, and Hartford, where the fuel crisis was most pronounced, a significant number resided in rural areas. Their pursuit of increased fuel efficiency and comfort is clear in their patent descriptions—for example, "in saving of fuel" and "an iron back log for warming rooms."[16]

These inventors would presumably not have patented their devices if they thought there was no market for them. Affordable, fuel-efficient heating systems had an obvious appeal for urban residents, but interest was increasing in rural areas as well, where the overwhelming majority of the population lived. Fuel prices in these regions remained low,[17] but procuring and preparing firewood was tremendously time-consuming and physically demanding. In the early 1780s, J. Hector St. John de Crèvecoeur reported that "firewood is an immense addition [to a farmer's labor], although the wood costs nothing."[18] Contemporaries estimated that a "general average man" could cut an acre of timber (yielding approximately twenty-five cords of firewood) in seven to ten days. Three men with a yoke of oxen could clear an acre a day, cutting the trees into four- to fifteen-foot lengths.[19] Further sawing or chopping was necessary to prepare the wood for domestic use. It is difficult to ascertain the number of man-hours required to perform this back-breaking labor, but Richard Beeman calculates that farmers in "relatively temperate" southeastern Virginia in the late eighteenth century spent roughly 40 percent of their working hours between 1 October and 31 March gathering and preparing firewood.[20] In colder regions, even more time would have been required.

The diary kept by Abner Sanger, a farmer and laborer in Keene, New Hampshire, documents more specifically how much time American men in the early national period spent processing domestic fuel. Sanger rented a small farm where he lived with his mother, sister, and several boarders. The farm provided food, but Sanger relied on odd jobs for income. He also had to fell, haul, cut, and split the family's firewood. In 1781, Sanger spent all or part of thirty-two days felling and hauling trees for fuel for his own household. The task kept him occupied throughout the year (July was the only month with no entry for these activities), but he was busiest in the winter, when snow cover facilitated sledding.[21] A typical entry reads, "Afternoon I go up to Henry Ellis's and cut a jag of wood. I have his team to fetch it home. He helped me load it."[22]

A "jag" was about half a cord,[23] so Sanger's family consumed at least sixteen cords of firewood during 1781, all of which had to be cut and split. This work was so routine that Sanger sometimes included it under the general description "I take care," a phrase that referred to daily tasks such as feeding livestock and milking. But he specifically mentioned either cutting or splitting firewood for his own household on thirty-eight days, at least once in every month except June. Typical entries read, "I tend upon fetching water for Rhoda to wash, and cut and split wood" and "I take care, cut wood, oven-wood and etc."[24] Regrettably, it is impossible to determine how many hours Sanger spent cutting and splitting firewood. He rarely worked a full day at the task, usually devoting instead a "forenoon," an "afternoon," or just "three-quarters of an hour."[25]

Procuring and preparing firewood were central features of Sanger's life. In fact, when he was not cutting wood for his own household, Sanger often performed the task for others. In 1781, he cut wood on thirty-one days for fourteen different families. Sanger's customers were evidently people of some means; they included "goldsmith Farr," "Captain Ellis," and "lawyer Stiles."[26] The exhaustive detail of Sanger's diary explains why these men hired him to cut their firewood: the job of keeping a household supplied with fuel was both arduous and never ending.

In this context, anything that promised to reduce fuel consumption was attractive. After all, if a man invested in a fuel-efficient fireplace or stove, he could devote the time saved to other activities. Domestic comfort was also an issue. No matter how much wood someone piled in a conventional fireplace, the results were far from satisfactory. While visiting Rhode Island in the early nineteenth century, Charles Janson observed that New Englanders' houses provided "but an indifferent protection from the cold." "Water," he added, "will freeze within a few yards of a large fire in ten minutes."[27]

Janson's experience was not unusual. Even after decades of effort, American masons and builders had failed to perfect the fireplace. A. William Hoglund has estimated that before 1830 three-quarters of the firewood used in the United States was burned in inefficient fireplaces that lost 80 percent of their heat up the chimney.[28] Nevertheless, the experiments went on, evidence of the tenacious Anglo-American preference for the open fire.

Benjamin Franklin remained a key figure in these efforts. After introducing his Pennsylvanian Fire-Place in 1744, he had continued to tinker with domestic heating systems. While in London in the late 1750s, he developed a "simple machine" to improve fireplace function that he thought would prove useful in cities "where firing is often dear." The secret was to construct a chimney with a narrow throat and equip it with an iron "sliding plate." When the fireplace was in use, the plate was drawn out "so as to leave a space between its farther edge and the back, of about two inches," which would, Franklin promised, be "sufficient for the smoke to pass." With the rest of the chimney blocked, drafts would be reduced and most of the warm air generated by the fire would be directed into the room.[29] Franklin's English friends were impressed. "Since I first us'd this Contrivance," he reported, "many Hundreds have been set up . . . and they have afforded general Satisfaction." The "Contrivance," he declared, had "Simplicity, Cheapness, and Easy Execution . . . to recommend it."[30]

Franklin was also interested in improving kitchen fireplaces, although information about his work in this area is sketchy. After he returned to Philadelphia in 1762, he began planning an "avant-garde" house with a number of "European refinements," including an up-to-date kitchen. Work began the next year, but slowed after he was sent back to England in 1764. In letters to his wife, Franklin tried to ensure that construction of the house was proceeding according to his directions, fretting about everything from curtain hanging to rubbish disposal.[31] The kitchen, in particular, concerned him. "I . . . wished to have been present at the Finishing of the Kitchen," he wrote in 1765. "It is a mere Machine, and being new to you, I think you will scarce know how to work it."[32] Unfortunately, the details of this "Machine" are unknown. Franklin's letter suggests that it was modeled on the European range, a row of iron or copper vessels built permanently into brick fireboxes to the side of a fireplace.

Franklin's familiarity with European cooking systems was rare in America, but his fear that his wife would prove unable to manage the complicated "Machine" he had planned reflects an attitude about gender and technology common in his day. Invention, even for the home, was a man's field. After the Revolution, American inventors continued their efforts to improve domestic heating systems. Lacking culinary experience, most chose to concentrate on the heating fireplace. The few who did design kitchen equipment emphasized fuel economy and warmth rather than the taste of food or the ease of its preparation.

In 1797, artist and museum founder Charles Willson Peale tried his hand at the "art of economizing fuel" because he recognized that the "saving of fuel and the rendering of our habitations comfortable is an object of vast importance."[33] Peale proposed a "thorough reform" that would "not fail to obtain much warmth from small fires."[34] According to his explanation, "The whole art of warming rooms consists simply in preventing the escape of the warm air, and the intrusion of cold air." With his son Raphaelle, Peale designed an improved fireplace that he felt met these requirements. Slanted jambs and spaces in the side and back walls increased the amount of warm air conveyed into the room. A damper, which could be set in a number of positions, made it easy to provide a "proper vent" for smoke, thereby reducing the amount of warm air escaping up the chimney. He also added a "sliding-mantle," a metal panel installed in grooves along the side walls, which could be raised or lowered over the fireplace opening as required. Peale claimed his fireplaces would save "an immense quantity of fuel" because closing the damper and "sliding-mantle" at night would slow combustion.[35]

To prove its flexibility, Peale adapted his improved fireplace for kitchen use. He claimed that most kitchen fireplaces were larger than required and "so badly constructed, as not only to be subject to smoke, but . . . they make an unnecessary waste of wood, almost exceeding calculation." Peale solved these problems in his own kitchen by installing two fireplaces, each equipped with a damper and "sliding-mantle." One, "large enough to hold a large kettle and a pot on the same crane," was used for occasional big jobs such as laundry, and the other, smaller and more fuel-efficient, served for daily cooking. The flue from the smaller fireplace also heated the oven, whose temperature could, he claimed, be "increased or diminished at pleasure." In such a kitchen, Peale boasted, "provisions for a family of twenty persons may be cooked with great ease."[36] He failed to point out, of course, that the expense of building two kitchen fireplaces would have seemed exorbitant, especially to families with fewer than "twenty persons."

Peale's fireplace may have been superior to those in common use, but it was not cheap. After being granted a patent in 1797, he charged $10 for the right to alter a single fireplace and chimney, "besides payment of the tradesmen's bills." Although individual homeowners would have considered this fee excessive, institutional application of Peale's design made sense. The next year, New York City hired Peale to oversee construction of six fireplaces in its Alms House "as an Experiment to cure the Chimnies from smoking." In just one winter, the modifications "made a saving of fuel equal to the . . . cost of the Patent right, and paid also the expences of the alterations." Buoyed by this success, Peale awaited customers. "I ought to make a fortune," he concluded hopefully.[37]

Peale did have competition, however. Other inventors were hard at work trying to improve the fuel efficiency and convenience of domestic heating and cooking systems. In fact, it is likely that Peale based some of his ideas on the work of Benjamin Thompson, a Massachusetts-born Tory who left America for Europe after the Revolutionary War and spent eleven years in Bavaria as a military advisor and strategist, earning the title Count Rumford. One of his many interests was the economical use of fuel. He claimed that fireplaces with narrow flues, sharply angled side walls, and shallow hearths would reduce fuel consumption while increasing heat radiation. His recommendations were published in England in 1792 and reprinted six years later in America, eliciting considerable favorable response. According to historian Samuel Edgerton, the Rumford fireplace "received immediate and universal acceptance."[38]

Like Peale, Thompson was also interested in improving cooking equipment. In fact, he claimed that his devices would save up to 90 percent of the fuel consumed in traditional kitchens. His principles were simple: produce heat only when required and insulate cooking vessels to retain that heat. Rumford kitchens, characterized by large cast-iron kettles and cylindrical roasting ovens set in massive brickwork (illus. 3.1), were undeniably fuel efficient, but they were also expensive and difficult to install. As a result, they were employed in Europe primarily in institutional settings and in the homes of the wealthy.[39]

Thompson's influence on American kitchen design is difficult to trace. Certainly Peale was familiar with his recommendations, informing Thomas Jefferson in 1801 that "I have embraced Count Rumford's Idea's." Constructing cooking utensils that would "lessen labour, ward off danger, ensure cleanlyness, command the power of fire, and economise fuel," Peale continued, was of "no little consequence to the Citizens of America." In pursuit of these goals, he combined Thompson's devices with "other engenious inventions." "My Pots," he explained, "are all set in brick-work, with flues imbracing them . . . the air admitted below . . . and a damper to retain the heat." Peale's kitchen was also outfitted with three insulated ovens of different sizes and several "Steam Kettles." With this equipment, he claimed, only a small fireplace was needed, used primarily for roasting. The result was a kitchen "warm in Winter, and very cool in Summer" that saved 50 percent on fuel costs.[40]

3.1. J. L. Bridgman, *The Basement Kitchen, No. 2 Chestnut Street, Salem, c. 1850–56,* 1915. Black-and-white watercolor drawn from actual measurements. Courtesy of the Society for the Preservation of New England Antiquities, Boston, Mass.

Peale was also concerned with comfort and convenience. He vented his steam kettles into the chimney to keep the kitchen "free of vapour," equipped dampers and pot covers with wooden handles, and arranged flues with ease of cleaning in mind. A woman who used one of his kitchens "need have no fateague, nor a red face," he boasted. In fact, "the Mistress of a family and her daughters would . . . find amusement [rather] than trouble . . . in . . . their Kitchen."[41]

Despite Peale's efforts, there is little evidence that Rumford-style kitchens became widely popular in the United States. As in Europe, they appeared primarily in institutions and in the homes of the well-to-do. In 1805, for example, Peale supervised the installation of a Rumford kitchen at the Pennsylvania Hospital in Philadelphia.[42] At Monticello, Jefferson also converted at least partially to Rumford technology. When he heard in 1809 that a man named Henry Foxall was installing "irons of casting for the . . . stew-holes" in the White House kitchen, he wrote him to request eight for his own household "as they are indispensable in a kitchen."[43] About the same time, Massachusetts teenager Sarah Anna Smith visited the coastal town of Newburyport and was impressed to find in the kitchen of her uncle's "mansion" a "Rumford Cookery," which she described as a "huge contrivance of brick and masonry" with "several boilers of different sizes, and other devices to facilitate domestic purposes, with apertures under each for a wood fire."[44] Homes in Boston, too, occasionally incorporated similar equipment. When Jonathan Jackson died in 1810, for example, he left an estate worth nearly $17,000; in his kitchen, appraisers found a "Rumford . . . Apparatus."[45] Farther south, in Baltimore, Judith Riddell spent $85.60 in 1810 to equip the kitchen of her new $15,000 home with "a Rumford roaster w[ith] grates and Fire door complete, 1 Boiler with Cock etc., [and] a set [of] Steemers & stoppers."[46]

Full-scale Rumford kitchens were unusual in America, however, largely because of their expense. Jane Nylander contends that "more than five hundred Rumford apparatuses were operating in New England kitchens by 1826,"[47] but that does not seem a high figure considering the fact that Americans had been aware of Rumford's innovations for nearly three decades. In 1827, when Asher Benjamin reprinted his popular builder's guide, he knew of only one Boston manufacturer who could supply Rumford equipment.[48] Such reluctance to embrace new technologies understandably frustrated inventors. Years earlier, Peale had been dismayed that so few of the "Gentlemen and Ladies" to whom he showed his kitchen chose to adopt his ideas. "How extremely difficult is it to turn people . . . from their old customs!" he complained.[49]

Overcoming habit was not the only obstacle. In addition to their high cost, Rumford kitchens were permanent fixtures that had to be left behind if a family moved. They were also complex to operate and difficult to repair.[50] Elizabeth

Watters noticed another flaw, writing her aunt in 1803 that she was "pleased with
. . . Rumfordising the mode of Cookery for the summer but agree with the Cook
that the sight of the Fire is far to be prefered in Winter."[51] Aesthetic preferences
aside, Rumford kitchens also required a good deal of work. Scrubbing large kettles that could not be removed from their fireboxes was a challenge, something at
which Peale only hinted when he remarked that "the only Trouble of the Kitchen
falls on the scullion."[52] A woman with servants could, of course, leave this arduous task to them, but women who had to wash their own pots would not likely
have applauded such a system.

For all of these reasons, the Rumford kitchen did not meet the needs of most
families. American consumers valued fuel economy, but they wanted smaller,
transportable cooking appliances. In the early national period, inventors began
trying to satisfy this demand, patenting twenty-five cooking devices between
1796 and 1815. Although these efforts were unsuccessful, they nevertheless indicate what entrepreneurs thought consumers wanted. Fuel economy and porta-
bility were the top priorities, as suggested in several patent descriptions: "a
perpetual oven," "a portable kitchen," and "a moveable kitchen."[53] In 1797, the
New York Daily Advertiser called Thomas Passmore's "conjurer for cooking and
boiling," the first of these appliances, "a very useful & valuable machine" that
made possible "great saving of fuel." It could supposedly cook a steak in three
minutes or boil water in six minutes using only "a sheet of paper, a few shavings,
or any combustible." However, the advertisement added that the "conjurer" was
"particularly convenient for masters of vessels" or "gentlemen [boarding] in
Chambers," suggesting that it could not fulfill a typical family's cooking needs.[54]

Five years later, Nicholas Boureau patented an "Economical house & ship
steam kitchen" that he hoped would enjoy greater success. Perhaps assuming that
customers would be more likely to accept new cooking equipment if it echoed a
familiar form, he had attached a "copper cylinder boiler" to a ten-plate stove.
Meat and vegetables could be "separately & completely boiled in less time than
is usually done . . . by means of a tin pipe [attached to the boiler] & extended to
any direction," he claimed. "I have fully tested [the stove and boiler]," he reported, "& am happy to find . . . that not only the wealthy, but also the poor,
from the great saving of fuel, will be greatly benefitted."[55] It is difficult to imagine that Boureau's stove worked as well as he promised. Certainly a tin pipe "extended to any direction" would not have retained heat well and would probably
have leaked. There is no indication that this device was manufactured or sold in
quantity.

The success of inventors such as Boureau was likely hampered by reports that
stove-heated air was unhealthy. In 1776, stoves were removed from Philadelphia's

Independence Hall after members of the Continental Congress complained that the stoves were affecting their "Health and Eyesight."[56] The next year, John Adams was dismayed to learn of similar side effects. After visiting the single women's dormitory in the Moravian community at Bethlehem, Pennsylvania, he wrote his wife that the "Rooms were kept extreamly warm with Dutch Stoves and the Heat, the Want of fresh Air and Exercise relaxed the poor Girls in such a manner, as must I think destroy their Health."[57] Nancy Shippen of Philadelphia also thought stoves were dangerous, noting in her journal in 1784 that she "was much alarm'd by . . . Mamma's being taken suddenly ill in consequence . . . of her sitting too near a stove."[58]

Peale seems to have shared these concerns. Heat from an open fire was, he thought, "more agreeable" than that produced by "heated metals." He was also put off by the clumsy appearance of most stoves. "A well-formed . . . fireplace may . . . render . . . heat nearly equal to that produced by any kind of stove," he asserted, "and . . . be made very elegant."[59] By implication, stoves and the people who used them were not refined. Stove critics such as Peale failed to recognize, however, that "agreeable," "elegant" heat was a luxury. To most Americans, staying warm in winter was a matter of survival. What they wanted was inexpensive heat—the kind that could be generated most efficiently by a closed stove. If cooking tasks could be accommodated as well, so much the better.

Nevertheless, Anglo-Americans tried to combine the advantages of closed stoves and open fireplaces whenever they could. One compromise developed in the early 1780s was the "Rittenhouse stove," an improved version of the Franklin stove. Rittenhouse stoves had sharply angled back plates to reflect more heat into the room and side plates cast in the shape of the letter Z. As a result, they had less surface area than Franklin stoves, making them lighter and thus less expensive to manufacture and transport. They were especially popular in Pennsylvania. In January 1795 alone, one Philadelphia merchant ordered 136 Rittenhouse stoves from a single furnace.[60] The following year, French expatriate Moreau de St. Mery found them in common use in the city.[61]

Americans who traveled to Philadelphia on government business grew accustomed to open stoves and helped introduce them in other parts of the country. In August 1797, for example, George Washington wrote from Mount Vernon to ask Clement Biddle to buy him an open stove like the one he had used during his stay in the city. Although the stove in Washington's Philadelphia study had smoked, he was willing to put up with this annoyance in order to be warm in winter. "I do not . . . see any occasion," he told Biddle, "for the second turn w[hi]ch that Pipe takes; and which probably is the cause of its smoking; an evil to be avoided if possible." Biddle failed to respond to this request, however, so, as the weather grew colder, Washington bought a stove in nearby Alexandria. Again, he was willing to compromise. "Although it is not altogether such as I wanted," he informed Biddle in mid-October, "a very good shift can be made with it."[62] Thomas Jefferson was equally impressed with open stoves. In November 1804, he asked Benjamin Latrobe of Philadelphia to procure "3 of the handsomest stoves, of the kind called . . . Rittenhouse."[63]

Open stoves remained popular for many years, probably because they combined the benefits of traditional fireplaces and closed stoves, yet their ability to warm rooms was limited. When Joseph Shoemaker Russell painted a Tiverton, Rhode Island, dining room as it looked in the winter of 1814–15 (illus. 3.2), he depicted an elderly man warming himself and reading next to a cheerful fire in an open stove, but the many layers of clothing the man is wearing suggest that the room is rather chilly, despite the stove's presence.

Henry Vanderlyn experienced other problems when he acquired an open stove for his Oxford, New York, law office in 1829. He had recently had the fireplace bricked up in anticipation of the stove's arrival, and at first the damp mortar caused it to smoke. After the wall had dried, however, the stove began to draw and Vanderlyn was "very much pleased with a most comfortable & ornamental fire place. It is far preferable to a common fireplace."[64]

3.2. Joseph Shoemaker Russell, *Dining Room of Dr. Whitridge's, Tiverton, Rhode Island, As It Was in the Winter 1814–1815: Breakfast Time (Pot-Apple Pie)*, c. 1848. Courtesy of the Old Dartmouth Historical Society—New Bedford Whaling Museum, New Bedford, Mass.

It is unclear why Vanderlyn chose an open stove instead of a more efficient closed model; perhaps he thought an "ornamental fire place" would make a better impression on clients. His contemporaries knew that when warmth was the primary goal, an open stove was not the sensible choice. However, it took a long time for Anglo-Americans to reconcile themselves to the closed stove. For many years, inventors struggled to come up with a heating appliance that worked as well as, but did not otherwise resemble, the box stoves common in Pennsylvania German homes.

Benjamin Franklin, who acknowledged in 1773 that "those that live . . . [with Stoves] get no colds,"[65] was one of the first to attempt such a system. Two years before, he had developed a "smoke-consuming" urn stove for use in his London lodgings. This device (illus. 3.3) resembled an open fireplace but functioned like

3.3. Benjamin Franklin, design for urn stove, 1771, in *Transactions of the American Philosophical Society* 2 (1786). Courtesy of the American Philosophical Society, Philadelphia, Penn.

a closed stove. Unlike other stoves, however, it did not need a stovepipe, which many people considered unsightly. Franklin placed the stove inside an iron-lined niche to maximize heat radiation. Smoke collected inside the urn in the center and was drawn back down through the fire by means of an opening in the floor.[66] Despite Franklin's love of an open fire, in this device it remained invisible, which likely explains the compensatory decorative "flame." Franklin used this stove for several years but was not entirely happy with it, dismissing it as an "oddity." The stove suffered from "several inconveniences," he told a friend. "It requires too much attention . . . to be controlled by ordinary servants, which is why I could not recommend its use even though I use it myself."[67] Moreover, it was expensive to cast and required a chimney with a very strong draft. There is no record that Franklin's urn stove was ever produced or sold in America.[68]

Twenty years later, other American inventors took up the challenge of designing a heating system that combined the best features of stoves and fireplaces. Ironically, Peale was one of the leading participants in this effort. At the same time that he was advertising his improved fireplace, he was also experimenting with stoves. In the 1790s, he built and installed in his Philadelphia museum two brick stoves of the type developed by French architect Francois Cointeraux. In 1796, Peale reported the results of a test of their "utility in the saving of fuel." He had placed one stove about a foot from the wall in a large room with a fifteen-foot ceiling. Early on a January morning when the outside temperature was thirty-five degrees, he opened the windows for an hour and twenty minutes. After closing them, he built a fire in the stove. When the wood was consumed, he covered the coals with ashes, closed the stove door and damper, and waited to see what would happen. A thermometer hanging in the middle of the room registered the results. At 9:20 A.M., the reading was forty-two degrees; by 1:30 P.M., the temperature had reached fifty-four degrees. Moreover, the heat generated by this stove was "regular and agreeable," unlike that produced by iron stoves. Peale was impressed, calling on his fellow citizens to join him in bringing brick stoves "into general use." Unfortunately, constructing these stoves was tricky. He reported in 1798 that "several" had been built in Philadelphia, but that "for want of attention to proper materials . . . there are not many of them now standing."[69]

Peale refused to give up. In the late 1790s, he designed a new stove shaped like a column, complete with pedestal and cornice and surmounted by a classical bust (illus. 3.4). Built of brick like his previous design, this stove was covered with plaster and painted to resemble marble. Inside, smoke was drawn back down through the fire for recombustion, while a subfloor pipe drew off the heated air. Peale installed at least two of these "smoke-eater" stoves in his museum. They "answer a double purpose," he boasted in 1802; "they not only warm

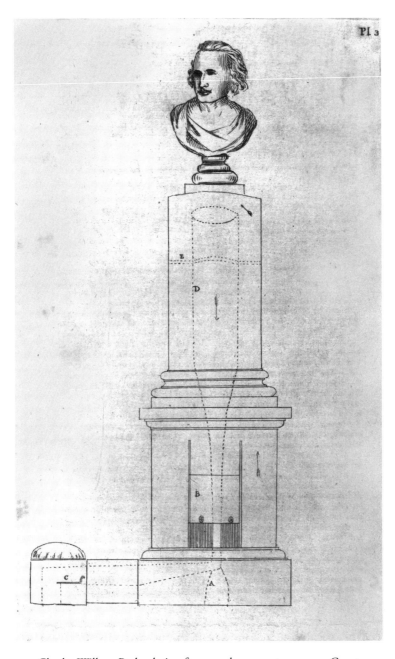

3.4. Charles Willson Peale, design for a smoke-eater stove, 1799. Courtesy of the American Philosophical Society, Philadelphia, Penn.

the Rooms compleatly but also excite much wonder." Regrettably, the smoke-eater stove was expensive to manufacture and complex to install and regulate. It never came into common use.[70]

Although unsuccessful, Franklin's and Peale's efforts demonstrate how reluctant some Anglo-Americans in the early national period were to accept the closed cast-iron stove. Most of their countrymen, however, valued fuel efficiency and warmth above looks and were willing to sacrifice style to performance. Fortunately, a number of improvements in iron-founding technology made their decision easier by enhancing both stove durability and appearance. In the Philadelphia region, the introduction of air furnaces allowed pig iron to be remelted for casting. Castings produced from remelted pig iron proved more closely grained and stronger than those cast directly at the furnace, and they had a longer life expectancy. Simultaneously, the adoption of flask casting made it possible to produce stove plates that were thinner, lighter, and easier to transport and assemble. Flask-cast plates could also be curved, which reduced cracking, and they had raised designs on both sides, which allowed for the addition of grooves and collars to improve fit and reduce smoke leakage between plates. More delicate ornamentation also became possible.[71]

By the early nineteenth century, cast-iron stoves exemplified the best of Federal design. In 1801, for example, the New York *American Citizen and General Advertiser* announced the availability of "Pyramidal Stoves . . . with lion's feet, the bust of General Washington on top—the arms of the United States on each side . . . the whole . . . finished in a masterly stile."[72] Adamesque ovals were popular motifs as well, as were classical urns and overflowing cornucopias (illus. 3.5 and 3.6). These celebrations of the new nation's democracy and abundance suggest that stove manufacturers were trying to make their products more acceptable to consumers. As Samuel Edgerton has observed, "the intrusion of rococo and . . . Adam tendencies into stove design is very important in showing how 'people of quality' were trying to adjust this new comfort improvement to their . . . sophisticated surroundings."[73]

The pace of stove adoption remained slow, however. According to one observer, Anglo-Americans were still "prejudiced" against closed stoves,[74] a sentiment that may have stemmed, at least in part, from lingering anti-German feeling. In 1794, Timothy Dwight criticized the lifestyle of the nation's "stinting Germans" while celebrating the "social circles" gathered around the "nutwood fire" in Anglo-American homes. To Dwight, being cold imparted important benefits that would be lost if stoves became common. "Every . . . blast," he argued, "brings health, and life, and vigour . . . / Innerves the steely frame, and firms the soul."[75]

3.5. New Orleans Victory ten-plate stove, Henry Schreiner, Philadelphia, c. 1820. Courtesy of Old Sturbridge Village, Sturbridge, Mass.; photograph by Henry E. Peach.

3.6. Side-plate detail, Henry Abbett ten-plate cookstove, Philadelphia, c. 1820. Collection of Donald Carpentier.

The high cost of stoves was an even more important factor retarding their dispersion. As had been the case before the Revolution, stoves were still too expensive for most families. In 1784, wholesale prices at the Atsion Furnace in Burlington County, New Jersey, ranged from £3.5.0 for a small six-plate stove to £5.7.6 for a ten-plate stove.[76] Retail prices were substantially higher; Josephine Peirce estimated that in 1785, Philadelphians paid £6 for a "large" six-plate stove and £10 for a ten-plate stove.[77] Prices would have been even steeper in regions distant from stove-manufacturing centers in the middle states.

Nevertheless, the economics of stove use was making more and more sense to those responsible for heating public buildings. Throughout the early national period, manufacturers and dealers emphasized that their products were especially suited to "church[es], Public Office[s], Halls or large Stores" as well as "meeting-houses, or school-houses."[78] In 1789, the trustees of the University of Pennsylvania resolved "that Stoves be erected in the English and Latin Schools." Built the same year, Philadelphia's Congress Hall was equipped with one closed and eight open stoves. According to Edgerton, by the 1790s "probably every public building in Philadelphia that could afford it [*sic*] was heated by stoves."[79]

Stoves were becoming increasingly familiar in rural Pennsylvania, too. Even though genre artist John Lewis Krimmel set his 1813–14 village tavern scene in May (illus. 3.7),[80] apparently the weather was still cool enough to make stove use attractive. The open door and the casual demeanor of the individuals grouped in the center suggest that the room is not particularly cold, but the man at the far left seems to be warming himself. He is seated next to a large ten-plate stove with his feet propped comfortably on the hearth plate. A beverage warms in a tankard on the stove top, and a pair of tongs leans nearby, ready for the periodic task of fire tending.

Stove use in public and institutional settings was becoming more common outside Pennsylvania as well. Levi Beardsley, born in upstate New York in 1785,

3.7. John Lewis Krimmel, *Village Tavern*, 1813–14. Courtesy of the Toledo Museum of Art, Toledo, Ohio.

3.8. Lewis Miller, "In Side of the Old Lutheran Church in 1800, York, Pa.," n.d. *Lewis Miller: Sketches and Chronicles* (York, Penn.: Historical Society of York County, 1966), 13. Courtesy of the Historical Society of York County, York, Penn.

always remembered his first encounter with the new technology. At age four, he had accompanied his parents to a country store, where, he recalled, "I first saw a stove . . . [which] I recollect from putting my hand on it and getting burned."[81] In 1793, leaders of the Shaker community in nearby New Lebanon decided to install "two or three stoves in the great house[,] . . . the first used [here]."[82] By 1795, their coreligionists in Shirley, Massachusetts, had placed stoves in every room of their large dwelling house.[83] Six years later, residents of Danville, Vermont, put a stove in their county courthouse.[84] Comfort and the desire for fuel savings were presumably the factors influencing these decisions. As Quartermaster General John Wilkins Jr. explained in 1797, when he shipped twenty stoves to the army garrison in Detroit, "[They] will aid in making the soldiers more comfortable and [will] save firewood."[85]

These sources gloss over the fact that installing a stove, especially in a large space, was far from easy. If centrally located to maximize heat radiation, as in the Lutheran church in York, Pennsylvania, depicted in illustration 3.8, a stove needed a lengthy stovepipe that had to be supported by strands of wire every few feet. Experience quickly proved the flaws of such an arrangement. "Horizontal pipes," noted Rev. William Bentley of Salem, Massachusetts, were "found inconvenient from their soot and if not carefully suspended to be dangerous."[86] The result was also unattractive. Samuel Edgerton has pointed out that "discriminating visitors to the Pennsylvania Supreme Court in the 1790s must have been highly offended at the sight of two hundred and thirteen pounds of [stovepipe] angling among the finely fluted Georgian pilasters."[87] Stovepipe could also mar a building's exterior. A 1799 engraving of Independence Hall (illus. 3.9) shows two pipes protruding awkwardly from windows on the building's otherwise elegant west facade.[88]

Americans also worried about the moral influence of stoves. In the late eighteenth and early nineteenth centuries, New Englanders, in particular, debated the propriety of installing stoves in the public structure most closely identified with their spiritual heritage—the church or meetinghouse. After its restoration in 1783, Boston's Old South Church was heated with stoves, an innovation viewed with considerable suspicion in some quarters. After all, the "Ancient Christians" had been pious without being comfortable, an anonymous poet pointed out. But, he sneered, in "these modern velvet days" church members wanted "the way to heav'n" to be "smooth and even." "The sacred fire of love" had become "extinct," this critic complained, and worshipers' "zeal [had] grown cold and dead." He concluded bitterly, "In house of God we fix a stove, / To warm us in its stead."[89]

3.9. William Birch, Independence Hall, 1799. Engraving. Courtesy of the American Philosophical Society, Philadelphia, Penn.

Controversy accompanied the introduction of stoves in other places of worship as well. When William Bentley became minister of the East Congregational Church in Salem, Massachusetts, in 1783, no church in town was heated by stoves, but a pronounced "change in public manners" occurred over the next several decades. The Quakers, perhaps influenced by coreligionists in Pennsylvania, were the first to adopt stoves. Other congregations followed suit—first the Congregationalists in the North and "Old" parishes, next the Episcopalians, and then the Baptists. By 1810, Bentley reported, "the Cry is now all for Stoves," but he was a technological conservative. Two years before, he had approved the use of a small charcoal stove in his church's "singing gallery," but he was reluctant to sanction a stove anywhere else. Many members of his flock favored stoves, but he thought their "inconveniences are not without claim upon notice." Apparently

Bentley's reservations were respected, at least for some years. In 1818, his church was one of the few in town not yet heated by stoves.[90]

Voters in Spencer, Massachusetts, struggled with a different dilemma when they considered installing a stove in the town's meetinghouse in 1821. Because the structure served as both a place of worship and the site of town meetings, a question arose as to whether the funds to heat it should come from tax revenues. Congregationalism was still the state religion in Massachusetts, but support for the separation of church and state was growing. Town leaders decided that a stove could be installed in the building, but only "by subscription, and without any cost to the town." For several years, townspeople even refused to permit tax revenues to be used to buy fuel for the stove.[91]

Connecticut residents could be equally contentious. Samuel Goodrich, born in Ridgefield in 1793, recalled that the inhabitants of "a certain country town" had been sharply divided over the introduction of stoves in their meetinghouse. Torn between the "Demon of Progress" and the "Angel of Conservatism," they split into a "Stove Party" and an "Anti-stove Party." "The battle raged portentously," with the minister caught in the middle. "Finally," Goodrich remembered, "the progressionists prevailed [and] great was the humiliation of the antistoveites." On the Sunday after stoves were installed, "Mrs. Deacon P," a leader of the "Anti-stove Party," came to church looking "pale but calm, as a martyr should." When the minister preached from Romans 12:20 about "heaping coals of fire on the head," she "slid from her seat, and subsided gently upon the floor." Concerned bystanders rushed her outside for fresh air and asked why she had fainted. "It is the heat of those awful stoves," she replied. "Mrs. Deacon K," a leader of the "Stove Party," pointed out that the stoves were not being used that day because the weather was unseasonably warm, causing her embarrassed opponent to slink home "in a manner suitable to the occasion." While this dispute raged, it "threatened to overturn society," but, Goodrich implied, the right side had triumphed. "All improvement is gradual," he observed, "and frequently advances only by conflict with prejudice."[92]

A similar debate divided Rev. Thomas Robbins's congregation in East Windsor, Connecticut. Robbins, privately a stove advocate, noted in his diary on 14 December 1821 that "there is some difference of opinion . . . about procuring a stove for the meeting-house." Five days later, he commented: "I fear trouble respecting our meeting-house stove." Unfortunately, the diary is silent as to how this "trouble" was resolved. Robbins may have overcome the "antistoveites" by spearheading a drive for donations; he contributed $7.50 himself. He merely noted on 6 January 1822 that "we have two stoves set up in the meeting-house," which were "a great relief from the cold," despite the fact that they "smoke some."[93]

Robbins was wise to work behind the scenes. Ministers who publicly supported the introduction of stoves ran the risk of alienating parishioners. After the Rev. Merrill of Lyndeborough, New Hampshire, began lobbying for a stove, an elderly member of his flock groused, "I have attended church these fifty years; I have fought the British . . . ; I have slept . . . on the frozen ground. . . . I have trod the snow path with bleeding feet . . . and if Mr. Merrill needs a fire, let him go to the place where they keep one year round."[94] As Robert Cray has pointed out, the debate over stove use in New England communities such as Lyndeborough was symptomatic of deeper divisions over theology and values. Fixed stoves lessened the need for individual footstoves, which had long been popular with the social elite. Thus, the new technology rendered these "important social props" obsolete and threatened to "democratize" the meetinghouse.[95]

Despite the concerns of stove opponents, however, heating stoves became increasingly common in public buildings during the early national period. While touring Vermont in 1819, Levi Woodbury noted that "almost every place of public worship in this quarter is well warmed by stoves."[96] Stoves were gradually being introduced in more private dwellings as well. In 1795, Thomas Jefferson informed Thomas Mann Randolph that he had begun to install stoves at Monticello, "much to our comfort & the economy of wood," and concluded, "I believe I shall adopt the general use of the stove against next winter."[97] Martha Saunders Salisbury, widow of a merchant in Worcester, Massachusetts, would likely have agreed with Jefferson about the comfort stoves provided. When she died in 1792, probate assessors found in her home a "stove & fraim" worth £4.[98]

By the first decade of the nineteenth century, less-wealthy Americans were also beginning to acquire heating stoves, especially for use in workshops and stores. When Festus Bliss, a joiner in Springfield, Massachusetts, and Israel Pierce, the owner of a general store in nearby Northampton, died in 1810, for example, probate assessors found stoves in their places of business. To the east, in Worcester County, stove use was also becoming more common. Heating stoves are listed in two of the inventories recorded there in 1810; in both cases, they were used in stores or workshops.[99] But the fact that only four of the 123 estates probated in these two counties in 1810 include stoves suggests that stove adoption was proceeding slowly. New England city dwellers were only marginally more committed to the new technology. Stoves are listed in only three of the fifty-eight probate inventories recorded in and around Boston in 1810, and only two of the twenty Providence, Rhode Island, households inventoried the same year were equipped with stoves.[100]

In contrast, Anglo-Americans in the mid-Atlantic states were beginning to rely more heavily on stoves. More than 40 percent of the 1790s estate inventories

3.10. John Lewis Krimmel, "Woman at Hearth," 4 July 1819, Sketchbook, 6.
Courtesy of the Joseph Downs Collection of Manuscripts and Printed
Ephemera, The Winterthur Library, Winterthur, Del.

Joan Jensen examined from Chester County, Pennsylvania, and New Castle
County, Delaware, list "stoves and ovens."[101] In 1805, Margaret Bayard Smith,
wife of a Washington, D.C., newspaper publisher, informed her sister that a
stove had made a big difference in her household. "I have had a close stove put
up in the kitchen," she reported, "which saves one half of the wood that used to
be consumed."[102]

Although fuel-efficient, box stoves could not yet replace the kitchen fireplace,
however. Even a ten-plate stove could not comfortably accommodate all cooking
tasks, and its oven was too small for large amounts of baked goods. In fact, as an
1819 sketch by John Lewis Krimmel reveals (illus. 3.10), in summer a ten-plate
stove might be useful only as a table. An anonymous inventor was correct when

he argued in 1796 that the closed stove of the period was "far from solving" Americans' need for improved heating and cooking appliances. "By being unattended with a free circulation of air it is insalubrious," he noted; "it is also expensive."[103] Americans who agreed with these sentiments would have to wait a few years for a more satisfactory stove. Beginning in the 1810s, developments in iron manufacturing led to improved stove design, and expanding transportation networks lowered freight costs. Simultaneously, inventors developed the first successful full-function cookstoves.

4

"A Great Variety of Stoves Just Received"

BETWEEN 1815 AND 1840, the American economy continued its rapid growth. Immigration and a high rate of natural increase boosted the population from 7.2 million in 1810 to more than 17 million thirty years later.[1] Manufacturing expanded dramatically as well; by 1840, the United States ranked second behind only Great Britain in industrial development.[2] Improved roads as well as a steamboat and canal boom lowered freight rates and made a variety of goods, including anthracite coal, more widely available.[3] These changes accelerated the adoption of both heating and cooking stoves in American homes, a process that can be reconstructed by examining the experiences of those involved in what Ruth Schwartz Cowan has aptly termed the "consumption junction"—the inventor, the manufacturer, the retailer, and the consumer.[4]

As Jean Matthews has pointed out, the "American mind" of the early national period "expressed itself most characteristically in the conquest of matter for utility and power."[5] John Kasson has likewise noted that antebellum Americans were "seized by a mania for invention." They "glorified" machines, "not simply as functional objects but as . . . symbols of the future,"[6] substantiating the statements of lawyer turned essayist Timothy Walker, who argued in 1831 that "the more work we can compel inert matter to do for us, the better will it be."[7] Ralph Waldo Emerson shared this faith in the transformative power of technology, noting in his journal two years later that the "progress of art" would soon "equalize all places." He predicted that "Anthracite coal, Nott stoves, coffee and books will give Greenland the air and ease of London."[8] By 1857, children's author Samuel Goodrich could claim that this day had arrived. "The miracles of antiquity are between thumb and finger now," he asserted; "a friction-match gives us fire and light. . . . We have summer in our houses, even through the rigors of winter."[9]

The nation's inventors played a crucial role in this process. In the 1790s, only twenty-seven patents were granted each year on average; in the 1830s, the figure was 572.[10] Although stoves have received far less attention than innovations such as the cotton gin and power loom, they were the focus of much of this activity. In fact, the commissioner of patents told Congress in 1845 that "the number of models of this invention far exceeds any other."[11] Between 1790 and 1814, fifty-three patents were issued for stoves and stove attachments (2.4 percent of patents for the period). Between 1815 and 1839, the pace accelerated, with 329 of these devices receiving patents (3.6 percent). Although much early attention focused on heating stoves, cooking stoves were becoming increasingly important; between 1835 and 1839 alone, 102 cookstoves were patented.[12]

Much of this inventiveness was inspired by the nation's continuing fuel crisis, a connection recognized by New York City merchant John Pintard, who observed in 1832 that the high cost of fuel had produced "great improvements in the construction of Cast Iron Stoves."[13] The wholesale price index for "fuel and light" had doubled between 1800 and 1815.[14] Although firewood prices dropped somewhat after the War of 1812, concern about fuel availability and cost did not abate. In 1817, *Niles' Weekly Register* argued that "economy in the consumption of fuel . . . is every year growing . . . of greater importance."[15] English visitor Frances Trollope would have agreed; she spent the winter of 1828–29 "shivering and shaking" near Cincinnati, "half-ruined in fire-wood (which . . . is nearly as dear as at Paris, & dearer in many parts of the Union)."[16]

Many observers felt the solution to this problem lay in a new fuel—anthracite coal. Jacob Cist, an early participant in the industry, asked in 1814, "How many miserable wretches, who shiver over . . . wood fires, which cost them 6 and 8 dollars per cord, could be made comfortable [with coal] at half the price?"[17] Cist may have been overly optimistic, but James Ronaldson of Philadelphia calculated the next year that using anthracite instead of wood for all domestic and manufacturing purposes in the city would produce savings of 25 percent.[18] Pintard agreed that coal was the best domestic fuel. During the "excessively severe winter" of 1830–31, he wrote his daughter that "general consumption of this article can alone render poor people comfortable at a cheap price."[19]

As far as cost was concerned, Pintard was right. As canals made coal more available in eastern markets, its price fell dramatically; the wholesale price index for anthracite declined nearly 60 percent between 1815 and 1825, and dropped another 45 percent during the 1830s.[20] As a result, fuel savings were considerable. The steward of Philadelphia's Pennsylvania Hospital reported in 1825 that switching from wood to coal had saved the institution more than $1,000 a year.[21]

Some consumers were convinced. In 1825, *New England Farmer* reported that residents of Wilkes Barre, Pennsylvania, used coal as their "principal fuel . . . both in parlours and kitchens." According to this account, coal had several advantages over wood: it burned more cleanly and kept a fire going longer, and its "durability, during combustion, save[d] two thirds of the trouble of attendance on fires."[22] The next year, Yale chemistry professor Benjamin Silliman called anthracite an "invaluable combustible" and observed that "the heat produced by a [coal] stove . . . is very mild and agreeable." He preferred coal to wood because it was cheaper, safer, and less smoky, and it reduced soot buildup. A coal fire also required less maintenance than one fueled by wood and, if carefully managed, could last overnight.[23]

But there was one major obstacle to overcome before Americans would accept coal, despite its low cost. Because anthracite required a higher temperature for combustion than wood, it was much more difficult to light. Consumers who switched to the new fuel quickly learned that even years of fire-building experience were of little help. In 1827, Robert Roberts enlightened readers of *The House Servant's Directory* about the "great mystery" of making fires with coal. "Let the grate be perfectly cleared," he directed. Next a layer of kindling wood was laid, followed by live coals from another fire, followed by pieces "about the size of a half-pint tumbler." Even if these instructions were followed to the letter, however, success was not assured. "If the process . . . fails," Roberts concluded discouragingly, "begin all over again."[24]

A decade later, Americans were still struggling with the new fuel. Denison Olmsted, professor of mathematics and natural history at Yale, noted in 1837 that "the community is . . . but imperfectly acquainted with the proper management of anthracite." Many families, especially during the first year of using coal, "fail[ed] to derive from it any of its peculiar advantages, while they suffer[ed] many inconveniences." Only after a "long and troublesome probation" did they achieve a "well-constructed fire," he concluded.[25]

Despite these problems, inventors and entrepreneurs did what they could to popularize coal. In 1826, the Franklin Institute offered a prize for the best coal cookstove design of the year.[26] Five years later, the institute's Committee on Premiums announced that mine owners had added $20 to its own $100 award for the best new coal-burning cookstove.[27] Inventors apparently responded to these enticements, patenting at least thirty-five coal stoves between 1825 and 1840.[28]

The effort to convince Americans to adopt coal as a domestic fuel was only minimally successful, however. Sales of anthracite increased from 365 tons in 1820 to more than 180,000 tons in 1830, but as late as 1850 wood still accounted for roughly 90 percent of the nation's fuel.[29] Except in northeastern cities, where the firewood crisis was most severe, consumers were reluctant to change their ways.

They must also have been bewildered by the explosion in the number of stove models. In 1821, A. F. M. Willich explained why he had refrained from discussing the new technology in his book, *The Domestic Encyclopedia*. "Stoves are

. . . so numerous that a description . . . would occupy a volume," he claimed. Besides, "as improvements are making in them daily, the information of the present . . . would probably be useless a year hence."[30] To Lydia Maria Child, author of *The American Frugal Housewife*, the rapid pace of innovation in the stove industry was a metaphor for other social change; in 1838, she characterized Calvinism as "a faith that must be thrown aside like a useless stove of last year's patent."[31] Henry Colman, editor of *New Genessee Farmer*, chose a different analogy, remarking in 1842 that "it is now a days with stoves . . . as it is with Ladies' bonnets. The man who purchases one . . . must hurry home, or the fashion may change before it can be mounted."[32]

Many early-nineteenth-century cookstoves were, in fact, nearly "useless." They were often poorly conceived and unstable, like the ones depicted in illus-

4.1. H. Fossette, after Charles Burton, "Bowery Theatre, New York," 1831. Engraving. I. N. Phelps Stokes Collection, Miriam and Ira D. Wallach Division of Art, Prints and Photographs, New York Public Library; Astor, Lenox, and Tilden Foundations, New York, N.Y.

tration 4.1, evidence that inventors had not mastered the design process. It was difficult for male inventors to grasp the nuances of a traditionally female skill, so it is not surprising that sometimes their efforts fell short. In 1842, Mrs. A. M. F. Annan told readers of *Godey's Lady's Book* the story of Mr. Chancy, whose desire to be acknowledged as "the father of some remarkable invention" inspires him to design a model cookstove. He works for weeks, neglecting his business and falling into debt, and finally produces a stove "immeasurably surpassing in complexity" all others on the market. He hires a local foundry to manufacture a prototype and proudly has it installed in his own kitchen. "You never saw such a collection of conveniences before," he boasts to his wife. "Here are cast-iron boilers, and sheet-iron boilers, and tin boilers. Here are cast-iron pans, and sheet-iron pans, and tin pans; and iron roasters and tin roasters; and iron bakers and tin bakers, and here are an iron tea-kettle, and a copper one; and stew-pans . . . and a large griddle and smaller ones, besides different sized gridirons, and preservers and picklers."[33]

His wife is far from impressed, however. "You don't pretend to call that monstrous thing a cooking stove?" she demands. How is anybody . . . to learn the twistings and turnings of such a machine as that?" "A cooking stove ought to be comprehended without any reasoning power," she explains patiently. "Everything about it ought to be plain at first sight." But Mr. Chancy insists that she give his stove a trial, so she reluctantly complies. Predictably, she finds that it is too large to heat evenly and economically, and she is unable to master the intricacies of its "cranks, and flues, and inclined planes." When he blames her troubles on lack of knowledge, she fumes, "Really, Mr. Chancy! As if it were a matter of course that we should get people to suit our stoves, instead of stoves to suit our people."[34]

Stove inventors failed consumers in other ways as well. The differences between models were often small, suggesting a rush to market products without thorough planning and testing. In reviewing one purportedly new stove in 1832, the editors of the *Journal of the Franklin Institute* snapped, "We think that the invention must be . . . microscopic, as we are unable to discover it with spectacles."[35] Three years later, they observed, "There is, in general, so little of new invention manifested in cooking, or other, stoves, and their number is so great, that we rarely think it necessary to give the particulars."[36] The commissioner of patents agreed that stove inventors lacked originality, telling Congress in 1845 that a "large number of applications for patents for stoves have been rejected, as presenting nothing more than mere changes of form."[37]

The high number of stove patents that were granted created a perplexing patchwork for manufacturers hoping to enter the industry. As William Keep pointed out in 1931, "in those days [stove] inventors worked independently. . . .

Means of communication were so poor that one invention may not have been known outside the immediate neighborhood."[38] Confusion sometimes resulted. In 1839, for example, inventor James Wilson complained to the New York firm Morse & Son, "I have just seen A Cooking Stove . . . said to be Made by you Passing the Fire Entirely Round the Oven by means of Dovetail or [Fanlight?] Dampers that Improvement belongs to me by Virtue of A Patent dated 12 Sept 1834."[39]

Even if inventors and retailers did not violate someone else's patent, they had difficulty separating themselves from the hundreds of other entrepreneurs seeking to profit from stoves. In 1837, stove dealers Kimball & Page in Bradford, New Hampshire, tried hyperbole to sell the recently patented Moore cookstove. In lyrics set to the tune of "Yankee Doodle," they addressed readers of the *Argus Spectator*:

> One Johnny Moore of Yankee blood,
> A cute and cunning fellow,
> He made himself a Cooking Stove—
> By gosh! It was a whaler.
> Four holes upon its top it had,
> And rims both big and little,
> So he could boil his dinner in
> Most any kind of kettle.
> A darn'd great oven, too, it had,
> As big as Granny's apron,
> In which he always baked his bread,
> While Molly fried the bacon.
>
> It took but mighty little fire
> To cook a rousing dinner;
> 'Twould bake his bread and boil his pot,
> And warm a chilly sinner.[40]

These overblown claims did not convince experts of the Moore stove's benefits. In fact, the editors of the *Journal of the Franklin Institute* thought it had "nothing in it meriting particular notice."[41] But even unsuccessful stove designs reveal what inventors believed consumers wanted. In the 1820s and 1830s, a number of "combination" stoves were introduced that supposedly possessed both the efficiency of cookstoves and the charm of fireplaces.[42] One of the more fanciful efforts was George Richards's Alterable Cooking and Franklin Stove (illus. 4.2), which folded up into a "handsome open Franklin fire place" or down into a bilevel cookstove. In 1829, Richards announced that changing the stove from one position to the other was "an easy process" that took only a minute,[43]

Anvils and Vices and various other goods which
together with the former stock makes a complete assortment and is offered for sale on very favorable
terms.   2wd   nov 28

A REAL CONVENIENCE.

THE Alterable Cooking and Franklin Stove,
which may be altered (by an easy process) in
one minute, from a Cooking Stove, to a handsome
open Franklin fire place. It has an excellent oven
and will operate four or five boilers at once, with
the quantity of fuel usually required for *two*, in
other stoves, and when altered into a Franklin, the
oven and two boilers may still be kept in operation.
The plate shows the stove in both forms.

The subscriber having invented a new and useful
improvement, which eminently combines in its construction, all the advantages of the *Cooking and
Franklin Stove*, has obtained Letters Patent for the
same duly executed according to law, signed by the
President of the United States, now offers for sale
the *Right* to make use and vend the afore-
said *Improvement* in any of the States, or coun-
tries, (not already sold) on terms very favorable to
the purchaser. Those engaged in casting or selling
stoves will find it greatly to their advantage to purchase the right. All persons are forbid making, using, or vending said improvement, without leave
first had and obtained of the Patentee in writing on
penalty of the law.

N. B. These Stoves will be for sale in about six
weeks by the subscriber at his residence, No. 30,
Pawtuxet Street. GEO. RICHARDS, Patented.
nov 9   2mo

BAKE HOUSE.

THE Bake House now occupied by Stephen
Wrightington, under the Fall River Hotel,
kept by NEWHALL, will be rented after the first

4.2. Advertisement for George Richards's Alterable Cooking and Franklin Stove,
Providence Journal (1 Dec. 1829), 1. Courtesy of the Rhode Island Historical Society,
Providence, R.I.

but the editors of the *Journal of the Franklin Institute* were not persuaded, arguing that most people would "deem it inconvenient rather than otherwise."[44]

Richards's stove was occasionally advertised in New England,[45] but it apparently never achieved significant sales. Other combination stoves were even less successful. The model the Woodbridges of South Hadley, Massachusetts, acquired in 1835, for example, "made after the style of an old iron fire frame," proved a "crude affair" that they abandoned within two years.[46] The editors of the *Journal of the Franklin Institute* were unimpressed by such stoves, observing in 1841 that "the idea of combining an open Franklin with a cooking stove is not new; it has often been attempted, but has never gone into extensive use."[47]

The failure of combination stoves demonstrates that cookstove buyers were more interested in saving money on fuel than in retaining the sight of the fire. Many inventors and dealers recognized this distinction and stressed fuel economy above other considerations. In 1819, for example, James & Cornell of New York claimed that their cookstove would "do all kinds of cooking, washing, and heating of rooms, with a small quantity of fuel."[48] Nottage & Belcher of Providence, Rhode Island, echoed this assertion in 1833, reminding patrons that "the cold season is now fast approaching and fuel is a heavy tax on the laboring class." They boasted, "We will sell you a Stove that will save one half the fuel."[49] Five years later, a competitor who carried "Granger's Patent Elevated Oven Rotary Cooking Stove[s]" promised, "I will warrant them susceptible of performing one third more business with one third less fuel than any [other] stove."[50]

Although they celebrated the fuel savings their products made possible, these manufacturers and retailers conveniently failed to mention that preparing wood for stoves was very time-consuming. Most stoves in this period had small fireboxes, which required pieces of wood as short as one foot, compared to the four-foot lengths suitable for fireplaces.[51] As Michael Williams has pointed out, it made little sense to rural Americans "to waste more man-hours by cutting up wood any smaller . . . in order to economize on the use of a seemingly abundant resource."[52] Some inventors, such as Nathan Parrish of Mendon, New York, addressed this problem directly, though ineffectively. In 1832, he patented a ten-plate stove that had a rectangular box attached to the front plate in order to accommodate longer wood. The editors of the *Journal of the Franklin Institute* were not impressed, commenting: "If instead of burning longer wood, this addition would cause wood to be burned longer, we should think more favourably of the contrivance."[53] Later in the decade, J. Cross of Chenango County, New York, introduced a stove that may have met with more approval—its number one advantage: "wood may be used 2 ft. & 2 [in.] long."[54]

Stove height was also a concern. Early-nineteenth-century cooking vessels were heavy and difficult to maneuver,[55] so stove manufacturers developed cooking stoves with low boiling holes to minimize the amount of lifting required of cooks.[56] The 1820s No. 2 James "saddlebags" cookstove (illus. 4.3) is a good example of this effort. Although this model was the next to largest size manufactured by the firm, it measures just twenty-eight inches from stove top to floor. Competitors' cookstoves were even shorter, ranging in height from nineteen to twenty-five inches.[57]

In the 1830s, inventors approached the problem of stove height in a different way, introducing the "step" or "horseblock" cookstove. In 1834, the editors of the *Journal of the Franklin Institute* reported approvingly of the model designed by Levi Kingsbury of Livonia, New York, that "the lowness of the upper plate of the box is spoken of as greatly facilitating the management of pots and kettles."[58] The 1830s Perfect Premium step stove (illus. 4.4) may have been based on Kingsbury's ideas. Its hearth plate is only eight and one-half inches from the floor, and the two lower boiling holes are just nineteen inches off the ground.

Low stoves were not without drawbacks, however. Women accustomed to waist-high brick ovens were now forced to stoop to check on the progress of baking items. In the late 1830s, a number of manufacturers introduced cookstoves with elevated ovens (illus. 4.5) to alleviate this difficulty. These models were also free from another flaw that plagued many early cookstoves; when the firebox was placed directly beneath the oven, as was typical, food was apt to burn on the bottom unless it received close attention. Other inventors, such as Joseph Page of Philadelphia and George Prentiss of Smithfield, Rhode Island, experimented with revolving ovens to minimize this problem; Allen and James Barnett of Louisville, Kentucky, moved the firebox and installed flues inside their stove in an effort "to distribute the heat equally."[59]

Although there is no evidence that their cookstoves were manufactured in quantity, Page, Prentiss, and the Barnetts were on to something: temperature management was crucial to culinary success. Stabilizing oven heat would prove a stubborn problem, but inventors had better success in other areas. Knowing that women adept at open-hearth techniques could achieve an almost infinite variety of temperature adjustments by moving food closer to or farther from the fire, they worked to develop a stove that would reproduce this flexibility. In 1833, for example, Elisha Town of Montpelier, Vermont, borrowed an old idea, patenting a cookstove with "cranes, so constructed . . . as to be made the . . . resting places, for pots . . . by which they may be easily swung on or off the fire, thereby regulating the quantity of heat applied to them."[60] Other inventors broke new

4.3. William T. James no. 2 cookstove, c. 1820. Courtesy of Old Sturbridge Village, Sturbridge, Mass.; photograph by Henry E. Peach.

4.4. Perfect Premium step cookstove, 1830s. Courtesy of Old Sturbridge Village, Sturbridge, Mass.; photograph by Henry E. Peach.

4.5. Granger's Patent Air-Tight cookstove with elevated oven, Ransom & Co., Albany, N.Y., 1846. Collection of the Albany Institute of History and Art, Albany, N.Y.; gift of Mrs. Dorothy M. Francis.

ground in their efforts to facilitate temperature management. In 1834, for example, Elisha Payne of New York City patented a cookstove with a revolving firebox; in the following year, Isaac McNary of Stafford, Connecticut, patented one with an adjustable grate that could be raised or lowered by a winch.[61]

The rotary cookstove, invented by Henry Stanley of Poultney, Vermont, in 1832, was the most successful of these efforts (illus. 4.6). The next year, the *Journal of the Franklin Institute* published this description: "Instead of the kind of top usually employed there is to be a circular plate of such size that only about one-third of its area will lie over the fire chamber. . . . This is covered by a second plate, supported by a rim, which rises it from the first. . . . By means of cogs upon the edges of the upper plate, it may be turned around . . . a pinion and crank being fixed for that purpose. The upper plate is perforated to receive pots, kettles, and other cooking apparatus, and a large tin cover, operating as a reflector [oven], is provided to cap the climax."[62]

The journal editors were impressed by Stanley's originality, but the rotary stove posed special challenges for consumers. M. N. Stanley & Company's 1835 instructions for stove buyers suggest some of the adjustments they had to make as they adapted to the new technology. The pamphlet begins on a positive note, however, the manufacturers explaining that the stove's "principal advantages . . . are in . . . equalizing the heat . . . and for obtaining such a degree of heat as may

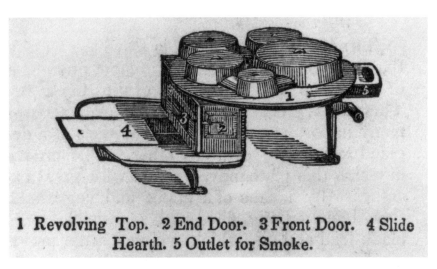

1 Revolving Top. 2 End Door. 3 Front Door. 4 Slide Hearth. 5 Outlet for Smoke.

4.6. Title page, M. N. Stanley & Co., *Remarks and Directions for Using Stanley's Patented Rotary Cooking Stove* (New York: G. F. Bunce, 1835). Courtesy of the Printed Book and Periodical Collection, The Winterthur Library, Winterthur, Del.

be required for either boiling or stewing, and likewise in the great saving of fuel." The small firebox also supposedly made cooking in summer more bearable.[63]

The manufacturers recognized, however, that the rotary stove looked odd. They acknowledged that customers' first impressions were "frequently unfavourable on account of the small size of the fire room," but they claimed that "the stove is sufficient to warm large rooms." Apparently, some users were unconvinced. "Care is necessary," the pamphlet warned, "not to overcharge the stove" with fuel; otherwise, it was "liable to being injured by being overheated."[64] Baking was also a problem. The tin reflector oven designed to be set on the stove top was "objectionable . . . to some who have been accustomed to the common oven." With the heat source directly below the food, maintaining an even temperature was difficult. In fact, the manufacturers instructed cooks to place bricks under baking items to prevent burning. If women used the "under roaster" for baking instead, they were supposed to set "the front part of the rack on the second slide . . . and the back part . . . on the third slide, giving it a small inclination, and thus equalizing the heat."[65] No mention was made of the likelihood that cake batter or pie filling placed on a slant would ooze onto the bottom of the "roaster" and burn.

The dispersion of cookstoves was slowed by design problems such as these. Manufacturers' efforts were further hampered by the persistence in some circles of the "erroneous idea that stove plates [had to] be made directly from the ore; that plates made at a second melting would crack."[66] An important geographic shift had taken place in the iron industry, however, that slowly broadened the area in which stoves were available. Beginning shortly after the turn of the century, iron manufacturers moved into the Albany-Troy area of New York because of the region's combined resources: ore from mines near Lake Champlain, limestone for flux, and the molding sand needed to produce high-quality castings.[67] After the opening of the Erie Canal in 1825, iron manufactured in Ohio, which proved "very tough," also found a ready market in Albany-Troy area foundries. Business grew; in 1830, one Albany stove founder reported annual profits of 10 percent.[68]

Retailers throughout the Northeast began to take advantage of these developments. In 1812, Lyman Kendal, a hardware and dry goods dealer in Greenfield, Massachusetts, advertised his interest in contracting with local artisans for 300 barrels, 200 kegs, and a ton of nails; he also announced the availability of a "small assortment" of stoves.[69] To the south, in Hartford, Connecticut, interest in stoves appears to have been stronger as two dealers vied to offer the latest products. In January 1815, Miles Beach & Son announced "a GREAT variety of stoves, just received from New York and Philadelphia."[70] Not wanting to be left behind, the Beaches' competitors, Ward, Bartholomew & Brainard, proclaimed in October that they had "received a greater variety [of stoves] than has been offered in this market. . . . Various patterns of Philadelphia Cooking [stoves], Pipe and Chimney Franklin, Box and Sheet Iron d[itt]o."[71] The Beaches responded to the challenge. By the next fall, they were selling a cookstove patented only sixteen months earlier: "Postley's PATENT COOKING STOVES . . . manufactured in New York, and for sale at New York prices."[72]

In their eagerness to appear up-to-date, these dealers failed to mention the fact that the stove business was still experimental. Retailers entered the trade cautiously, usually combining it with other activities. In Providence, Rhode Island, for example, hardware dealer and ship chandler Peter Grinnell began selling stoves by 1818, but in 1832 he still carried a wide variety of other items, including paint, oil, turpentine, varnish, lanterns, sheet lead, loom shuttles, anvils, wire, tape measures, knives, forks, window glass, and cordage.[73] Henry Miller, a Worcester, Massachusetts, hardware dealer, made a similarly modest commitment to the new appliance. When his store was damaged by fire in 1837, insurance adjusters found that his inventory had been dominated by hinges, locks, lamps, cooking utensils, candlesticks, looking glasses, and tinware. Damage to the three cookstoves and nine box stoves he had on hand represented only 2.6 percent of his claim.[74] Manufacturers of stove utensils had to be equally flexible. In 1825, Rice & Miller, metal workers in the same city, produced "Tin and Copper Furniture for Cooking Stoves," but they also made "Cotton Cans, Tin Roping Spools, . . . Cast Steel Spindles . . . [and] Spring Shuttles" for the region's growing textile industry.[75]

As the century progressed, more entrepreneurs began to manufacture and sell stoves. In 1824, Providence had six hardware stores, two of which carried stoves. As we have seen, Peter Grinnell sold stoves as an adjunct to his ship chandlery business. His competitors, J. Congdon & Son, also offered a range of products, advertising "Wilson's, Tallmadge & Parker's, and James & Cornell's Parlour, Cooking and Box Stoves" together with their traditional stock of andirons, fire shovels, tongs, wire, bolts, latches, lamps, hoes, axes, and the like.[76] By 1832, there were twelve hardware firms in the city, as well as fifteen tin-plate workers, nine of whom worked for James Eames, who carried stoves as part of his stock. This year was also the first that a "stove dealer" (John C. Cass) and a "stove manufacturer" (George Richards) appeared in the city directory.[77] Eleven years later, the city supported three specialized stove establishments, one of which (Lincoln & Barstow) was also involved in stove manufacturing. In addition, there were eight hardware dealers and twelve tin-plate and sheet-iron workers in the city, many of whom also sold stoves.[78]

As their numbers grew, stove retailers tried to appeal to consumers by offering a wider variety of models. Brand name identification strengthened as unsuccessful designs were weeded out of the marketplace. In 1834, J. & S. Pierce of Greenfield, Massachusetts, placed the following advertisement in the *Greenfield Gazette and Franklin Herald*: "STOVES! STOVES! The subscribers have on hand a complete assortment of Cooking, Parlour, Franklin, Oven, & Box Stoves,— Among the Cooking Stoves are Stanley's celebrated rotatory top, Richard's alterable Stove, . . . [and] Bidwell's patent stove, a late Connecticut invention. Also Hoyt's, Wilson's, Moore's and James's which are well known and approved in the country."[79]

Stoves were also making their appearance farther west. The same year, J. Mayhew & Company of Buffalo, New York, announced their intention to enter the "wholesale business of STOVES, HOLLOW WARE AND PIG IRON." They procured stove plates from several blast furnaces in Ohio, and advertised the Wilson cookstove in six sizes, the James in four sizes, the Improved James in two sizes, and ten-plate "oven stoves" in four sizes.[80]

Enterprising men began to see opportunities in the business, especially as increasing numbers of Americans migrated to western New York and the Ohio Valley. In 1836, Robbins Douglas considered moving from Canaan Four Corners, New York (near the Massachusetts border), west to Oswego. He asked his brother-in-law, S. B. Ludlow, to make inquiries in Albany about the possibility of becoming a stove dealer. Ludlow responded enthusiastically, informing Douglas that an inventor named French was willing to license him as the exclusive agent of his Rotary Cap Stove. "This will be a good business," Ludlow predicted. "A vast deal of money has . . . been made on this sort of stoves: and, as there are none at Oswego, I think you will be able to sell a great many."[81]

Lucius Hoyt, a farmer's son from New Haven, Vermont, also hoped to move west and make his fortune selling stoves to new settlers. In 1833, he visited his sister Delia and her husband, who operated a general store in Niles, Michigan, and decided to move there to open a "foundry and smithy." Although he planned to produce agricultural implements and mill castings as well, he counted heavily on stoves for success. "Prospects . . . appear Flattering," he wrote his sister Eliza. "I can sell 100 Cooking & Box Stoves during the Fall at a Proffitt of more than 100 p[e]r c[en]t. . . . I ask but a full swing from now till the 1st of next May to make $4000."[82]

Ludlow's and Hoyt's enthusiasm suggests that consumer interest in stoves was increasing. Certainly significant progress had been made in overcoming the greatest barrier to stove dispersion — high cost. Early in the century, many stove dealers had wisely avoided mentioning specific figures. In 1818, for example,

Peter Grinnell of Providence merely informed potential buyers that his new cookstoves were "offered at the manufacturer's prices."[83] George W. Brown of New York was equally vague, noting at the end of one 1818 advertisement that his stoves were available "at the lowest prices for Cash, or approved Credit."[84]

When dealers did list prices, consumers may well have experienced "sticker shock." The "large and elegant" cookstove that Lyman Kendal of Greenfield, Massachusetts, offered for sale in 1812, for example, cost $50,[85] a figure likely inflated by transportation costs. Stoves were expensive even close to the site of manufacture, however. In 1819, J. & S. Gleason of Philadelphia advertised five sizes of their "IMPROVED PATENT Steam Kitchen Stoves," ranging in price from $43 to $90.[86]

Prices dropped somewhat during the 1820s. In 1822, Rice & Miller of Worcester, Massachusetts, advertised cookstoves costing between $20 and $60.[87] The next year, James & Cornell advertised eight sizes of their cookstove; the cheapest cost $15 and the most expensive $50.[88] These advertisements suggest that affordable cookstoves were becoming available, but it is difficult to tell whether a typical family could have made do with a small stove costing $15 or $20. The account book kept by Greenfield, Massachusetts, stove dealers Samuel Pierce & Son indicates that most consumers in this period were interested in larger models. Between 1821 and 1826, the firm sold twenty-four cookstoves ranging in price from $27 to $43.54, with an average cost of $32.11.[89]

During the next decade, stove prices were still quite high, but some less-expensive models did enter the market, and dealers made an effort to make stove purchase possible for moderate-income families. During the winter of 1834–35, Samuel Pierce Jr. of Greenfield sold twenty-two cookstoves with an average price of $31.88, but his low-end options were more varied than had been the case in the early and mid-1820s. He carried "oven stoves" (ten-plate models) ranging in price from $11 to $15 and rented top-of-the-line cookstoves for $5 to $6 a year.[90] Other stove dealers began to offer secondhand stoves, another way to make the new technology more affordable.[91]

Gradually, American consumers responded to these efforts. In doing so, however, they had to overcome their long-standing habit of modest investment in cooking equipment. When Asa Bates of Palmer, Massachusetts, died in 1810, for example, he left an estate worth $101.12, but his cooking utensils — "2 pots, dishkettle, skillet, tea kettle, bake pan, p[ai]r Hand irons, gridiron, shovel & tongs & [a] spider" — were valued at only $3.52 (3.5 percent). Bates's better-off neighbors made do with much the same equipment, although they typically owned more cooking vessels. Benjamin Scott — a wealthy Blanford, Massachusetts, farmer who left an estate valued at $5,106.81 at his death in 1810 — had also invested few resources in food preparation; his kitchen tools were worth just $17.73 (0.3 percent).[92] In the prestove era, urban kitchens were also outfitted simply. James Murry, a Boston hackman who owned an estate worth $120.50 at his death in 1810, had prepared meals using only a skillet and an iron pot worth $1 (0.8 percent). Stephen Goff, a Boston housewright who died the same year, was substantially wealthier than Murry (with an estate valued at $3,894.33), but his cooking equipment amounted to only $19.43 (0.5 percent).[93]

These figures demonstrate that buying a cookstove in the early nineteenth century was a dramatic departure from previous practice, yet some Americans chose to be technological pioneers. Identifying their motivations is difficult, but saving labor on fuel preparation was doubtless on many people's minds. After all, "to feed the family fire in those [prestove] days, during the severe season, was fully one man's work."[94] Saving work for women may also have been a consideration. As Margaret Hindle Hazen and Robert M. Hazen have recently pointed out, open-hearth cooking required "constant maneuvering, adjusting, and vigilance."[95] A cook might have to manage many fires simultaneously, one in the oven, one in the fireplace, and several more on the hearth. In a stove, however, a single fire could be used for a number of different cooking tasks at the same time, including baking.

Saving time was also an issue. Once a fire was lit in a cookstove, its oven could be used in ten or fifteen minutes, whereas it took an hour or more to heat a brick oven. Preparing an entire meal using traditional techniques could be a lengthy ordeal. While living in Illinois in the late 1830s, Eliza Woodson Farnham found that a neighbor intending to serve "tea" at 6:30 P.M. had to begin cooking at 1:00. The meal consisted of gingerbread, biscuits, and pumpkin pie baked sequentially in a reflector oven before the fire, accompanied by tea, dried beef, pickles, honey, and plum preserves. But even with five and a half hours in which to cook, Farnham's hostess ran into trouble; the "naughty pie" "would not bake" and was not ready until the guests got up to leave shortly before 8:00.[96] Women familiar with these challenges must have been intrigued by the possibility of simultaneously preparing several dishes using a stove.

Open fires could also cause discomfort, making the idea of enclosing fire in a stove seem sensible. After moving to Michigan in the mid-1830s, Caroline Kirkland discovered how troublesome open fires could be, especially in summer. "There was no end to the bread that the children ate . . . while a tin reflector was my only oven, and the fire required for baking drove us all out of doors," she complained.[97] Robert Roberts pinpointed other problems that many people hoped stoves would reduce or eliminate, commenting in 1827 that a cook had to live with "continual and inevitable dangers" such as the "glare of a scorching fire and . . . smoke . . . baneful to the eyes and the complexion."[98]

The warmth cookstoves provided in winter was an even greater attraction. In the early national period, American homes, especially in the northeastern and midwestern states, were chronically and often bitterly cold. The narrator of Harriet Beecher Stowe's *Oldtown Folks* (1869), a novel set in New England in "ante-railroad times," remembers when the kitchen fire was "the only means of warming." Every night, the fire was raked up to preserve a few coals for morning. During the winter, the first person awake might find the back of the fireplace "sparkling with . . . frost crystals." Even during the day, when a "forest" of logs was burning, the kitchen was not much warmer: "Aunt Lois, standing with her back so near the blaze as to be uncomfortably warm, yet found her dish-towel freezing in her hand, while she wiped the teacup drawn from the almost boiling water."[99]

Mary Palmer Tyler of Guilford, Vermont, experienced similar conditions and welcomed the comfort provided by the new technology. In the 1860s, she felt "disposed to vote a monument to the memory of the first inventor of family stoves"—adding with some asperity, "The people of this age know little of the horrors of winter."[100] Tyler had been an early convert. In 1822, after her husband Royall, a lawyer and noted playwright, fell ill and her son John, a Boston merchant, went bankrupt, the Tylers acquired a heating stove for their "back room," probably a money-saving move. Two years later, Mary noted in her diary: "This day by the advice of my husband I . . . traded away our chaise for a cooking stove."[101]

Tight finances may also have helped convince the Bascoms of Phillipston, Massachusetts, to abandon the open hearth. In 1819, Ruth Henshaw Bascom and her husband, a Congregational minister, bought a cookstove for $30, 13 percent of their expenses for the year (by comparison, a barrel of flour cost them $9.50, five pounds of coffee $2.55, and a quart of brandy $.74).[102] Making ends meet was difficult for ministers' families, who often depended on sometimes haphazard parishioner donations. Under these circumstances, investing in a cookstove to save money on fuel made sense.

Diaries and account books demonstrate that cooking stoves were making their way into northeastern homes in increasing numbers after 1815, but they reveal little about the pattern of stove dispersion. Probate inventories provide important clues about this process, but it is important to keep in mind that these records doubtless underestimate the presence of stoves because many estates—particularly those of younger, more mobile decedents—were not appraised.[103] Moreover, because inventories list possessions at death, young and middle-age adults are underrepresented, thereby skewing the chronology of consumption.[104]

Despite their flaws, however, inventories provide evidence of consumption trends unavailable elsewhere. The probate records of Boston, for example, demonstrate urban Americans' increasing reliance on stoves. The 104 inventories recorded in 1820 list ten heating stoves (9.6 percent) and two cookstoves (1.9 percent). Five years later, seventeen of the eighty-one estates probated (21 percent) included heating stoves, and six (7.4 percent) included cookstoves. The individuals who owned heating stoves were merchants or artisans who typically used the appliances in their workplaces.[105] Cookstove owners, in contrast, were willing to introduce stoves into their homes. Although some of them continued to use open fires in their primary living spaces, others made a full commitment to the new technology by installing both a heating stove and a cookstove.[106]

Most of these cookstove owners were wealthier than their neighbors,[107] but some poorer Boston families did acquire stoves in these years, presumably to save money on fuel. Moses Atwood, a "trader" who may have kept boarders, lived in modestly furnished rented quarters. In fact, at $14, his cookstove was his most valuable possession. Significantly, Atwood had entirely embraced the new technology; assessors who recorded his property in 1820 also found a $3 heating stove. Stoves thus comprised nearly 17 percent of the value of his estate.[108] Jonathan Lawrence, the lighthouse keeper on Long Island in Boston Harbor, was also likely interested in saving money. At his death in 1825, his $393.20 estate included a "Cooking Stove No. 5 Apparatus Complete" (likely a James model) worth $20.[109] This investment made particular sense in his case because of the labor and expense involved in transporting fuel to an island.

Providence, Rhode Island, probate inventories reveal a somewhat different pattern. None of the fifty-six estates probated in 1820 and 1825 included cookstoves, and only five (8.9 percent) included heating stoves, suggesting that the city's fuel crisis was less acute than Boston's. However, eight of the fifty inventories (16 percent) recorded in 1830 and 1835 list cookstoves. These cookstove owners were neither poor nor wealthy;[110] in Providence, at least, acquiring the new appliance made most sense to middle-income individuals, those who could afford stoves but were also interested in saving money on fuel.

As in Boston, commitment to the new technology was incomplete. None of the eight Providence cookstove owners also owned heating stoves. Several of them probably lived in quarters small enough to be heated by just a cookstove, but the desire to heat primary living spaces with open fires was still strong. David Borden, for example, outfitted his parlor with a Franklin stove; Nathan Jackson chose a "Lehigh [coal] grate"; and Nicholas Sheldon, Power Knowles, and Russell Proctor preferred traditional andirons.[111]

Stove use spread even more slowly in rural areas, where surviving woodlots helped keep firewood prices down. Probate inventories from Barnstable County, Massachusetts (Cape Cod), record no stoves in household use in 1820 or 1825, although William Sandford of Falmouth had installed a "caboose" (galley stove) aboard his sloop.[112] During the next decade, however, stoves became more common; six of the seventy-three estate inventories from 1830 and 1835 list cookstoves (8.2 percent). Unlike the situation in Providence, these cookstove owners were well-off, with a estate value more than three times higher than the median,[113] suggesting that Cape Codders in this period may have regarded cookstoves more as status symbols than fuel savers.

The inventory of one of these households illustrates how the transition from fireplace to cookstove often occurred. When Paron Cook of Provincetown died in 1835, he left an estate worth $2,953.92. In his kitchen, assessors found a $23 "Cooking Stove & all the apperatus," but they also noted a $2 "fire set and crane" in the "porch," probably a summer kitchen used for laundry, butchering, and other tasks that required a large fire. In his primary living space, Cook combined tradition and modernity, relying on a "fire frame & fire set" (a Franklin-type stove).[114]

Stove use was even rarer in Worcester County, in central Massachusetts. Inventories there recorded no cookstoves and only two heating stoves in 1820, both of the latter in workshops. Ten years later, inventories listed only three shop stoves and a single cookstove.[115] Despite its aberrance, this last record is important because it describes the household of a young family, the kind usually absent from probate documents. Thirty-five-year-old Henry Ballard, a farmer in Lancaster, had died after being struck by a tree he was felling. He left a thirty-year-old pregnant widow and three children under age seven. The household also probably included several relatives or employees because the inventory lists eight beds. The family lived well; at $4,465.94, Ballard's estate was nearly ten times more valuable than the median. Although not extravagant, he liked nice things; the inventory lists an eight-day clock worth $15, fourteen silver teaspoons, and an imposing militia uniform. Assessors also found "1 Cooking Stove and Apparatus" valued at $13.67.[116] The Ballards were typical of early cookstove owners in the rural Northeast. Well-off enough to afford a still expensive appliance, they were also young enough to adapt to a new system of domestic heating and cooking, and their household (with children too young to be much help with chores) was large enough to make saving labor on fuel procurement attractive. Regrettably, complete information about early stove-owning households such as this one is difficult to come by.

Unlike probate inventories, dealers' sales records reveal exactly when someone acquired a stove, what it cost, and how many models were available. The account books kept by the Pierces of Greenfield, Massachusetts, the most complete stove dealers' records known to survive, document the development of the trade.

Between 1821 and 1826, the firm sold 127 stoves, including twenty-four cook-stoves (18.9 percent), to customers in Greenfield and surrounding agricultural communities. Most of the cookstoves were James models, but the Pierces may have carried several other styles by the middle of the decade.[117] Fifteen of the in-dividuals who bought cookstoves from the Pierces could be located in the 1820 census. Although enumeration categories are too broad to pinpoint the ages of these individuals, seven of them were in their thirties or early forties and eight were forty-five or older when they acquired cookstoves. Their households had on average 12.4 members, an indication that large families were among the first to invest in the new appliance.[118]

The characteristics of the Pierces' five customers from the farming village of Shelburne are worth detailed examination. Captain Parker Dole led the way, buying a cookstove for $43.54 in December 1821. Dole, a fifty-seven-year-old farmer with only seven people in his household, owned an impressive brick house uncharacteristic of the village's conservative architecture.[119] He seems to have acquired a cookstove for comfort and convenience rather than out of any pressing need to save money. An enterprising individual, he probably realized that the labor no longer required to procure firewood could profitably be di-verted to some other activity.

Dole's neighbors appear to have bought cookstoves for other reasons. Inn op-erator Joseph Severance's livelihood depended in large part on the efficient preparation of meals, so business considerations were likely uppermost in his mind when he invested $41.50 in a cookstove in March 1826.[120] Farmer David Long also probably valued efficiency. His unusually large household included fourteen people, six of them under age sixteen. When Long spent $40.58 on a cookstove in March 1824, he may well have hoped it would reduce the work of preparing firewood and cooking for such a crowd.[121]

David Fiske and William Long were more typical of cookstove purchasers. Fiske, who worked at an axe and scythe factory, was thirty-two when he bought a cookstove for $28.76 in January 1824. He and his wife Laura had been married for ten years and had three children. In 1820, Fiske's household also included two additional adults.[122] Long, a farmer, was thirty-eight when he bought a cookstove for $31.36 in January 1825. In 1820, his household included him, his wife, their two children, and four other adults.[123] Although their households were average size,[124] Fiske and Long may have decided that purchasing a cook-stove, although an immediate financial drain for a young and growing family, would more than pay off in future savings.

The next Pierce account book, which covers 1834 and 1835, documents the spread of cookstoves in the Greenfield area. In these years, Samuel Pierce Jr. carried at least eight different models, ranging from an $11 "oven stove" to a $46.45 no. 3 Stanley rotary. In contrast to the previous decade, more than 40 percent of the stoves he sold were cookstoves, even though their average price had dropped only slightly.[125] Some of Pierce's patrons were even willing to buy a new, little-tried model—if it promised both fuel savings and flexibility. Despite their recent introduction, Pierce sold five Stanley rotaries in this period, for an average cost of $39.53.[126]

These records also indicate that cookstove use was becoming possible for families of modest means. One purchaser, evidently short of cash, paid for his "oven stove" with an unspecified amount of wood.[127] Eight other customers chose a new option—stove rental. With the bewildering number of models entering the market, it must have been difficult to make a choice. By renting, a family could try out a stove first. Top-of-the-line cookstoves priced at more than $35 were made available by Pierce for just $6 per year. Thus, if a stove did not work out, as evidently happened to three of Pierce's customers, it could be returned at minimal cost.[128]

Although the Pierce accounts contain valuable hints about consumer motivations, they reveal little about the actual experience of buying and using a cookstove. Customer testimonials provide additional information. In an advertising pamphlet published in 1837, W. A. Arnold & Company of Northampton, Massachusetts, printed the following letter signed by twenty-four area residents: "We, the subscribers, having in use one of 'Arnold's Patent Yankee Cooking Stoves,' say with confidence we believe it to be decidedly the best Cooking Stove ever offered to the public, both for economy and convenience. In this stove are combined all the good qualities requisite to such an article. Washing and all kinds of Cooking, such as Boiling, Baking, Stewing, Frying, Broiling, or Roasting, all can be done at the same time, and in the best manner, without one branch interfering with another; and for saving of fuel it is excelled by none."[129]

Fourteen signatories lived in Northampton. Of those enumerated in the 1840 census, there were seven manufacturers or artisans, two merchants, two farmers, and a bank cashier, suggesting that town dwellers bought stoves more often than farmers in this period, probably because they were less likely to own sizable woodlots. Cookstove owners in Northampton were also younger than average and, like the Pierces' customers, lived in larger households than their neighbors.[130]

Available quantitative data demonstrate that cookstoves were no longer a novelty in the northeastern United States by 1840, but it is difficult to recover the qualitative experience of living and working with the new technology. How did consumers find out about stoves? How did they learn to use them? How much and what kind of work did stoves require? How well did they perform? Answers to these questions may be found in diaries, letters, and personal reminiscences.

Acquiring a stove was a watershed event. Mary Janette Elmore vividly recalled the arrival of her family's first cookstove in 1838, although she was only six years old at the time. "One morning," she wrote in 1911, "we children were told that a new stove was coming that day so we went out into the dooryard and gathered large bunches of twigs and small pieces of wood to burn in it." She continued, "It was a cooking stove of large size, and the furniture that came with it was large and very heavy. The oven was a great cylinder set up some distance above the stove."[131]

Elmore evidently considered the new appliance a curiosity, but many of her contemporaries were more fearful. The narrator of a late-nineteenth-century folk song recounts the effect of her father's purchase of a Wilson-Benton stove: "The people how they wondered when we got the thing to go / They swore 'twould burst and kill us all some fifty years ago."[132] Susan Baker's father caused similar commotion in Thornton's Ferry, New Hampshire, when he bought the town's first cookstove in the mid-1830s. "The neighbors said we would all be sick before Spring," his daughter remembered. But, she continued, "in a year or two all the neighbors had one, after they saw that we came out all right."[133]

Overcoming these fears was just the beginning. Once a stove had been delivered, it had to be properly installed. To facilitate draft, it was wise to close off the kitchen fireplace, leaving only a hole for the stovepipe. It was also important to ensure that all joints in both stove and pipe were tight, or the stove would not draw well. The next step was to set the stove a "sufficient distance" from the wall on a protective brick or stone platform or sheet of metal.[134] In 1837, W. A. Arnold & Company recommended that stoves be placed a "considerable distance" from the chimney so that the pipe could radiate heat more effectively.[135] An 1849 painting by Tompkins Harrison Matteson (illus. 4.7) shows that some families failed to follow this advice. Here, the cookstove has been set into the fireplace opening, an arrangement that may well have permitted the escape of warm air up the chimney. Like many early cookstoves, this model is also inconvenient; it is so low to the ground that the woman using it must bend over nearly as far as she must once have done to reach cooking vessels on the hearth.

Matteson's painting does not reveal how ticklish stove installation could be. Ensuring sufficient draft and protecting surrounding woodwork from the risk of fire were crucial. Samuel Rodman, a merchant in New Bedford, Massachusetts, faced a tough challenge after buying a rotary stove. One day in October 1834, he noted in his diary: "P.M. occupied in arrangements for and putting up one of Stanley's cooking stoves . . . which promises to be very economical of fuel and easy of management." He also spent most of the next morning "completing the arrangements of the new mode of cooking," but things did not go smoothly. A week later, he had to get the mason to return to "stop the throat of the chimney more completely." Fortunately, this modification "quite remedied the difficulties [with the new stove] which had before embarrassed its advantages."[136]

Once in place, a stove required more care than a fireplace. Ash removal was a continual chore. Keeping oven flues and draft openings clear was necessary but difficult.[137] Stoves also had to be "blacked" to keep them free of rust. For this

4.7. Tompkins Harrison Matteson (American, 1813–1884), *Now or Never*, 1849. Oil on canvas. Clark Collection, The Parrish Art Museum, Southampton, N.Y.; photograph by David Preston.

task, the author of *The American Housewife* (1839) recommended either "Black lead" or British Lustre powder mixed with cold water. This paste was applied to the stove, rubbed into the surface, and allowed to dry. Then the stove was gone over with "a dry, stiff . . . brush, till clean and polished."[138] Blacking had to be done when the stove was cold, of course, which necessarily complicated meal preparation.

Stovepipe also had to be cleaned periodically to keep it soot free, an awkward, messy undertaking that could cause domestic friction. Frances Breckenridge, who grew up in Meriden, Connecticut, in the 1830s, described what happened in one household when "something ailed the kitchen stove." "Angelina" told "Edwin" that the first thing to do was to take the stovepipe down and clean it. On hearing this, "Edwin . . . was obliged to meet a man on important business," so "Angelina" tackled the job herself. A difficult hour followed. "She burned her hands and blackened her face and dress," but finally got the pipe cleaned and back "more or less in its place." It refused to fit together properly, however. In frustration, "Angelina" hit it successively with a hammer, a hatchet, tongs, a rolling pin, a potato masher, and a pair of shears, but the "sheet iron fiend" would not budge. Her final embarrassment came when "Edwin" returned. "You did not get that stovepipe quite straight," he remarked tactlessly, and then he tapped it on each side, at which point it "settled . . . firmly in its place."[139]

Spring brought new difficulties, as many families moved their cookstoves away from the center of the house to minimize the heat from the cooking fire during the summer. In April 1840, Tobias Walker, a farmer in Kennebunk, Maine, recorded the task in his journal: "Move the stove from the kitchen to the portch."[140] Walker's terseness obscures the fact that moving a stove that weighed several hundred pounds was far from easy. Lucretia Warner Hall of Canaan, New York, was more candid, observing in her diary the following March, "Very Warm moved the Stove hard Days Work."[141]

This annual chore also often revealed hidden problems. Broken fire-brick linings had to be patched or replaced. In coal stoves, any "concretions" inside the firebox had to be removed. Denison Olmsted recommended in 1837 that stove owners "commit the whole work of cleaning and refitting to the stove-dealer," but he recognized that some people might wish to avoid this expense and so supplied a recipe for a putty that could be used to repair broken linings.[142] Stove owners also had to be prepared for the possibility of cracks because many inventors evidently failed to provide adequately for the "unequal expansion of the plates" due to changing temperatures.[143] Thomas Fessenden told readers of *The Husbandman and Housewife* (1820) that "a crack . . . in a stove . . . may be completely closed . . . with a composition consisting of wood ashes and common salt, made into a paste with a little water."[144]

Even if stove owners did not face these problems, they nevertheless had to learn how to use their stoves properly. They needed to know when to add fuel to a fire they could not see and how to adjust a stove's dampers to maintain an even temperature. Stoves were fickle creatures, sensitive to variations in air currents or fuel quality, factors over which their owners had little control. In November 1841, for example, as Martha Coffin Wright sat writing her sister, suddenly "whack! went the stove equal to a cannon." She opened the windows to let the smoke escape, and then, just as it had dispersed, and the room was beginning to warm up, "Bang! goes the blamed stove again." In frustration, Wright closed the dampers, at which point the stove "chosed to puff."[145]

Some manufacturers tried to ease the transition from fireplace to cookstove by designing stoves that could accommodate familiar tools. In 1835, M. N. Stanley & Company assured customers they could roast "in the common reflector which most families have." "The various sizes of [the] holes for boilers," they continued, "will enable families to use most of the utensils . . . they may have on hand."[146] But it must have been difficult for a woman accustomed to the divided nature of open-hearth and brick-oven cooking to learn to boil, fry, broil, roast, and bake simultaneously.

Baking, in particular, was different in a stove. In 1837, W. A. Arnold & Company reminded owners of their Patent Yankee Cooking Stove to be careful to keep the passage under the oven free of obstructions. They also had to remember to open the correct damper so that the hot air could pass under as well as over the oven. "After a little practice," the manufacturers promised, "you will be able to bake as well in this as in any brick oven."[147] Sarah Josepha Hale, author of *The Good Housekeeper* (1839), did not entirely share their confidence. "Baking can very well be done in a stove," she acknowledged, "but the stove must be carefully watched or there is a danger of scorching."[148]

As Hale's warning indicates, early-nineteenth-century cookstoves did not always perform well. Frances Breckenridge remembered that the crank of her mother's rotary "had a trick of becoming useless, and the tongs had to take its place."[149] Sophia Draper White experienced a different problem. In 1839, she wrote her parents about the difficulty of doing laundry with a stove whose boiler could heat only "half a pail" of water at a time. Even worse, White's stove was "not convenient to heat the irons without making such a hot fire you can hardly stay in the room."[150] Eliza Woodson Farnham also struggled with her cookstove, complaining about its "inelastic capacities" and noting that "getting up a formal dinner was an affair quite beyond . . . comprehension." Even boiling water for tea was a challenge because the kettle had to be squeezed into the space provided. This task posed no risk when the water was cold, but removing the kettle after the water had boiled was "quite another affair." Baking was even trickier. Farnham used a traditional tin reflector oven; its front legs rested on the stove hearth, but its back legs had to be propped up with chips of wood. "Sometimes," she grumbled, "my oven . . . went over and poured out the half-baked loaves upon the floor."[151]

Despite "mechanical obstacles" like these,[152] however, most cookstove purchasers seem to have been pleased with the new technology. Two early models, the James "saddlebags" and the Stanley rotary, were especially popular. The James stove, introduced in 1815, was the first successful multifunction cookstove; by 1823, 5,000 models had reportedly been sold.[153] Abijah and Rhoda Wilder of Keene, New Hampshire, were probably among the firm's customers. In 1821, Rhoda's eighty-two-year-old father, Abner Sanger, who lived with the Wilders, was impressed by their cookstove's flexibility. "They boil all sorts of victuals at one and the same time," he marveled.[154] The Harrises of Warner, New Hampshire, were equally satisfied with the James cookstove they bought in 1827; in fact, the family used it for more than eighty years. In 1915, Amanda Harris called it "a marvel of convenience in every respect." She particularly remembered that "the two doors could be set wide, and . . . the effect was that of the open fireplace."[155] The James stove's success may well have been due to this combination of innovation and tradition.

Purchasers of the Stanley rotary cookstove, patented in 1832, were just as loyal. In 1835, George Weems wrote the manufacturer that the rotary he had installed aboard his steamboat "occupies a very small space and consumes so much less wood that I find my kitchen . . . free from that excessive heat produced by the . . . other cooking stoves that I have had." Samuel Mahon was equally pleased with the rotary he had acquired for his packet boat. The same year, he wrote the manufacturer, "I have made [a] full trial . . . and find it to answer a most valuable purpose. We are able to cook the usual varieties of meats, vegetables, puddings, &c. for 60 persons."[156]

Families who bought rotaries liked them, too, but they also acknowledged their flaws. Jane Eliza Johnson, born in Newtown, Connecticut, in 1837, commented in 1917, "I often wish, when I must lift a heavy kettle from one part of the stove to the other, that I had my mother's old rotary." "If it could have had a good oven," she continued, "I am sure none could be better."[157] The Rodmans of New Bedford, Massachusetts, would likely have agreed with this assessment. In 1840, Samuel Rodman noted in his diary that a new grate had been put into the "Stanley improved rotary cooking stove for coal" he had purchased three years before, but he expected it to be the last, "as the verdict of the family is decidedly against a continuance of the 'Rotary,' the defect . . . in baking being the most important objection."[158]

If the members of the Draper family were troubled by this "defect," they ignored it, emphasizing instead the comfort that rotaries provided. In December 1838, William Rice wrote from Ware, Massachusetts, to his sister-in-law, Sophia Draper White, who had recently moved to Cleveland. "I should like to see you here along side of our rotary," he told her. "I reckon it is warmer here than on the borders of that frozen lake." Rice's wife also liked the stove. William, a store clerk, often had to leave her alone in the evening to work. "I feel rather lonely," Emeline wrote her sister, "but have become quite reconciled[,] . . . a stove you know is pleasant company."[159] Four months later, Calista Draper, a cousin who lived in Worcester, Massachusetts, wrote Sophia in much the same vein. "I am seated," she reported, "in my small stuffed Rocking-Chair in our . . . sitting room which is warmed principally by a Stove Pipe which runs from the Rotary in the kitchen."[160]

Americans who chose other cookstove models also generally praised them. In 1827, New York City merchant John Pintard informed his daughter that "your brother is engaged in fixing a Fire Range to burn Schuylkill coal in the kitchen." He commented approvingly that "It is very economical and prevents smoke."[161] About the same time, the Janneys of Loudoun County, Virginia, also acquired a cookstove, the "first . . . ever seen in the neighborhood." The women of the family, John Janney recalled, "soon learned to love" the stove because "it took much less wood than the fireplace, did the cooking just as well, and with much less discomfort."[162] Margaret Patten Baker of Thornton's Ferry, New Hampshire, also liked the cookstove she began using about 1836 because "it was easier to cook [with] than the fire place."[163] Faith Silliman Hubbard, who lived in Hanover, New Hampshire, made the transition from hearth to stove cooking about the same time. In 1837, she wrote her parents that "we do all our cooking by a stove and thus far I am much pleased with it, and think it saves a great deal of work."[164]

It is significant that Hubbard did "all" her family's cooking with a stove. By the late 1830s, some younger women (Hubbard turned twenty-six in 1837) had begun cooking entirely without open hearths and brick ovens. When thirty-three-year-old Emeline Draper Rice moved with her husband into new quarters in Worcester, Massachusetts, in 1839, she wrote her sister with obvious satisfaction that the house had "stoves in every room, not a fire place or an oven [anywhere]."[165]

Rice's mother, Lucy Watson Draper, who lived in nearby Spencer, was more conservative. Born in 1788, she was fifty when she learned to use a cookstove. She also lived in an older house that probably had a brick oven. Both of these circumstances likely delayed her complete conversion to the new technology. Yet Draper welcomed stoves; in 1839, she wrote her daughter Sophia, "We have a stove like Mrs. W. Bemis's with the addition of an oven where the cross piece is, it is made large and lined, with a door at each end. I am very much pleased with it. It is very warm and convenient. . . . I do almost all my cooking in it."[166]

For women such as Lucy Watson Draper, the cookstove was a transitional appliance. Many families still occasionally employed traditional culinary techniques, much as modern cooks alternate between electric or gas stoves and microwave ovens. In the 1830s, Lucy Battle Griggs of Dover, Massachusetts, decided not to close up her "ancient fire place" when her cookstove was installed so she could continue to enjoy an open fire from time to time.[167] Anne Langton, who lived in southern Ontario, was also caught between two culinary systems. She prepared "many a nice meal" using a "dilapidated cooking stove" whose oven "was out of repair," and she thus was delighted when the men of the household made time to build her a brick oven, which she considered "a great relief."[168]

Jane Eliza Johnson recalled much the same arrangement in her parents' Newtown, Connecticut, home. In one room, a rotary stove was used for "ordinary work," but "extraordinary work" such as laundry and butchering was done using the fireplace in another room. The stove also proved inadequate for "general baking," so the family continued to use a brick oven.[169] The Barnards of Peru, Vermont, worked out a similar compromise after acquiring a Conant cookstove for their former tavern. The stove proved useful for boiling and frying food as well as for heating water for washing, Nancy Barnard Batchelder remembered, but the family "still kept a fire in the old bar-room . . . where Mother . . . hung a sparerib up to roast, since she could not bake them in the oven." The fireplace had another attraction as well. "It made us almost homesick when the big [kitchen] fireplace was shut up," Batchelder commented. In the evenings, the family usually sat around the hearth fire in the "bar-room" instead.[170]

The Barnards' fondness for the open fire was widely shared. In November 1825, a Connecticut schoolgirl named Delia Hoyt visited her grandparents in New Haven, Vermont. In a letter home, she described an idyllic domestic scene: "We are seated thick as bees around the kitchen fire . . . Grandfather and old Aunt Nabby are chatting their youthful tales—Grandmother is talking about you Robert is reading Mary and Nelson are eating apples Rufus & Abby in the corner & Mary Williams ironing—so you can imagine how we look."[171] City dwellers also appreciated the cozy charm of open fires. In a February 1834 letter to her sister, Margaret Bayard Smith described an evening get-together in her Washington, D.C., parlor. Two women sat on one side of the fireplace playing chess while Margaret and another woman sat chatting on the other. The rest of the guests clustered nearby, the women "winding worsteds" or doing embroidery while the men talked. Smith asked her sister to imagine "all [of us] circled round a blazing fire, while without doors it was cold and lowering."[172]

Celebrations of the traditional fireplace also appear in nineteenth-century domestic fiction. Interestingly, they suggest that gender influenced how Americans responded to the cookstove. In several female-authored New England local-color novels set in the antebellum period, male characters complain about the displacement of the fireplace by the cookstove. Sarah Orne Jewett, a careful observer of domestic life, commented perceptively that "women . . . knew better than their husbands did the difference this useful invention had made in their every-day work."[173] Men, she suggested, could more easily afford a sentimental attachment to the open fire than women because their work did not revolve around the kitchen. Jewett was not the only female author to notice this phenomenon. "Deacon Blake," a character in Sarah Anna Emery's *My Generation,* "didn't want any of these durned black, iron cooking stoves . . . in his kitchen."[174] Cephas Barnard, a character in Mary Wilkins Freeman's *Pembroke,* agreed. Despite the fact that his wife thought a cookstove "might save a sight of work," he was "set against" getting one.[175]

A similar disagreement divides men and women in Jewett's *A Country Doctor.* Mrs. Martin Dyer is delighted with her cookstove, telling a friend that it is "such a convenience [because] the fire's so much handier," but her husband is unimpressed. One night while his wife is out, Dyer's brother Jake stops by. The two men, who consider the cookstove "a poor exchange for the ancient methods," dismantle the "plaguey thing" and take it out to the woodshed. They then remove the fireboard from the old fireplace and look "smilingly upon the crane and its pothooks and the familiar iron dogs." After gathering wood for an "old-fashioned fire," they sit by its "crackling blaze," and Jake remarks that he wishes his own cookstove "could be dropped into the river."[176] The "old gentlemen" Adeline D. T. Whitney knew as a child shared the Dyer brothers' poor opinion of cookstoves. In a short story published in 1887, Whitney remembered "when there were no cooking-ranges, and . . . how the old gentlemen grumbled when the new inventions first came, and couldn't eat their roast beef that was no longer cooked by a wood-blaze."[177]

Such sentiments, rare in the 1820s and 1830s, became more common after 1840. As Americans grew accustomed to the comfort and convenience stoves provided, they began to forget the bitter cold of the prestove era and became less tolerant of the drawbacks of the new technology. Simultaneously, middle-class, Anglo-American social critics who were struggling to adjust to bewildering social, economic, and political change sentimentalized the past and transformed the open hearth into an emblem of tradition and stability. To them, stoves, especially cookstoves, became disquieting symbols of the permeability of the barrier between the supposedly "separate spheres" of home and world.

5

"Near a Stove the Heart Builds No Altars"

A s consumers' reliance on stoves increased in the mid–nineteenth century, a chorus of antistove rhetoric arose among northern, middle-class Anglo-Americans—an excellent example of what Charles Sellers has called the "cultural schizophrenia of capitalist transformation."[1] Stove critics were among those who responded to industrialization, urbanization, and immigration by creating a "cult of domesticity" that constructed the home as a refuge from the frenzied, amoral world of business.[2] Disturbed by the extent to which manufactured goods and commercial relations had compromised the integrity and independence of the household, they were reluctant to advise women to embrace modern appliances and sought to isolate cookstoves, together with the servants who often tended them, from the heart of the home. Fireplaces, in contrast, were celebrated as symbols of gentility and ease.

The denigration of stoves and the veneration of the open hearth were part of a larger effort, already under way, to glorify the preindustrial past. New Yorker Samuel Woodworth wrote his sentimental paean to the "old oaken bucket" in 1818. Five years later, John Howard Payne of Massachusetts penned the effusion that typified the "cult of domesticity" for the rest of the century—"Home, Sweet Home." These celebrations of tradition were inspired by apprehension about the present. Industrial development and the improved standard of living it made possible were particularly worrisome. In 1855, novelist George Lunt asked, "What . . . can be said of an age, the best . . . energies of which are devoted . . . to the betterment of our material welfare?" "To be mechanical is no doubt useful," he conceded, "but the utility is of an inferior . . . character."[3] Philadelphia attorney Sidney Fisher agreed, observing in 1844 that "the great error generally made is in supposing that material prosperity is real advancement." In fact, Fisher asserted, American society was characterized by "an absorbing passion for gain, gross and sensual tastes and the mean trafficking spirit of merchants," a circumstance he called "ominous of trouble." "Machinery," he concluded, "cannot help us to combat dangers from within."[4]

To Americans who shared these fears, stoves were both symbol and cause of many "dangers from within." *New England Farmer* reported in 1839, for example, that "the innumerable complaints to which persons are subject during the winter . . . are produced by stoves."[5] Yale professor Denison Olmsted agreed, claiming that the "burnt, disagreeable odor" of stove-heated air was "unwholesome."[6] Thomas Webster and Frances Parkes, authors of *The American Family Encyclopedia* (1854), were more specific, alleging that the "sulphureous smell" of stoves caused "headaches, giddiness, and even stupor."[7] Elizabeth Ellet likewise contended in *The Practical Housekeeper* (1857) that "a stove . . . is apt to give the air a close or disagreeable smell, and produce headache and stupor."[8]

Perhaps convinced by arguments such as these, influential domestic advisor Catharine Beecher became more critical of stoves over time. She had already concluded by 1841 that there were three "chief objections" to the new technology: the "dryness of the air," the "disagreeable smell," and the "coldness of the lower stratum of air" in stove-heated rooms.[9] By 1856, she had become even more wary, asserting that "close stoves make it almost certain that the inmates of a room will constantly breathe impure air, which will act as a slow poison." This danger, she recalled wistfully, had been unknown in the days of the "broad-mouthed chimney . . . [which] secured a constant flow of . . . pure air."[10] A contributor to *New England Farmer* also decided that the "confined and unhealthy air, and the great heat [produced by stoves] . . . must have . . . debilitating effects." The damage was not just physical: "Stoves," he continued, "work a portion of . . . the dejection and low spirits which are common."[11] Frank Hastings Hamilton shared these views, telling the medical graduates of the University of Buffalo in 1859 that "our houses have been . . . pillaged . . . of the domestic hearth, toward which so many associations have always centered, for which the blood of nations has been poured, and which in all ages has been . . . the symbol of home." Stoves, he concluded, "have . . . abridged . . . human life."[12]

Other stove critics were equally vehement. In 1850, Dr. J. A. Kennicott of Illinois wrote architectural reformer Andrew Jackson Downing, fuming that "This . . . state is the land of stoves. I hate the whole breed of them." Although admitting that stoves were useful, perhaps even "necessary for cooking," he nevertheless felt a "strange hankering for the old 'trammel' and hooks." In fact, his antipathy to stoves was so strong that he had built a cabin with a "primitive sitting-room" heated by an open fireplace. Here he sat in winter before a "rousing fire," "with the free air constantly sifting through," enjoying "much comfort" and reportedly remaining free of the "'colds,' and 'croups,' and 'quinzies' . . . that 'flesh is heir to,' in . . . air-tight rooms, heated by 'air-tight stoves.'"[13]

Downing went even further in condemning stoves, calling them "the national curse," "secret poisoners" "more insidious" than "slavery, socialism, mormonism . . . tobacco, patent medicines, or coffee."[14] In 1860, a proponent of McNeil's Hot-Air Moistening Register likewise warned readers of *Scientific American* that "of all the agencies which the grim King of Terrors has marshalled to his service—War, Famine, Fever, Plague, Cholera, Rum—the great leader in the Harvest of Death is Dry Air. . . . Hence the necessity . . . of making ample provision for moistening air which is heated by stoves."[15]

Reformers such as Downing were in the vanguard of the antistove movement. In *The Architecture of Country Houses* (1850), he acknowledged that "there are few 'notions' of which our people are fonder than stoves," but he protested against them "boldly and unceasingly," explaining that "Close stoves are not agreeable, for they imprison all the cheerfulness of the fireside; and they are not economical, for though they save fuel they make large doctor's bills."[16] Downing made much the same point in an editorial in *The Horticulturist.* "Even in the midst of the country," he griped, "the farmer will sell . . . wood and buy coal, so that he may have a little demon—alias a black, cheerless . . . stove—in the place of that genuine, hospitable . . . friend . . . , an open wood fireplace."[17]

Lewis Allen, author of *Rural Architecture* (1852), shared Downing's views. The introduction of stoves had been "carried to an extreme," he contended. In their zeal to avoid the "hardships" and "inconvenience" of the prestove era, Allen's misguided countrymen had sealed every door and window, and had installed "air-tight" stoves to create a "snug, close house." According to Allen, these actions had put every inhabitant of such a home "on the high road . . . to a galloping consumption."[18] His colleague Solon Robinson was equally blunt but more succinct. "Red-hot stoves in close rooms are among the abominations of the age," he seethed. "They save heat and waste health."[19]

Cookstoves were considered even more dangerous than heating stoves. One manufacturer (who claimed to have solved the problem he identified) asked consumers, "Did you know that nearly all Cook Stoves . . . are the source of terrible disease . . . [which] arise[s] from the poisonous gases . . . saturating our food during the baking process, and infecting the rooms where the process is carried on?"[20] The authors of *Science in the Kitchen* (1863) sounded a similar alarm, advising readers to ensure that the covers that fit into the boiling holes on the cookstove top were always firmly in place because "the gas which . . . escapes into the room . . . is a fearful poison."[21]

Cookstoves were also suspect because they had changed the way Americans prepared meals. In 1853, the editor of *Harper's New Monthly Magazine* announced "that the coming-in of cooking-stoves threatens to be the going-out of *broiling.*" "We hardly like to soil this page with the . . . unpleasant truth that in many . . . places the national steak is—*fried!*" he lamented.[22] The trend toward baking meat in stove ovens instead of roasting it before the fire was equally disturbing. The author of *Eighty Years of Progress in the United States* (1861) conceded that "stoves and ranges [have] rendered cooking much more convenient," but he regretted the passing of "the better old fashion of roasting."[23] Solon Robinson was even more upset. "Simplicity in cooking went out when cooking-stoves came in," he complained in 1860. "These iron monsters, that save fuel and consume human life . . . have driven the old wood fire and . . . huge oven almost out of memory." He insisted that "To be sweet, nutritious, and delightful to the palate, a roast must be cooked in the open air." It was, he continued, "as impossible to make good bread in one of these cast-iron monsters as it is to roast meat."[24]

Robinson and his colleagues knew they were fighting a losing battle. Even Downing was forced to admit in 1850 that "nine-tenths of all the houses in the northern states . . . are . . . heated . . . by close stoves."[25] The authors of *Village and Farm Cottages* (1856), who shared Downing's "great fondness for an open . . . fire," reached the same conclusion. But "what would it avail?" to oppose stove use, they asked. "The stove has become universal. All through the country, even where fuel is still abundant and cheap, it has supplanted the fireplace."[26]

5.1. "Discovery of Three Half-Starved Alms-House Children in the Room of a Hired Nurse, 152 East Thirty-Fourth Street," *Harper's Weekly* 3 (19 Feb. 1859), 116.

Reformers failed to appreciate the fact that consumers chose heating and cooking systems based primarily on financial, not aesthetic, considerations. To their critics, however, stoves represented the triumph of necessity over gentility. Unable to hide their distaste of the new technology, some midcentury artists and writers even began depicting stoves as symbols of poverty. In 1854, for example, novelist George Canning Hill described a "dismal" poorhouse with "stained and spotted" walls and cracked plaster. "The stove that went part of the way towards warming it in winter" was used mostly as a trash receptacle. "Into its gaping mouth were thrown bits of tobacco, stained pipe stems . . . , fragments of old teacups, and scraps of used-up newspapers."[27] Five years later, *Harper's Weekly* depicted an equally sordid scene (illus. 5.1) in which New York City officials are removing three "half-starved alms-house children" from the care of an incompetent "hired nurse." The children's malnourished condition and the room's sparse furnishings clearly spell poverty. Against one wall stands an emblem of the woman's struggle to make ends meet—a tiny cookstove with a single boiling hole. For this "nurse," as for the rest of the working poor, open fires were economically impossible. The young woman featured in Anna Bache's novel *Scenes at Home* (1852) supports herself by painting decorative fire screens for wealthy customers although she has no use for such an item. In keeping with her scanty income, she lives with her father in a small room heated by a "battered and rusty" ten-plate stove.[28]

These negative representations of stoves arose out of concern over deteriorating social conditions. In the antebellum period, middle-class Americans were convinced they were surrounded by an insidious, invisible enemy—"bad air."[29] Its major causes— urban overcrowding and "vice"—were difficult to address, but the "foul air" of stove-heated rooms was an easier target. "Ventilation mania" gripped the nation.[30] Stove critics conveniently overlooked a key fact, however: by midcentury, only those with substantial means could afford the fresh air of open fires.

"Ventilation mania" was a product of the "cult of domesticity." As middle-class social critics turned inward and idealized the home as a haven, a "firm, unchanging center" for lives daily growing more complex and confusing, they transformed the fireplace into a "domestic icon."[31] Joel Pfister has found that, by the 1840s, "the hearth was associated with the . . . preservation of sentiment, sincerity, authenticity, and spiritual light in an uncertain capitalist world."[32] Margaret Hindle Hazen and Robert M. Hazen have likewise concluded that the "family hearth" became the "altar of a curious new religion" for nineteenth-century Americans, who believed that the "energy emanating from an open fire helped the human spirit—as well as the human body—to do its work."[33]

This "cult of the fireplace"[34] emerged in the 1820s and 1830s, just as stoves were beginning to become common in northeastern homes. To the proponents of the open hearth, the grave implications of abandoning it were clear. After all, as the editor of *The Young Ladies Class Book* (1831) noted, "the domestic fireside is the great guardian of society against the excess of human passions."[35] Samuel Goodrich echoed this view, reminding readers of *Fireside Education* (1839) that "the fireside . . . is a seminary of infinite importance. . . . There are few who can receive the honours of a college but all are graduates of the hearth."[36]

Over the next several decades, artists and writers elaborated on this theme, turning the open hearth into a powerful symbol of domestic "stability and constancy."[37] The frontispiece of a novel published by the American Tract Society in 1862 (illus. 5.2) is a good example of this effort. Three generations of a prosper-

5.2. Frontispiece, *Maple Hill; Or, Aunt Lucy's Stories*
(Boston: American Tract Society, 1862).

ous family gather cozily around a blazing parlor fire. The children sit quietly and listen attentively to old "Aunt Lucy's stories." Even the dog and cat sleep peacefully side by side. The scene is a privatized version of Edward Hicks's "peaceable kingdom" folk paintings of the 1830s and 1840s,[38] except that here it is domesticity, not Christianity, that has created utopia.

Similar nostalgia enveloped the old-fashioned kitchen fireplace. In 1855, *Ballou's Pictorial* published a "felicitous representation" of "a New England fireside" (illus. 5.3) in which fourteen people cluster in companionable groups in a kitchen suffused with the glow from the "wide-yawning fireplace." A "sturdy yeoman" sits reading while two other men talk by the front door. Women sew or cradle babies. Two children nestle in the chimney corner eating apples while a third pops corn on the hearth. The "primitive purity and attractiveness" of the atmosphere is heightened by strings of dried apples, a tall case clock, a braided rug, and andirons with hooks for spits.[39] This room is the kind that novelist

5.3. "A New England Fireside," *Ballou's Pictorial* 8 (10 Mar. 1855), 145. Courtesy of the American Antiquarian Society, Worcester, Mass.

George Canning Hill had in mind when he described a kitchen in which "dancing flames went roaring up the chimney . . . filling . . . the apartment . . . with visions of comfort, and plenty, and home." Such fires, Hill believed, drew people "in a magnetic circle around them," inspiring "sacred home feeling."[40]

If the open fire imparted such benefits, then why had so many Americans switched to stoves? In 1840, poet Ellen Sturgis Hooper asked Fire, "[Why] art thou banished from our hearth and hall, / Thou who art welcomed and beloved by all? / Was thy existence then too fanciful / For our life's common light?"[41] Americans, she hinted, had gotten so caught up in improving their standard of living that they had lost touch with "fancy." Nathaniel Hawthorne reached a similar conclusion. Like increasing numbers of his countrymen, he was willing to do without the romance of the open fire to enhance personal comfort, but stoves troubled him nonetheless. In November 1842, he wrote his sister that he was "well contented" to stay in Concord, Massachusetts, for the winter because he had acquired two heating stoves and a cookstove that made his house "perfectly comfortable."[42] In his private notebook, however, he expressed a quite different reaction. "We have had three stoves put up," he commented, "and henceforth no light of a cheerful fire will gladden us at even tide. Stoves are detestable in every respect, except that they keep us perfectly comfortable."[43]

Hawthorne's stoves soon made him even more ill at ease. In "Fire Worship" (1843), he bewailed the "almost universal exchange of the open fireplace for the cheerless and ungenial stove." Although confessing that he had installed stoves in his home, he decried their "barren and tedious eccentricities," which included a penchant for scorching fingers, singeing clothing, and emitting "volumes of smoke and noisome gas."[44] Hawthorne lamented the loss of the open fire's "invaluable moral influences" and predicted dire consequences if stove use continued to spread. "Social intercourse cannot long continue what it has been, now that we have subtracted from it so important . . . an element as firelight," he declared. In stove-heated homes, "there will be nothing to attract . . . children to one centre. . . . Domestic life . . . will seek its separate corners." The fate of the nation itself was at risk. "While a man was true to the fireside," Hawthorne claimed, "so long would he be true to country and law," and further scoffed, "FIGHT FOR YOUR STOVES! Not I."[45]

It would be interesting to know what Hawthorne's wife thought of stoves, considering that she was probably more intimately involved than he in their use. Regrettably, no record of her opinion survives. But even Hawthorne could not deny that stoves kept his house warm in winter. His tirade against them masked a deep-seated fear that, in David S. Reynolds's words, "togetherness, the family, and moral values" were "giving way before fragmentation, debate, and atomism."[46] Stoves were merely convenient scapegoats to help explain the social de-generation he found so distressing.

Henry David Thoreau shared many of Hawthorne's reservations about stoves. During his second winter in a cabin beside Walden Pond, he decided to install a "small cooking-stove for economy," but reported that "It did not keep fire so well as the open fireplace." It also took up valuable space, "scented the house" unpleasantly, and, even worse, "concealed the fire." "I felt as if I had lost a com-panion," he complained.[47]

Antistove sentiment and nostalgia for the open hearth grew during the 1850s and 1860s. Probably because they worked with stoves less often than women, men were especially upset by the abandonment of the fireplace. In 1851, influen-tial minister and advice writer Horace Bushnell reminisced about the "friendly circles [which had] gathered so often round the winter's fire" in his youth, "not the stove," he specified, "but the . . . hospitable fire."[48] Poet John Greenleaf Whittier also remembered the open fireplace of his youth with affection. In "Snow-Bound" (1866), he recalled a December night when his family had as-sembled around the kitchen fire, which "burst, flower-like, into rosy bloom" and produced a "tropic heat." "What matter how the night behaved?" Whittier asked. "What matter how the north-wind raved? / Blow high, blow low, not all its snow / Could quench our hearth-fire's ruddy glow."[49] James Russell Lowell, another popular poet, agreed that the open fire was preferable to stoves. In the mid-1860s, he set "The Courtin'" in an old-fashioned kitchen where "a fireplace filled the room's one side / With half a cord o' wood in— / There warn't no stoves (tell comfort died) / To bake you to a puddin'."[50]

About the same time, social critic John F. W. Ware bemoaned the disappear-ance of such rooms in *Home Life: What It Is, and What It Needs* (1864). "The large, cheerful, generous old kitchen was the home in those golden days ere its sacred economies were handed over to . . . ignorant domestics," he explained. "There were no modern labor-saving appliances" in such kitchens, he admitted, but "the home went on more wisely and happily than now. The kitchen was the sanctum of the home, the nursery . . . of virtues which have seemed to wane with the coming in of carpets and curtains and conveniences."[51]

George Canning Hill was even more explicit about the damage "conveniences" had done to the nation's homes. "We are all . . . natural fire-worshippers," he as-serted in 1867, "but the Age we live in . . . invades every nook and corner . . . and with its . . . other vaunted improvements . . . [it] has pushed forward an army of . . . stove-fitters . . . who have . . . camped down in the . . . pleasantest rooms of all the households in the land." Moreover, "They have drawn their curtains of sightless brick-and-mortar across the dear old fireplaces . . . [and] have mounted a grim cylindrical invention . . . and bidden the shivering household gather around it." Echoing Hawthorne's lament in "Fire Worship," Hill concluded, "There are to be no more household gatherings as of old . . . for the vestal fires are all gone out. A stove . . . is not a hearth; heat is not fire; warmth is not blaze. . . . Near a blackened stove the human heart builds no altars."[52] Hill overlooked the fact that the "army of . . . stove-fitters" he found so objectionable had entered American homes at their owners' request. Considering his point of view, however, this omission is not surprising; his motivation was rooted in domestic ideology, not in reality.

Some women writers also regretted Americans' growing reliance on stoves. Susan Fenimore Cooper told readers of *Rural Hours* (1850) that "a fine, open, wood fire is undeniably the pleasantest mode of heating a room." But, she concluded sadly, "our living forest wood must . . . give way to black, dull coal; [and] the generous, open chimney to the close and stupid stove!"[53] Harriet Beecher Stowe shared Cooper's preference for the fireplace. In *House and Home Papers* (1865), she insisted that it was more than a nicety that promoted family togetherness; it was "an altar of patriotism." "Would our Revolutionary fathers have gone barefooted and bleeding over snows to defend air-tight stoves and cooking-ranges?" she asked. "I trow not. It was the memory of the great open kitchen-fire . . . that called to them . . . to keep up their courage, that made their hearts warm and bright with a thousand reflected memories."[54]

For women like Stowe, sentimental fiction proved an effective platform for condemning stoves. In best-selling novels published in the 1850s, Susan Warner, Stowe, and Ann Sophia Stephens all suggested a link between feminine prestige and the continued use of traditional cooking techniques, a connection not emphasized by male stove critics. In *The Wide, Wide World* (1851), for example, Warner described the mysteries of the "good-sized, cheerful-looking kitchen" in Miss Fortune Emerson's New England farmhouse. Its "enormous fireplace" and "great oven" astound little, city-born Ellen Montgomery, who watches Miss Fortune cook with "great curiosity" but is never able to discover the "magic" behind her "good . . . country coffee," "excellent . . . brown bread and butter," and "entirely satisfactory . . . fried pork and potatoes." Ellen is even sent out of the room when the coals are swept out of the oven in preparation for baking, as though she might prematurely learn a trade secret known only to adult women.[55]

Warner elaborated on the idyllic quality of rural domesticity in *Queechy* (1852). Her heroine, Fleda Ringgan, has two aunts who exemplify the extremes of women's experience. Lucy Rossitur, a city dweller who does not do her own housework, is upset when financial reverses force the family to move to an isolated farmhouse. Her husband tells her they cannot afford servants and speculates about the house's equipment. "I suppose you'll find . . . every fireplace with a crane in it," he muses. Lucy is puzzled; to her, "crane" means "nothing but a large water-bird." Fortunately for Fleda, her Aunt Miriam is a different type of woman. A competent country housewife, she runs her household without the aid of either servants or stoves. She is completely at home with cranes and other traditional cooking devices, and clearly in control of a process that Fleda finds compelling. Entranced, Fleda watches Aunt Miriam's "tall figure . . . stooping to look in at the open mouth of the oven" at "great loaves of bread" and a "perfect squad of pies and pans of gingerbread."[56] Surrounded by symbols of eighteenth-century domestic prowess, Aunt Miriam is, Warner suggested, a far better role model for American girls than Lucy Rossitur.

Queechy was overshadowed by another novel published the same year—Stowe's *Uncle Tom's Cabin*. This book, best known for its antislavery message, also features a woman who continues to uphold culinary tradition. Dinah, the slave who supervises the kitchen in Augustine St. Clare's New Orleans household, is a "native and essential cook" who works without system but somehow manages to achieve spectacular results. Her master tries to convince her to exchange the "great old-fashioned fireplace" for a "modern cook-stove," but she refuses, remaining "inflexibly attached to time-honored inconveniences." To the horror of St. Clare's carefully trained cousin Ophelia, Dinah uses "sixty-five different sugar bowls" and washes dishes "with a dinner-napkin one day, and with a fragment of old petticoat the next." But, as St. Clare remarks appreciatively, "she gets up glorious dinners . . . and you must judge her . . . by her success."[57]

As far as Dinah and St. Clare are concerned, preparing good meals required innate female skill, not modern appliances or organizational principles. Salina Bowles, a character in Stephens's *The Old Homestead* (1855), would have agreed. "With . . . reverence for ancient usages," she, like Dinah, "set herself resolutely against all cooking-stoves, ranges and inventions of that class," declaring "that no decent meal could ever be cooked by any of these new-fangled contrivances."[58]

Mrs. Gray, whom Stephens introduced in *Fashion and Famine* the previous year, held similar views. A Long Island "huckster-woman" who makes a living selling produce in New York City, she exhibits "the perfections of an old-fashioned New England housewife." Born in Maine, Mrs. Gray takes the then-regional holiday of Thanksgiving very seriously. "You should have seen her," Stephens relates, "surrounded by raisins, black currants, pumpkin sauce, peeled apples, sugar boxes, and plates of golden butter, her plump hand pearly with flour." Seated in a "splint-bottomed rocking chair," Mrs. Gray expertly chops mincemeat ingredients with "a soft, easy motion" and "a quiet and smiling air." With little assistance, she fixes an impressive meal, including roast turkey, chicken pie, "sucking pig," roast beef, and Indian pudding. "Kitty," her "awkward Irish girl," is allowed only to tend the potatoes, a task for which she is "qualified by birth." Best of all, despite the amount of work involved in preparing this feast, Mrs. Gray still uses a fireplace and brick oven, having "not yet degenerated down to a cooking-stove."[59]

Like male stove critics, Stephens, Stowe, and Warner were motivated by a specific social agenda. As Mary Kelly has demonstrated, middle-class sentimentalists such as these responded to American materialism by expressing "nostalgia for an imagined past and a demand that society return to supposedly traditional . . . values."[60] One of the most publicly sensitive issues, which helped shape the debate over cookstove use, was the question of who would perform the "traditional" work of the household.

During the antebellum period, a number of domestic advisors, many of them men, criticized middle-class women's penchant for leaving housework to servants. In 1837, for example, William Alcott argued that domestics disrupted the "order of families" and were bad influences on children. Even worse, employing servants magnified class distinctions "already sufficiently apparent."[61] But Alcott knew that women were eager to turn the dirty work of their households over to servants whenever they could. He blamed this phenomenon on "fashionable life," which inspired in women an "unreasonable prejudice against cookery, washing, mending, &c." It was time, he thought, for housekeeping to be "taken by wise and discreet mothers into their own hands, instead of being committed to those who have no interest in it."[62] The author of *Cookery As It Should Be* (1853) shared Alcott's views, complaining that the United States was "the only country . . . where women in the middle ranks of social life consider domestic avocations as unladylike," and recalling that "Time was when ladies looked to the ways of their household." As this writer saw it, "Now such matters are left to inexperienced foreigners."[63]

The comment about "inexperienced foreigners" is revealing. Although the impact of nativism on the nation's politics and labor relations is better known, it also influenced the debate over domestic work. Faye Dudden has discovered that relations between middle-class Americans and their "help" changed markedly after 1820. New opportunities in schools and factories reduced the number of native-born women willing to enter domestic service. Their places were increasingly filled by Irish immigrants, a circumstance that troubled Anglo-Americans trying to protect their homes from alien influences. Fear of Roman Catholicism exacerbated the tense relationship between mistresses and servants, but class differences were equally important. New standards for genteel conduct and a greater emphasis on family privacy gave Anglo-Americans two additional reasons to widen the gulf between themselves and their "unwashed," "ignorant" servants.[64] Domestics also represented the "extension of marketplace relations" into the supposedly separate domestic sphere. Although necessary for "mundane, repetitive, and rather primitive" household chores, servants undermined the "cult of domesticity." The solution, increasingly popular after midcentury, was to isolate them in basement kitchens and service areas, and to restrict their traffic to back stairways.[65]

Stoves, typically tended by servants in families able to afford "help,"[66] were also beginning to be treated as unwelcome "strangers in the gates."[67] Cookstoves, in particular, were relegated to the "back" of the house, where the soot and odors they emitted would not sully the pristine atmosphere of "front" rooms reserved for family and friends.[68] According to conventional wisdom, it was unseemly for genteel ladies trained in the niceties of parlor etiquette to grapple with cookstoves. As early as 1833, a writer in *American Ladies' Magazine* claimed that middle-class women believed "it would degrade a lady to be seen in her kitchen at work."[69] Twenty-one years later, social critic Ellen Chandler Moulton complained, "We have learned that it's really a *bona fide* disgrace for a young lady to do house-work. She may . . . walk over half the streets of the city, or fatigue herself with music-lessons . . . but, if she would not lose caste, let her avoid the kitchen."[70]

'Lena Rivers, the heroine of Mary Jane Holmes's 1856 novel of the same name, knew from personal experience that kitchen work could damage a genteel young woman's image. After her uncle's cook falls ill, she agrees to supervise a company dinner, but the guests arrive before she can wash or change her clothes. As she discovers, "bending over hot stoves . . . is not very beneficial to one's complexion," and her "cheeks, neck, forehead, and nose" have turned an unbecoming "purplish red." A few days later, another kitchen stint results in her "burning herself until she was ashamed to appear at the table."[71]

Stove maintenance, too, was represented as a task best left to hirelings. In an 1857 cartoon from *Frank Leslie's Illustrated Newspaper* (illus. 5.4), Mr. Tibbs scolds his wife for not having called in a professional to "physic" the family's cookstove, which is spewing smoke and has ruined dinner. The situation is especially embarrassing because the "darkey stove doctor" knows more about the stove than its white owners. Disgusted, Mr. Tibbs "vanishes," leaving his wife groveling on the floor in front of the unruly stove. The next year, *Harper's Weekly* published another cartoon ridiculing a middle-class woman's ignorance of stoves (illus. 5.5). Here, a fashionably dressed young woman is trying to learn to cook because she must let her servants go "in consequence of the Hard Times." She

5.4. "Darkey Stove Doctor," *Frank Leslie's Illustrated Newspaper* (12 Dec. 1857), 32. Courtesy of the American Antiquarian Society, Worcester, Mass.

5.5. "Novel and Alarming Incident," *Harper's Weekly* 2 (9 Jan. 1858), 32.

has put too much fuel in the stove, causing the kettle to boil over, and stands, enveloped by a cloud of steam, feebly clutching a poker and asking her cook what to do next.

The period's domestic advice fiction likewise suggests that cookstoves caused friction between servants and employers. With some reason, cooks believed stoves existed for their convenience and resisted employers' efforts to interfere with their management. As Elizabeth, a servant in *Plain Talk and Friendly Advice to Domestics* (1855), explains, "I like to have my mistress stay in the parlor, and be after minding business of her own, and not be preaching to me."[72] Dinah, the cook in Sarah Josepha Hale's *Keeping House and Housekeeping* (1845), is equally assertive, insisting that her employers, the Harleys, buy a new range like the one to which she is accustomed. Otherwise, she claims she cannot be held accountable "if she burn[s] the meat, or but half bake[s] the bread." Mr. Harley, who is planning a party for business associates and whose wife knows nothing about housework, has no choice but to accede to Dinah's demand.[73]

The servants in Timothy Shay Arthur's *Trials and Confessions of an American Housekeeper* (1859) prove even more difficult. Margaret is the first good cook the Smith family has been able to find, but she has to be fired for habitual drinking. Biddy, her successor, steals from the household stores, so she, too, is sent packing. Kitty, the next cook, proves to have an inconvenient fondness for sensational fiction. One day, Mrs. Smith tells her that her husband is bringing a friend to dinner and will be sending home a turkey that she is to prepare "in the best manner." Doubting Kitty's culinary skill, Mrs. Smith decides to make the puddings herself, telling Kitty to "be sure to have a good fire in the range, and see that all the drafts are clear." But when she enters the kitchen just half an hour before dinner is to be ready, she witnesses the distressing scene depicted in illustration 5.6: Kitty sits before the range, engrossed in a "pamphlet novel," oblivious to the fact that the puddings are burning and the cat is gnawing on the uncooked turkey.[74]

Inattention was not the only tactic available to a disgruntled cook. Biddy, the cook in another fictional household described by Arthur, considers the kitchen "her castle" and takes revenge against her interfering employers by damaging the most expensive thing in reach—their cookstove. One day when dinner is late, Mrs. Brown investigates. "This is no kind of fire," she exclaims. "The coal won't burn," Biddy answers. "It always has burned," Mrs. Brown retorts. "No wonder . . . with this damper half closed, how could you expect coal to burn without a free draft?" she asks. Biddy's "spirit of opposition" is awakened by this exchange, and she retaliates by delaying dinner even further.[75]

5.6. "Showing Why the Dinner Was Late." In Timothy Shay Arthur, *Trials and Confessions of a Housekeeper* (Philadelphia: J. W. Bradley, 1859), 20.

Matters worsen when Mr. Brown intervenes. Biddy has continued to abuse the range, and a new one has been installed. Anxious to avoid a repetition of the problem that ruined its predecessor, Mr. Brown shows Biddy how to use the new appliance. "You must never let the coal come above this fire-brick," he explains. "If you do, it will neither burn so freely nor give such a good heat. . . . Moreover, if you build the fire up to the top plate, you will crack [it] . . . with the intense heat." But Biddy, a "sharp-witted Irish girl" who has no respect for a man willing to involve himself in domestic work, pays no attention. Mr. Brown returns to the kitchen the next day and discovers that "the fire-chamber of the range was so full that portions of the ignited fuel projected . . . through the hole in the top plate." After this encounter, he "occasionally" suggests to Biddy that she is not managing the range properly. "All, however, availed not. The coal was still piled to the top plate that, in a few weeks, was cracked in two pieces."[76]

Servant-employer confrontations over cookstoves did not always have to end so badly. In *The Lady at Home* (1844), Arthur told the story of another mistress whose cook is "slow, awkward, and untidy." One day when dinner is delayed, Mrs. Elmwood scolds Hannah sharply, but shortly afterward she reads a story that advises patience and forbearance as the secrets to successful household management. Contrite, she returns to the kitchen and, speaking in a "mild, encouraging voice," offers to help Hannah get dinner. "I don't think you understand my stove yet," she says tactfully, "for your fire does not seem lively." Mrs. Elmwood then "took up the poker and cleared the fire of an accumulation of ashes, examined the dampers, and found that they were all wrong; rearranged the dishes . . . so as to bring them into more advantageous positions, and then showed Hannah what [she] had done, explaining to her . . . the whole action of the cook-stove." Hannah is won over by her employer's tone and attitude and magically becomes "clean, tidy and industrious, and always to the minute with her meals."[77]

As his fiction demonstrates, Arthur believed middle-class women had to be sufficiently knowledgeable about housework to supervise their servants. In 1842, he railed against the "false idea which has begun to prevail . . . that it is a perversion of [a woman's] true character . . . to make her thoroughly . . . acquainted with the details of domestic life."[78] Other advisors shared this view and tried to convince women that housework was ennobling, a crucial element in the success of male breadwinners and the rearing of future citizens. "Homes," explained Harriet Beecher Stowe in 1865, "are the work of art peculiar to the genius of woman. . . . She comprehends all, she balances and arranges all; all different tastes and temperaments find in her their rest, and she can unite at one hearthstone the most discordant elements. . . . To make such a home," she concluded, "is ambition high and worthy enough for *any* woman."[79]

To create idyllic homes, middle-class women had to be properly educated. But because domestic advisors were edgy about the impact of technology on the home, they emphasized attitude and process, not equipment. Catharine Beecher's *A Treatise On Domestic Economy,* for example, reprinted almost annually from 1841 to 1856, taught women to establish a stress-free home environment by the application of logic.[80] Beecher outlined weekly housework schedules, discussed the organization of storage facilities, explained the division of household labor among family members and servants, and gave directions on everything from cutting and fitting clothes to lubricating carriage wheels.[81] Her aim was to transform the household into a domestic factory that functioned so smoothly that it appeared to run itself. Mary Cornelius, another popular domestic writer, gave women similar advice: "Do everything in its proper time. Keep everything to its proper use. Put everything in its proper place. . . . This habit promotes order and system, and gives quietness and ease to the . . . whole family machinery."[82] The author of the *American Ladies' Memorial* (1850) employed an

analogous metaphor, observing that "a well-ordered house has been fitly compared to a watch, all the wheels and springs of which are out of sight."[83]

This celebration of domestic duties was part of an effort to compensate for the
diminishing relevance of what Mary P. Ryan has termed the "corporate character
of family economies." During the first half of the nineteenth century, many tasks
that women had hitherto performed at home, especially those involving textiles,
shifted to factories. Many households also stopped producing soap, candles, and
medicines,[84] and the nation's food supply changed as agriculture grew more specialized and transportation networks expanded. City dwellers had access to bread
from bakeries, as well as to milk and produce raised on nearby farms. Improvements in ice-cutting and storing technology made it possible to eat fresh meat
throughout the year. Refrigerated railroad cars, introduced in the 1840s, transported fresh food to distant consumers. Processed meat, milk, fruits, and vegetables also began to appear on store shelves.[85]

The growing distance between food producers and consumers, together with
the appearance of unscrupulous middlemen, troubled social critics, who responded by reemphasizing the importance of women's role as cooks. In the
1830s, dietary reformer Sylvester Graham concluded that the expansion of the
market economy and the depersonalization of trade had destabilized the nation.
He pleaded with Americans to reassert control over one of the few aspects of
daily life still within their power—their food. "A very large proportion of all the
diseases . . . of civic life," he explained, "are originated by . . . diet."[86] Bread, the
first staple product manufactured in quantity outside the home, was a special
concern. Graham insisted on bread made from coarsely ground, unbolted flour
and baked at home by "the wife, the mother only," maintaining that it was "she
alone . . . who will ever be inspired by that . . . unremitting affection . . . which
will excite the vigilance . . . requisite to . . . a perfect bread-maker."[87]

Other domestic advisors also believed that women's lack of interest in cooking
was having serious consequences. In 1848, Perrin Bliss complained about "fashionable females" who thought it a "disgrace . . . to make good bread." To his dismay, he discovered that these misguided women were bringing up their
daughters without instruction in domestic duties. "No wonder," Bliss concluded, "that our females, especially in cities . . . , are so enfeebled."[88] The nation's economy might also suffer from such ignorance, as Mary Cornelius
pointed out in 1846: "The health of many a professional man is undermined and
his usefulness curtailed, if not sacrificed because he habitually eats bad bread."[89]
Inept cooking could even affect foreign policy. In 1847, Caroline Kirkland, editor of *The Union Magazine of Literature and Art,* declared, "Of all the reforms,
none is more loudly called for than one in . . . cookery. . . . Who knows but the
Mexican war may be traced to an ill-cooked . . . dinner."[90]

Domestic advisors pleaded with middle-class women to prevent such catastrophes. American mothers had to stop training their daughters "for the ballroom," argued the author of *Cookery As It Should Be* (1853). "The first object of a woman's care must be the family laboratory—the kitchen."[91] Solon Robinson echoed this sentiment, asserting seven years later that "domestic happiness is greatly dependent upon the manner in which the cooking department of the household is managed."[92]

If done by middle-class Anglo-American housewives, good cooking could achieve remarkable results and give the women who did it a sense of achievement. Ann Allen, author of *The Housekeeper's Assistant* (1845), asserted that "the most devoted husband is better pleased with having good bread and butter . . . than the most learned dissertation in Latin . . . or the most splendid performances upon the piano forte."[93] Sara Willis Parton, a popular writer whose *Fanny Fern's Family Cook Book* appeared in 1856, also believed the "secrets of the kitchen" were "far more important to domestic felicity than the drawing-room." Mastering the "art of cookery," she argued, would give a woman the power "to hold her lord of creation in leading-strings for the remainder of his days."[94]

Despite their efforts to elevate the "art of cookery," however, domestic advisors devoted little attention to the modern tools that might have helped women achieve the results they promised. Cookbooks and domestic economy guides published in the 1840s and 1850s rarely acknowledged the increasing presence of cookstoves in American homes. Catharine Beecher, for example, scarcely mentioned stoves in *A Treatise on Domestic Economy* (1841), despite dedicating one chapter to "fires and lights," one to the "preparation of healthful food," and one to the "care of the kitchen, cellar, and storeroom." Only in her discussion of house construction did she casually note that some households were equipped with the new appliance.[95]

Eliza Leslie, author of *The House Book* (1841), was one of the only advisors in this period to make specific suggestions about cookstoves, but she recommended a ten-plate stove with a single boiling hole, a style long since superseded by improved designs.[96] She also gave readers instructions on heating brick ovens and provided a list of items needed to cook with an open fireplace.[97] The author of *The American Matron* (1851) was also uncertain about what advice to give her readers. About bread baking, she commented, "So many and so various are the inventions of modern times to accomplish this branch of cookery— some using cooking stoves, heated by wood or by coal, some coal ranges; others, again, the brick oven, heated by wood—that but few rules can be laid down."[98]

Mary Cornelius likewise referred to multiple cooking techniques throughout *The Young Housekeeper's Friend* (1846) to ensure that her instructions would be applicable to all circumstances. Tomatoes, she advised, "are much the nicest when cooked in a stove, or brick oven"; cornbread was to "bake in a stove, or a baker before the fire"; sausages would take twenty minutes to cook if fried in a "spider" over coals, but on a stove they would require half an hour. Like Leslie, Cornelius also provided readers with step-by-step directions for baking in a brick oven.[99] When she issued a revised edition in 1860, however, she prefaced the section on baking with this disclaimer: "Stoves and cooking-ranges have so generally taken the place of brick ovens that the following directions, which were appropriate when this book was first published, will seldom be of use now."[100]

Cookbook authors knew, of course, that the transition to cookstoves was happening gradually, especially as far as roasting and baking were concerned. Their advice demonstrates some of the challenges of adapting to the new appliance. Early stove ovens were notorious for uneven temperature and were believed by some to saturate food with poisonous gases. Ann Allen recommended that cooks revive the "good old custom of roasting meats before the fire," but she also knew that it was easier to use a stove. If meat were to be baked in a stove, she continued, "have good heat, and open the doors a trifle, and it will improve the flavor, as air lets off the strong fumes . . . rendering it more delicate."[101] Elizabeth Lea gave similar advice in *Domestic Cookery* (1846). "A . . . turkey . . . is best done before the fire in a tin oven," she asserted. "Baking [meat] in a stove requires more water in the dripping pan, as the heat is greater and dries it up; care should be taken to turn it often. If done carefully," she concluded, "meat is almost as good roasted in the stove as before the fire."[102]

The diminished reliance on brick ovens also bothered cookbook authors. In 1848, Perrin Bliss argued that "there is no oven so good . . . as the old fashioned brick oven."[103] Sarah Josepha Hale agreed, insisting nine years later that a brick oven was "far superior . . . for baking . . . , being much more easy to regulate, as well as more economical, than an iron one."[104] Hale's last remark is puzzling. If there was one thing on which her contemporaries agreed, it was the fact that stoves were "economical." Hale may have meant that the large size of brick ovens made it possible to bake more items at one time, but her conclusion still rings false.

Hale's attachment to the brick oven was likely motivated by the same concerns that led other middle-class social critics to champion traditional cooking techniques and tools as emblems of stability. It was difficult for proponents of the "cult of domesticity" to come to terms with the new technology of domestic heating and cooking. Some of them even tried to deny the existence of stoves, at least symbolically. Although *The Kitchen Companion and House-keeper's Own Book* was published in 1844, its cover (illus. 5.7) depicts an eighteenth-century kitchen unprofaned by modern technology; neither processed foods nor stoves are visible. A similar illustration appeared the next year as the frontispiece to Esther Howland's *The American Economical Housekeeper* (illus. 5.8). The "habits of

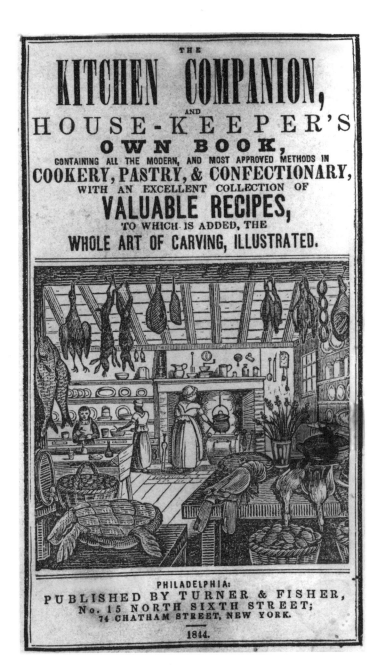

5.7. Cover, *The Kitchen Companion and House-keeper's Own Book*
(Philadelphia: Turner and Fisher, 1844). Courtesy of the American
Antiquarian Society, Worcester, Mass.

system and order" so dear to advocates of "domestic economy" have influenced the organization of this kitchen, but the scene is nevertheless dominated by an open fireplace, complete with crane and pothooks.

These images had little in common with the kitchens most northern families were actually using. As part of their campaign to celebrate a supposedly simpler, healthier, more moral past, middle-class social critics tried to downplay the impact of technological change on the household. As Ann Douglas has indicated, the efforts of "domestic economy" advocates "were robbed of vitality by the intrusion of technology into the kitchen; mother-at-home was forced to play hostess to male inventions."[105] Because cookstoves were the most noticeable of these "male inventions," they were marginalized in the ideal home, despite their growing presence in the nation's real households. In subsequent decades, it would prove more difficult to ignore them.

5.8. (*Opposite*) Frontispiece, Esther A. Howland, *The American Economical Housekeeper* (Cincinnati: H. W. Derby, 1845). Courtesy of the American Antiquarian Society, Worcester, Mass.

6

"We Have Got a
Very Good Cooking Stove"

DESPITE THE OUTCRY against stoves between 1840 and 1865, Americans were buying the appliance in increasing numbers. Stove manufacturers expanded output, lowered prices, and improved both performance and appearance. Northerners, accustomed to the benefits of cookstoves, began to consider them necessities, and as more and more of them moved west, they spread stove use to places such as Kansas, Wisconsin, and California. But consumers remained impatient with the shortcomings of the cookstove and continued searching for new ways to reduce the burdens of housework.

The gap between consumer behavior and domestic advice is easily explained. Stove critics, like other champions of the "cult of domesticity," were atypical. David Reynolds has found ample evidence in nineteenth-century American popular fiction "to explode the long-standing myth that there was an all-powerful cult of domesticity that governed daily behavior."[1] Ann Douglas has highlighted the paradox at the heart of the myth: the era's sentimentalists asserted that "the values a society's activity denies are precisely the ones it cherishes." She concludes that sentimentalism made it possible "to protest a power to which one has already in part capitulated." Consumers' growing acceptance of stoves in the midst of widespread denunciation of their use is an excellent example of what Douglas terms the "cultural bifurcation" evident in nineteenth-century America.[2]

Midcentury artists and writers captured this tension in their work. As we have seen, many of them portrayed stoves in an unflattering light. Some, however, did not. Genre painter Francis W. Edmonds, for example, depicted several household interiors with cooking fireplaces and traditional tools,[3] but he also appreciated the benefits of the new technology. *The Wind Mill* (illus. 6.1), painted about 1858, shows a man demonstrating a toy while a child and dog watch entranced. To the right, set into the fireplace, is an up-to-date range, complete with hot-water reservoir, a recent innovation. Tongs and a skimmer, appropriate for either

6.1. Francis W. Edmonds, *The Wind Mill*, c. 1858. Robert L. Stuart Collection, New York Historical Society, New York, N.Y.; on permanent loan from The New York Public Library. Copyright © Collection of the New-York Historical Society.

fireplace or stove cooking, share space with a rimmer, a ring that reduced the size of a boiling hole on the range top. In this scene, at least, a modern stove compromises neither tradition nor sentiment.

The impact of the cookstove on women is demonstrated in the work of another genre artist, Lilly Martin Spencer. Her 1854 painting *Shake Hands* (illus.

6.2) depicts a modishly but sensibly dressed and coiffed woman who frankly offers to greet the viewer, despite the fact that her right hand is covered with flour. As Elizabeth Johns has pointed out, handshaking was an important "ritual of male equality" in nineteenth-century America. She notes that the equality this woman seeks is "limited . . . because she is rooted in the domestic sphere," but she also concludes that "resistance to domestic subordination [is] embedded in the motif of the picture." Spencer's painting "shows a woman in command of her world,"[4] with the cookstove serving as an integral part of this world.

Shake Hands is, as Johns observes, a "celebration of female domesticity in its most practical form." It also proved popular. Spencer exhibited it several times and sold it to the Cosmopolitan Art Union in 1857, which produced an engraving for distribution to members. Spencer's 1856 painting *The Young Wife: First Stew,* of which only a study survives (illus. 6.3), did not enjoy similar success. Perhaps, as Johns has suggested, Americans resisted the implication that women's culinary skill was "learned rather than natural."[5] Public response notwithstanding, it is significant that the same cookstove appears in each painting. Spencer wanted women to know that although they might struggle to learn to cook, with time they could master the secrets of the kitchen, including those of the most modern appliance found there.

Some midcentury fiction writers, most of them women, also approved of stoves. In Alice Haven's *The Coopers* (1858), for example, when Mr. Cooper asks his bride whether they should begin furnishing the parlor or the kitchen, she responds, "Oh, the kitchen! Aunt Agnes used to say: 'Do have your kitchen well furnished. . . . If you don't, you will always be in some trouble.'" Mr. Cooper sees the wisdom of this argument, so the couple's first purchase is an $18 cookstove.[6] The central characters in Eunice White Beecher's *From Dawn to Daylight* (1859) face much the same choice. A young minister and his bride have only $30 to outfit their new quarters, but, fortunately, the minister's brother and sister-in-law offer a practical wedding gift. "We would be most happy to present you with a cooking stove," they tell them, "*that* being a very important article in housekeeping."[7] Even the tenants in the "dark" and "dirty" tenement described in Catherine Sedgwick's *Married or Single?* (1857) rely on the new appliance; each apartment is furnished with a "wretched cooking-stove." Sedgwick's adjective might imply antipathy to stoves, but she was actually pleading for even more "modern improvements" — steam heat, gas lighting, "dumb waiters and speaking pipes."[8] Only in this context could the by now familiar cookstove appear "wretched."

Mary Andrews Denison also examined the impact of stoves in her fiction. In *Orange Leaves* (1856), she praised the "wondrous machinery" that had done so much to improve the lot of housekeepers. "First and foremost," she decided, was

6.2. Lilly Martin Spencer, *Shake Hands,* 1854. Courtesy of the Ohio Historical Society, Columbus, Ohio.

6.3. Lilly Martin Spencer, study for *The Young Wife: First Stew,* 1856. Courtesy of the Ohio Historical Society, Columbus, Ohio.

"the cooking-stove—a warm old friend that makes little mischief because it is always at work."[9] Children's book author Abraham Oakey Hall likewise recognized the benefits of cookstoves. In *Old Whitey's Christmas Trot* (1857), he described the New York City boardinghouse operated by Mrs. Mount. Her kitchen (illus. 6.4) is dominated by a "little stove" over which she stoops, protectively tending a kettle of soup. Hall presents the stove from a male perspective. As Mrs. Mount works, one boarder crouches snugly against the wall reading a newspaper while another stretches comfortably in his chair. Mr. Mount and his son enter the room eagerly, drawn by the "savory odor" that also attracts another lodger, who works in a hardware store. In contrast to the stoves he sells, which are "as shining and as cold as the exterior of a man of fashion," Mrs. Mount's stove is "a jolly piece of iron" that gives a "glow to everything about."[10]

These artists and writers were responding to a trend that was difficult to ignore. By midcentury, cookstoves had become common in the North. Thirty of the fifty-four estates (56 percent) probated in Providence, Rhode Island, in 1840 and 1845, for example, included cooking stoves.[11] Commitment to the new technology varied, however. Whereas John Atwood owned "8 small [heating] stoves"

6.4. Mrs. Mount's kitchen. In Abraham Oakey Hall, *Old Whitey's Christmas Trot* (New York: Harper and Bros., 1857), 117.

and "one James's patent [cook]stove," Robey Barker was more tentative. He owned a "cooking stove" and a "small coal stove," but his inventory also lists two pairs of andirons, evidence that open fireplaces were still being used in his home. Fourteen other residents in this sample made a similar decision, choosing to own both cookstoves and andirons or firesets.[12]

The probate inventories of Barnstable County, Massachusetts (Cape Cod), reveal a similar pattern. As in Providence, stoves had become the most common means of preparing meals; sixty-nine of the 117 estates recorded in 1840, 1845, and 1850 included cookstoves (59 percent). The appliance was found in both modest and wealthy households; both the poorest and the richest men in this sample owned cookstoves. Stoves were also spread evenly across the economic spectrum; twelve of the sixteen estates valued below $200 included cookstoves, as did seven of the eight valued above $5,000.[13]

These inventories also reveal differing levels of stove use. Twenty of the households in this sample had both stoves and andirons, firesets, or Franklin stoves.[14] The inventory of Joshua Loring, a Barnstable fisherman who died in 1851, illustrates the compromise between tradition and innovation that was common at midcentury. Loring's estate was valued at $1,368.75, slightly above the median, but his family lived quite simply. His $600 "homestead" had five rooms: an "east front room" (a sitting/dining room), a kitchen, a "milkroom" (for food and utensil storage), and two bedchambers. The milkroom and the "square chamber" were both unheated, but assessors found a shovel and tongs in the "east front room" and a pair of andirons in the "back chamber," indicating that both spaces were warmed by open fires. In the kitchen, however, they discovered a $10 cookstove.[15]

Although consumers such as Loring often still preferred open fires in their parlors, probate inventories demonstrate their increasing willingness to install stoves in their kitchens. Fortunately, innovations in the iron industry had resulted in substantially lower stove prices. In 1833, Frederick Geissenhainer patented a method of smelting iron using anthracite coal and a hot blast of air. Because anthracite could support more ore and flux in the blast furnace than charcoal, it was possible to build larger furnaces, which increased output and reduced the cost of pig iron.[16] Casting technology improved as well. As long as manufacturers believed that stove plates had to be cast directly at the furnace, stove sales suffered because transportation costs drove up retail prices. In the 1830s, however, Jordan Mott of New York experimented with remelting pig iron in a cupola furnace. To the surprise of industry experts, castings produced by these furnaces proved more durable than those manufactured in the traditional way. Mott was thus able to introduce a "light, smooth, sharp cut, and elegant . . . stove plate" instead of the "rough castings" previously in use. Moreover, because cupola furnaces burned coal instead of charcoal and were smaller than the blast furnaces used on iron plantations, they could be set up in urban areas.[17]

As news of Mott's work spread, inventors and manufacturers competed to take advantage of it. Between 1840 and 1864, 796 patents for stoves and stove attachments were granted, compared to 329 in the previous twenty-five years.[18] Victor Clark estimated that at midcentury 150,000 stoves were manufactured annually in both Philadelphia and New York, plus 50,000 in Cincinnati, 30,000 in Providence, and 20,000 in Pittsburgh.[19] By 1850, 230 firms had entered the stove business, producing stoves valued at $6.1 million annually. This placed stove manufacturing forty-third out of 184 industries nationwide, a good showing for a business only some thirty years old.[20] In fact, the stove industry may have expanded too rapidly, at least in some areas. The population of Providence, for example, increased 119 percent between 1840 and 1860, yet the number of stove dealers rose from three in 1843 to twenty-two in 1860. The number of stove manufacturers also increased, from one in 1843 to six in 1860.[21]

As their numbers grew, stove dealers had to work harder to attract customers. A thriving secondhand trade developed, bringing stove ownership within reach of more consumers. In 1844, for example, Gloucester, Massachusetts, stove dealer Calvin Putnam informed the public that he would exchange "Old Stoves [for new ones] at their full value."[22] John Burleigh, a stove dealer in Douglas, Massachusetts, was equally obliging. In the late 1840s, he bought several used stoves from local families. Horace Emerson, a frequent customer, paid Burleigh $19.50 for "1 Sec[ond] Hand Stove" in October 1846 and returned five months later to sell him "1 old Stove" (perhaps the same model) for $10. Burleigh was also willing to accept goods and services in lieu of cash. In 1847, for example, he sold a "stove and fixtures" for $15.81 to a teamster named Brown, who paid him with a combination of corn and free hauling.[23]

The account book kept between 1852 and 1855 by Greenfield, Massachusetts, stove dealer George Pierce provides additional insight into the options available to stove buyers and the flexibility required of retailers. In these years, Pierce sold sixty-nine new cookstoves. He carried several unnamed models, including one with an elevated oven, as well as the Bay State in four sizes, the Challenge in four sizes, the Fashion of Troy in four sizes, the Farmer's Bay State, the Grecian, the Buena Vista, the Forrest, and the Mohawk and Hudson. These stoves ranged in price from $2 to $55 with an average cost of $21.87, 31 percent lower than in the mid-1830s. Pierce also sold thirty-one parlor cookstoves, a new design that added one or two boiling holes and sometimes a small oven to a heating stove. These stoves ranged in price from $8 to $18.50 with an average cost of $13.04. Pierce also provided ways for stove buyers to lower their out-of-pocket expenses. Nine of his customers chose secondhand cookstoves, paying between $5.13 and $18.97, and three bought secondhand stovepipe. Pierce was also willing to accommodate cash-poor clients. Twelve of the people who bought new cookstoves from him traded in old stoves, earning credits of between $1.50 and $15.50. He also accepted goods as payment. In November 1854, for example, Pierce sold Wellington Barnard a No. 4 Bay State cookstove for $22, "payable by 3 loads [of] wood not to exceed 3¾ cord[s] and the Bal[ance] in cash the first of April next." The next month, he sold John Arms a $10 cookstove "to be [paid] in corn to amount of ten bushels within one month."[24]

Pierce's customers were much like their neighbors. Twenty-seven of the people who bought new cookstoves from him could be traced in the 1850 census. The youngest was twenty-five and the oldest seventy-two, an age range considerably greater than that among stove purchasers in the 1820s and 1830s. Household size also varied widely, ranging from one to ten, with an average of 5.6. Thirteen of these households had fewer than six members, suggesting that large family size was a less significant factor in stove acquisition than had been the case earlier. The sample also includes nine farmers, indicating growing reliance on stoves among rural Americans. Variations of income, household type, and birthplace are also evident. Six of these individuals owned no real estate, whereas two owned real estate valued at $9,000 or more. Seventeen households contained only nuclear families; the other ten included boarders or employees. And at least three of these stove buyers were immigrants, two German and one English.[25]

The individuals who bought parlor cookstoves from Pierce were even more diverse. Ten of those located in the 1850 census lived with fewer than five people, and three were unmarried. For them, a parlor cookstove made sense. After all, why spend extra money for a full-size cookstove when you could manage without one? Other consumers chose parlor cookstoves because they were less expensive than full-size models. Solomon Wheeler, a thirty-six-year-old farmer, probably had this in mind when he bought a $9.50 parlor cookstove from Pierce in October 1852. He also bought nearly twenty pounds of stovepipe and three stovepipe elbows, which suggests that he wanted the stove to be a primary heat source. The Wheelers owned no real estate and had one boarder, more evidence that they were struggling to make ends meet.

For larger and wealthier families, a parlor cookstove was usually an adjunct to a full-size cookstove. Four of Pierce's customers bought both cookstoves and parlor cookstoves between 1852 and 1855. Charles Mirick, for example, spent $18 on a parlor cookstove in December 1853 and returned eleven months later to buy a No. 3 Bay State stove for $24.32. Mirick, who turned forty-two in 1853, was a printer who owned real estate valued at $700. His household included his wife Caroline, their five children, two men who worked in his printing shop, and five women, presumably either servants or boarders.[26] With fourteen people to feed,

Caroline Mirick had her hands full, even if she did have domestic help. A parlor cookstove would have given her more flexibility in cooking equipment and location, in addition to helping keep the home warm in winter.

The popularity of parlor cookstoves in the Greenfield area is only one indication of consumer interest in a broadening variety of cookstove types. During the mid–nineteenth century, inventors and manufacturers worked to develop more reliable, attractive, and affordable stoves. Competition at the wholesale and retail levels was good news for consumers, who were offered a wider range of models than ever before. In 1854, for example, those with limited incomes could buy a basic No. 6 Barstow Lilly Dale cookstove for only $8.[27] Of course, stoves with all the latest improvements were more expensive. In 1856, Henry Martin of Milwaukee bought a top-of-the-line cookstove, complete with food-warming closet, hot-water reservoir, and wash boiler, for $44.73, a price that included seven and a half feet of stovepipe, a stovepipe elbow, a dripping pan, a gridiron, two basins, and a $1 installation fee.[28]

Although far from perfect, the cookstoves available in these years were substantially better than earlier models. In 1847, Owen Evans reported that the Exhibition of American Manufactures in Philadelphia was "remarkable for the number of good cooking stoves and ranges." "The competition in this business within the last few years has produced such great improvement both in the principle and form of cookstoves, that culinary operations are now rendered easy," he noted.[29] Thirteen years later, an English observer declared that the American stoves displayed at a London industrial exhibition were to be "commended for beauty, comfort, cleanliness, and the saving of fuel."[30]

As these encomiums demonstrate, American stove designers and manufacturers had made progress since the early decades of the century, a trend they celebrated whenever possible. In 1843, Lynn, Massachusetts, stove dealer Jesse Hutchinson wrote a newspaper advertisement praising Isaac Orr's new air-tight stove. "To give a true description fair, / Of the most wonderful Tight Air / Would fill a newspaper complete," he gushed. He then devoted two columns of dubious poetry to the merits of this stove and others he carried, applauding their "breadth and length, and plain utility,— / [Their] Beauty, Strength, and Durability." All his stoves, Hutchinson promised, were "of [the] Heaviest kind" (to "last a dozen year[s]") and made "in splendid style" with "ornaments both new and fine."[31] His emphasis on durability and appearance suggests that stove buyers were beginning to focus on these issues, a rare phenomenon in the 1820s and 1830s, when fuel economy dominated the discussion about stoves.

Stove-naming patterns had also changed. Gone were the matter-of-fact models named for their inventors. Patriotism was a common theme, as the nation's newspapers filled with advertisements for Sentinel, Young America, Roger

Williams, and Statesman stoves. For heating stoves, manufacturers often chose exotic names such as Crystal Palace, Island Princess, Fairy, and Orion, whereas cookstoves were more likely to have names that stressed function, such as Green Mountain Rotary or Silver Star Respiratory.[32]

In the middle decades of the century, the difference between heating and cooking stoves grew as Americans increasingly divided their homes into "front" and "back" regions.[33] As one advice author explained in 1857, the "internal machinery of a household should . . . be studiously kept out of view."[34] Because heating stoves were difficult to hide, manufacturers tried to make them fashionable, embracing what Joel Pfister has aptly called "ornamental fecundity."[35] Beginning in the 1840s, consumers could choose parlor stoves that mimicked the latest architectural revival (illus. 6.5) or the naturalistic motifs popular in furniture and decorative arts (illus. 6.6).[36] It was particularly important to disguise the humble function of parlor cookstoves. In one example (illus. 6.7) — manufactured by the New York City firm Johnson, Cox, Lesley & Company about 1855 — boiling holes and oven are carefully concealed by decorative plates. Of course, as Margaret Hindle Hazen and Robert M. Hazen have observed, a person "could be burned by a pretty stove just as easily as by an ugly one, but an overlay of decoration transformed the overpowering rawness of a fire into genteel 'warmth' and 'radiant beauty.'"[37]

Because cookstoves were designed for the home's functional "back" region, they required little "overlay of decoration." The divergence of heating stove and cookstove design is evident in an 1855 city directory advertisement from Lowell, Massachusetts (illus. 6.8); although the heating stove has both ornamental urn and cornice, the cookstove is unabashedly utilitarian. C. Foster & Company, stove dealers in nearby Worcester, made much the same distinction, informing area residents in 1846 that they carried several models of "new and beautiful" heating stoves as well as "the most convenient and economical [cook]stove ever made."[38]

Inventors and manufacturers realized that cookstove buyers were more interested in performance than looks, so they worked hard to solve the problems that had plagued early models. Philo P. Stewart, one of the founders of Oberlin College, contributed several key improvements. According to William Keep, who interviewed him early in the twentieth century, Stewart had become frustrated trying to keep a fire going in a cookstove with a traditional square firebox. Because the fire kept dying down on the "broad, flat bottom," it occurred to him that a firebox with sloping sides would concentrate the fuel as it burned, thus making it possible to keep a fire going longer with less wood. In 1838, he patented a "summer and winter air tight cooking stove" that went into production at Fuller, Warren & Company in Troy, New York.[39] The stove quickly

6.5. Temple parlor stove, Vose & Co., Albany, N.Y., patented 1854. From the collections of Henry Ford Museum and Greenfield Village, Dearborn, Mich.

6.7. Home parlor cookstove. Johnson, Cox, Lesley & Co., *Spuyten Duyvil Foundry Stove Works Catalog* (New York: C. A. Alvord, 1855), unpaginated. Courtesy of the American Antiquarian Society, Worcester, Mass.

6.6. (*Opposite*) Four-column parlor stove, Johnson, Geer & Cox, Troy, N.Y., patented 1844. Courtesy of the Albany Institute of History and Art, Albany, N.Y.; gift of Mr. and Mrs. Richard C. Rockwell.

became known for its quality workmanship. *Scientific American* reported many years later that "it is one of the traditions of the foundry that if [Stewart] could insert the edge of a piece of paper between an oven door and its frame, the door had to be rehung."[40]

But the Stewart stove had other, more notable features. In addition to a more efficient firebox, it was equipped with a built-in ash pit to facilitate cleaning and a large hot-water reservoir at the back of the top plate through which the stove-pipe passed (illus. 6.9). Thus, waste heat from cooking could keep a supply of hot water always at hand—as long as someone remembered to fill the reservoir. The Stewart stove also came with insulated tin covers that were attached to the top, bottom, front, back, and left side in summer to minimize the heat in the kitchen. According to Keep, even "on a warm day the heat from the covered stove was not uncomfortable."[41]

The Stewart cookstove was popular for a number of years. Judges at an 1844 industrial fair reported, "After testing all the Cooking Stoves, we find . . . Stewart's . . . the best, as it took but thirteen minutes to boil two gallons of water, and baked biscuit in the same time, and broiled beefsteak, and all [was] done in the best manner . . . in thirty minutes from the time the fire was put in."[42] Others who tried the stove were equally impressed. Greenman & Northrup, the Stewart stove's Boston sales agents, sold more than 1,200 in less than two years. In 1844, they published a pamphlet that included letters from satisfied customers. "I do not hesitate to give [the Stewart stove] the preference to any that I have used," wrote Rev. Edward Beecher of Boston, "for economy in . . . fuel, and for the efficiency, rapidity and ease with which it performs the various processes involved in cooking." Troy, New York, mayor Gurdon Corning agreed: "It is the best cooking stove we have ever used. . . . It boils, roasts and bakes better, and consumes less fuel, than any stove I have ever seen." Five "citizens of Boston" were especially pleased with the stove's flexibility. "When clothed in summer dress," they commented, the Stewart stove "almost entirely shuts out the heat from the room and performs every branch of cooking in the most perfect manner; while, without the summer dress (which is easily removed) it will give sufficient heat for the largest kitchen."[43]

Despite the Stewart stove's initial success, the manufacturer worked to "perfect, simplify and systematize" it. In 1863, the company continued to extol the care with which the stove was manufactured and emphasized the comfort and convenience provided by the hot-water reservoir and removable summer covers.

6.8. (*Opposite*) Treadwell & Wallingford advertisement, *Lowell Directory* (Lowell, Mass.: n.p., 1855), 7. Courtesy of the American Antiquarian Society, Worcester, Mass.

6.9. P. P. Stewart's Patent Summer and Winter Cooking Stove, Fuller, Warren & Co., Troy, N.Y., patented 1838. Courtesy of the Rensselaer County Historical Society, Troy, N.Y.

6.10. (*Opposite*) American Hot Air, Gas Burning Cooking Stove. Shear, Packard & Co., *The American Hot Air, Gas Burning Cooking Stove* (Albany, N.Y.: C. Van Benthuysen, 1863), front foldout. Courtesy of the American Antiquarian Society, Worcester, Mass.

But some changes had been made, most notably the addition of a "double-sheet bottom flue" to heat the oven more evenly. The firebox had also been improved by constructing it of three separate pieces, each of which could be replaced when necessary without disassembling the stove.[44]

Like everyone else in the stove industry, Fuller, Warren & Company faced growing competitive pressure. Shear, Packard & Company, whose plant was in nearby Albany, challenged them head-on in 1863, alleging that although the Stewart stoves had performed "extraordinary feats" at expositions, they had been "fitted up expressly for that purpose." The stoves that consumers bought were not similarly equipped, Shear, Packard & Company charged, and were thus "of no practical value." Naturally, Shear, Packard & Company knew which cookstove to recommend—their own "American Hot Air, Gas Burning Cooking Stove"—a typical midcentury design (illus. 6.10). By this time, most cookstoves had four boiling holes, a firebox directly below the front of the top plate, a

bilevel oven, and a wide front hearth with an ash pit below. Many models, like this example, also had an extension top that included a hot-water reservoir and warming closet. The American cookstove, its manufacturers explained, "has no complicated machinery. . . . [It] is square and compact . . . ; the . . . design is plain, bold, and very neat." All plates exposed to the fire were "of extra thickness," all joints were sealed with fire cement, and the bottom and back plates were filled with nonconducting material to help retain heat. In sum, the stove was "all that can be desired."[45]

Like their opposition, Shear, Packard & Company also recognized the publicity value of testimonials. In 1863, the firm published a pamphlet filled with customer letters comparing the relative merits of the Stewart and American cookstoves. "I . . . formerly was of the opinion that the Stewart was the best," wrote George Luther, "but since I have used the American Cooking Stove, I have altered my mind." Mrs. B. B. Sanders had a similar experience. "In answer to your enquiry how I like the American Hot-Air Cooking Stove," she wrote, "I would say it gives the most perfect satisfaction in every respect, and we like the stove far better than the Stewart stove which we used formerly." If these testimonials are to be believed, customers were especially pleased with the baking capabilities of the American. Fanny Pattison called the stove "absolutely perfect — baking like a brick oven, with perfect evenness in all parts . . . without turning the pans." "The general arrangements of the stove," she concluded, "combine beauty, convenience and utility." Joseph Annin was equally impressed, saying that the stove "will bake equal to the best brick oven and with equal ease." A writer for the *Palmyra Courier* was even more enthusiastic, calling the American "the best Family Cooking Stove in the market. It is economical, quick and sure. The oven . . . can be heated . . . in fifteen minutes; the broiling apparatus is complete and simple, and in fact, there is not a single fault to be found."[46]

Cookstoves like the American suited most families, but large households, boarding houses, and hotels required something bigger. Here, too, stove inventors and manufacturers worked hard to satisfy demand. The most popular solution was the range, which one observer described as a "modified stove bricked into a fireplace instead of standing out in the room."[47] Ranges took up less floor space than stoves and were usually equipped with a hot-water tank. They also supposedly gave a "character and social appearance to the kitchen possessed by no other cooking apparatus."[48] Modest ranges, such as the one installed in Washington Irving's Hudson River Valley home in the mid-1850s (illus. 6.11), had six boiling holes and two ovens. More lavish versions were up to twenty feet long with as many as six ovens.[49] The primary benefit of owning a range was increased cooking capacity. The Stimpson Improved Range, for example, was available in "various sizes to cook for 25 to 150 persons," and the oven of the No. 3 Improved Union Range could accommodate sixteen pies.[50]

Consumers who wanted these features paid more for them than for a basic free-standing cookstove. In 1844, for example, James Beekman of New York City spent $53.50 on "1 large size Kitchen Range" complete with "Hot water Back, Iron pipes, couplings, etc."[51] Prices remained at the same level for some years. The least expensive range manufactured by Gardner Chilson of Boston in the mid-1860s cost $32, but adding a "water back," warming closet, and "hot air fixtures" (to heat an adjacent room) raised the price to $57.[52]

Some people considered the extra expense of a range worthwhile, especially if they could get someone else to foot the bill. In 1846, Mrs. B. K. Wyeth consulted

6.11. Newport Range, Boynton Furnace Company, New York, N.Y., c. 1855. Courtesy of Historic Hudson Valley, Tarrytown, N.Y.

the cashier of the Essex Company cotton mills in Lawrence, Massachusetts, about her upcoming duties as keeper of one of the firm's boardinghouses. "I wish to ask you if the Corporation will not put in a good Cooking Range to the House I am going to Have," she wrote. "The Chimney is Left for a Stove, which . . . is very injurious to the Paint as well as the Wood Work of a House, there being no chance for the Steam . . . to pass off in the flue, while a Range is so constructed as to carry [off] all the Steam."[53]

Although increasing numbers of Wyeth's countrywomen shared her enthusiasm for stoves and ranges, they did not always match her in assertiveness. After all, buying a stove meant dealing with the men who sold and installed it, something for which a woman's prior experience may not have prepared her. In many families, men were in charge of the household budget, even when it came to purchases that would be used primarily by women. For example, Mary Ann Waterman of Clear Branch, Virginia, wrote her cousin in 1852 that "Mr. W. bought me a cooking stove."[54] When the Forbeses of Westborough, Massachusetts, bought a new cookstove the same year, Catharine White Forbes noted in her diary, "Mr. F. and myself went into town [and] bought a cooking stove."[55] Forbes had been managing a household for ten years, so she presumably had the expertise to pick out a cookstove by herself. But the only other purchases recorded in her diary are fabric and fashion accessories, so it is unlikely that she had charge of large sums of money. Decision making in the Brown household of Epsom, New Hampshire, was handled in a similar way. In the same month that the Forbeses bought their stove, Susan Brown traveled with her father to nearby Pittsfield to do some shopping. Twenty-eight at the time, she probably went along to advise her father, but, as she phrased it, "he brought home a new cooking stove."[56]

Seven years later, Brown married Alexander Forbes, a Boston store clerk. The couple lived on a tight budget, and Susan took in boarders to make extra money. Because she was running a business, she assumed more control of stove buying. In 1863, she went "stove hunting" by herself and picked out a new range. The next year, when the new heating stove she had bought proved "not right," Forbes returned to the store to exchange it.[57]

"Charlotte S.," wife of a New York congressman, had to be prodded to show similar initiative, even though her cookstove "smoked and leaked . . . [and] could neither bake nor broil." One day in 1854, Charlotte "shed tears" while telling Elizabeth Cady Stanton about her "kitchen misadventures." Stanton asked her why she had not replaced the balky appliance. "Why, I have never purchased a darning needle . . . without consulting Mr. S.," she replied, "and he does not think a new stove necessary." "What does he know about stoves?" Stanton retorted. "My advice is to buy a new [one] this very day!" Charlotte hesitated, but Stanton persisted, pointing out that the advantages of having a new stove outweighed the risk of "Mr. S.'s" displeasure. This logic was "irresistible," so Stanton and "Mrs. S." set off on their errand. Once at the store, Charlotte grew bolder. First, she "selected the most approved, largest-sized [cook]stove" and then allowed Stanton to talk her into buying a new heating stove as well. "Mr. S. will probably be no more surprised with two stoves than with one," the latter remarked, "and, as you expect a hot scene . . ., the more you get out of it the better."[58]

After the stoves were installed, the cook was "delighted," and the "S." children were glad to have a warm playroom, but the biggest change was in Charlotte herself—she was "jubilant with . . . [a] newborn feeling of independence." When "Mr. S." came home and saw the stoves, he erupted as expected, but Charlotte said nothing, and he "looked so ridiculous flying around . . . like popcorn on a hot griddle" that he eventually realized the humor of the situation and calmed down. He was also hungry, so he allowed his wife to persuade him to sit down to eat. "We had a good dinner," Charlotte later told Stanton, "and I have not heard a word about the stoves since."[59]

Some years later, Stanton told this story in "Mr. S.'s" presence. For the first time, he understood how his meek, obedient wife had "emerged from . . . thraldom and manifested such rare executive ability." "I am . . . obliged to you," he told Stanton, "for the most comfortable part of my . . . life. Charlotte . . . did just right . . . and she has been a happier woman ever since. She now gets what she needs." After all, he observed, "[H]ow can a man know what implements are necessary for the work he never does?" "Of all the agencies for upsetting the equanimity of family life," "Mr. S." concluded, "none can surpass an old, broken-down kitchen stove!"[60]

Stanton was one of many midcentury Americans who believed stoves were necessary for domestic comfort, but the new technology was not evenly dispersed throughout the country. In 1849, the American Medical Association Committee on Public Hygiene reported that nearly all of the houses visited in Portland, Maine, and Concord, New Hampshire, were "warmed by wood or coal close-stoves." Most homes in Cincinnati were also heated by coal stoves. In Baltimore, too, stoves were "in almost universal use among the labouring population," and houses in Louisville, Kentucky, were "warmed, for the most part, by stoves." In the moderate climate of Charleston, South Carolina, however, stoves were "comparatively rare."[61] Joseph and Laura Lyman likewise observed eighteen years later that "in many parts of the country, particularly in the South, stoves and ranges are very little used."[62]

Other sources corroborate these findings. Former slaves interviewed in the 1930s recalled that open-hearth cooking had still been the norm on Georgia plantations in the 1850s.[63] To the north, in Washington, D.C., cookstoves were also unusual; the White House was not equipped with one until 1850. When Millard Fillmore succeeded Zachary Taylor as president, he was dismayed by the "temple of inconveniences" in which he and his wife Abigail were expected to live and entertain.[64] Considering their modest lifestyle early in their marriage and the fact that they were from upstate New York, the Fillmores were probably familiar with stoves. One of the first improvements Abigail introduced was a coal range, but things did not go smoothly. The White House cook, accustomed to preparing state dinners over an open fire, was so baffled by the new appliance that "the President himself had to inspect the Patent Office model in order to give directions for operating its complex system of drafts."[65]

Southerners may have been slow to adopt stoves, but Americans in colder regions embraced them eagerly. Thomas Hubka has discovered that after 1830 increasing numbers of rural New Englanders added ells to their farmhouses designed to accommodate cookstoves.[66] Bernard Herman found a similar pattern in central Delaware.[67] Some new housing in this period was specifically planned for stoves. Park Place, for example—a Portland, Maine, row house development built in the late 1840s— had no fireplaces.[68] Josiah Hammond approved of such construction, arguing in *The Farmer's and Mechanic's Practical Architect* (1858) that "the housekeeper who continues to use an open fire-place for all her cooking . . . where the seasons are cold and fuel is scarce . . . does not know her own wants."[69]

Diaries, family correspondence, and personal reminiscences confirm northerners' growing dependence on cookstoves. The Conklins of Herkimer County, New York, for example, began using stoves in the mid-1840s. In 1844, Henry Conklin's father, struggling to support a wife and thirteen children as a tenant farmer and laborer, moved his family into a small house without a fireplace. "Father got a little cook stove somewhere," Henry recalled, which "took wood only a foot long." Because the stove had just two boiling holes and an oven that could hold only one loaf of bread, Mrs. Conklin had to work hard to prepare meals. She also found the adjustment from fireplace to stove cooking difficult. Her bake kettle, she discovered, was now useful only as an ash receptacle, and her reflector oven "was used up for a plaything." The next year, when the Conklins' circumstances improved and they built a bigger house, the first thing they did was to set up the cookstove, "for they thought it would be cheaper to use a stove than to make a fireplace." "That summer father had gotten quite a good cook stove somewhere almost new," Henry recalled. "It was the first style of the elevated oven and took in wood about two feet long."[70]

Urban northerners also switched from one stove model to another as better designs were introduced, even if they had to learn new skills. Sophia Draper

White, who had used a small and not entirely satisfactory wood cookstove while living in Cleveland, switched to coal after moving to New York City. "We have got a very good cooking stove," she wrote her mother in 1847; "it is level on the top, with four *griddles*. We burn coal in it, the fire is in front at the top, the oven is under, the whole size of the stove. It bakes *beautifully* if I pay proper attention to the fire. It took me a long time to learn to cook with coal, if the fire gets *down,* it takes a long time to start it."[71]

Stoves were becoming common in the Midwest as well. In 1851, for example, when Scottish widow Jane Griffiths Baker arrived in St. Louis to prepare for her family's migration to Oregon, her first purchase was a $14 "cooking stove . . . with all the utensils belong[ing]."[72] Ellen Spaulding Reed, who set up house-keeping three years later in Burke, Wisconsin, agreed that "we must have [a stove] to begin with." She and her husband had only $50 to buy necessities and were stunned by local prices. "We went to Madison . . . and got a few things," Ellen wrote her mother back in Vermont, "but they are so high here that our money . . . failed us. . . . We got a stove for which we gave twenty seven dollars."[73]

Homesteaders elsewhere in the Midwest also considered cookstoves necessary, even if prices were exorbitant. Hannah Anderson Ropes, who settled in Kansas in the mid-1850s, wrote her mother in Massachusetts shortly after her arrival, "First . . . we must have a stove. The price, thirty-three dollars! is quite frightful; but it will bring many conveniences with it; a thought of much moment in be-ginning . . . civilized house-keeping."[74] Miriam Davis Colt, another new Kansan, would have sympathized with Ropes's assessment of what it took to be "civilized." In 1856, she wrote her family about her husband's vision of their fu-ture: "[He] says we shall have . . . a neat little log cabin. . . . When we come to get our goods, have our carpets . . ., [and] our nice little stove to cook by . . . [then] we shall be comfortably situated."[75] Philip Marshall Moore also consid-ered a cookstove important. Before his marriage in 1860, he scrimped to equip the three-room home where he and his wife, Melissa, were to live. "He furnished it as best he could," she recalled. "Somewhere he had found a little cookstove. . . . There were [four] lids . . . and an oven, which would hold only one pie. But it was a stove, and there were few of them in Kansas at that time."[76]

Despite Melissa Moore's claim that there were "few" stoves in the Midwest, other evidence indicates that many families considered the appliance a necessity. In 1864, when a widow named Samary Sherman moved to Brown's Island, Ohio, with her five children, the first things she acquired to set up housekeeping were bedsteads, chairs, a table, and a secondhand "cooking stove & aperatus."[77] Sev-eral years earlier, Susan Stevers Wyatt, who had been left to care for five children after her husband's desertion, had bought a cookstove for her Iowa home to symbolize her new self-sufficiency. When her daughter "put . . . stove black on the new stove and polished it . . . Susan's pride was boundless."[78]

Elsie Strawn Armstrong would have understood Wyatt's feelings. When she was in her late sixties, her independence hinged on a stove. Born in Pennsylvania in 1789, she had married Joseph Armstrong in 1808 and moved to Ohio, where she bore six sons. In 1829, she left her husband because of his "love for company and liquor" and took her sons to Illinois. There, she ran her own farm for twenty-five years, but after suffering a mild stroke in 1856, she decided to sell and move to the town of Ottawa. Her sons urged her to come live with one of them, but she refused. Shortly thereafter, her ability to live alone was threatened. "She had much trouble with her stove smoking," her grandson recalled, "and [she] was almost persuaded to yield to their pleading." As Armstrong debated what to do, her son George came to examine the recalcitrant stove, took down the stovepipe, and discovered that the draft was being obstructed by a brick that had fallen from the chimney. Once he removed it, the stove worked fine, and Armstrong was able to continue living alone for five more years.[79]

Women like these, who had successfully made the sometimes difficult transition from fireplaces to stoves, were reluctant to return to traditional methods. The exigencies of westward migration often made this retrogression necessary, however. In describing life in Michigan in the late 1830s, Caroline Kirkland complained that "woman's little world is over-clouded for lack of the old familiar means and appliances."[80] Mollie Dorsey, born in Indianapolis in 1838, would have concurred. Having grown up in a world where stoves were the norm, she was startled on moving to Nebraska in 1857 to see women cooking without them. "Mrs. Blake gave us a splendid dinner," Mollie wrote in her journal, "and however she got up such a variety puzzled me, as she cooks by the fireplace and does her baking in a small skillet."[81]

Charlotte Haven of Portsmouth, New Hampshire, had a similar experience. In 1843, she moved to Nauvoo, Illinois, with her brother and sister-in-law, and was shocked by the primitive living conditions she encountered. The family's parlor/dining room was heated by a stove, but the kitchen had only a fireplace. Haven and her sister-in-law were unused to open-hearth cooking so, as Charlotte wrote home, "Mrs. C. [a neighbor] kindly offered to get dinner . . . a herculean task it seemed to me, with the fire-place and such cooking utensils." "But we had a nice dinner," she concluded with some surprise, "venison, hot biscuits, potatoes roasted in the ashes." Several weeks later, after Haven's brother had hired a "girl" to do the housework, the family had a party at which everyone dined on roast turkey that "was cooked by being suspended by a string from the mantel-piece, with the 'spider' beneath to catch the gravy. It was pronounced excellent by all." However, Charlotte continued with satisfaction, "our 'spider' is now cast into the shade by a Yankee Notion cooking stove."[82]

Women on the Overland Trail faced an even more daunting prospect: they had to cook outside for several months without the stoves to which they had grown accustomed. As Jane Holbrook Gould remarked in her diary in 1862, three days after setting out for California, "having no stove it is rather unpleasant cooking."[83] Miriam Davis Colt experienced comparable difficulties in Kansas in 1856. "[We] have a fire out of doors to cook by," she wrote in her journal. "It is not very agreeable work. . . . The bottoms of our dresses are burnt full of holes."[84] Ellen Pennock explained the challenges of trail cooking in more detail: "It was a whole day's job to bake a panful of cookies or a few pumpkin pies, as only four cookies or one pie could be baked at one time. The lid [of the bake kettle] had to be lifted and the hot coals removed often. If your hand should suddenly lose its grip . . . down the lid would come and the coals . . . [would] land inside the kettle." Like Colt, Pennock found that camp cooking had other drawbacks. "The fronts of my dresses would be scorched, the toes of my shoes burned, and my face blistered," she remembered.[85]

Some families tried to mitigate the problems of trail cooking by taking cookstoves with them. Traveling to California with her brother and sister in 1852, Eliza Ann McAuley remarked in her journal, "We have . . . a good sized tent and a . . . camp stove which can be set up inside, making it warm and comfortable, no matter what the weather. . . . Our stove," she continued, "is furnished with a reflector oven which bakes very nicely."[86]

Unfortunately, camp cookstoves did not always perform as well as their owners hoped. Constructed of thin sheet iron, they proved far less durable than their cast-iron cousins. Elizabeth Wood, on her way from Illinois to Oregon, noted in her diary in 1851 that "a storm arose, [which] . . . capsized our stove with its delicious viands, [and] set one wagon on fire."[87] Although Wood's stove survived this accident, the Frinks, who had made the trip from Indiana to California the previous year, were not so lucky. Before leaving Cincinnati, Ledyard Frink had bought "a small sheet-iron cooking-stove," which his wife found "useful" until a mishap in Wyoming forced them to leave it behind. "We had always carried it lashed on the hind end of the wagon," she explained, and "some careless person . . . drove his team up too close . . . and the pole of his wagon ran into the stove, smashing and ruining it."[88]

Margaret Frink was thus forced to demonstrate her culinary flexibility. She and her husband "adopted a plan, which was very fashionable on the plains. We would excavate a narrow trench . . . in which we built the fire. The cooking vessels were set over this, and . . . we found it a very good substitute for a stove."[89]

Louisa Cook, on her way from Ohio to Oregon in 1862, agreed that this method worked well. "We have three stoves among us," she wrote in her journal, "but I prefer a fire on the ground. G[eorge] digs a little short trench . . . just wide enough to let the frying pans and camp kettles rest on the edge and we can cook capitally."[90] Some of Cook's predecessors on the Overland Trail had also reached the conclusion that camp cookstoves were worthless. In only the second week of her trip from Illinois to Oregon, Eugenia Zieber wrote disgustedly in her diary that "we were obliged to leave our cooking stove behind . . . it being a perfect humbug."[91] Many other emigrants evidently had the same experience. In 1852, Lucy Rutledge Cooke, on her way to California, wrote her sister that "we heard great talk of things being thrown away on the road but we saw little that was any good excepting stoves and there were plenty of them." "I never should think of taking one," she went on, "as a bakeoven . . . with [a] frying pan and [an] iron pot . . . is far preferable."[92]

Despite the problems westward migrants encountered with camp stoves, most women were eager to resume using cookstoves once they arrived at their destinations. Of course, the transition took some time, as Phoebe Newton Judson learned after arriving in Oregon in 1853. "How strange it seemed to be . . . cooking over a stove once more," she recalled.[93] But women readjusted very quickly. Luzena Stanley Wilson, who moved to Sacramento with her husband and two children in 1849, observed later that "the great majority of people lived . . . in houses made of canvas. . . . The furniture was primitive: a stove (of which there always seemed plenty), a few cooking vessels, a table . . . , two or three boxes . . . and a bunk."[94] Moving to the same city the next year, Sarah Bayliss Royce described a similar arrangement. For several days after their arrival, she and her husband and daughter lived in their wagon "till sufficient lumber was secured to lay a good floor, and over it was stretched a well made tent. In this our large cook-stove and several other newly-procured household conveniences were placed," she remembered.[95]

There may have been "plenty" of stoves in the far West, but Wilson and Royce failed to mention that the high cost of transportation had made them appallingly expensive. Nevertheless, families who considered them necessities paid what was asked. In 1852, Mary Jane Cole Megquier, living with her husband in San Francisco, wrote her children in Maine, "We have purchased some cane seat[ed chairs for] sixty dollars . . . [a] rocking chair [for] twelve [dollars, a] stove [for] fifty [dollars], [and] other things in proportion."[96] Lt. Orsemus Boyd and his wife—stationed at Camp Halleck, Nevada, in the 1860s—were equally shocked by such prices. "We found . . . that we must have at least two stoves," Frances Mullen Boyd wrote later, "one for cooking and the other for heating.

. . . Their combined cost was one hundred and seventy-five dollars"—adding tartly, "Both could have been bought in New York for about twenty dollars [but] if we ever rebelled . . . the cost of freight would be alluded to."[97]

Some westerners offset the high cost of stoves by using them to make money. In 1850, Ledyard and Margaret Frink rented an unfurnished house in Sacramento for $175 a month with the intention of opening a hotel. Ledyard built a dining table and benches, and bought a $50 cookstove; within a month, "Frink's Hotel" had turned a $200 profit.[98] Luzena Stanley Wilson also used her cookstove to earn a living, charging miners in Nevada City, California, a dollar a meal in the early 1850s.[99] As her experience demonstrates, a woman's culinary ability was prized in the West, with its highly transient, male-dominated population. In 1852, *Hunt's Merchants' Magazine and Commercial Review* published a letter written by a woman in a California mining town to friends in Connecticut. "I have made about $18,000 worth of pies," she boasted, "about one-third of this has been clear profit. . . . $11,000 [worth] I baked in one little iron skillet, a considerable portion by a camp fire. . . . But now I have a good cooking stove, in which I bake four pies at a time. . . . I bake on average about 1,200 pies per month, and clear $200." "There is no labor so well paid," she concluded, "as women's labor in California."[100]

Having an adequate cookstove was crucial if a woman hoped to make a living preparing meals. In 1860, Mollie Dorsey was living in Gold Hill, Colorado, with her new husband, Byron Sanford. "By is to do the blacksmithing for the [mining] company," she confided to her journal, "and . . . I am to cook for the men. My heart sinks . . . when I see there are 18 or 20. . . . I have . . . mustered my small cook stove into service, but that will only hold one loaf of bread. I fear I shall sink under this burden." Ten days later, she wrote: "The week has been spent in monotonous routine. Cook, cook, bake, bake! The fire . . . is . . . so hot that it almost burns my face to a blister."[101]

As Sanford's experience suggests, cooking remained a formidable task in this period, even with stoves. Despite lower prices and substantial design improvements, midcentury cookstoves remained imperfect. In their eagerness to profit from the rapid growth of the industry, some manufacturers had cut corners. In 1849, *Scientific American* complained that "stove plates are generally made now too thin. . . . They last but a short time . . . at least those . . . exposed to the fire."[102] The next year, an observer at the New York State Agricultural Fair confirmed that "the majority of [stoves] are specimens of unsound devising."[103] The editor of *Scientific American* agreed, griping in 1853 that "we are far from having arrived at perfection in . . . stoves. With all our extensive practice, where is there a stove . . . that has not some glaring defects?" he asked. "We have never seen a stove of a perfectly convenient construction, especially in the cleaning out arrangement, and for kindling the fire. . . . The patents . . . are very numerous, but the right kind of stove has yet to be invented." One trend especially bothered him. "Stove designers seem to be smitten with the idea that . . . flowers, scrolls, &c. constitute the very perfection of their art."[104]

Mrs. M. L. Varney of San Francisco also noticed this tendency. In 1859, she wrote *Scientific American* to suggest some improvements in stove design. "If the raised work . . . is placed thereon simply for ornament, I would have it dispensed with," she observed, explaining that a "plain stove would be much more easily kept clean."[105] Several months later, E. M. Richards of Moore's Ordinary, Virginia, wrote to endorse Mrs. Varney's views, but he believed designers also needed to improve stove function. "A good method whereby the clinkers and non-combustible refuse could be easily removed . . . without disturbing the fire would," he thought, "add still more to the value of that 'woman's friend.'"[106] Mrs. John Fruit of Camden, New Jersey, agreed; four years later, her husband informed *Scientific American* that she wished someone would invent "some improvement in the grates of cook stoves whereby the cook could at any time remove the stones and clinkers from the bottom of the fire, without dumping or letting down the whole and consequently putting the fire out."[107]

As these comments indicate, stoves still required much upkeep. As had been the case earlier, installation could be a formidable obstacle. Eliza Woodson Farnham and her husband endured a "siege of the stove" after moving to California in the early 1850s. First, they discovered that "a rod or two" had broken during shipment. Farnham's husband tried to put the damaged stove together anyway but soon gave up. Next, two neighbors took up the challenge. "Their labors continued to a late hour," Farnham recalled, "but [they] finally failed, and I . . . also failed." By the third day, everyone had been "thoroughly tamed" and had "come to [the stove's] terms." They finally put it together by omitting several "refractory rods, plates etc." and found to their surprise that it functioned adequately without them. After this experience, all agreed "that stoves could not have been used in the time of Job, or all his other afflictions would have been unnecessary."[108]

Once a stove was set up, it required regular maintenance. In the 1840s, a Nashua, New Hampshire, stove manufacturer published directions that suggest some of the challenges stove owners faced: "Take the ashes wholly out . . . once in two or four weeks. . . . Once in a month or two bring the whole stove nearly to a red heat . . . and as soon as cooled, scrape off the soot with a pretty sharp shovel . . . and scrape the pipe about the damper with a case-knife."[109]

Rust was also a perennial problem, making "blacking the stove" a domestic ritual. In 1841, Eliza Leslie provided exhaustive instructions: "Take half a pound of black lead finely powdered and . . . mix with it the whites of three eggs well beaten; then dilute it with sour beer or porter. . . . Having stirred it well, set it over hot coals, and let it simmer twenty minutes. When cold, pour it into a stone jug, cork it tightly, and keep it for use." Only then could the actual work begin. Stoves had to be blacked when they were cold, which disrupted household routine. First, all the ashes were removed and then the stove was wiped free of dust. Next, the concoction was "rubbed on . . . with a soft brush, and then polished off quickly with a clean hard brush." As a last step, Leslie advised readers to buy "an excellent black varnish" to be applied "when the iron is cold," and she warned, "No dust or ashes must be allowed to get to [the stove] till the varnish is perfectly dry, otherwise you will have to do it all over again."[110]

Even stoves that received proper care could still cause trouble. In 1845, Esther Howland told readers of *The American Economical Housekeeper* that "cracks in stoves . . . are readily closed by a paste made of ashes and salt with water."[111] The next year, *Scientific American* similarly advised, "When a crack is discovered in a stove . . . the aperture may be readily closed . . . with a composition . . . of wood ashes and common salt, made into a paste with a little water."[112]

Despite such counsel, stove owners were sometimes forced to hire professionals. In October 1842, for example, James Beekman of New York City paid Henry Earley $5 for repairing two grates and resetting a range oven. Two months later, he paid Benjamin Valentine the same amount for cleaning and relining a stove.[113] Harriet Beecher Stowe would have been glad of this kind of aid in the fall of 1849. As she explained in a plaintive letter to her husband, "our cooking stove [which was still downstairs in the summer kitchen] smoaks — and I can't get anybody to help me move it upstairs yet . . . and it draws so poorly that we can't bake in it at all."[114] Caroline Dustan had a similar problem in 1861. When her range ovens were out of order, she resorted to baking a pudding in front of her parlor fire.[115]

Even women untroubled by such malfunctions could find it trying to cook with a stove. In 1854, the authors of *The American Family Encyclopedia* told readers that "some . . . [ovens] perform very well, while others have been found to be useless." If they were burdened with one of the latter, cooks were advised to put "a tile or a dish with some sand" under baking items to prevent them from burning on the bottom.[116] Six years later, Mary Cornelius explained that "to roast meat in a cooking stove, it is necessary to attend carefully to the fire, lest the meat should burn. Lay it into the pan with . . . water in it," she advised, and "turn the pan around often, that the parts may roast equally."[117]

To compound these problems, meat baked in stove ovens had an unfamiliar taste. Some people disliked it so much that they continued to use traditional culinary methods. Caroline Howard King of Salem, Massachusetts, never forgot the "contemptuous expression on [her] father's face the first time a turkey baked in a range was placed before him . . . and he always maintained that meats had a wholly different flavor . . . when they were roasted before an open fire." This opinion, she noted, "was shared by many old-fashioned people." One "very energetic" woman of King's acquaintance went so far as to roast her Thanksgiving turkey "in a tin kitchen, before the fire, in her back parlor."[118]

Dissatisfied with the "high-oven, spider-legged" stove her family had acquired in 1848, Sarah Brewer Bonebright of Newcastle, Iowa, would have applauded this woman's choice. "We used the cook stove very little," she remembered, "preferring the more laborious fireplace methods."[119] Maria Foster Brown, whose husband was a partner in a general store in Athens, Ohio, was more specific about what was wrong with her cookstove. "When we went to keeping house in 1845," she told her granddaughter, "Dan'l . . . bought me a little iron stove. . . . It was no good, and would only bake things on one side. I soon went back to cooking at an open fireplace."[120]

Other Americans continued to complain about the bad effect stoves had on health. In 1849, members of the American Medical Association Committee on Public Hygiene reported that the ventilation of the New York City homes they visited was "as bad as it can possibly be, the atmosphere being rendered worse . . . by the . . . stoves for burning anthracite coal." They discovered a similar situation in Philadelphia, where "ventilation . . . is more defective than formerly, when houses were chiefly heated by wood in open fire places."[121] *Scientific American* elaborated, reporting: "Every one knows that smoke and gas . . . escape from the joints of the common stove when the door is open, and also when the damper . . . is shut."[122]

Stoves were especially dangerous to children and the elderly. In 1850, Elizabeth Sullivan Stuart of Detroit wrote her son about a recent domestic "scene." "A few mornings since, young Alex went into Uncle's room and found all his hair singed. . . . He had been reading," she explained, "and I suppose got asleep and his hair caught fire! He will in spite of all remonstrance leave his stove door open."[123] Six years earlier, two-year-old Elizabeth Babcock Leonard suffered more serious injuries when she "fell against the hot stove, . . . burning her face slightly and both hands badly leaving the skin on the stove."[124]

The hot-water boilers attached to kitchen ranges posed an even greater risk. In 1852, *Scientific American* reported that a servant had been killed in New Orleans when a stove boiler exploded. The accident, the author speculated, had been caused either by "too short a supply of water, or improper confinement of the steam." With macabre relish, he concluded, "A fragment of the broken stove cut off all the front part of the poor girl's head, and death was, of course, the almost immediate result."[125] Seven years later, J. G. Whitlock told *Scientific American* readers how to avoid such tragedies. "If the water is not drawn as soon as it commences to boil," he observed, "steam will be generated, the feed water driven back through the pipe, and if the fire is active there will soon be a 'tempest' in the kitchen." Such "bursts and collapses" could be prevented, however, if cooks were always sure, "whenever the water is near the boiling point, to commence drawing it off even if it is not wanted for use, because this brings cold water into the back, and prevents the generation of steam."[126]

Although Norwegian immigrant Elisabeth Hysing Koren never experienced this kind of calamity, her diary and correspondence provide a valuable record of the ups and downs of living and working with midcentury stoves. For several months after their arrival in Iowa in 1853, she and her husband lived with the Egge family in a small cabin heated by a cookstove. At first, Elisabeth found the stove comforting, noting in January 1854 that she and Vilhelm had spent most of one evening sitting "on a bench by the stove, in which the fire was burning merrily; outside, the storm was howling and caused us . . . to appreciate how pleasant it was in a warm room."[127]

But Koren soon discovered that life in a small stove-heated space could be uncomfortable. On 24 February, she wrote, "We spent the greater part of the evening near the open door, behind us a stove that was red-hot because of some peas which . . . had to be cooked for a long time." As this mishap demonstrates, stove management was not easy. It was even more difficult if a woman were distracted. A week later, Koren wrote, "I just laid aside my knitting and Irving's Sketch Book. . . . My attention was divided between them and looking after the fire in the stove (with which I have great trouble, running out time and again for chips)."[128]

Koren witnessed another of the challenges posed by stoves when she and her husband visited the Bekkens in April 1854. The Bekkens' cookstove had already been moved to its summer location, and Aase Bekken was kept "extremely busy running downhill to . . . her stove, and up to the house again." The next month, after the Korens moved into their own cabin, Elisabeth faced a different problem. "We now have our stove with which I am greatly pleased," she wrote her father. "I have had a shed built in which to put it. . . . It is out of the question," she explained, "to have it inside . . . during the summer." "I have begun to bake bread," she went on, but "something went wrong the first time and I was quite disgusted . . . , but I found a man who taught us how to operate it. . . . Now all goes well."[129]

For the Korens, as for many of their contemporaries, stoves were part of daily life. Most of the time they were praised for the comfort and convenience they provided, but sometimes they caused problems. In the fall of 1854, when the

Korens finally moved into their permanent home, they did not feel completely settled until their stove was set up. "It is really good to have the pipe up for the stove," Elisabeth wrote on 21 October. "Now I can sit here cozy and comfortable with the fire crackling in the stove while outside, the rain is pouring down."[130]

Despite the challenges of using stoves, most midcentury Americans preferred them to traditional methods. Some families residing in older homes compromised—using stoves for some cooking, but continuing to use fireplaces and brick ovens from time to time. Americans who lived in newer homes, as well as those who moved west, were less likely to have this option, however. Yet some of them, too, remained hesitant about stoves even though they used them. In 1856, for example, when Maria Foster Brown and her husband moved from Athens, Ohio, to a farm near Augusta, Iowa, she recalled, "We stopped in St. Louis long enough to buy . . . a cookstove. It was a good stove—there never was a better." But Brown remained ambivalent. Stoves "kept our house warm and comfortable," she admitted, but she thought it "pathetic" when her young son asked her what a mantelpiece was, and she, too, found she missed the "open fires of Ohio."[131]

In 1857, while still living in Nebraska, Mollie Dorsey made a similar comment about children who grew up without open fires. "We fixed up the little folks what we could," she wrote in her journal on Christmas Day. "Poor little tots, they attribute the absence of Santa Claus to not having any chimney. Our stove pipe goes thro[ugh] a hole in the roof." Three years later, married and living in Colorado, Mollie did not worry that her future children would face this disappointment. She had arranged her home "real nicely": "I have an oiled wagon cover on my . . . floor, white curtains to my . . . window . . . [and] my cook stove," she noted on New Year's Day in 1861, but the house also had a "large fireplace." "We . . . pile the pine logs on, and . . . I feel as if I am in a palace," she concluded.[132]

Although many Americans, such as the Sanfords, were comfortable balancing tradition and modernity, others lobbied for additional inventions to ease the burdens of housework because they felt that stoves had created as much work as they had saved. These individuals were responding to an unanticipated effect of the "cult of domesticity" and the partial mechanization of the household. In 1869, Henry Ward Beecher shrewdly remarked that "housekeeping . . . grows less simple . . . as society advances in refinement." "It is true," he conceded, "that . . . mechanical improvements have rendered each specific art in housekeeping easier than formerly, but in doing so, they have introduced such multiplicity and variety, that *care* is augmented in proportion as labor is decreased." In particular,

"The care of the table" had increased dramatically, he thought, becoming "four fold more onerous than it was a hundred years ago."[133]

Beecher's last observation was correct. By the mid–nineteenth century, expert opinion held that meals had to be varied to be healthy. Cookbook author Sarah Josepha Hale explained the new thinking in 1857: "The commonly received idea, that what goes under the denomination of 'good plain living'—that is, joints of meat, roast or boiled—is best suited to all constitutions, has been proved to be a fallacy. Many persons can bear testimony . . . that 'elaborate culinary processes are frequently necessary in order to prepare food for the digestive organs.'"[134]

Ruth Schwartz Cowan's research demonstrates that Americans followed this advice. Because cookstoves made it easier to prepare several dishes at the same time, they "augured the death of . . . one-dish meals—and . . . probably increased the amount of time women spent in preparing foodstuffs."[135] Mary Ryan's research on family life in Oneida County, New York, confirms that "cooking had become [by the 1850s] something more than simply preparing food for human consumption. Even publications addressed to farm women contained increasingly elaborate recipes . . . all recommended as symbols of domesticity as well as for their nutritional value."[136] These new expectations placed a significant burden on women. "It is quite certain," Dr. J. H. Hanaford asserted in 1868, "that . . . woman's labor is sufficiently onerous. . . . [Yet] not a few of our housekeepers, for the sake of . . . setting as good a table as their neighbors . . . are wasting the energies which might otherwise be better employed." Husbands were guilty, too, he believed, because they permitted their wives "to toil . . . over a stove . . . simply to gratify . . . a low appetite." The solution, Hanaford concluded, was a return to "simple, unstimulating, and easily prepared" meals.[137]

Some of Hanaford's contemporaries had other ideas about how to reduce kitchen drudgery. In December 1859, Mrs. M. L. Varney of San Francisco asked *Scientific American* to plead with inventors to turn their attention to the development of better tools for housework. "In the Shop, where . . . men daily labor, desirable improvements are readily seen," she commented perceptively, "but in the House, few . . . men come directly into contact with the . . . implements of housekeeping," so they devoted little effort to updating them.[138] Four months later, she wrote again to explain that improved stoves, washing machines, dishwashers, and the like would not compromise the sanctity of American homes. Quite the contrary—"whatever lightens the labors and cares of the house," she argued, "helps to bring comfort and cheerfulness . . . to the . . . *home*."[139]

Varney's linguistic separation of "house" and "home" is significant. As household appliances became more common, it grew increasingly difficult to uphold the fiction that the home was isolated from the world of commerce and industry. During the next several decades, Americans continued to struggle with this dilemma. Conservatives responded by increasing the separation between the functional and affective parts of the household, whereas radicals advocated the removal of housework from the home. Americans in the middle continued to live and work with stoves, taking pride in their successes, lamenting their failures, and hoping for even better appliances.

7

"This Necessary Evil— The Cooking Stove"

After the Civil War, Americans remained ambivalent about the cookstove. Whereas some observers celebrated stoves as emblems of the nation's industrial achievement, others, accustomed to their benefits, grew increasingly frustrated over their flaws. Although manufacturers offered popular accessories such as hot-water reservoirs and warming closets, and continued to introduce design improvements, they could not hide the fact that wood and coal stoves were sometimes unsafe, often difficult to manage, and always dirty. Yet a successful struggle with such a stove empowered women and, if domestic advisors are to be believed, typified their subtle yet vital power within the home.

In *Motherly Talks with Young Housekeepers* (1873), Eunice Beecher expressed this mixed response to stoves in a single chapter, beginning with a complaint and closing with a compliment. "Next to perplexities . . . with servants, there is nothing that so severely afflicts the careful housekeeper as the . . . cooking-stove," she claimed, calling the appliance "this necessary evil." Yet she concluded by saying that "housekeepers have reason to be well satisfied with the many excellent ranges and stoves now in general use." Beecher was unsure how she felt about the mechanization of the household. She lamented the passing of "mother's great brick oven" and pleaded with readers to use open fires "in their family room at least," but she also hoped that gas technology would some day make wood and coal cookstoves obsolete.[1]

As Beecher's contradictory comments indicate, the cookstove had become a problematical symbol of American domestic life. In 1882, during a tour of the United States, English aesthete Oscar Wilde freely expressed his disapproval of his hosts' taste. He was especially critical of "the small iron stove which they always persist in decorating with machine-made ornaments" such as "funeral urns," calling it "as great a bore as a wet day."[2] Many Americans were outraged. Cartoonist Thomas Nast responded by depicting a fussy, effeminate Wilde leap-

7.1. Thomas Nast, "Oscar Wilde on Our Cast-Iron Stoves," *Harper's Weekly* 26 (9 Sept. 1882), 575.

ing awkwardly off a beloved "American Institution"—the "Red Hot Stove" (illus. 7.1). To Nast, a cookstove—complete with elaborate decoration and the tongue-in-cheek motto "I Can Stand It If You Can"—represented America's cultural independence from Britain. Poet Eugene Field likewise contrasted the chill of England's "barny" fireplace-heated rooms with the welcome warmth of American homes. "Go, guzzle in a pub, or plod some bleak malarious grove," he advised Wilde's countrymen. "But let me toast my shrunken shanks beside some Yankee stove."[3]

Other Americans, however, found Wilde's criticism valid and tried to make stoves more fashionable. Having made a "special study" of stove decoration, Henry Gleason told *Scientific American* in 1887 that Wilde's comment had sparked "a craze for stoves ornamented with fancy tiles and bronze images." "Roman warriors, gladiators, Knights of the Red Cross . . . , Charles V, Joan of Arc . . . and . . . 'Mikado' characters" had begun appearing on one "giddy" stove after another. "The stove has now got to be as ornamental as any other part of the house," Gleason explained.[4] By 1893, when stove manufacturers Fuller, Warren & Company displayed their wares at the Columbian Exposition in Chicago (illus. 7.2), nickel-plated decorations and elaborate low-relief images had become

7.2. Fuller, Warren & Co., "Exhibits of Stoves and Heaters," 1893. In Rossiter Johnson, ed., *A History of the World's Columbian Exposition,* 4 vols. (New York: D. Appleton & Co., 1897–98), 3:311. Prints and Photographs Department, Chicago Historical Society, Chicago, Ill.

de rigueur for both heating and cooking stoves. The exhibit's designer heightened the contrast between the massive, ornate stoves of the late nineteenth century and their smaller, plainer predecessors by tucking a circa 1840 Stewart cookstove modestly into the display's front row.

Domestic advisor Laura Holloway drew still another lesson from Wilde's remark. Admitting that much of what he had said during his tour had been "trite and threadbare," she nevertheless agreed that "American stoves . . . are destructive of the perfect ideal of a home." As far as Holloway was concerned, no amount of ornament could make a stove fit for the domestic sphere. "One cannot . . . conceive a happy thought or genuine inspiration to have been suggested by, or derived from, the modern stove," she maintained, insisting that only "live coals burning on the altar-hearth of Home" could keep the nation's families "safe from physical and spiritual harm."[5]

These divergent reactions to Wilde's comment reveal continuing uncertainty about the proper place of stoves in American life. To some observers, late-nineteenth-century stoves exemplified the nation's democratic values and manufacturing prowess. In 1880, for example, the editors of *Scientific American* declared that "perhaps no one thing has contributed . . . to the increased comfort of American homes as the great improvements which have been effected in stove manufacture within the lifetime of men who are not yet old." "There are none so poor, but they have the advantages of stove[s]," they concluded.[6] In the same year, Maria Parloa, author of several cookbooks and domestic advice manuals, concurred, claiming that American stove manufacturers had come "so near perfection . . . that it would be difficult to speak of possible improvements."[7] In 1885, a publicist for the Barstow Stove Company of Providence graciously agreed, announcing that "the AMERICAN STOVE . . . is . . . one of our crowning triumphs," "fully as conspicuous" as the steamboat, cotton gin, sewing machine, revolver, telegraph, telephone, or typewriter.[8]

The cookstove was a particular source of national pride. In 1872, the authors of *The Great Industries of the United States* boasted that "in the manufacture of cooking-stoves . . . America is in advance of all the world."[9] Twenty years later, the author of *The Housewife's Library* called the "standard modern cooking stove" "splendid," both "beautiful" and "effective," with a "marvelous" cooking capacity. A home without such a stove, he declared, was "behind the times and below its privileges."[10] Perhaps inspired by such praise, one composer even wrote a polka in honor of a cookstove and its manufacturer (illus. 7.3).

In some households, the cookstove had become almost a member of the family. Sappho, a character in Pauline Hopkins's *Contending Forces* (1900), is

7.3. "Peerless Polka" sheet music cover (Boston: G. D. Russell, c. 1868).
Courtesy of the American Antiquarian Society, Worcester, Mass.

prouder of her "very convenient" parlor cookstove "than a daughter of Fortune would have been of the most expensive silver chafing-dish." When a friend visits, they lock the door "to keep out all intruders" and luxuriate in comfort, Sappho "lazily stretching her . . . feet toward the warm stove, where the fire . . . glowed so invitingly . . . through the isinglass door."[11] The "very large" cookstove with "bright nickel trimmings" in one of the Nebraska farmhouses memorialized by Willa Cather was equally cherished because it kept the kitchen "safe and warm . . . like a tight little boat in a winter sea."[12] A similar domestic utopia is depicted in Marietta Holley's 1875 novel *My Opinion and Betsy Bobbet's* (illus. 7.4). Just before sitting down to an "awful good supper," Josiah Allen stands "with his back to the fire . . . , a lookin' serenely round that bright warm room. . . . 'There haint no place quite so good as home, is there, Samantha?'" he asks his wife. The Allens obviously value their cookstove highly, both for its contribution to domestic comfort and for the "good dinners and breakfess'es" it makes possible.[13]

Cookstoves provided psychological reassurance as well — to a mother rocking her child (illus. 7.5) or to a lonely widower mourning the loss of his wife (illus. 7.6). They could even serve as role models. The heroine of Dorothy Richardson's *The Long Day* (1905) considers the Little Lottie stove in her New York City lodgings the room's "one . . . cheerful object" and contends that "there was

7.4. "The Pleasant Supper." In Marietta Holley, *My Opinions and Betsy Bobbet's* (Hartford, Conn.: American, 1875), 430.

7.5. Eastman Johnson, *Mother and Child,* 1869. Courtesy of Howard Godel, Godel & Co., New York, N.Y.

7.6. "He Rose and Took His Old Wooden Arm-Chair by the Stove." In Sarah Orne Jewett, "A Second Spring," *Harper's New Monthly Magazine* 88 (Dec. 1893), 116.

something whimsically, almost pathetically, human about it because of the sufferings it had borne." The "brave, bright, merry little cripple of a stove" encourages her in her own struggle to survive. "In the red-hot glow of its presence, and with the inspiring example of courage and fortitude which it presented, how could I have felt otherwise than optimistic?" she asks.[14]

Some of Richardson's contemporaries—who, like her, had grown up with stoves—imbued them with a host of homely virtues. In 1899, a woman named Lucelia Clark wrote a poem in honor of a cookstove she had recently replaced after twenty-five years of hard use. "Oh! My old kitchen cookstove, to time now surrendered, / How well I remember the day you were new, / As so proud in your newness you stood in my kitchen, / So black and so shiny and fair to my view," she recalled. Clark reminisced about sitting by the stove to cuddle her first-born child and waxed eloquent about the "dear little feet" that had crowded around its hearth. Sadly, "Time's ghostly fingers" had touched the stove—the oven door had been replaced, the front door was "warped out of form," and the firebox was missing a hinge. Although Clark understood the need for a new stove, she was melancholy nonetheless. "For hours I have sat, a batch of bread tending," she remembered, "feeding the fire, for you always cried, 'More!' / And often at eve watched the fantastic pictures / So coyly revealed through that broken front door." She concluded, "Many changes have come since we first were acquainted, / Some that are happy, and some sad to tell, / But through every one you have ever stood faithful / My shattered old stove that has served me so well."[15]

The Sherwood sisters of North Benton, Ohio, also considered their cookstove a friend. In 1908, they wrote the Baxter Stove Company to express their regret at having to replace a Baxter Banner model they had been using for forty years. Like Lucelia Clark, one of the sisters sought solace in poetry. "During forty biting winters, when the mercury was low, / It fed and warmed and cheered us, as no other could, we know," she remembered. She went on to praise the stove's faithfulness in keeping fires going overnight and its success in turning out "rich dainties." "The Baxter did its duty," she concluded with pride, "we shall ever feel its loss, / For when it comes to cookstoves, it surely was the 'Boss.'"[16]

Not surprisingly, stove manufacturers seconded such sentiments, pointing with satisfaction to expanded production and numerous design improvements. According to the National Association of Stove Manufacturers, founded in 1872, the nation's 275 stove firms more than doubled their output between 1860 and 1870. New York and Pennsylvania still led the way, but the Midwest was gaining as more foundries were established in cities such as Cincinnati, Detroit, and St. Louis. The numbers were impressive; in 1870, 2.5 million stoves were manufactured in the United States compared to just 375,000 twenty years before.[17]

The nation's inventors had been busy, too. In the 1860s, 722 patents were issued for heating and cooking stoves compared to only 332 in the previous decade. An additional 270 patents were granted for stove attachments such as draft regulators, water reservoirs, and ash sifters, up from only thirty-three in the 1850s. The pace of invention accelerated thereafter. In the 1870s, 827 patents were issued for wood and coal stoves, and another 735 for stove attachments.[18] The increasing focus on attachments suggests that inventors were turning their attention to refining rather than altering the basic stove types that had proven popular with consumers. Their primary goal was to make already fuel-efficient stoves easier to use. The developer of "Falardeau's coal and ash sifter" (illus. 7.7), for example, promised to eliminate "annoyance and inconvenience," implying that previously dirty and time-consuming stove maintenance could now be "easily done," even by small children.[19]

One of the most welcome improvements, added to both heating and cooking stoves, was the "self-feeding" or "base-burning" fuel magazine that made it possible to add coal on top of the fire without disturbing combustion at the bottom. A fire could thus be kept going overnight or even for several days or weeks if stove owners remembered to refill the chamber twice a day. The first "truly successful" base burner was introduced by Albany's Littlefield Stove Manufacturing Company in 1855. In subsequent years, other manufacturers rushed to add the feature to their lines, some including other improvements such as "clinkerless grates" that required no shaking and only daily cleaning with a poker.[20]

Manufacturers devoted special attention to cookstove performance in an attempt to address long-standing consumer concerns. In 1870, for example, the Double Reservoir Stove Company of Troy, New York, reported that it had solved many of the problems that had plagued earlier designs. The firm's new Mansard Cook Stove, equipped with four "large Mica lights" placed "upright on a sloping surface, like the new Mansard or French Roof," was simultaneously fashionable and functional. "The effect is most beautiful," the manufacturers exclaimed, "making the room bright and cheerful." Even better, the windows could be removed entirely, turning the stove into an "Open Fire-place." But the Mansard Cook Stove was more than ornamental. The manufacturers went on to say that "most of the waste . . . of fuel [in stove use] arises from overloading the Fire Box . . . by servant girls." They had mounted bars at the top of the fuel magazine to indicate its maximum capacity so that "if a servant girl is inclined to load the Stove with coal . . . the lady of the house can see for herself," a feature that may have facilitated the sometimes ticklish task of managing domestic workers.[21]

If advertising claims can be believed, the ventilated ovens, warming closets, hot-water reservoirs, and enclosed ash receptacles that manufacturers were adding to cookstoves improved the taste of food and eased the burdens of stove

7.7. "Falardeau's Coal and Ash Sifter," *Scientific American,* n.s., 57 (15 Sept. 1887), 243. Courtesy of the American Antiquarian Society, Worcester, Mass.

care, meal preparation, dish washing, and laundry. In 1869, it took Troy stove manufacturers Swett, Quimby & Perry thirty-two pages to describe the wonders of their "New Empire Hot-Air, Gas and Base-Burning Cooking Stove for Wood and Coal." They "respectfully" called the public's attention to the stove's "Auxiliary Air Chamber . . . [which] produce[d] perfect combustion" and its new cast-iron water reservoir, "the best . . . in [the] Market." Other noteworthy features included an oven "higher and more capacious than that of any other first-class Stove" and a "dumping and shaking" coal grate, which supposedly made it possible to clean the ash pan "without a particle of dust . . . escaping."[22] According to Boston stove manufacturers Pratt & Wentworth, such "entirely new and very desirable features" remedied the "defects known to exist in all . . . [previous] cooking stoves."[23]

In the midst of this hyperbole, Americans shopping for a cookstove may well have been confused by the growing number of options. The basic model of the 1850s could now be augmented in a variety of ways. In addition to improvements such as "base-burning" fuel magazines and "clinkerless grates," inventors had developed an array of attachments specifically for cookstoves; between 1865 and 1880, 147 patents were granted for items such as broilers, oven shelves, and ventilators.[24] As a circa 1875 broadside (illus. 7.8) produced for the Littlefield Stove Manufacturing Company reveals, the combination of possible features posed a number of questions for stove buyers. Would the firebox be more convenient on the left or right side of the stove? Would a high warming closet be better than a low one, or was it worthwhile to have both? Was a stovepipe shelf desirable? Could one get by without a hot-water reservoir?

Consumers who patronized other manufacturers faced similar choices. The Iron Clad wood-burning cookstove offered by New York's S. W. Gibbs & Company in 1868 was available in three sizes (with seven-, eight-, or nine-inch boiling holes), each of which could be equipped with any combination of the following: hollowware, griddle, gridiron, hot-water reservoir, and warming closet. The Improved American cookstove introduced by Albany's Perry & Company the next year came with even more features, including a fourteen-inch boiling hole. The stove could also be outfitted with an extension top (to add more boiling holes), an enamel- or copper-lined hot-water reservoir, a reservoir cover, a warming closet, and grates and frames for either wood or coal.

Consumers faced with such options must have deliberated carefully before deciding which combination would best meet their needs. Price, of course, was still a factor. Purchasers of the Iron Clad cookstove could spend as little as $15.50 or as much as $41. Similarly, customers could economize with a basic No. 7 Improved American wood-burning stove for $24.80 or splurge on a coal-burning

THE West Shore Range

With Triple Oven Door, Separate Flue from the Oven, Simplex Grate, and Boiling Reservoir.

Single Oven and Base.   Reservoir and Base.   Single Oven and Low Closet.   Reservoir and Low Closet.

ngle Oven, Base and Pipe Shelf.   Reservoir, Base and Pipe Shelf.   Single Oven, Low Closet and Pipe Shelf.   Reservoir, Low Closet and Pipe Shelf.

ngle Oven, High Closet and Base.   Reservoir Base and High Closet.   Single Oven, High and Low Closet.   High and Low Closet and Reservoir.

os. 8.18, 8.20 and 9.20 with Left-Hand re-Boxes, Coal or Wood Fixtures and ater Fronts for all Sizes.

Nos. 8.22 and 9.22 with Right-Hand Fire-Boxes, High and Low Closets, Shelves, Reservoir and Water Fronts to Both Sizes.

8.22 and 9.22 Right-Hand West Shore

7.8. Advertising broadside for West Shore range, Littlefield Stove Manufacturing Co., Albany, N.Y., c. 1875. Courtesy of the American Antiquarian Society, Worcester, Mass.

no. 10 model with an extension top, copper-lined reservoir, reservoir cover, and warming closet for $63.75.[25]

The editors of *The Household* understood that readers needed guidance about which cookstove attachments were worth the extra expense. They recommended "a stove with an extension top, cast iron water-tank and tin heater, in which to keep things warm," arguing that the additional $10 or $12 investment would pay for itself in saved labor. Instead of having to wait until after a meal was cooked to begin heating dish water, a woman with a cookstove like the one described would always have it ready "in no stinted supply." "We need not enlarge on the value of the tin heater," they continued, "to warm the mince pie, to keep John's supper warm when he comes home late . . . or in which to raise . . . bread," and concluded, "If we can by the use of [such] improved stoves . . . lessen the labor of the kitchen, we shall . . . increase the comfort of our wives and daughters."[26]

"Lessen[ing] the labor of the kitchen" and "increas[ing] the comfort of [the nation's] wives and daughters" were goals rarely associated with cookstoves in the antebellum period. Then, as we have seen, the primary concern was saving fuel, but now consumers expected more. In 1874, the Littlefield Stove Manufacturing Company appended extracts from 117 customer letters to a pamphlet advertising its Morning Glory Hot-Blast Cooking Stove. Sixty-nine correspondents mentioned fuel economy as a key reason for their satisfaction with the stove, but eighty-one praised its improved oven, thirty-one applauded the stove's portable hot-water reservoir, twenty-four commented on how easy the stove was to use, twelve discussed how attractive and easy to clean it was, ten were pleased by how well the stove heated their kitchens, and four liked its durability. Mrs. S. Webb's response was typical. "The No. 7 Morning Glory Cooking Stove I purchased of you is beautiful," she reported; "[I have] never had anything bake like it." Mrs. John B. Cotton concurred, noting that the stove "works in every way as recommended. The oven has a uniform heat, bakes quickly and well, and I find the 'Extension' with the hot water tank very useful."[27]

Similar testimonials suggest that Americans who acquired other "improved" cookstoves in this period were equally pleased. Twenty-five of the thirty-seven letters included in Pratt & Wentworth's 1866 advertising brochure commented favorably on the fuel economy of the Peerless cookstove, but an equal number applauded its baking performance. Other correspondents complimented the stove's roasting capabilities, the ease with which it could be regulated, the cleanliness of its enclosed ash pan, and the "nicety of its finish." Charles Hatch expressed his reaction succinctly: "The 'Peerless' is the only stove . . . that is entirely free from . . . faults." John Hudson was also impressed, reporting that he "would not part with [the stove] for twice the price."[28]

Swett, Quimby & Perry's customers were just as outspoken in praising the New Empire cookstove. The company's 1869 advertising pamphlet included eighty-six letters from satisfied purchasers. Fifty-three writers were pleased with the stove's fuel economy, reporting savings of between 25 and 85 percent compared to other models, but a number of other aspects of the stove's performance were also singled out. Thirty-one correspondents applauded the stove's "quick and even" oven, six going so far as to call it "equal to a brick oven." In addition, nineteen people liked the fact that they could keep a fire going for lengthy periods, twelve others mentioned how easy the stove was to manage, and five commended its workmanship.[29]

It is important to keep in mind, however, that customer testimonials are suspect as historical sources. For one thing, 221 of these 240 letters were written by men, despite the fact that men were less likely than women to be familiar with cookstoves. To be sure, many of these men probably sought women's opinions; in fact, several specifically mentioned their wives' assessment of the stoves in question. But male correspondents were more likely to emphasize a stove's fuel economy, whereas females tended to highlight its performance, which suggests that they valued cookstoves differently. Of equal concern, a number of these extracts include phrases such as "in reply to your question" or "in regard of your request for my opinion," indicating that the letters had been solicited.[30] It is reasonable to assume that customers who responded to such requests felt strongly about the stove they had purchased and that complaints were not included in promotional literature. Thus, the letters that were selected almost certainly exaggerate consumers' positive reactions.

Read another way, in fact, these testimonials suggest that all was not well in the stove business. In 1869, Parker Houghton congratulated Swett, Quimby & Perry on the "good operation" of their New Empire cookstove, but he noted that he was comparing it to "common cheap stoves." J. Curtis and L. B. Curtis, stove dealers in Red Hook, New York, also thought that many of the stoves on the market had "come far short of their recommendations."[31] Other letters provide important clues about cookstove lifespan. C. S. Burt, for example, had used his American cookstove for only two years before replacing it with a New Empire, and George Mark bought the same model to replace a cookstove he described as "new."[32]

Unfortunately, neither Burt nor Mark explained why they had discarded stoves acquired only recently, but several of these testimonial letters indicate that many models were still unsatisfactory. In 1868, for example, H. L. Grose wrote that he was buying his fourth cookstove in twenty-five years. Six years later, W. J. Hernstreet admitted that his household had used six cookstoves in the previous twenty years, and Andrew Randall reported using five cookstoves in seventeen years. H. D. Booth was even harder to please. He claimed to have exhausted twenty-five cookstoves by 1869—a remarkable feat. Even if he had acquired his first model in 1815 (the year the James "saddlebags" stove was introduced), each of his cookstoves had lasted on average only a little more than two years.[33]

Other sources confirm that the cookstoves of the post–Civil War period were still flawed. In 1870, the editors of *The Household* reported the conclusions of a committee that had examined the models exhibited at a recent state fair. "In looking through the whole list, we fail to find one that . . . comes up to the requirements of what a cook stove ought to be," committee members complained. Four-hole "square stoves" were especially inflexible. On wash day, the laundry boiler occupied the two holes over the firebox, making it impossible to renew the fire without moving the boiler first. These stoves also had inadequate oven flues, which contributed to imperfect combustion and caused an inefficient and dangerous accumulation of soot in the stovepipe. Stoves with extension tops were better, committee members acknowledged, but too often their water reservoirs were constructed of flimsy "tinner's copper."[34] L. H. Bingham of Harmor, Ohio, also believed manufacturers were cutting corners and informed *Scientific American* in 1880 that "in one type of cooking stove—a very . . . popular pattern—the flue divisions are not half thick enough . . . and the door frames are equally deficient."[35] But what was a family to do? "Until our stove makers give us something better," the editors of *The Household* conceded, "we must . . . make the best of the present condition."[36]

Even some stove industry spokesmen were beginning to suggest that manufacturers had made bad decisions in their pursuit of customers. In 1881, Buffalo, New York, stove manufacturer John R. Chapin read a paper before the National Association of Stove Manufacturers "deprecating the tendency to profuse nickelplating."[37] Eight years later, George Barbour, president of the organization, likewise criticized his colleagues' emphasis on decoration. "Who of us ten years ago would have thought stove manufacturers would . . . adorn our stoves at a cost of one to two dollars [per unit]?" he asked.[38]

The increasing number and complexity of stove options were also causing problems. Even a cookstove relatively free of ornament, such as the one depicted in Sidney Morse's 1908 book *Household Discoveries* (illus. 7.9), had enough parts to overwhelm all but the most experienced homemaker. Consumers were beginning to make their displeasure known. In 1872, the nation's 275 stove manufacturers had generated an annual "volume of business" of $37.6 million; by 1894 (admittedly a difficult depression year), the figure had declined 35.6 percent, and the number of firms had dropped to 215.[39]

Popular humorist Edgar Wilson "Bill" Nye agreed that stove manufacturers had mistaken their priorities. In 1881, he described his battle with a new "Fearfully and Wonderfully Maid" stove. "At the first stroke of the piston, I saw that something was wrong with the reversible turbine wheel," he explained. Undaunted by his self-confessed "ignoran[ce] of the workings of the stove," he "attempted to remedy this trouble without first reversing the boomerang . . . [and] in a few moments the gas accumulated so rapidly that . . . the right ventricle of the buffer-beam was blown higher than Gilroy's kite." Nye called his mistake "careless" and assured readers that "there is nothing more simple than the operation of one of these stoves." "Before starting your fire," he directed, "see that the oblique diaphragm and eccentric shaft are in their true position[,] . . . reverse the guide plate, . . . force the stretcher bar forward and loosen the gang-plank. . . . [Next] throw open the lemon-squeezer and right oblique hydraulic, see that the tape-worm pinion and Aurora Borealis are well oiled, bring the rotary pitman forward until it corresponds with the maintop mizzen . . . and the stove cannot fail to give satisfaction."[40]

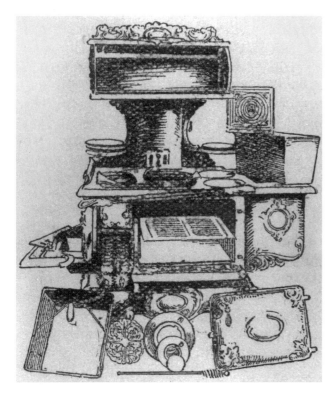

7.9. "See If Any Parts Are Needed." In Sidney Morse, *Household Discoveries* (New York: The Success Co., 1908), 296.

Nye's sarcasm aside, operating a stove incorrectly could be dangerous, even fatal. In 1866, four members of the Garey family of New York City were discovered unconscious in their lodgings; although two were reported "likely to recover," sixty-seven-year-old Rosanna and four-year-old Francis died. "No other cause can be assigned than the escape of some noxious gas from a small cooking-stove," noted the *New York Times.*[41] Nine years later, a similar accident occurred in Seekonk, Massachusetts, when Annie Waterman and her two children "were found in their room insensible from coal gas escaping from a stove, the damper of which was improperly turned." One child recovered quickly, but the other died, and Mrs. Waterman was reported to be "in a critical condition."[42]

A more spectacular but less serious disaster struck the Kirkpatrick household in Pittsburgh in 1870. Shortly before breakfast, family members heard a "terrible explosion" followed by screams. They rushed to the kitchen and found their cook, Martha Wylie, with one leg broken and her clothing on fire. Every pane of glass in the room had been shattered, the woodwork was "on fire in several places," and the range ("of first-class Cincinnati manufacture") had been "reduced to atoms." At first, the Kirkpatricks assumed the explosion had been caused by the cook's failure to turn on the water valve to the range's reservoir before she lit the fire. Wylie, however, specifically recalled adjusting the valve properly. The "most probable hypothesis," concluded the *New York Times,* was an "obstruction of some kind in the pipes" leading to the reservoir that had caused a dangerous build-up of pressure.[43]

Unstable stove legs also posed a serious risk, especially as cookstoves grew taller and more top-heavy. Cast separately from the rest of the stove, most legs were designed to slide into slots in the bottom plate. If not secured, they could work loose over time—with devastating consequences. In 1870, E. G. Patter of Bellevue, Iowa, informed *Scientific American* that his cookstove had tipped over after a leg slipped out of place, narrowly missing one of his children. He also reported that a neighbor's child had been scalded to death in a similar incident when the contents of a cookstove's hot-water reservoir cascaded to the floor.[44] A child in Ansonia, Connecticut, barely escaped the same fate when her family's cookstove toppled over after "one of the legs . . . was discovered to have fallen out."[45]

Over the next several decades, the nation's inventors tried to address this problem by developing new stove-leg designs and fastening systems.[46] They also attempted to ease what had long been one of the most unpleasant features of stove ownership—the semiannual ritual of moving the stove. In 1876, for example, H. M. Hockman of Berwick, Pennsylvania, patented the elaborate "devices for lifting stoves" depicted in illustration 7.10. Five years later, Thomas Lindsay of Fort Edward, New York, tried a simpler method, introducing a detachable stove handle. A. Mey of Buffalo, New York, approached the problem from a different angle, patenting "stove-leg casters" (illus. 7.11) in 1877. Other inventors focused on the problem of assembling stovepipe; between 1865 and 1880, 285 patents were issued for stovepipe and pipe accouterments such as elbows, collars, and supporters.[47] Despite these efforts, however, little could be done to simplify the dreaded chore.

Moving stoves in the spring was tricky because, as Hazel Webb Dalziel recalled, "after the long winter the pipe was always full of soot and the least little jar would send the stuff billowing over everything."[48] Replacing a stove in the fall created different problems. If the circa 1895 stereograph in illustration 7.12 can be believed, it could even mark the beginning of a husband's "troubles." The *New York Times* commiserated with such men, asserting that "it requires more

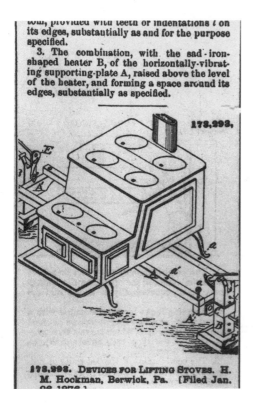

jom, provided with teeth or indentations *t* on its edges, substantially as and for the purpose specified.

3. The combination, with the sad-iron-shaped heater B, of the horizontally-vibrating supporting-plate A, raised above the level of the heater, and forming a space around its edges, substantially as specified.

173,293.

173,293. DEVICES FOR LIFTING STOVES. H. M. Hockman, Berwick, Pa. [Filed Jan.

7.10. Patent drawing for H. M. Hockman's "Devices for Lifting Stoves," No. 173,293, *Official Gazette of the United States Patent Office* 9 (8 Feb. 1876), 283.

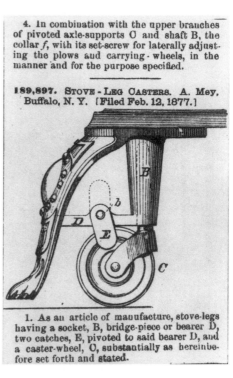

4. In combination with the upper branches of pivoted axle-supports O and shaft B, the collar *f*, with its set-screw for laterally adjusting the plows and carrying-wheels, in the manner and for the purpose specified.

189,897. STOVE-LEG CASTERS. A. Mey, Buffalo, N. Y. [Filed Feb. 12, 1877.]

1. As an article of manufacture, stove-legs having a socket, B, bridge-piece or bearer D, two catches, E, pivoted to said bearer D, and a caster-wheel, C, substantially as hereinbefore set forth and stated.

7.11. Patent drawing for A. Mey's "Stove-Leg Casters," No. 189,897, *Official Gazette of the United States Patent Office* 11 (24 Apr. 1877), 703.

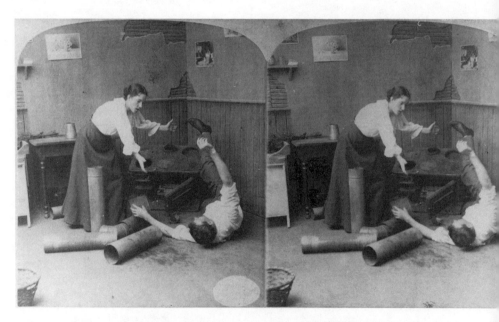

7.12. "When a Man's Married His Troubles Begin." Stereograph, c. 1895, Griffith & Griffith, Philadelphia. Photograph courtesy of Robert M. and Margaret Hindle Hazen.

brains to put up a stove than to manage a political campaign." The stovepipe was "always the crucial test of temper." "Like the scorpion, . . . the stove uses its . . . pipe as its instrument of attack and defense," the *Times* reporter observed, and only "profanity, perspiration, and pounding" could tame it.[49] Years later, Ben Logan remembered his father's strikingly similar assessment: "By God, there's nothing in this world ornery as a piece of stovepipe. When they're just right, they bend like paper. When you want to bend them, they're like cast iron."[50]

Dialect humorist Marietta Holley was also familiar with the complications of stove moving, but she understandably viewed the task from a woman's perspective. Samantha Allen, the heroine of Holley's *Samantha among the Brethren* (1892), describes what happened in her household one fall: "Josiah wuz a-bringin' in the cook stove from the summer kitchen. . . . He wuz at the worst place, too. He had got the stove wedged into the entry-way door, and couldn't get it either way" (illus. 7.13). "He had acted awkward with it, and I told him so," Samantha went on tactlessly. "Oh! the voyalence and frenzy of his demeanor as he stood there a-hollerin'," a reaction exacerbated by the unexpected appearance of a neighbor.[51]

7.13. Josiah Allen moving the stove. In Marietta Holley, *Samantha among the Brethren* (New York: Funk and Wagnalls, 1892), 56.

Mark Twain would have sympathized with Josiah's predicament. In 1870, he called putting up a stove a "job . . . as severe and vexatious as humanity can possibly endure." Because stoves weighed several hundred pounds,[52] the responsibility fell primarily on "the head of the family." A man's first step, Twain explained, was to don "a very old and ragged coat." Then he assembled the stovepipe, invariably blackening both hands and face. Next he wrestled the stove into position and lifted one side to install the legs, only to have them slip out of place while he worked on the opposite side. Once this problem was resolved, he fiddled with the stovepipe, which always proved too short, too long, or the wrong diameter. Then he found to his dismay that the stove did not sit flat on the floor, so the whole process had to be repeated. "Job never put up any stoves," Twain grumbled. "It would have ruined his reputation if he had."[53]

Emily French, a self-described "hard-worked woman" who did housework and laundry for neighbors in Elbert, Colorado, probably never read Twain's essay, but the diary she kept in 1890 records a similar litany of struggles with stoves. On one occasion, she had to clean a heating stove "covered with hen drop and rust" because it had been stored in a barn all summer, and on another, the wind ripped off her skirt as she perched on a roof trying to set up a stovepipe. At least three times that year, she had to take down and clean a stovepipe because a stove was not drawing properly. One entry describes the chore: "I got up early determined to clean the stove in the kitchen, it dont burn good. I took the pipe off, cleaned it out. . . . It was a big ugly job." Even after being cleaned, French's stove did not always perform satisfactorily. On 14 January, her cookstove smoked so badly that she prepared breakfast in her front room fireplace to let the fire in the stove die out. Then she took down the stovepipe and cleaned it, "but no use, it [still] drew [smoke] into the kitchen." The problem proved stubborn. Three days later, she complained, "How the stove does smoke almost all the time, no let up." Two days after this, she wrote, "The stove smokes near all the time, we can scarce cook a meal. I made an onion stew on Mrs. Sloan's stove."[54]

French was not alone in her battle with balky stoves. In 1871, Susan Brown Forbes of Springfield, Massachusetts, noted disgustedly in her diary: "New stove stands with its leaking 'water front' in the little kitchen. Alex asked Mr. Beebe to come and see to it, but he did not." The next day, another specialist was called in, but apparently to no avail. A week later, men from the stove dealership finally came and took away the ironically named Peerless stove.[55]

The cookstoves in Anne Ellis's Colorado households in the 1880s and 1890s exhibited other problems. The stove she had used as a teenager "would not draw and left things doughy." In later years, she started a baking business but was hampered by "the usual discouragements of a smoky stove and an oven which refused to bake on the bottom."[56] Carrie Young recalled similar challenges faced by her mother in North Dakota in the early twentieth century: "Her oven . . . didn't bake evenly, so she had to keep turning the pans and trading them off from the top shelf to the bottom shelf."[57]

Advice writers and authors of domestic fiction knew that the "improved" stoves of the post–Civil War years were still difficult to manage and required a great deal of upkeep. Building and maintaining fires, for example, remained a challenge. In 1874, Barbara Brandt recounted woes with which many readers of *The Household* surely identified. She began by wadding up paper and laying kindling in the stove's firebox. "A . . . blaze springs up encouragingly . . . accompanied by a noisy crackling," she noted, but this "is succeeded by a faint splutter, which . . . dies away entirely. Dismayed, you take off one of the covers . . . and peep in. The 'blackness of darkness reigneth.' There is no help for it, you must begin anew." The next attempt seems more promising, "but [then] the room is full of smoke, the stove refuses to 'draw,' and the tea-kettle won't boil. . . . You open the stove [and] give the fire a vigorous poke . . . while volumes of smoke . . . blind your eyes."[58]

Inexperience made such scenes more likely. Americans' struggles with coal fires had become legendary. In 1895, Erie, Pennsylvania, stove dealers Black & Gerner featured a tall tale about such battles in a pamphlet touting the benefits of their new Radiant Home model. "We had never had a coal stove," the narrator explains. "We filled the Radiant Home about half full of pine fence, and, when the stuff got well to going, we filled the artesian well on top with coal. It simmered and sputtered . . . and all went out." "We turned every dingus on the stove that was movable, and pretty soon the Radiant Home began to heave up heat," he continues. "In ten minutes that room was as much worse than a Turkish bath as Hades is hotter than Liverman's ice house. . . . We opened the doors, and snow began to melt as far up Vine Street as Hanscombe's house. . . . We went to bed, supposing that the coal would eventually burn out, but about twelve o'clock the whole family had to get up and sit on the fence. Finally, a man came along who had been brought up among coal stoves and he . . . turned the proper dingus and she cooled off. . . . If you buy a coal stove," he concludes, "learn how to engineer it, or you may get roasted."[59]

Youngsters learning to "engineer" stoves faced similar trials. In Susan Warner's novel *What She Could* (1870), twelve-year-old Matilda Englefield and her sister take over the family's housework after their mother falls ill. Having never been taught to manage stoves, they forget to open the draft damper before lighting the fire—with disastrous results (illus. 7.14). "This stove won't draw," Maria exclaims, "what is the matter?" "It always does draw," Matilda replies. "Well, it

7.14. "It Won't Draw. It Just Smokes." In Susan Warner, *What She Could* (New York: Robert Carter and Bros., 1871), 246.

won't today," her sister answers. "Did you put kindling enough in?" Matilda asks. "There's nothing but kindling!—and smoke," Maria retorts.[60] Jo March, heroine of Louisa May Alcott's *Little Women* (1868), also has trouble with her family's cookstove, becoming so engrossed in dinner preparations that she forgets to add coal, which means that later there is no hot water to wash dishes.[61]

Adults also struggled to start and keep up stove fires. "First draw out the dust-damper [and] free the grate entirely of ashes," Elizabeth Miller advised readers of *In the Kitchen* (1875). "A light layer of partly burned coal may remain," she explained; "shake it about . . . until no ashes adhere to it. Brush the tops of the ovens and all the inside iron within reach. Then put in a half a dozen loosely twisted rolls of dry paper . . . ; over these, running lengthwise, strips of light kindling-wood, and over these, in the opposite direction, sticks of hard, dry . . . wood . . . ; then a layer of coal. . . . Replace the covers," she concluded, and "take up the ashes, sweep the brick-work . . . and brush thoroughly the entire outside of the range. When all is clean and bright, light the fire, push in the dust-damper, and see that the dampers which affect the draught are pulled out."[62]

Miller's nonchalant directions to "free the grate entirely of ashes," "take [them] up," and make sure that everything was "clean and bright" significantly underestimated the challenges of stove care. Hazel Webb Dalziel recalled one of the most daunting tasks: "Ashes were taken out every day or so through the door at the bottom of the stove. This was a horrible messy job. . . . No one could prevent the . . . ashes from covering everything. Mother came nearest. One of my dearest recollections is seeing her . . . with the coal bucket on one side ladling them out, a shovelful at a time, and easing them into the bucket more carefully than if they were eggs." Dalziel also remembered that "it was always Mother who polished the stove . . . , every inch black and shining."[63]

Dalziel's contemporary Edgar Guest was also nostalgic about the stove care duties he remembered from his childhood, perhaps because he had not had to perform them. Every winter morning, he had awakened to the sound of his father shaking the stove grate to free it from ashes and clinkers. "He seemed to take a special glee / In shaking with a will," Guest recalled. "He flung the noisy dampers back, / Then rattled steel on steel, / Until the force of his attack / The building seemed to feel." Guest claimed to miss the days when he had awakened to a room so cold that the windows were "glossed . . . by old Jack Frost," but it was his father he missed most, musing, "And now that he has gone to rest / In God's great slumber grove, / I often think those days were best / When father shook the stove."[64]

These affectionate reminiscences considerably understate the demands of stove maintenance. In *Family Living on $500 a Year* (1888), Juliet Corson spelled out the steps involved in cleaning the appliance's exterior: "Blacken the stove when it is cool," she directed, "using any good polish moistened with cold water or vinegar, and then polish it with a brush. If there are steel fittings, polish them with a burnisher or . . . emery cloth." But the work of cookstove care did not stop there. "Always clean the stove from ashes and cinders before making the fire," Corson went on, "and take care that the water tank is filled, and the flues and tops of the ovens free from soot. . . . When an oven burns on the bottom, cover it . . . with . . . sand; if it burns on the top, put a layer of sand . . . over it."[65]

Corson's final comments suggest that cooks were still struggling with their ovens, even if they were scrupulous about stove upkeep. Other sources confirm this supposition. In 1879, Eunice Beecher advised women to "lay a large wire grate on the oven bottom, or place some nails or old pieces of iron on it" if their stove ovens proved too hot.[66] The next year, Adeline D. T. Whitney recommended a variation: "If . . . the oven proves . . . too hot . . . invert a shallow tin plate upon the floor of it, and set the baking-pan on that; and put a shallow dish or pan of cold water upon the . . . shelf . . . above."[67] "Mrs. Allspice" faced the opposite problem. "Unless my stove is red-hot on the top," she informed *Ladies's Home Journal* in 1884, "the oven will not bake, and this . . . is very trying in hot weather."[68]

In 1871, Thomas Beecher addressed another challenge faced by the nation's long-suffering cooks, expressing "surprise . . . that enterprising stove-builders . . . have not yet equipped a stove oven with some kind of thermometer. . . . [Now]," he pointed out, "the bread and cake-maker must learn to judge of the heat . . . by holding the cheek near it."[69] Rosetta Hastings agreed that oven thermometers were needed, observing in *The Household* in 1872 that "we talk about hot, quick and slow ovens, but it takes . . . long experience to enable one to tell by the feeling. . . . [O]ur whole system of cooking is . . . guess-work," she complained.[70] Unfortunately, frustrated cooks had to wait quite a while for manufacturers to introduce effective oven thermometers; the first numerically graded version was not invented until 1913, and reliable gauges did not become common for some years.[71] In 1916, cookbook author Mae Savell Croy was still advising women to test oven temperature in the time-honored fashion of seeing how long a handful of flour thrown inside took to brown.[72] As late as the 1940s, young Jerry Twedt of Iowa watched in awe as his mother tested the oven temperature in her wood range by putting her arm inside. Although her stove was equipped with a thermometer, he remembered that it "never seemed to work."[73]

Blaming inventors and manufacturers for cookstoves' shortcomings could do little to eliminate them. In the last third of the nineteenth century, domestic advisors began suggesting that consumers look elsewhere for the true cause of their culinary difficulties. As S. D. Farrar explained in *The Homekeeper* (1872), "[if] stoves . . . [are] not working well, the fault belongs more to the engineer than to the stove-maker."[74] Eunice Beecher concurred, arguing that her countrywomen did not understand their responsibilities in this area. She repeated a question she had heard numerous times from disgruntled housekeepers: "Is there no way to secure better . . . ranges, cook-stoves, and utensils belonging to them?" Beecher retorted, "It takes no large amount of common sense to become mistress of a . . . cooking-stove, and still less to understand how to keep them . . . in good working order." Problems with cracked stove plates, bent dampers, and burned-out grates, she contended, occurred only because women left stove care to their poorly trained and inadequately supervised "help."[75]

The solution was obvious. As architectural reformer Eugene Gardner explained in 1874, the "essential home work [of preparing meals] needs to be taken from the hands of indifferent, careless servants and confided to those who realize the nobleness of the responsibility."[76] Middle-class women had to begin managing their cookstoves themselves—and take pride in doing so. After all, devoting oneself to family cooking was a holy sacrifice. When the "Virgin of the Kettles," heroine of a 1903 short story by Elizabeth Hale Gilman, has to give up college to take charge of her family's kitchen, she is at first unwilling to submit to the cookstove's "scorching torment." Gradually, however, she discovers the dignity of her new calling. Every morning, while everyone else is still asleep, she creeps downstairs to tend the stove. "To slide the draughts open and draw the kettle [to the] front . . . is the work of a moment," but she realizes that it is a work of great significance. "It always impresses me as . . . a sacred rite," she concludes.[77]

But where were such women to look for reliable and suitably inspirational guidance? Compared to their predecessors, post–Civil War domestic advisors did a better job educating women about stove selection and operation. Catharine Beecher and Harriet Beecher Stowe, for example, devoted an entire chapter of *The American Woman's Home* (1869) to conduction, radiation, and reflection in "Stoves, Furnaces, and Chimneys." The best cookstove for most families, they concluded, was one "constructed on true scientific principles," with a corrugated firebox, slanted bottom flue plate, ventilated front door, grate with internal ash sifter, and extension top with hot-water reservoir. "If all American housekeepers could be taught to select and manage the most economical and convenient apparatus for cooking and for warming a house," Beecher and Stowe asserted, "many millions now wasted by ignorance and neglect would be saved." But saving money was not their only concern. They believed "every woman should be taught the scientific principles with regard to heat, and . . . their application to practical purposes . . . on which health and comfort so much depend."[78] Twenty-five years later, the author of *Smiley's Cook Book and Universal Household Guide* echoed their advice. "To get the best results out of a stove . . . requires intelligent treatment," he explained. "Every woman should understand the principles on which her stove is constructed and its scientific management."[79]

These calls for "scientific management" in the kitchen were part of a nation-wide movement to elevate the status of housework, an extension of the antebellum domestic economy movement. Fearing the effect of the removal of tasks such as spinning, weaving, and sewing from the home, reformers had created a new field for middle-class women—"home economics." After Congress passed the Morrill Land Grant Act in 1862, a number of educational institutions established programs such as Iowa State College's "Course for Ladies" (later called the Department of Domestic Economy) and Illinois Industrial University's School of Domestic Science and Art. In eastern cities, Juliet Corson, Mrs. D. A. Lincoln, and others founded cooking schools where women could learn to prepare

7.15. "Prang's Aids for Object Teaching: The Kitchen." Lithograph (Boston: L. Prang, 1874). Courtesy of the American Antiquarian Society, Worcester, Mass.

economical and nutritious meals.[80] According to Lou Allen Gregory, the first professor of domestic science at Illinois Industrial University, the goal was to give young women a "liberal and practical education, which should fit them for their great duties and trusts, making them the equals of their educated husbands and . . . enabling them to bring the aids of science and culture to the all-important labors . . . of womanhood."[81] Mary Welsh, founder of the Iowa State program, concurred, arguing that such training would lend "dignity to that part of [woman's] life work hitherto considered as menial drudgery."[82]

Much of this "life work," reformers agreed, revolved around cooking. In 1868, the editors of *The Household* bemoaned the fact that "we are . . . seriously deficient . . . in culinary labors" and expressed the hope that the "day be not distant when our culinary interests shall become permanently connected with our educational system."[83] Had they been able to see into the future, they would have been pleased. In 1884, Juliet Corson commented approvingly on the change she had witnessed: "Within the last decade . . . we have reconsidered one habit, which had come with our advancing prosperity and culture, that of leaving the treatment of our food supplies to untrained domestics."[84] James Fernald made much the same point, claiming in *The New Womanhood* (1891) that "cooking . . . will, to the end of the world, be part of 'woman's work,'" but he hastened to assure readers it was "a work not easily surpassed in substantial worth."[85]

If properly understood and implemented, the principles of home economics would, advisors promised, transform the relationship between the housewife and her tools. As Gardner explained in *Homes, and How to Make Them*, "We have only to elevate [the kitchen] morally and intellectually, make it orderly, scientific, [and] philosophical. . . . As the chief workshop of the house, the kitchen should be fitted up . . . as an intelligent manufacturer would fit up his factory. . . . Then if our housekeepers . . . will learn their . . . profession half as thoroughly as a mechanic learns a . . . trade,—we shall have a domestic reformation that will bring back something of the Eden we have lost."[86] The woman depicted in an 1874 lithograph (illus. 7.15) has taken Gardner's advice to heart. The dishes and glasses in her cupboard are arranged with mathematical precision, but the flowers and framed picture remind the viewer of her other talents. She stands at her work table, placidly rolling out pastry, undisturbed by other family members and confident that everything in her domain is under control. Unlike the real kitchens of women's diaries and reminiscences, there is no dirt, soot, or disorder. Instead of causing aggravation, this woman's most important tool—her up-to-date coal range—is a fully tamed ally.

Other sources confirm that the relationship between the housewife and her cookstove was changing—at least in popular art and literature. The author of *DeWitt's Connecticut Cook Book and Housekeeper's Assistant* (1871), described the new association: "Of primary importance is the cooking apparatus. It would be evidence of incapacity in an engineer, should he undertake to manage a steam engine without first becoming familiar with . . . all its parts. A cooking range or stove is but a piece of mechanism."[87] Master her "cooking apparatus," this author implied, and a woman would become a household "engineer" with the same status as her male counterparts in industry.

Mrs. Spofford, a character in Isabella Alden's *The Pocket Measure* (1881), shared this vision. When her neighbor, a "lady of leisure" who has previously relied on servants, is suddenly faced with having to do her own housework, she finds her cookstove a formidable foe. "I never made a coal-fire in my life," she exclaims, "and though I tried to set [it] going, the ugly black lumps looked fiercely at me and stayed as black as before." Fortunately, Mrs. Spofford, who "does her own work," comes to the rescue. A "skillful engineer," she has no trouble coaxing the "heartless black lumps" to burn, thereby illustrating the value of domestic skills.[88]

Women like Mrs. Spofford realized that their triumphs over cookstoves were worth celebrating. After all, subduing a late-nineteenth-century stove was no insignificant feat. One woman, who had only recently "outlived [her] own fiery ordeal in which [her] chief demon was the cooking stove," "yearn[ed] with a pity akin to love over neophytes in housekeeping" who had yet to achieve this victory.[89] Even the best advice manuals and cookbooks could do little to help. As Kathleen Smallzreid has pointed out, "the only way a woman could discover the private peculiarities of her own stove was to experiment, to fail once or several times, and to succeed at last only if she had the will to stay with her problem until it was solved."[90]

It was best to begin this process in childhood because cooking proficiency came only with long experience. Learning to gauge the temperature of a cookstove fire was particularly difficult. The little girls in Ella Farman's novel *The Cooking Club of Tu-Whit Hollow* (1886) take lessons in bread making from an accomplished housewife. "Now remember," Mrs. Halliday tells them, "there must be fire enough to begin with to complete the baking. A fresh blaze will burn the crust, while a steady fire will sweeten it." But learning to distinguish a "fresh blaze" from a "steady fire" was tricky. After Mrs. Halliday determines that the fire is just right, each girl "put . . . a hand in the oven, and sought to impress upon her memory how hot it ought to be."[91]

Matilda Englefield, the young heroine of Susan Warner's novel *What She Could* (1870), also seeks expert assistance. After filling the kitchen with smoke because of her ignorance of stoves, she begins cooking lessons with a neighbor, whose confidence she finds both impressive and puzzling. The two sit by Miss

Redwood's cookstove while their first batch of gingerbread bakes. "It'll be good," the woman assures Matilda. "I hope it will," the girl answers tentatively. "I know 'twill," her instructor replies. "You do your part right; and these sort o' things . . . never disappint." "But mamma has her cake spoiled in the oven sometimes," Matilda observes. "'Twarn't the oven's fault. Ovens don't do that for me," Miss Redwood retorts. "The fire's just right," she continues. "But how can you *tell?*" Matilda asks. "'Tell?' said the housekeeper; 'just as you tell anything else; after you've seen it fifty times, you know.'"[92]

Matilda was fortunate to have someone willing to teach her how to manage a cookstove. If a girl did not learn these lessons, the results could be devastating. In one of his *Whilomville Stories*, Stephen Crane recounted what happened when overindulgent parents gave their daughter a toy cookstove but failed to train her in its use. The events take place in the home of "Cora's" aunt and uncle, Dr. and Mrs. Trescott, during a Christmas visit. Experience has shown that Cora, outwardly "a nice child," is actually a "tyrant" capable of turning any household upside down. This occasion proves no different. The trouble begins shortly after the family's arrival, when Cora shrieks that her beloved stove has been forgotten. "It's all right," her doting mother assures her, as Dr. Trescott retrieves the stove, which he is surprised to find is a substantial "affair of cast iron, as big as a portmanteau." "[It's] just a toy of the child's," Cora's mother explains. "She's grown so fond of it . . . that if we didn't take it everywhere . . . she'd suffer dreadfully." Her prediction is amply justified when the child "burst into a wild declaration that she could not retire for the night unless the stove was carried upstairs and placed at her bedside." Her "lamb-eyed" father does what his daughter demands, repeating the process in reverse the following morning. "What are you carting that thing all over the house for?" Dr. Trescott asks. "If it makes the child happy . . ., why shouldn't she have it," Cora's mother replies.[93]

Later that day, while the adults are busy, Cora and her cousin decide to experiment with the stove. Jimmie, "made a serf" by Cora's "imperious way," follows her directions willingly. They carry the stove outdoors, and Cora dictates: "Now, Jim, get some paper. Get some wood. . . . Now we want a match. . . . Hurry up, now! No. *No!* I'll light it my own self. You get some more wood. There! Isn't that splendid?" Having gotten the fire going, Cora insists they need something to cook "else it ain't . . . real," but it begins to snow, and the fire goes out.[94]

Unwilling to give up her plan, Cora gets Jimmie to help her move the stove into the cellar, and they resume their game. "Now what'll we cook?" Cora asks. "Potatoes?" suggests Jimmie. "No," she replies pettishly. "I've cooked 'bout a million potatoes." Turnips, Cora decides, will be more interesting, so she packs four into the stove's oven and places three rows on its top. Even this is not enough to please the child. "Jimmie," she cries, "let's play we're keepin' a hotel, an' have got to cook for 'bout a thousand people." Since her stove cannot accommodate enough turnips to feed "'bout a thousand people" she directs Jimmie to shovel piles of the pungent vegetables into the furnace that heats the Trescott home, which he "obediently" does.[95]

Within minutes, the results are noticeable as the upstairs is pervaded by the "solemn odor" of burning turnips. "It's that damned kid of yours!" Dr. Trescott yells at Cora's father. Stunned by the enormity of Cora's "outrage," Dr. Trescott urges him to spank her, which he reluctantly does. Cora, who has never been disciplined in this fashion, "raise[s] to heaven a loud . . . howl" that immediately brings her mother to her side and prompts her father to apologize. The story closes with the "angel child" wrapped in the embrace of her mother, who glares "bitterly, scornfully, at the cowering father and husband."[96]

Crane's message is clear: males who failed to exercise proper authority over the females in their households were not fully men, and ignorant females unrestrained by custom could not be true women. But there was another important

7.16. "Hot Water." In Marietta Holley, *My Wayward Pardner; Or, My Trials with Josiah, America, the Widow Bump, and Et cet ery* (Hartford, Conn.: American, 1881), 407.

object lesson in this tale. Properly instructed and supervised, "little Cora" could have learned valuable lessons about domesticity from her cookstove. In her untrained, self-indulgent hands, however, it becomes dangerous, not only for the domestic havoc it creates, but because it helps her turn a male into a "serf."

Other sources confirm that the power of cookstoves in the hands of women was beginning to cause concern. After all, a hot stove could prove a tempting weapon to an angry woman. In Marietta Holley's *My Wayward Pardner* (1881), for example, a Mormon elder almost literally gets into "hot water" after proposing plural marriage to Samantha Allen (illus. 7.16). The body language of the two characters reveals their relative status. Having committed what Holley's non-Mormon readers would have considered an unforgivable sin, Elder Judas Wart cringes and holds up one hand to fend off an anticipated attack, while Allen stands commandingly over him, one arm outstretched in a gesture of condemnation, with her faithful cookstove at her side. "If you say that word seal to me agin," she cries, "I'll scald you." Elder Wart tries to explain that he had meant the proposal "in a religious way." "Wall," Samantha snorts, "I'll scald you in a religious way."[97] A similar exchange is depicted in an 1880s trade card for Rising Sun Stove Polish (illus. 7.17). Here, a woman outraged by the audacity of salesmen hawking inferior brands orders them to leave her kitchen immediately. If they refuse, she seems quite capable of clobbering them with the fire shovel she brandishes.

7.17. Trade card for Rising Sun Stove Polish, c. 1880. Author's collection.

Real women also used their cookstoves to retaliate against men. Shortly after Anne Ellis was married in the 1890s, she discovered that her husband occasionally disappeared to celebrate what he called "birthdays"—events he invariably marked by wearing a tall silk hat and getting rip-roaring drunk. After one of these binges, Anne took matters into her own hands. Herbert came in "daringly," she recounted, "as much as to say, 'Yes, I am drunk, and what are you going to do about it?'" Ellis silently served him supper, and while he was busy eating, she picked up his hat, took it to the kitchen table, "ram[med] the butcher knife into it, then hack[ed] it up, lift[ed] a stove lid and cram[med] it into the stove." Startled, Herbert "open[ed] his eyes rather wide, but never sa[id] one word." "It must have been the right thing to do," she concluded, "because there were no more birthdays."[98]

7.18. "Making It Hot for A Sewing Machine Agent," *The Day's Doings* 15 (9 Oct. 1875), 13.

7.19. "The American Housekeeper's Crest." In Julia McNair Wright, *Ideal Homes* (Chicago: J. H. Moore, 1895), 61.

An unnamed "plucky" woman in Leesport, Pennsylvania, was even more assertive. An agent had induced her to buy a sewing machine on installments, but
she was unable to keep up the payments after her husband's death left her in
"destitute circumstances." In fact, she desperately needed a refund of the money
she had already paid, but the hard-hearted agent refused her request, "insulted"
her, and tried to repossess the machine "by force." A New York weekly newspaper described the "tussle" that ensued: the widow "locked both . . . doors . . . and
. . . threw [the agent] over the hot kitchen stove, and finally succeeded in setting
him down on top of it and held him there" (illus. 7.18). Beaten, he "begged
piteously for mercy" and agreed to return "every cent." The woman, "satisfied
that he was severely scorched," pulled him off the stove but kept a firm grip on
him until he returned her money.[99]

Women like these seem to have known instinctively that they were born to
work with cookstoves and, if necessary, to use them in defense of their homes
and families. By the turn of the twentieth century, the cookstove had become a
badge of honor for housewives such as the one depicted in illustration 7.19 from
Julia McNair Wright's *Ideal Homes* (1895). Yet this effort to glorify feminine skill
and elevate the status of housework came at a cost. Men—such as "Blessed
Benedick," who was ridiculed in *Good Housekeeping* in 1911 (illus. 7.20)—were
disqualified by sex from cooking even a simple dinner. Even for women, training
could never replace innate talent. Docia, an African American servant described
in a 1908 short story by George Madden Martin, is so "blinded" by the "scientif-
ically tried and tested" principles of home economics she has learned at "an institution for the betterment . . . of her race" that she is incapable of applying
them to the demands of a real household. Her white employer pleads with her to
be more practical, but Docia is "fanatically obstinate." "Alas," Docia's mistress
laments, "she proved . . . to be singularly deficient in manual dexterity, as well as
in the simplest mechanical sense. She did not kindle a successful fire in her stove
the time she was with me, nor could she learn to manage the draughts and
dampers" (illus. 7.21).[100]

These sexist and racist episodes highlight a prevailing cultural prejudice:
middle-class white women were the only people destined and fitted to run their
households. But the torrent of advice they received on this subject in the late
nineteenth and early twentieth centuries suggests that many of them were not
listening. Women were understandably delighted if they could afford to pay others to do their housework. Cooking, in particular, remained a demanding and
dirty job. During the next several decades, Americans who were unconvinced
that the cookstove was a symbol of women's achievement continued to search for
ways to mitigate its impact.

His Experience

The Blessed Benedick leaned down
    O'er a red hot range at even;
He'd not been married very long,
    His home still seemed a heaven.
He had two cutlets on the grill,
    And spuds in the pot were seven.

His clothes, besmudged from neck to
        hem,
        Some grease spots did adorn;
    But a white apron of his wife's
    For service sweet was worn;
    And the egg that spilled along its bib
    Was yellow like ripe corn.

        It seems he scarce had been a day
        Trying to do the work;

            The cook had left them suddenly,
            And he was not a shirk.
            But heat and worry made him cross;
            He gave the pot a jerk.

    "I wish that she would come," he said;
        "I'm in an awful fix!
    Her bridge game must be over now,
    She said she'd leave at six
    And these potatoes boil so queer—
    I'm not on to their tricks!"

            I heard him growl. But soon that pot
            Began to bubble o'er;
            He grabbed it up—'twas awful hot—
            He dropped it on the floor.
            The steam surged up and scalded him;
            He swore. (I heard him swore!)
                        CAROLYN WELLS.

7.20. Carolyn Wells, "His Experience" (illustration by Strothmann), *Good Housekeeping* (Feb. 1911), 196.

7.21. "She did not kindle a successful fire in her stove the time she was with me" (illustration by Stanley Arthurs). George Madden Martin, "Fire from Heaven," *American Magazine* 67 (Dec. 1908), 141.

8

"The Disappearing Kitchen Range"

D URING THE late nineteenth and early twentieth centuries, the cookstove
began to "disappear" from its familiar but controversial place in American
homes. While inventors, architects, and domestic advisors explored new ways to
mask the dirt and odors associated with wood and coal stoves, social critics went
further. Some tried to diminish the stove's influence by reasserting the importance of the open hearth, and others proposed doing away with cookstoves entirely by removing food preparation from the household.

As we have seen, consumers had never been entirely satisfied with cookstoves.
Although huge improvements compared to the fireplace in terms of fuel efficiency and comfort, they did not always perform as advertised and did not make
possible complete control of the household climate. In May 1885, for example,
Julia Gage Carpenter complained in her diary about conditions she and her husband endured during a late season blizzard in the Dakota Territory: "Freezing
cold. Milk froze in cupboard, water in pails. . . . We suffered with cold all day."
The family's cookstove was not much help in these conditions. "I sat with my
feet in the oven most of the day," Carpenter continued. "Although we had a hot
fire the storm was so cold that my breath came out like smoke."[1]

Suffering from the other temperature extreme was even more common. In
August 1882, Emily Hawley Gillespie confided to her diary a sentiment that
must have been shared by thousands of other women who had sweated through
countless summer days preparing meals with a stove like the one in her Iowa
home. "I'm sorry I get so nervous when I am warm cooking over the hot stove,"
she wrote; "it seems just as if I burned up twenty years of my life by the heat off
the stove."[2]

Unfortunately, women in this period had few options. In the absence of reliable, affordable alternatives, they had no choice but to continue using wood and
coal cookstoves. They could, however, try to overcome their shortcomings. If
stoves were hot and smelly, which was undeniable, why not attack these problems directly? A number of inventors responded to the challenge by developing

contraptions to minimize the odors and moderate the heat produced by stoves. In 1876, for example, H. M. Hockman of Berwick, Pennsylvania, received a patent for a cookstove "ventilating device" (illus. 8.1), one of seventeen such items patented between 1868 and 1883.[3] Six years later, James Cowles of Chicago turned his attention to the problem of heat, patenting an impractical cookstove "fender" that limited radiation but also restricted access to both firebox and oven.[4]

It is unlikely that many of these unwieldy inventions were ever commercially successful, but Americans were beginning to appreciate the value of proper kitchen ventilation. In 1869, *The Household* had advised readers to install hoods above their cookstoves for this purpose.[5] Five years later, architectural reformer Eugene Gardner described the kitchen of a woman who had acted on this recommendation: "Over the entire stove . . . there's a sort of movable cover with a flue running into the chimney that carries off every breath of steam and smoke." In another kitchen of which Gardner approved, the cookstove was placed "in a . . . recess by the chimney, with tin-lined doors to shut it out of sight," an arrangement that would have reduced odors and smoke and lowered room temperature in summer.[6]

Eunice Beecher agreed that it was desirable to minimize the smells and discomfort associated with cooking, telling readers of *All Around the House* (1879) that "some kind of ventilator is important over the range or stove, by which steam and all disagreeable odors can be carried off." She applauded the solution implemented in one household, "where a very small room is built on the back part of the kitchen to prevent overheating the main room. It is just large enough for the cook-stove." She also suggested a less expensive option: a "screen or curtain . . . to hide the cook-stove."[7]

As these recommendations demonstrate, the preferred way to reduce a cookstove's unwelcome effects was to isolate it from the rest of the house. Architects understood this approach. As feminist Charlotte Perkins Gilman explained, they did not consider the kitchen stove "an inspiring altar,"[8] relegating it to a remote area as often as their clients' budgets allowed. In 1887, domestic advisor Laura Holloway described an elegant "brick residence" in which the dining room and kitchen were separated by a pantry, "serving in a measure to exclude the smells of cooking."[9] Katharine Budd would have approved of this arrangement. In 1906, she told readers of *The Outlook* about a "model kitchen wing" in which the range was placed as far as possible from the dining room and covered by a "canopy" to help "keep the room cool."[10]

The connection between income and the location of a home's service areas is exemplified by George Barber's *The Cottage Souvenir No. 2* (1891), which

173,294. Ventilating Devices for Cook-Stoves. H. M. Hockman, Berwick, Pa., assignor to himself, W. J. Knorr, and J. B. Withers, same place. [Filed Jan. 28, 1876.]

Brief.—The dome has a flexible joint-connection with the extensible pipe, and that is similarly joined to the exit-pipe.

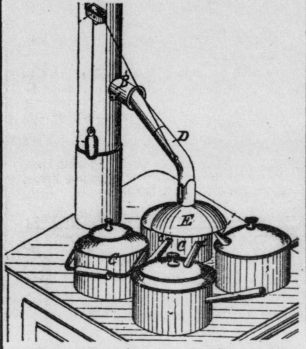

1. The adjustable and extensible pipe, having at its outer end the ventilating-dome, attached as described, and combined with the stove-pipe by means of a flexible joint, substantially as and for the purposes set forth.

2. The combination of pipe D, adjustable, extensible, and detachable, as described, collar B', stove-pipe B, and ventilating-dome E, with pots or vessels having nozzle or spout *c* in body or cover, substantially as and for the purposes set forth.

8.1. Patent drawing for H. M. Hockman's "Ventilating Devices for Cookstoves," No. 173,294, *Official Gazette of the United States Patent Office* 9 (8 Feb. 1876), 284.

includes designs for fifty-eight single family houses ranging in cost from $500 to $6,500. Fifty of the plans include a dining room, a space increasingly obligatory for middle-class families.[11] As Eugene Gardner explained in 1874, "the dining-room is a necessity. . . . The confusion usually attending the dinner-hour should be out of sight."[12] But hiding the "confusion" of cooking was not cheap. In twenty-three of the twenty-eight houses costing more than $3,000, the dining room is separated from the kitchen by a hallway, stairway, pantry, or partition; the same is true in only ten of the twenty-two homes costing less than $3,000. The two versions of Design No. 24 are good examples of the relationship between income and the ability to isolate the kitchen from the rest of the house. In Plan No. 1, estimated to cost $1,860, the kitchen is part of the main mass of the structure, and there is no dining room. Even here, however, the passage between the hall and the kitchen is fitted with double doors; "thus," Barber explained, "the odors of cooking are effectually cut off from all other rooms." Plan No. 2, which cost $490 more to build, drew a sharper distinction between function and gentility. It includes a pantry separating the kitchen from the dining room, as well as a back stairway to the "girl's room" on the second floor. In such a house, family members who wished to do so could largely ignore the demands of food preparation and stove care.[13]

Americans who could not afford to live in such a home or employ servants to do their housework also found ways to downplay the presence of cookstoves. In 1871, novelist Adeline D. T. Whitney recounted the story of the Holabirds, a widow and her grown daughters who respond to financial reverses by letting their Irish "girl" go and dividing the housework among themselves. To simplify meal preparation, they move their cookstove from the basement up to the dining room. At first, Mrs. Holabird wonders if it is possible to have a "real ladies' kitchen" with a stove in it. "I think that a cooking-stove, all polished up, is just as handsome a thing as there is in a house," her daughter Barbara assures her. But "it is clumsy," Mrs. Holabird complains, "besides being suggestive."[14]

The Holabirds' solution was ingenious—they tucked the stove into the dining-room fireplace and concealed it behind a "green screen," transforming it almost beyond recognition. In its new location, "the stove stood modestly sheltered, . . . its features softened to almost a sitting-room congruity." Previously the tool of an uncaring "Irishocracy," the Holabirds' cookstove is now really theirs. Suddenly it looks "smooth and enticing," and Mrs. Holabird quickly becomes its willing servant. She "let down the ashes . . . and set the pan into the out-room. . . . Then into the clean grate went a handful of shavings . . . , one or two bits of hard wood, and a sprinkle of small, shiny nut-coal. The draughts were put on, and in five minutes the coals were red." Everything is dainty and tidy, in keeping with nineteenth-century standards for Anglo-American femininity, and a marked contrast to "an Irish fire . . . with its volcanic . . . cinders and ashes."15

The Holabirds' "art kitchen" is even fit for receiving guests. As the women discuss plans for an upcoming party, they debate whether or not to lay out the festive supper there. "They'll see the cooking-stove," one of them objects. "They won't know it when they do," Barbara replies. The family's new domestic organization passes an even tougher test when "Madam Pennington" and her daughter Elizabeth drop by while Mrs. Holabird is preparing an apple pudding. Barbara is reluctant to take them into the dining room while her mother is cooking, but they assure her that they do not mind. The scene is idyllic: "mother sat with the . . . bowl in her lap, turning and mincing . . . the light, delicate . . . pastry. The sunshine . . . filled the room . . . with life and glory." "This is the pleasantest room in . . . your house," Elizabeth exclaims; "you don't mean that this is really your kitchen!" Mrs. Holabird calmly continues assembling the pudding while chatting with her visitors. When she is finished, "Barbara disappeared with it behind the damask screen, where a puff of steam went up . . . that told the pudding was in." After the table is cleared, there is "nothing but a low, comfortable bubble in the chimney-corner to tell of . . . dinner."16

Fifty years later, M. H. Carter recommended a strikingly similar kitchen arrangement in *Ladies' Home Journal.* The article begins with a conversation between two women who commiserate because "servants are impossible to get . . . and all the cooking falls on the housewife." They want to make the kitchen the "heart of the home—kitchen, dining room and living room all combined to save steps." But "what do you do with your surplus heat from the range when the family sits down to dinner?" one of them asks. "Maybe you haven't tried eating in the kitchen just after a big meal has been cooked, but . . . [i]t's awful in summer; and it's worse . . . in winter because you can't open the windows." The other woman mulls the problem over and then cries: "Eureka! I found it, the disappearing range! Now you see it; now you don't! When you want to get rid of the heat, shut it up—and there you are!"17

Carter described several versions of the "disappearing range," including a system in which the stove was separated from the rest of the kitchen by doors, placing it in "a neat little living room all to itself" (illus. 8.2). Once preparations for a meal were complete, "the surplus heat from the range . . . is disposed of by opening the window . . . and closing the . . . doors, which converts the kitchen into a dining room." Carter also had advice for women with summer kitchens, describing a housewife who owned two ranges—to save the "work and dirt" of moving one of them twice a year. In summer, she converted her "disfiguring winter range" into a sideboard by draping it with "bright muslin curtains and an embroidered cover" (illus. 8.3).18

8.2. "When You Want to Get Rid of the Heat, Shut Up the Range." M. H. Carter, "The Disappearing Kitchen Range," *Ladies' Home Journal* 48 (Apr. 1921), 96. Courtesy of the Library of Congress, Washington, D.C.

8.3. "The Disfiguring Winter Range." M. H. Carter, "The Disappearing Kitchen Range," *Ladies' Home Journal* 38 (Apr. 1921), 96. Courtesy of the Library of Congress, Washington, D.C.

Unfortunately, kitchen wings, alcoves, and decorative screens could only mask the problems associated with wood and coal stoves. The only way to resolve them permanently was to eliminate the appliance entirely, something that proved far easier in the sitting room than the kitchen. As central heating became more common in middle-class homes in the late nineteenth and early twentieth centuries,[19] the parlor stove was increasingly retired in favor of the furnace register. The new technology, depicted in an 1885 advertising brochure published by the Barstow Stove Company of Providence, Rhode Island (illus. 8.4), separated the dirty work of fuel handling (now consigned to a man in the cellar) from the refinement of the home's public rooms. In such a household, warm air swirled magically upstairs to keep tea-drinking ladies and curious babies comfortable without the intrusion of a "disfiguring" stove.

The growing popularity of central heating also contributed to renewed interest in the open hearth. After all, as David Handlin has pointed out, if the "furnace and its related equipment provided the bulk of the heating; the fireplace [could be] used . . . to create a homelike atmosphere."[20] "There must be somewhere in the house a common family rendezvous," explained a contributor to *The Household* in 1868, "a more radiant attraction than a black hole in the floor, through which hot air pours from a subterranean furnace."[21] Echoing the arguments of antebellum "fire worshipers," architectural advisors continued to stress the importance of the fireplace. In 1873, Frank and Marian Stockton, self-appointed experts on "the home[,] where it should be and what to put in it," pleaded: "In whatever way you heat your house, try to have an open fire in the family sitting-room. . . . It will not cost very much, and the little extra trouble it gives is not to be compared with the enjoyment the family will derive from it, to say nothing of . . . keeping the air pure and sweet."[22] Eugene Gardner was even more insistent, calling the fireplace an "essential . . . without which no house is complete." "Build a house as big as you please," he told readers of *Home Interiors* (1878); "fill the rooms with fountains and flowers . . . and heat them with hot air from the regions below." But in the home's most important room, he implored, "build upon an ample hearth a glowing fire of hickory-wood, and in the presence of that genial blaze . . . will congregate all that is good and kind and lovely of the household."[23]

These paeans to the open fire were meant to reassure middle-class Anglo-Americans that their traditions were safe in an era of rapid social and economic change. As Gwendolyn Wright has observed, "the image of the family gathered around the hearth was the most common way to call up the ideal of the home as a place of protection."[24] In 1906, antiques enthusiast Paul Huston asserted that "nothing stands for the real meaning of home and family quite so well as

8.4. "Interior view of cellar and first floor, showing a Barstow Furnace . . . in operation." Barstow Stove Co., *Fireside and Kitchen Ancient and Modern* (Providence, R.I.: for the company, 1885), unpaginated.

. . . the old-time . . . fireplace. Nothing can take its place—no coal grate, or stove, or registers, or steam heaters."[25] William Davis agreed, arguing the same year in *Plymouth Memories of an Octogenarian* that a sitting-room fireplace would help reverse the "disintegrating effect of civilized life" caused by "new means of heating . . . [which had] scattered the members of [the] family."[26]

Fireplaces were also altars for ancestor worship. Local-color writer Hamlin Garland recognized this, insisting that the house he built in Wisconsin about 1905 had to have this "most vital of all the requisites of a homestead." To Garland, the open wood fire evoked memories of "the days of the Kentucky rifle, the broad-axe and the tallow-dip" when "everybody had fireplaces." "Like most of my generation, I had been raised beside a stove," he lamented. His wife had likewise "hung her Christmas stocking before a radiator." But now with a young daughter to think of, they both began to long for "a hearthstone of the old-fashioned kind" instead of "iron stoves of varying ugliness." Garland's decision was difficult to implement, however, because the craftsmen he had hired did not know how to build an "old-fashioned" hearth. In fact, they thought his idea "comically absurd." But Garland's mind was made up. "That fireplace must be built," he insisted. When his wife hesitated over the cost, he retorted, "Hang the expense!" After numerous delays, the work was finally completed, and the first fire lit. "The color of . . . home-life is in that fire," Garland exclaimed delightedly. "Centuries of history are involved in its flickering shadows. We have put ourselves in touch with our Anglo-Saxon ancestors."[27]

The prestove kitchen, with its wide hearth and brick oven, was an even more powerful reminder of "Anglo-Saxon ancestors." Kenneth Ames has related how a significant number of nineteenth-century Americans—unsettled by modernization, urbanization, and immigration—celebrated "colonial" artifacts and placed "extraordinary emphasis on the kitchen as a purveyor of . . . values."[28] As Alice Morse Earle explained in *Home Life in Colonial Days* (1898), "the kitchen . . . was the most cheerful, homelike, and picturesque room in the house. . . . [It] had a warm, glowing heart that spread light and welcome, and made the poor room a home."[29]

Beginning in the 1860s, recreated "colonial" kitchens were popular features at fairs and expositions. In 1864 alone, six northern cities sponsored fund-raisers for Union soldiers that included "olde tyme" kitchen displays.[30] Those responsible for the Brooklyn and Long Island Sanitary Fair made an explicit connection between their "colonial" exhibit and the nation's embattled federalism. "The idea is to present a faithful picture of New-England farm-house life of the last century," they explained. "The grand old fireplace shall glow again—the spinning wheel shall whirl as of old. . . . We shall try to . . . illustrate the domestic life and habits of the people, to whose determined courage, sustained by their faith in God, we owe that government, so dear to every loyal heart."[31]

After the war, more elaborate "olde tyme" kitchens were featured at both the 1876 Centennial Exposition in Philadelphia and the 1893 Columbian Exposition in Chicago.[32] In the same period, historical museums such as Memorial Hall in Deerfield, Massachusetts, and the Golden Gate Park Museum in San Francisco installed "colonial" kitchens as period room displays.[33] Typically, these rooms bristled with antique artifacts unknown in all but the most well-to-do eighteenth-century households. A circa 1900 photograph of the Memorial Hall installation (illus. 8.5), for example, shows an astonishing amount of glassware and pewter and at least ten lighting devices. Cooking implements are also far too numerous; something is hanging from nearly every inch of the fireplace wall. But accuracy was not the goal of these recreations. As antiquarian Walter Dyer observed in 1910, the "vision of the huge kitchen fireplace, with its pewter-laden mantel, the old flintlock hung above, [and] strings of peppers and onions overhead," was meant to evoke memories of "our forebears gathered about it in

8.5. Memorial Hall Kitchen; photograph by Frances and Mary Allen, c. 1900. Courtesy of the Pocumtuck Valley Memorial Association, Memorial Hall Museum, Deerfield, Mass.

the ruddy glow."[34] Visiting such a site was a moving experience, as Huston attested in 1906 after a trip to Mount Vernon. "No one who has ever stood before the old-time, spacious fireplace . . . can have failed to feel a thrill," he asserted. "What an atmosphere of old-time ways . . . the very heart of the republic."[35]

In addition to their artifactual errors, these static exhibits also failed to depict the work of running such kitchens. Of course, sentimentalizing physical labor is difficult, especially while it is being done. Artist Thomas Hicks had the right idea. His painting *No Place Like Home,* popularized as an engraving (illus. 8.6), portrays two elderly people sitting companionably in front of their kitchen fireplace. The food has already been prepared, and the table is neatly laid, making it possible for the woman to sit quietly with her hands folded. The man is holding a pair of tongs, suggestive of activity, but his grip is relaxed, as though the implement is more prop than tool. In this scene, the artist has conveniently ignored the demands of food and fuel preparation.

Selective memories of the working conditions in prestove kitchens are also evident in other sources. Between 1865 and 1900, a generation of Americans old

8.6. Engraving from Thomas Hicks's *No Place Like Home.* In Barstow Stove Co., *Fireside and Kitchen Ancient and Modern* (Providence, R.I.: for the company, 1885), unpaginated.

enough to remember the warm glow of open kitchen fireplaces, but too young to recall the labor and discomfort associated with them, celebrated a technology they did not fully understand. In 1867, for example, Ann Howe devoted the frontispiece of her *American Kitchen Directory and Housewife* to an idyllic depiction of "our grandmothers kitchen" (illus. 8.7). Work is being done here— "Mother is preparing for baking . . . , the daughter is pounding clothes, [and] the son brings in wood and water"—but an atmosphere of tranquility nonetheless prevails. A dog sleeps peacefully in the middle of the room (where he would have been in the way), while a little girl sits reading between two roaring fires, the one on the hearth easily within singeing distance. The tall case clock, the spinning wheel, the Bible on the mantel, and the church visible through the window—icons of industry and social stability—remind the viewer of the nation's traditional values.

Two years later, Harriet Beecher Stowe described a similar kitchen in *Oldtown Folks* (1869), a novel set in late-eighteenth-century Massachusetts. The room's chief attributes are a "great fireplace" and a "jolly old oven" that "roared and crackled in great volcanic billows of flame." Every Thanksgiving, like a patriarch overseeing the gathering of his family under the ancestral roof, the oven "brooded over successive generations of pies and cakes . . . till . . . shelves and

8.7. "Our Grandmothers Kitchen," lithograph by Rising & Oerlach, New York, N.Y. In Ann Howe, *The American Kitchen Directory and Housewife* (Cincinnati: Howe's Subscription Book Concern, 1867), frontispiece. Courtesy of the American Antiquarian Society, Worcester, Mass.

pantries were . . . crowded."[36] In 1872, a contributor to *The Household* likewise praised the glories of "Grandmother's Houses." Sadly, she reported, the "wide, open [kitchen] fireplace holds now a patent cooking-stove, which projects glumly from its empty recess," but she fondly remembered "the time when great back-logs dozed there . . . and . . . kettles swung from the crane"; "[i]t was," she recalled, "a delight . . . to sit near the chimney . . . and see the . . . great fire playing over the . . . andirons, and converting the tin pans . . . into so many flashing suns."[37]

Emily Barnes, born about 1803, remembered with equal pleasure her grandparents' home in Walpole, New Hampshire. "There were no stoves . . . at that time," she wrote in 1888. "The kitchen fire was a marvel of comfort and convenience, affording ample room for a dozen persons . . . to make themselves comfortable before its . . . genial warmth."[38] George Hoar, born in Concord, Massachusetts, about 1830, shared Barnes's enthusiasm for the past. "The great kitchen fireplace" of his youth "presented a very cheerful appearance compared to the black range or stove of to-day," he averred in 1898. "No boy of that day will think there is any flavor like that of roast turkey . . . cooked by these open fires. . . . The fireplace was the centre of the household, and was the type and symbol of the home," he concluded.[39]

In 1883, Hoar's contemporary Ellen Rollins extolled the virtues of her grandfather's kitchen and the people who had labored there. By day "sombre," the room, "brightened by a roaring backlog, . . . was full of cheer" after nightfall. "Fire-changed," its "simple furnishings were enriched by shadows, and the pewter dishes . . . shone . . . like silver." To Rollins, humble artifacts—"leather-covered books," a "weatherwise almanac," the "cross-legged table and prim chairs," the "long crane with its hissing teakettle," the "settle in the corner"—symbolized a vanished, therefore valued, lifestyle. The people Rollins recalled were also dreamlike. "There was dignity in the . . . labor of my grandfather's kitchen," she insisted. "Its workers wrested from . . . their vocation some measure of . . . beauty. . . . Their daily walk was narrow . . . but this . . . was glorified by firelight and consecrated by use. The simple harmony of it . . . was reflected upon these women. They became a part of it, . . . not drudges . . . , but quaintly costumed life-studies."[40]

If Rollins's recollections are reliable, her "stately grandmother" handled her "clumsy utensils" with "a becoming deftness," did her work with "no hurry," always kept "her checked apron and muslin cap . . . spotlessly clean," and turned out three "well-cooked, sufficient, and wholesome" meals a day "with perfect order."[41] Katy Scudder, a character in Stowe's *The Minister's Wooing* (1859), was equally accomplished, possessed of that ineffable but crucial housewifely attribute "faculty." "To her who has faculty," Stowe maintained, "nothing shall be impossible. She shall scrub floors, wash, wring, bake, brew, and yet her hands shall be small and white. . . . She . . . is never in a hurry."[42]

It is difficult to reconcile these images of perpetually tidy and calm "quaintly costumed life-studies" with the heat and soot of open-hearth cooking, but they had a powerful appeal at a time when Anglo-Americans were flocking to "olde tyme" kitchen exhibits. Not surprisingly, the tendency to make nearly everything in the past preferable to almost anything in the present distorted memories already dimmed by time. Rollins unwittingly explained how such a misconstruction could occur. "I . . . sat hour after hour in that kitchen watching the backlog's slow consumption," she recalled, "half blinding my eyes with its flickering brightness. It was a . . . companionable thing, taking strong hold upon a child's fancy."[43]

Yet a "child's fancy" is hardly reliable as a historical source. Several late-nineteenth-century reminiscences that similarly glorify the open hearth also misrepresent Americans' reaction to stoves in the antebellum period. Born in Duanesburg, New York, in 1832, Henry Conklin remembered in the 1890s the "happy sweet days of childhood" when he had been "clasped in . . . a mother's arms before a great blazing . . . fire." With only partial accuracy, he asserted, "Stoves had not been invented then or if they had . . . people were too poor to buy them."[44] Lucy Larcom's recollection of the reception of early stoves is also suspect. Born in Beverly, Massachusetts, in 1824, she memorialized her "New England girlhood" in an autobiography published in 1889. "Primitive ways of doing things had not wholly ceased during my childhood," she recalled. "We . . . sat by open fireplaces. . . . There was a settle in the chimney corner, where three of us . . . could sit . . . and toast our toes." She also noted, "Cooking-stoves were coming into fashion, but they were clumsy affairs, and our elders thought that no cooking could be quite so nice as that . . . done by an open fire." Larcom's assessment of early cookstoves as "clumsy" is supported by the facts, but her bias against the new technology is also clear. "We younger ones reveled in the warm, beautiful glow [of the open fire]," she gushed. "There is no such home-splendor now. . . . The shutting up of the great fireplaces and the introduction of stoves marks . . . the abdication of shaggy Romance and the enthronement of elegant Commonplace."[45]

Albert Bolles, author of *Industrial History of the United States* (1879), went even further in condemning stoves. Entranced by the beneficent influence of the open hearth, he misrepresented the history of stove use, a fact overlooked by one recent scholar.[46] "The old fashioned fireplace will never cease to be loved for the beautiful atmosphere it imparts," Bolles contended, applauding "the snug and cheerful effect of an open wood-fire." He claimed that "When stoves were first introduced, a feeling of unutterable repugnance was felt by all classes toward . . .

them, and they were used for a generation chiefly in schoolhouses, court-rooms, bar-rooms, shops, and other public and rough places. For the home," he insisted, "nothing except the fireplace would do. The open fire was the true centre of the home-life, and it seemed perfectly impossible . . . to bring up a family around a stove."[47]

Of course, as we have seen, "all classes" had not felt "unutterable repugnance" toward stoves when they were "first introduced." In fact, it had seemed entirely possible to many people "to bring up a family" around their welcome warmth. But if Bolles's comments do not accurately reflect consumer response to stoves in the antebellum period, they do represent a significant segment of late-nineteenth-century opinion. Many people shared his suggestion that stoves were "rough" but fireplaces were "snug and cheerful." Portraits of the well-to-do in this period, such as the 1869 Eastman Johnson painting of the Brown family (illus. 8.8), were often composed to emphasize the warm glow of the open fire.[48] During the next several decades, some families even added a new fireplace-dominated space to

8.8. Eastman Johnson, *The Brown Family*, 1869. Courtesy of the National Gallery of Art, Washington, D.C.; gift of David Edward Finley and Margaret Eustis Finley.

their homes—the "living hall"—a supposed echo of medieval hospitality.[49] As Clarence Cook explained in *Scribner's Monthly* in 1876, "people have been finding out that though a furnace may be an excellent thing . . . , yet there are days . . . when a fire . . . seems to go more directly to the right spot." Being physically warm was not enough; only an open fire could make one psychologically warm.

Attended by a votary in classic garb, a fireplace like the one Cook recommended (illus. 8.9) could appease the "god of fire,"[50] but a stove had no such power. In fact, stoves were often portrayed in late-nineteenth-century popular art and literature as squalid accompaniments of an undesirable lifestyle. In 1873, for example, *Scribner's Monthly* told the story of the "hermit of Quidnit" who lived in a tiny, sparsely furnished cabin (illus. 8.10), his only companion a battered step cookstove. Seven years later, *Harper's New Monthly Magazine* described an even cruder domestic scene (illus. 8.11). Both author and artist went out of their way to highlight the alien quality of this New York City "squatter" family's life. The crucifix on the wall and the "mummy-like old woman" who sits

8.9. "Aha! I Am Warm—I Have Seen the Fire!" Clarence Cook, "Beds and Tables, Stools and Candlesticks: II," *Scribner's Monthly* 11 (Jan. 1876), 342.

8.10. "The Hermit of Quidnit," from a painting by George B. Wood. "Nantucket," *Scribner's Monthly* 6 (Aug. 1873), 395. Courtesy of the American Antiquarian Society, Worcester, Mass.

8.11. "An Interior." "Squatter Life in New York," *Harper's New Monthly Magazine* 61 (Sept. 1880), 568.

peeling potatoes and "talking Celtic between the puffs of her pipe" demonstrate that this household is the antithesis of an Anglo-American, middle-class, Protestant home. To complete the scene, a goat lies "curled up before the rusty little stove."[51]

Stephen Crane used a similar cookstove as a prop in a domestic-confrontation scene in the "gruesome" tenement he depicted in *Maggie: A Girl of the Streets* (1893). When young Jimmie comes home bloodied from a street brawl, his parents argue about how to deal with him. Jimmie's mother, standing "rampant" by the "seething stove," scolds her husband for interfering, but he merely sits quietly, "his great muddied boots on the back . . . of the stove," and "tranquilly" tells her to go to hell. She erupts, and he storms out. Left alone, she "shroud[s] herself . . . in a cloud of steam at the stove" to finish cooking dinner and then, after serving the children, sits by the stove "shedding tears and crooning miserably."[52]

Daisy Miller's family, whose plight was detailed in a short story published in *World's Columbian Exposition Illustrated* in 1891, lived in similar circumstances (illus. 8.12). Daisy, the eldest of five children, earns a pittance as a "cash-girl" in New York City, but her income is insufficient to save the family from eviction. Fortunately, she is discovered crying in the street by Hiram Horton, a farmer

8.12. New York City "back tenement." In J. B. Campbell, "How the Farmer Spent His Christmas," *World's Columbian Exposition Illustrated* (Dec. 1891), 23.

from the nearby countryside. He escorts Daisy home and is shocked by the "dark and dismal" lodgings she shares with her widowed mother, siblings, and a decrepit "stove of old make." Horton immediately formulates a plan to help the Millers and returns home, where family members pitch in to fill a crate with clothing and food (illus. 8.13). Significantly, they accomplish this good deed in an old-fashioned kitchen untouched by modern technology; there is even a crane visible inside the fireplace.[53]

The popularity of "olde tyme" kitchens in late-nineteenth-century American popular culture is undeniable, but the sentimental "colonial" re-creations

8.13. Kitchen in the Horton household. In J. B. Campbell, "How the Farmer Spent His Christmas," *World's Columbian Exposition Illustrated* (Dec. 1891), 18.

devised by antiquarians, artists, and writers bore little resemblance to the rooms where real women prepared meals. Inexorably, the skills required for open-hearth cooking were being lost. When young Matilda Englefield visits her minister in Susan Warner's novel, *What She Could* (1870), for example, she watches with "great curiosity" as he hangs an apple on a string in front of his library fireplace. "Did you ever roast an apple so?" he asks the child. "No," she replies, "we haven't got that way at our house . . . for we have no fires; nothing but stoves."[54] By 1903, when *Harper's Bazaar* published a retrospective of open-hearth cooking techniques and tools, the author could find only one "housekeeper of adventurous spirit" willing to do without "the hopelessly unpicturesque cooking-stove" to prepare meals "in real Colonial fashion."[55]

Although some households in the last half of the century continued to rely on brick ovens when a large amount of baking space was needed,[56] their use, like that of the kitchen fireplace, was becoming increasingly rare. Fewer and fewer families heeded S. D. Farrar's advice in *The Homekeeper* (1872) that "a good brick oven is needed . . . as no stove ever will equal it."[57]. Five years earlier, Ann Howe had argued that "brick ovens are . . . best for baking most things, particularly those . . . which require a long time," but conceded that "it is a good deal of extra trouble and expense to heat a brick oven when you have a good one attached to your cooking-stove," and admitted, "It will generally be found preferable to use the latter."[58]

Some savvy observers recognized that the attention lavished on the open hearth and brick oven was rooted in nostalgia. Mary Janette Elmore, whose reminiscence of life in South Windsor, Connecticut, was published in 1911 when she was nearly eighty, agreed with the champions of traditional culinary techniques that "food baked in . . . [brick] ovens was much better than what we now have." "But," she wondered, "perhaps the appetite, which in healthy growing children, gives such a relish to . . . food, may in part account for it."[59] Edward Everett Hale, born in Boston in 1822, had a similar experience. When, later in life, he and his siblings "were sounding the praise of wood fires, and talking rather sentimentally about their companionship and poetry, my mother would . . . say: 'You may take the poetry of an open wood fire . . . but to me . . . it was only dismal prose, and I am grateful I have lived in the time of anthracite coal.'"[60]

Even Harriet Beecher Stowe, an ardent admirer of open fires and the values they supposedly embodied, had to admit that cookstoves were "neat [and] labor-saving."[61] Mary Livermore, a prominent temperance and women's suffrage advocate, concurred. When she wrote her autobiography in the 1890s, she matter-of-factly recalled kitchen working conditions seventy years before. "There were no stoves, nor ranges . . . and the cooking was done in an open fireplace, by means of cranes inserted in the chimney, from which were suspended hooks for pots and kettles. There were 'bake-kettles' for . . . baking . . . over beds of live coals. . . . There were 'tin kitchens' for the roasting of meats . . . before the fire. . . . The kitchen conveniences of those days," she concluded, "would drive to despair our housekeepers of today."[62]

In 1870, an insightful contributor to *The Household* explained how the labor-intensive, dirty, and dangerous cooking of the prestove era (as well as the people who had done it) had come to be so celebrated. "Among all the jeremiads . . . upon the degeneracy of modern days, there is none more frequent . . . than the lament over the loss of housekeeping abilities," she commented. "So highly do men eulogize the domestic arrangements under which they spent their happy youth . . . that one would think the art of good housekeeping perished with our grandmothers." But, she pointed out, "it is always well to be sure of a fact before attempting to account for it; and we are not certain that the housekeepers of other days . . . were able to accomplish more than is possible at the present time. We remember dimly that their cookery was delicious, but forget that we ate it with the eager appetite of childhood." "Time . . . wraps everything in the roseate hue of distance," she concluded. "It is thus that we look back upon those old-fashioned mansions, and regret their happy, well-ordered cheer; but compared with the thousand . . . comforts of our modern dwellings, they would seem barren of attractions and the life which satisfied their inmates . . . intolerable."[63]

As this author recognized, most Americans in the late nineteenth century were unwilling to surrender the "comforts of . . . modern dwellings" for the technology of "old-fashioned mansions," no matter how much social critics glorified the latter's "well-ordered cheer." Domestic advisors were thus forced to compromise. In 1865, Stowe recommended that readers of *House and Home Papers* supplement furnace heat with "fireplaces to keep up a current of ventilation," but for kitchens she suggested a range equipped with a water back.[64] Two years later, Joseph and Laura Lyman, authors of *The Philosophy of Housekeeping,* came up with a similar solution: "a cheerful, open fire" in the family sitting room and a cookstove (which they admitted had "been brought . . . to a wonderful degree of perfection") in the kitchen.[65] In 1869, a contributor to *The Household* neatly summarized this combination of tradition and modernity: "I would not do away with the advantages of the cooking stove, but I would confine it to a small room . . . and then I would have a fireplace to live by."[66] Nathaniel and Matey Prentiss, the New England couple memorialized in a 1908 short story by Dorothy Canfield, organize their household along just these lines—they have a coal stove in their kitchen but an open fire in their parlor (illus. 8.14).[67]

Like the Prentisses, most Americans preferred open fires for family gathering places but agreed that cookstoves were necessary. Some domestic reformers, however, were unhappy with the incomplete mechanization of the household

8.14. "Oh, Mother, Don't! I Can't Stand It" (illustration by Edwin B. Child). In Dorothy Canfield, "The End," *American Magazine* 66 (June 1908), 138.

and lobbied to remove housework from the home—a goal that, if realized, would have banished the cookstove as well. As early as 1834, author Caroline Howard Gilman had suggested that households should utilize the division of labor being introduced outside the home. "We have a partial system which might easily be carried through the whole order of social life," she maintained. "We have our chimney-sweeps, our wood-sawyers, our bakeries; why not have our grand cooking-establishments?"[68]

Gilman's dream remained unfulfilled in the antebellum period, although increasing numbers of Americans in these years did reduce the burden of housework by boarding or by moving into hotels or apartment houses.[69] It was not until after the Civil War, however, that the reorganization of housework was attempted on a substantial scale. The middle-class home, reformers argued, had become outmoded. "*Habitations* we have," a supporter of boarding told readers of *The Household* in 1869, "but . . . Biddy or Topsey has become mistress in fact, though not in name. We may stigmatize the idea of *Boarding*, yet [many] . . . so-called housekeepers are no more than boarders with their servants." According to this author, the solution was "aggregation," which would improve efficiency without sacrificing privacy. After all, "a dozen families may live as isolated under one roof, being served by one cooking range, and the same retinue of servants, as though living in . . . twelve houses, with twelve ranges and three or four times as many servants."[70]

Eunice Beecher agreed there was a problem. "If something cannot be found to lessen the heavy burden which fashion binds on our housekeepers," she argued in 1879, "hotels and boarding-houses will be the *shelter* of our families, and homes . . . one of the myths of the past." The "style of housekeeping" had become too "elaborate," she thought, and servants were "less competent and amenable" than in the past. "It is difficult to see how our homes are to be preserved," she concluded mournfully. For cities, she recommended the construction of "spacious hotel[s]" with central courtyards where laundry and cooking could be done collectively by hired workers.[71] Harriet Beecher Stowe envisioned a similar arrangement, predicting in 1868 that the "future model village" would have a laundry "fitted up with conveniences such as no private house can afford," a bakery "where the best of . . . bread . . . shall be compounded," and a "cook-shop, where soups and meats may be bought, ready for the table."[72]

J. V. Sears also believed that modern tools and industrial organization could free women from domestic drudgery, enthusiastically describing his ideas in *Atlantic Monthly* in 1881. "Housekeeping, as now conducted, is too big a job for those who undertake to do it," he claimed. Fortunately, "magic appliances" would soon consign its "severe labors . . . and . . . dirt-making toils . . . to an organized establishment [to be] brought under subjection to steam and electricity,

[and] to combined effort and discipline." Sears imagined a "domestic depot," centrally located to serve fifty homes and equipped with a "steam generator," an "electric light apparatus," a "hotel range," a "laundry with modern machinery," and, interestingly, a "good old-fashioned brick oven." Housekeepers would place orders by telephone and receive deliveries via pneumatic tube. The "depot" would also supply homes with "heat . . . for all purposes" and "light, probably electric." Thus, he promised grandly, "the household is to be relieved of the heavy and gross labors . . . connected with cooking, washing, ironing, heating, and cleaning." The only thing missing from Sears's "domestic depot" was the people who would operate its equipment and produce the items ordered. "Details," he remarked casually, "will be settled by experience."[73]

Although Sears's utopian vision was never realized, contemporaries did establish a variety of "cooperative housekeeping" ventures. As Dolores Hayden has demonstrated, these "material feminists" wanted to effect a "grand domestic revolution" that would produce a "complete transformation of the spatial design and material culture of American homes."[74] As feminist Zona Gale put it, "the private kitchen must go the way of the spinning wheel."[75] A number of reformers agreed; at least thirty-three cooked-food delivery services and cooperative dining clubs were founded in the East and Midwest between 1869 and 1921.[76] Most lasted only four or five years, however, victims of the "artificial privatism" that made Americans suspicious of proposals to alter traditional family life. Many people also had trouble accepting the idea that housework had a cash value that had to be paid for when it was performed outside the home.[77]

Benjamin Andrews, a professor at Columbia, shared the discomfort of those who were reluctant to make radical changes in their domestic arrangements. He admitted in 1915 that "progress for the home . . . is to be accomplished either by transferring housework outside the home to the machine, or by bringing the machine to the work left within the house" and agreed that some tasks, such as laundry, should eventually be handled by "large industrial units." But Andrews was concerned about more sweeping efforts to remove domestic chores from the household. "There is an irreducible minimum . . . of work which must stay within the home," he asserted. "The care of the house . . . and its furnishings, the immediate preparation of food and the family table, the care of the child — these things . . . cannot go outside the home."[78]

As Hayden's research and Andrews's comments demonstrate, most Americans found socialized housekeeping unacceptable. A less controversial approach was to change the way work was done within the home. Drawing on the principles of scientific management being introduced in the nation's factories, Christine Frederick proudly announced what she called "the new housekeeping" in 1913. She analyzed household tasks using motion study and rearranged appliances and furniture to minimize steps. She also recommended "businesslike equipment" for the home and stressed detailed paperwork: daily schedules, library and medical records, clothing storage lists, and clippings files on every imaginable subject from home entertainment to infant hygiene. Aware that thousands of women were entering the paid labor force, Frederick hoped to convince middle-class housewives that their domestic duties were equally interesting and important. "It is just as stimulating to bake a sponge cake on a six-minute schedule as it is to monotonously address envelopes," she maintained; "it is just as . . . great a test of cleverness to 'dispatch' a six-course dinner as it is to . . . teach a graded school." "Housework," Frederick concluded, "can be the most glorious career open to any woman— one that will not stultify nor degrade, but [one] which offers her peculiar talents their widest and most varied scope."[79]

Hayden has called the efforts of reformers such as Frederick "antifeminist," the "final corruption of home economics,"[80] but the "domestic engineers" and the "material feminists" had at least one thing in common. Despite their differences, they both concentrated more on the organization of housework than the tools with which it was done. Frederick did discuss the value of "fuel-savers," "step-savers," "labour-savers," and "time-savers," but she insisted that the crucial factor was how a device was used, not how it was designed. "Too many women put over-emphasis on the tool and too little on themselves," she complained. "If a woman is inefficient, how can she use a tool except in an inefficient way?" She felt "strongly that women's liberation from drudgery lies not so much in tools as in her own improved methods of work."[81]

Some "material feminists" were more sensitive to the relationship between housework and its tools, but they, too, rarely gave housewives specific guidance. For example, Ellen Swallow Richards, an instructor in "sanitary chemistry" at the Massachusetts Institute of Technology, acknowledged that the "mechanical setting" was "an important factor" if "homemaking . . . [was to] be worked out on engineering principles,"[82] but her advice was vague, particularly in view of her broad practical experience. When she and Mary Hinman Abel established the New England Kitchen in Boston in 1890 to provide inexpensive, nutritious meals to the public, they had installed the latest "scientific" inventions, including Edward Atkinson's Aladdin Oven, which used heat retention to cook food slowly and keep it warm.[83] Of course, outfitting a large enterprise such as the New England Kitchen was very different from equipping a single household. It is likely that Richards found less resistance to putting cutting edge technology in public kitchens than in private homes.

Domestic advisors who did want to tell women which tools to use faced a familiar difficulty: household appliances continued to be plagued by problems. The choice of a kitchen stove, the "most important possession of the home,"[84] remained a special challenge. Some of the women involved in the "grand domestic revolution" acknowledged the flaws of wood and coal cookstoves. The traditional kitchen, asserted Mary Livermore in 1886, was "a purgatory" because the stoves used there gave housewives "an experience like that of 'Shadrach, Meshach, and Abednego' in the fiery furnace."[85] Richards and Abel were more offended by the inefficiency of such stoves, griping in 1893 that "the common kitchen range seems to have been calculated for the express purpose of devouring fuel."[86]

Charlotte Perkins Gilman was even more pointed in her critique of American kitchens and the stoves used there. In *The Home: Its Work and Influence* (1903), she complained that "the preparation of food is still the main business of housekeeping; its labour, the one great labour of the place; its cost, the main expense." She estimated that "the cooking, service, and 'cleaning up' of ordinary meals," plus the "contributary processes of picking, sorting, peeling, washing, etc., and the extra time given to special baking, pickling, and preserving" consumed six hours of an average farm wife's day. "Cooking," she continued, "makes cleaning; the two main elements of dirt in the household being grease and ashes."[87] Gilman recognized that neither reformers nor inventors had given American housewives enough help in reducing the physical burdens of these tasks. Even after manufacturers began making stoves with rolled sheet steel plates and asbestos linings to improve durability and performance,[88] the hard work of fire management and stove care continued.

"Are you content," Gilman asked a "young wife" in 1893, "To clean things dirty and to soil things clean; / To be a kitchen-maid, be called a queen,— / Queen of a cook-stove throne?"[89] In another poem, she protested, "Six hours a day the woman spends on food, / With fire and water toiling, heat and cold; / Struggling with laws she does not understand." Gilman knew that for the typical woman, food preparation was a "career, so closely interknit / With holier demands as deep as life / That to refuse to cook is held the same / As to refuse her wife and motherhood."[90] The smoke-spewing, soot-producing cookstove symbolized this bondage. In a poem with the tongue-in-cheek title "The Holy Stove," Gilman noted that the "soap-vat," "pickle-tub," "loom and wheel" had left the home. Even baking and laundry were increasingly being done elsewhere. But cooking, she knew, was still a vital element of the American domestic ideal. "Bow ye down to the Holy Stove, / The Altar of the Home!" Gilman commanded sarcastically. "The wood-box hath no sanctity; / No glamour gilds the coal, / But the Cook-Stove is a sacred thing / To which a reverent faith we bring / And serve with heart and soul."[91]

Gilman's fellow poet, Elizabeth Akers Allen, had told an even sadder tale of domestic woe in 1886. After "Madge Miller" gives up a life of satisfying independence as a milliner to marry, she is trapped by ever-more daunting family and household responsibilities: "Week by week did she drudge and toil / And stew and pickle, and roast and boil . . . / And bathe the children, and brush their locks, / Button their aprons and pin their frocks." The toll was heavy. "She lost her airy and sportive ways, / The pretty charm of her girlish days." "For how can a playful fancy rove," Allen asked, "when one is chained to a cooking-stove?" Ultimately, Madge dies of strain and overwork, returning to haunt her husband with a vision of how much better her life would have been had she remained single.[92]

Most women of this generation were unwilling to abandon traditional domesticity, of course, but they would have welcomed more help with cooking. In the turn-of-the-century period, nearly a hundred years after the introduction of the cookstove, women continued to struggle with the often cantankerous appliance; as late as 1930, 7.7 million of the nation's households still relied on wood or coal for cooking.[93] In the early 1980s, when more than 200 elderly women were interviewed for the National Extension Homemakers Council oral history project, they recounted divergent experiences with wood and coal stoves. Elizabeth McAdams of Alabama, for example, had "really enjoyed cooking on a wood stove" because it was "cozy" and "baked beautifully," and she regretted having to replace it with an electric model in 1951. Her contemporary, Marjorie Whitney of Illinois, was less enthusiastic. She acknowledged that her "two-tone tan" range was "beautiful" but concluded that she and the stove had never been "compatible." "If I wanted it hot, it just sort of simmered along," she remembered. "If I wanted it medium, it would just get red hot. I never really mastered the big old range," she conceded.[94]

In 1984, Beulah Meier Pelton described similar conditions in her Iowa farm-house in the 1930s. "The focal point of the kitchen was the big, black cook-stove," an old model with "lots of fancy, nickel-plated scrollwork." Pelton and "Devil," as she called the stove, "carried on a continuing feud." "Most of my day was taken up . . . shoving the fuel into his belly, and taking out the resulting ashes," she remembered. "You had to be careful to turn his damper just right. If you left it too far open you soon found that all the heat had gone up the chimney. . . . [But] if you shut the damper too tightly Devil . . . spewed foul-smelling gas." "He seemed to be a living thing," she went on, "his sole purpose in life to thwart my will. He never got hot until long after I . . . had reached the boiling point. At such times I would . . . give him a good, swift kick . . . and yell, 'Get hot, damn you!'"[95]

Despite these problems, which would have been familiar to her nineteenth-century predecessors, Pelton eventually conquered "Devil" and learned to respect his "admirable qualities." "I was never fond of him," she admitted, "but I recognized his versatility. He kept us unmercifully hot in the summer, but he kept us comfortably warm in the winter." "Devil" also did some things better than the gas and electric stoves Pelton used later in life; he baked angel food cakes of unmatched "lightness and fluffiness," and his large size made it easier to cook for many people. "There have been many times when I've had to cook for a large crowd . . . and wished I had him back," she remarked, "ugly and dirty and crotchety though he was."[96]

Pelton's pride in learning to manage her "crotchety" cookstove cannot obscure the fact that her life as a young housewife had been difficult. "You had to have the strength of a Percheron, the speed of a gazelle, and the patience of a saint," she recalled. It was not considered important for her to have up-to-date tools to do housework, but things were different elsewhere on the farm. Whereas Pelton's house "had been built with [only] one purpose in mind—to put a roof over one's head," the family's barn had been designed "with an eye to the convenience of the man who worked in it and the comfort of the creatures who inhabited it." She wryly summed up the situation: "It was livestock that counted—not women."[97]

Years before, Mary Wager had noticed the same phenomenon, griping in *The Household* in 1871 that rural Americans were technologically conservative when it came to their homes. "Every farmer must have a reaper and mower, a horse-rake and a drill, . . . just as rapidly as he can pay for them, but how about labor-saving machines and inventions indoors?" she asked. "In nine cases out of ten, labor-saving affairs are brought to the help of man first." The consequences of this behavior worried her. "It is no wonder that good mothers are so scarce, step-mothers so common, and invalid women not a rarity," she commented. Wager believed women were partly to blame because they were so used to doing their work by "back and elbow power" that they looked "askance at new-fangled things." The time had come for change. "We do not believe women are so well able to endure incessant labor as men," she concluded, "so we argue that labor-saving machines should come first to the housewife."[98]

The habits Wager criticized were difficult to break, however. In 1909, social scientist James Van Cleave tried to account for the hard times being experienced by the nation's stove manufacturers. Farmers, he explained, placed the highest priority on their own implements; children's "winter shoes" and "Sunday-school hats" ranked next. Only after these wants had been supplied might a man consider buying a new cookstove for the "drudge of the family." The stove trade, he concluded lugubriously, resembled the coffin business because "no one ever buys a stove . . . until dire necessity forces the issue, and no one ever buys two because they are cheap."[99]

Van Cleave's pessimism about farmers' buying habits is confirmed by other sources. In 1913, the U.S. secretary of agriculture wrote the wives of the department's 55,000 volunteer crop correspondents "asking them to suggest ways in which the . . . Department . . . could render more direct service to . . . farm women." The 2,025 replies shared one "universal grievance": "that any device which will lessen the labor in the fields is purchased without hesitation, but that no labor-saving devices are introduced into the house to lighten the woman's work." "We do not feel so . . . neglected by the department as by our men," one Michigan woman wrote. "In many of our farm homes . . . , the women must still . . . work much as their mothers . . . did. There are no modern conveniences . . . while the men have all the modern machinery . . . their work requires." A Missouri woman begged, "Teach the men that we need . . . improvements in our homes as much as they in their fields," and concluded bitterly, "So many of us are cooking on the same old stoves we first began housekeeping with . . . [while] the men . . . have bought automobiles, mowers, rakes, hay racks, and new patent stackers, sulky plows and harrows, cultivators and wagons. . . . Whenever they see something that will lighten their labors, they immediately write a check."[100]

A number of respondents asked for advice about stoves. "Information is badly needed . . . on the economical management of the kitchen range," a Virginia man wrote. "The average woman can destroy a range and bankrupt the coal bin in the shortest conceivable time." Among the letter writers who focused on heating and cooking systems, "the feeling [was] general that the . . . wood or coal range [was] antiquated and should be replaced by less cumbrous and troublesome methods." What the farm wife needed most, asserted one Idaho man, was a cookstove "that will burn crude petroleum, so she can get a uniform heat that she cannot get out of wood or coal." A New Hampshire woman had a different suggestion—a "system of lighting the house . . . with acetylene gas [that] would provide a stove for cooking [and] save the farmer's wife from chopping wood . . . and warming up the house in summer." A Minnesota man likewise pleaded for "the adoption of a fuel other than wood or coal in cooking . . . to reduce the amount of dirt and dust the housewife combats daily," suggesting denatured alcohol as the most "reasonable solution."[101]

It was left to a farm wife from Kentucky to summarize the benefits expected once alternatives to wood and coal cookstoves became widely available. "If there is one thing more than all else that would be the greatest . . . help, it would be to have gas or electricity to cook . . . with," she wrote. "A smoking coal range has come nearer making me lose the little religion I . . . have than all else pertaining to housekeeping," and explained how "This everlasting fire making, emptying of ash pans, cleaning [off the] top of [the] range, [cleaning] out [the] soot box, and so on gets to be repulsive in the extreme. If we could be supplied with some [other] kind of heat we could depend on it would certainly be a relief."[102]

Mabel Stranahan Pattison, author of *Principles of Domestic Engineering* (1915), agreed that improved cooking appliances would make a world of difference to the nation's overtasked housewives. If forced to rely on wood or coal cookstoves, women continually faced the question, "How is the fire?"—which, she contended, made it "mentally impossible [for them] to think in a concentrated . . . way upon any subject unrelated to the . . . kitchen stove." Some day, the cooking situation would be better: "We can foresee the time . . . when the equipment necessary to feed the family shall be beautiful in form and . . . simplicity."[103]

Mrs. Harding, a farm wife featured in Gene Stratton-Porter's novel *Michael O'Halloran* (1915), had the chance to experience the benefits of improved domestic technology. But, like many of the nation's real farmers, her husband first had to be educated about the importance of up-to-date household equipment. "If you don't hurry," his observant young friend Mickey tells him one day, "she's going to have them nervous prostrations." He suggests that Mr. Harding go into her kitchen and "cotton up to that cook stove and imagine standing over it while it is roaring, to get three meals a day. . . . If there was money for a hay rake, and a manure spreader, and a wheel plow, and a disk, and a reaper, and a mower, and a corn planter, and a corn cutter, and a cider press, and a windmill, and a silo, and an automobile," Mickey continues with pointed thoroughness, "there should have been enough for . . . the pump inside, and a kitchen sink, and a bread-mixer, and a dish-washer; and if there wasn't any other single thing, . . . the kind of a summer stove that's only hot under what you are cooking, and turns off the flame the minute you finish."[104]

Chastened, Peter Harding sets aside $6,000 for his wife's use. She plans her purchases carefully, installing a furnace in the basement and a bathroom on the second floor. Electricity from a nearby trolley line provides lighting, as well as power for a "whole bunch of conveniences," including an iron, a vacuum cleaner, and a washing machine. In the kitchen, as Mickey eagerly tells a friend, "there's a big sink with hot and cold water, and a dish-washer. There's a bread-mixer and a little glass churn, both of which can be hitched to the electricity. . . . There's a big register from the furnace . . . for winter, and a gas cook stove that has more works than a watch." Overcome by these marvels, Mrs. Harding "just stands and . . . laughs and cries, 'cause *she's so glad*."[105]

The domestic transformation that so delights Mrs. Harding was under way in the nation's real households as well. Having tried, with limited success, to mask the smoke, soot, and heat produced by wood and coal cookstoves, more and more housewives were turning to new domestic fuels. The first gas cookstove was patented in 1854,[106] but many years passed before inventors and entrepreneurs were able to develop stoves and fuel distribution systems sufficiently reliable and affordable to supersede the cookstove.

9

"A Nice, Clean Fire Whenever Needed"

IN THE LATE NINETEENTH and early twentieth centuries, a growing number of inventors and manufacturers tried to convince American consumers to switch from wood and coal cookstoves to stoves fueled by gas, petroleum, or electricity. Unfortunately, early models were expensive, awkward, and plagued by poor performance. Thus, their story parallels that of the artifact they eventually replaced—the cast-iron cookstove.

Scottish engineer William Murdoch had pioneered a technique for manufacturing gas from the controlled combustion of bituminous coal in 1782, creating a system for illuminating streets and public buildings that won rapid acceptance in Europe and, more slowly, in the United States. In 1816, Baltimore became the first American city to charter a gas-manufacturing plant; by 1860, more than 300 municipal gas lighting companies had been established across the nation.[1] But cooking with gas posed a special challenge because it required a burner that generated a hot flame and little smoke instead of the cooler, dirtier flame used for illumination. Beginning in the 1840s, inventors experimented with burners that mixed air with coal gas or liquid fuels. Between 1854 and 1865, thirty-one patents were issued for gas and "vapor" stoves,[2] some of which quickly appeared on the market.

Hopes for these inventions were high. "It would be one of the greatest blessings ever conferred upon the human race if by the simple turning of a faucet, the dinner could be cooked," observed the editors of *Scientific American* in 1850. The prospect of what such a system would displace was equally appealing. "Just think of all the clamjamfrey of stoves . . . and all their attendant dirt, lumber and trouble, being at once abolished," they exulted.[3] Just two years later, they thought this glorious day had already arrived. "A fire can be made . . . in a single minute," they reported in a review of an experimental English gas stove; "the heat is intense and the flame clean; there is no ashes, no smoke and the amount [of gas] burned according to the degree of heat desired . . . can be regulated with the utmost nicety."[4]

However laudatory, media reviews such as this one failed to tell readers what they most wanted to know. How did gas stoves perform in people's homes? What did they cost to buy and operate? Did they alter the taste of food? Were they safe?

One of the first models to appear on the American market, Morrill's Erovapor Cooking Stove, was advertised in Boston in 1858. Fueled by liquid "alcohol, . . . camphene, naptha [or] benzole . . . mixed with about eight parts of Atmospheric Air," the Morrill stove was purportedly "adapted to all kinds of Cooking and Ironing." The inventor promised that "These Stoves are Perfectly Safe!" and "[They] can be . . . managed by a child; will not get out of order; are portable; need no pipe; can be used in any part of the house; make no dirt; will not heat the room . . . ; can be kindled as well as extinguished in a moment. Will Heat Flat Irons, Boil, Broil, Fry and Bake Quicker and Better than any other System of Cooking now in use." The stove, he continued, "has met with the universal appreciation of the Press and of the practical housewives of Boston and vicinity, together with that of every scientific man who has given it his attention"—concluding modestly, "It is destined to supersede all other cooking apparatus now in use."[5]

Several years later, William Shaw began advertising his "patent gas range" in the same city, claiming to have sold 2,180 models in 1859 alone. "These stoves are constructed upon entirely different principles from any other gas stoves before offered to the public," Shaw explained—perhaps a hint that the Morrill stove was not without flaws. "They do not produce smoke or disagreeable odors of any kind, if the directions for use are complied with; have no connection with any chimney; and can be used in any part of an apartment." "In the apparatus furnished by me," he went on, "economy, comfort, neatness, convenience, uniformity of result, and improvement in the quality of food have been attained. . . . Meats retain all their juices, and acquire a rich and delicate flavor which no other process can impart. Much time and labor are saved in . . . making of fires, etc." He concluded, "The apparatus is not at all complicated."[6]

Elizabeth Nicholson was convinced. "The sciences . . . have descended to aid woman in . . . her daily task-work," she proclaimed in *The Economical Cook and House Book* (1857). "Instead of the cooking range, with its bushel of coal, to prepare our dinners while the thermometer ranges at ninety degrees, we shall ere long forget, in our beautifully systematized gas cooking, that our houses were heated from the kitchen, through our protracted summers." Nicholson knew what she was talking about. She had been using a gas stove for three months and gave it "a decided preference over every other kind of cooking." "The usual objection to gas for cooking has been that it is expensive," she continued, but "we have not found it so—and for labour-saving and cleanliness, nothing can equal it." The taste of food had not suffered either. "Bread baked by gas is not to be surpassed," she claimed, "and meats retain their flavour and tenderness more perfectly than when roasted by any other means."[7]

It may not be coincidental that Nicholson's account reads like a promotional brochure. Unlike other domestic advice authors, who rarely recommended specific household devices, she made sure to tell readers that "the best [gas] apparatus is Gleason's Patent, to be had of Gleason & Sons, No. 463 Market Street [in Philadelphia]." This recommendation raises the possibility that the firm had given her a stove hoping she would like it and publicize its merits. But even if the company had done so, Nicholson was not blind to the drawbacks of gas stoves. Their "superiority over every other mode of cooking is obvious for the summer," she commented, an indication that she was aware that gas stoves were of little use for heating. She seems to have identified other problems as well, concluding vaguely, "There is really nothing to be desired but some improvement in the apparatus."[8]

Nicholson also failed to mention the high price of gas stoves. In 1858, a single-burner Morrill stove cost $10, and a two-burner model cost $14.50; neither would have met the needs of most households. The gas stoves that so impressed Nicholson were even more expensive, costing $20 to $30. In the early 1860s, William Shaw charged between $12.25 and $21 for his basic stoves depending on the number of burners, but additional equipment (most of it necessary) meant extra expense. A four-burner Shaw stove with oven, tea kettle, steamer, broiler, and two flatirons was priced at $27.61, and a five-burner model, optimistically described as "designed to cook for a family of twenty-five," cost $38.63.[9] Prices remained high for a number of years. In 1864, Boston boardinghouse keeper Susan Brown Forbes spent $34.75 on a gas stove, tea kettle, and boiler, the equivalent of three and a half months' wages for her maid. She also spent nearly $10 a month on gas and continued to need a parlor stove for heat.[10]

As Forbes's experience indicates, the high cost of fuel substantially increased the expense of adopting gas stoves. In 1852, the editors of *Scientific American* complained that New York City's $3 charge per thousand cubic feet of gas made cooking with the new fuel prohibitively expensive.[11] Fifteen years later, they lobbied for public ownership of municipal gas works, contending that monopolization in the industry had inflated prices. Gas that cost manufacturers only $1.88 per thousand cubic feet to produce was being sold for between $2.50 and $4 per thousand cubic feet.[12] Prices were even higher elsewhere; consumers in Kansas City and Denver were paying $4.50 and $5 per thousand cubic feet respectively.[13]

The *New York Times* echoed these complaints in 1866, noting that the "terror of a heavy gas bill" was the biggest factor preventing consumers from adopting the new technology. One of the paper's reporters decided to see for himself if the conventional wisdom proved true. He bought a $25 gas stove and used it in his home for a month to cook and wash for a household of six. He then calculated that the fuel for these purposes had cost $5.65 compared to $10.50 for coal and kindling wood during the same month the previous year. For "comfort, cleanliness and a sure economy," he concluded, gas stoves were the obvious choice.[14]

The poor performance of early gas stoves was a concern, however. As was the case with wood and coal stoves, proper installation and maintenance were essential. William Shaw closed his advertising pamphlet with "directions to gasfitters," telling them firmly, "Never connect these Stoves with a less supply than would be required for a gas chandelier with the same number of burners, [because] if the supply of gas is insufficient, the Stoves will not give satisfaction."[15] Gas leaks were also worrisome. After a "Mr. Wilkins" came to "fit the pipes" of Susan Brown Forbes's new gas stove, she noted in her diary: "Stove burner leaks—got to be fixed."[16]

Erratic fuel supply was another obstacle. As Kathleen Smallzreid has explained, "in the hours of heavy fuel consumption the pressure dropped, and the flame under the pans became . . . too small to keep the food cooking."[17] In the early twentieth century, a West Virginia man recalled how such a problem could disrupt daily routine: "We children sat . . . waiting for the hired girl to fry the pancakes . . . [but] the butter lay . . . in a dense . . . sheet. . . . Coffee was given up as a bad job. Eggs hardly changed color. . . . To provide us one hot bite, mother would put bread in a toaster rack and brown it over the [coal] fire in the dining room grate."[18] Even worse, in cold weather, "moisture condensed in the lines and froze . . . and put out the fire entirely."[19] Susan Brown Forbes recorded such an occurrence in her diary in January 1866: "The gas froze. Mr. Smith, Alex and I thawed it with irons and hot water."[20]

Cooking with gas also required new skills. "Regulate the heat in the oven," William Shaw directed, "by partly closing the gas-cock, and by [adjusting] the slide damper in the back," a ticklish process that had to be learned by experience. If a flame burned too weakly to make cooking possible, he continued, "the gauze surfaces require . . . cleaning . . . (which can be easily done by the use of a small paint brush . . .). If . . . a one-sided flame is produced, . . . remove with a pin any obstruction . . . in the . . . burner." If these directions were followed carefully, Shaw insisted, "[my] . . . Stoves cannot be made to emit smoke or odors."[21]

It is difficult to believe that learning to cook with gas was as easy as Shaw implied. In fact, the illustration on the back cover of his advertising pamphlet (illus. 9.1) suggests how difficult it would have been to move about freely in a room filled with gas appliances. Rubber tubes hang loosely from wall fixtures;

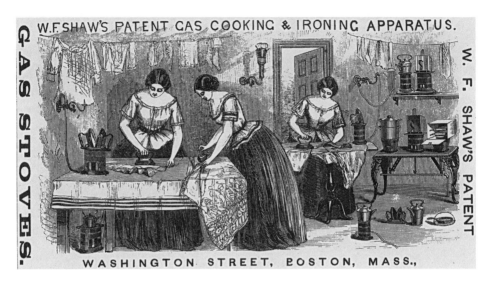

9.1. "W. F. Shaw's Patent Gas Cooking & Ironing Apparatus." In William F. Shaw, *Illustrated and Descriptive Catalogue of Gas Heating and Cooking Apparatus* (Boston: Damrell and Moore, c. 1860), back cover. Courtesy of the American Antiquarian Society, Worcester, Mass.

knocking over a burner with a scalding flatiron or steaming pot on top of it would have been alarmingly easy. And how was a short person to reach the tea kettle perched on the fixture near the door? The stove, too, looks inconvenient. Despite the fact that it is one of Shaw's larger models, it is well below waist height and looks too frail to stand up to the rigors of daily usage.

In 1863, Henry Ward Beecher recounted the challenges of cooking on a first-generation gas stove. He had returned to Brooklyn several days early from a trip and decided to fix his own meals until the rest of the family rejoined him. Heretofore, the household's "little gas-stove" had been used mostly to boil water for tea, but now Beecher required more flexibility. "To broil was beyond its skill—or . . . beyond our knowledge of its capacity," he reported, so he "rummaged the shops" for a broiler attachment and tried to cook a steak. "The broiler was very much like two iron pot-lids soldered together, with a hollow handle," he explained. "The gas came through the handle . . . and the lower section . . . was covered with blue jets. The meat was placed on a tin dish, [and] this blazing cover was placed on . . . supports just over it, and shot its heat downwards." "It is a capital contrivance," he continued; "the juice . . . and the fragrant fumes attempting to escape, were driven back into the meat, and . . . such was the force

. . . that they were driven out of the plate and . . . on to the dining-room carpet."[22]

The situation quickly worsened as the gas supply tube slipped off the broiler handle and "shot a flame across our hands." "With astonishing celerity," Beecher understandably dropped everything on the floor. Next the tube refused to stay in place, so he held it "on to the broiler with one hand, and manipulated the meat with the other. We salted it, we peppered it, we turned it twice, the first time on to the floor." Then he found that the steak had stuck to the surface of the broiler so that he could not turn it over. "At length we put out the gas, uncovered the meat, took both hands, and triumphantly reversed the obdurate steak." Beecher's struggle to cook a simple supper gave him "a profound sense of a man's dependence on women for domestic comfort"— concluding, "We admire and revere the genius that conducts so intricate a campaign as must be every single day's housekeeping."[23]

A number of Beecher's contemporaries identified other problems with gas stoves. A reporter for *Leslie's New York Journal* admitted in 1856 that the new appliance had "come . . . into vogue of late," but he was worried about the consequences of using it without venting fumes to the outside. He was also annoyed that most gas stoves proved unable to roast meat properly, leaving its surface pale and "sodden by water."[24] Fourteen years later, the editors of *The Household* also criticized gas stoves, "at least such as provide no escape for the gases of combustion. They may, perhaps, be admissible in summer for culinary purposes when doors and windows are opened wide," they conceded, "but we should as soon think of sleeping in an apartment connected by an open pipe with the nearest sewer, as in a close room warmed by a gas-stove."[25]

If concerned about these reports but nevertheless eager to replace their wood or coal cookstoves, consumers did have another option. After oil was discovered in western Pennsylvania in 1859, inventors began working on ways to use the new fuel for domestic purposes. In the 1860s, eighteen patents were issued for coal oil, kerosene, gasoline, and petroleum stoves.[26] Outwardly, they resembled early gas stoves (illus. 9.2), but they had the significant advantage of being independent of a municipal fuel distribution network. Some models were also more flexible. The oil stove manufactured by the Florence Sewing Machine Company, for example, could be converted from cooking to heating "by simply changing the drum." When set up as a heating stove, it doubled as a "powerful lamp," and when set up for cooking, its advertised performance was impressive. "There is no kind of cooking it will not do, and do better than any wood or coal stove," a company brochure proclaimed. "The heat is under instant and perfect control. Bread, cake and pies . . . are like those baked in the old-fashioned brick oven.

9.2. Advertisement for Florence Oil Stoves, *Providence Directory* (Providence, R.I.: n.p., 1879), 674. All rights reserved, the Rhode Island Historical Society, Providence, R.I.

. . . Steak can be broiled quicker and better than over hickory coals. Boiling, frying, toasting, stewing and roasting can be done with neatness and dispatch. . . . Three operations . . . can be carried on at once, and a handsome dinner . . . prepared in the shortest possible time."[27]

Oil stoves were also competitive with gas stoves in terms of price. In 1881, the Chicago firm Adams & Westlake advertised a two-burner model equipped with an extension top, oven, broiler, and flatiron heater for $13; a three-burner model cost $16.50, and one with four burners cost $2 more.[28] Two years later, the Florence Sewing Machine Company offered a double-wick stove with base, cook drum, three-hole extension top, oven, and broiler for $19.50. People who required larger models could buy a similarly equipped four-wick stove with extension top for $29.[29]

By the early 1890s, the company was manufacturing an even larger "double oil stove with extension top" designed to resemble contemporary wood and coal stoves (illus. 9.3). According to the author of *The Housewife's Library* (1892), this model afforded "ample accommodation for a family of six." It "performs all the offices of the most elaborate kitchen range," he went on, "and for roasting meats, broiling and baking is unequaled by them, for the reason that in no stove . . . is the fire . . . so completely under control of the cook." Florence stoves, he added,

9.3. Florence Manufacturing Company, "Double Oil Stove with Extension Top." In *The Housewife's Library* (n.p.: n.p., 1892), 276.

utilized "the most approved principles of construction, and are especially happy in the effects obtained, the trimmings being elaborately nickled and . . . very handsome." Stove operation and maintenance were straightforward, too. Any "good" kerosene would do, although "to avoid odor" this author recommended "the best water white oil, of not less than one hundred and fifty degrees fire test." Wicks were to be replaced every four to six weeks, and the stove kept "perfectly clean." "With care in observing such . . . hints," he concluded, "the oil stove may become a very helpful and convenient accessory in the affairs of every house."[30]

Some consumers agreed with this assessment. In 1886, a woman wrote the editor of the *Ladies' Home Journal* to praise her Florence Junior Oil Stove with extension. It "does our cooking nicely," she reported, "and . . . with the heater attached, gives out a most pleasant warmth on a . . . cold morning. The saving in labor, as well as heat, is wonderful. No wood to split, no hungry fire to feed, simply a reservoir full of oil, to begin each baking, and then the heat regulated by turning the wick up or down. Would that every weary, flurried housewife might have both labor and heart lightened," she concluded, "as ours have been, by a Florence Oil Stove."[31]

Mr. and Mrs. J. W. Alexander of Waynesboro, Mississippi, were equally satisfied with their oil stove. "We . . . are pleased with it beyond our most sanguine expectations," Mr. Alexander wrote in 1895, claiming that the stove had saved $1.30 a month in fuel costs. Moreover, "we . . . have a nice, clean fire whenever needed, no trouble, no wood to handle, no fire to kindle— compact, and for cooking, oh my! the best bread and pastry, pie, roast, and everything, done to a turn." Alexander's wife was especially pleased with the amount of work the stove saved. "She would not return to the wood stove if she was made a present of one and a servant thrown in to keep up the fire," he reported. She also "found it to be just as safe as . . . wood cookstoves, and much freer from the danger of fire."[32]

Oil stoves had a dubious reputation, Alexander's comments to the contrary notwithstanding. Although more flexible and less expensive to operate than gas stoves, they smelled, especially if low-grade fuel were used. In the early 1880s, the Florence Sewing Machine Company noted that many oil stoves (not its own, of course) were plagued by the "difficulty of overcoming the . . . odor."[33] Manufacturers had trouble correcting this situation. In the early 1980s, sixty-seven-year-old Betty Trout of Blackford County, Indiana, remembered, "When we first went to housekeeping, we had an oil stove. . . . I can almost smell it yet."[34]

Baking with an oil stove could also be a challenge. In 1888, the editors of *Scientific American* reported that "occasional complaints are made that the ovens of gasoline stoves do not bake well." The problem, they thought, was "more than likely the fault of the operator," and explained, "A frequent trouble in baking is that the bread, meat or pastry is put in as soon as the burner is lighted, instead of waiting until the oven is thoroughly warm. It is impossible to obtain good results when this is done."[35] Neva Schlatter of Pulaski County, Indiana, could have benefited from this guidance. Recalling her housekeeping arrangements in the early twentieth century, she remarked, "We bought a three-burner oil stove with an oven that sat on top. I never did like those ovens—[they] didn't bake too well, or else I didn't know how to use them."[36]

Unpleasant odors and refractory ovens were doubtless annoying, but the risk of fire and explosion associated with oil stoves was far more serious. In 1888, the editors of *Scientific American* emphasized how important it was for stove dealers to give detailed directions to buyers about when and how to fill fuel tanks. The task was never to be undertaken while the stove was in use, they explained, and if any fuel spilled during the process, it had to be completely cleaned up and the room thoroughly aired before the stove was lit. "It is only by the grossest carelessness or most willful refusal to adhere to instructions . . . that an accident is possible," they insisted.[37]

Despite such warnings, mishaps with petroleum stoves occurred fairly frequently. One Missouri editor recalled that in the 1890s newspapers often featured stories about the "death and destruction incident to explosions in kitchens" equipped with gasoline stoves.[38] Replenishing the fuel reservoir was particularly tricky. In 1877, for example, a Mrs. Timmens of Cleveland was filling her gasoline stove when it "suddenly exploded with terrific report." She was "instantly enveloped in flames," her husband and daughter were burned when they came to her rescue, and the family's house and furniture were "considerably damaged." The woman's injuries were "said to be very serious, but it is hoped not fatal," a *New York Times* report concluded.[39]

Mrs. Timmens may have been dealing with a common situation—the fuel tanks on such stoves "had a mean way of going dry while a roast . . . was in the oven."[40] Hilda Thomas of Jackson County, Indiana, experienced a different kind of accident caused by liquid stove fuel. One day "the coal oil didn't work quite right" in her table-top stove and caught fire. "Grandpa Thomas," who was sitting at the table eating lunch, "just grabbed that thing and took it outdoors and slung it on the ground. I would not have another one of the stoves," Thomas remarked wryly.[41]

Gas stoves, whether fueled by reservoirs or municipal supply pipes, could also explode. Russell Lynes recounted what happened in one woman's kitchen after she replaced an empty tank with a full one and was then distracted. She forgot to light the gas for several minutes, so when she did, a "loud explosion" resulted. The oven was "torn from its moorings," and there was a "terrible mess of baked turkey, dressing and gravy."[42] Vernell Saltzman of Posey County, Indiana, had a similar problem after she switched from a kerosene stove to a "crazy" gas model. "Every doggone time I lit [the oven]," she remembered disgustedly, "that thing would blow up . . . and I would run out the back door. . . . The lady next door . . . said she knew when I was getting ready to bake . . . because she would see me running."[43]

One way to prevent such occurrences was to develop a less volatile fuel. Beginning in the 1890s, experiments with electric cooking appliances attracted considerable attention. Although electric stoves did not become common in American homes for decades, the publicity they received made wood and coal models seem increasingly antiquated. Still rare in the nation's households (in 1907, only 8 percent of homes were wired),[44] electricity had a magical, almost utopian quality. Cooperative housekeeping had failed to eliminate cooking from the home, and gas and oil stoves had proven less perfect than manufacturers claimed, but perhaps electricity would finally make cooking easy. "With the entrance of Electricity into the home, . . . [the] true regeneration of housework begins," averred home economist Mabel Stranahan Pattison in 1915.[45]

In 1890, *Scribner's Magazine* forecast the impact the new technology would have on domestic life. "The adoption of electrical appliances is daily becoming more widespread," author A. E. Kennelly observed; "in the near future we may anticipate a period when [electricity's] presence in the homestead will be indispensable." He was particularly impressed with the changes promised by electric lights, telephones, and small motors. "There is no household operation capable of being mechanically performed, of which . . . electricity cannot become the . . . willing slave," he announced. Electric cooking intrigued him, too, despite its high cost. "Even now," he argued, "there may be . . . occasions where heat is required to be applied very locally, in culinary purposes," citing the example of a man who worked at night who would benefit from an electric "coffee-heater" in his bedroom. In such cases, Kennelly concluded, "cleanliness and convenience might outweigh the objection of extra expense."[46]

Three years later, visitors to Chicago's Columbian Exposition had a chance to see this new technology in operation. Organizers had designed a "modern ten-room residence" in which electricity heated water and powered the "most improved machinery" for doing laundry. The home was even cooled by an experimental form of air conditioning and outfitted with fireplaces containing "electric log[s]." But it was the kitchen that was expected to prove most interesting to "ladies." Exhibit engineer William Primm explained its features: "The conventional range . . . will be absent, and in its place will be . . . a marble slab with a switch-board. . . . The cook wishing to broil a steak, places the broiler on the slab, connects the wires . . . with the switch-board by simply pushing a plug into a hole, [and] turns the switch. . . . Stewing, boiling and frying will be conducted similarly, while the oven, which bothers the housewife so often, will be a dream of delight. Top, bottom and sides are provided with separate coils and the heat may be applied just as it is needed."[47]

In 1896, R. R. Bowker showed readers of *Harper's New Monthly Magazine* what such a kitchen might look like (illus. 9.4). Six separate appliances sit on a bilevel wooden table, all busily frying, steaming, or boiling. Despite the fact that this "stove" appears to have neither an oven nor a vent to disperse the large cloud of steam, Bowker asserted confidently that "when electricity becomes cheap enough, all of us who can get it will do our cooking . . . by it."[48] Katharine Budd agreed, telling readers of *The Outlook* in 1906 that "the ideal kitchen is that where cooking is done by electricity. In the near future we may expect to see this universally used," she predicted, "but, as yet . . . it is . . . a charming novelty."[49]

Pioneers in the field were busy trying to turn the "charming novelty" into reality. In 1898, the *New York Times* described the array of electric household appliances displayed at a recent industrial exhibition: "There are the oven, hot-water urn, . . . teakettle . . . , double boiler, coffee pots, broilers, chafing dishes, griddle-cake cookers, flat-iron heaters, plate warmers, and . . . disk stoves." The latter, the reporter gushed, "look so clean and simple and attractive that they are a delight," and preparing griddle cakes was "almost poetical." But the article also suggests a hint of consumer suspicion. Thomas Edison Jr. attended the event to publicize the domestic use of electricity and made a point of drinking tea and eating biscuits prepared with electric appliances. "If the son of the 'Wizard' can eat electrically cooked food," the reporter remarked, "other mortals can do the same."[50]

Performance was also a concern. In the first decade of the twentieth century, both General Electric and Westinghouse developed prototype electric stoves; in 1908, three models appeared simultaneously on the market. But, like their wood, coal, gas, and oil predecessors, first-generation electric stoves were beset by problems. Because the current delivered by utility companies could not heat elements of more than 600 watts, it took up to an hour to heat the oven to a sufficiently high temperature for baking. The weak current also made it nearly impossible to use the oven and the stove-top burners simultaneously.[51] To make matters worse, these stoves "were filled with temperament and subject to frequent breakdowns and the almost constant ministrations of service men."[52]

In the 1910s, the substitution of nickel-chromium alloys for copper and platinum in wires and heating coils alleviated some of these difficulties,[53] and domestic advisors, who had hitherto largely ignored electrical appliances, began to take notice. In *The Efficient Kitchen* (1914), for example, Georgie Boynton Child

9.4. "An Electric Kitchen." In R. R. Bowker, "Electricity," *Harper's New Monthly Magazine* 93 (Oct. 1896), 725.

applauded electrical cooking because it did "not exhaust the oxygen in the air." She also liked the fact that table-top burners could be installed in a smaller space than that needed for conventional cookstoves.[54]

Helen Kinne and Anna Cooley, authors of *Foods and Household Management* (1915), were more fulsome. "The advantages of electric cooking are obvious," they asserted. "The heat is directly conducted to each utensil, and a minimum amount is lost in radiation. The degree of heat is perfectly under control. . . . There are no waste products, and no matches to light. . . . If the wiring is properly done, there is no danger of fire. The one present disadvantage," they acknowledged, "is cost." Because of this obstacle, they concluded that electricity was "the method of the future for the average family."[55] Child reached the same conclusion. In the areas she surveyed, electricity typically cost $.10 per kilowatt hour, and prices as high as $.12 to $.15 were "not at all unusual." Appliances were expensive too; electric ranges cost between $60 and $125.[56]

Over the next several years, small electric appliances such as irons and vacuum cleaners began to become popular,[57] but cooking by electricity remained rare. Only 3.4 percent of the 1,300 electrified homes in Philadelphia surveyed by the National Electric Light Association in 1921, for example, had electric ranges.[58] They were equally unusual in Muncie, Indiana. In a six-month period in 1923, retailers there sold 3,977 electric appliances for household use, but only three were ranges. Sociologists Robert Lynd and Helen Merrell Lynd found that even though 99 percent of the community's households were wired for electricity, "very few" used it for cooking.[59] Perhaps the residents of Muncie had experienced the same problems as the consumers described by H. Bohle in *Electricity* magazine in 1924: "Some people who tried electric cooking gave it up again on account of the excessive repair bills and the inconvenience connected with the burning out of elements." There were, he concluded, "many defects still connected with electric cooking appliances and room for considerable improvement."[60]

Despite their problems, electric stoves significantly expanded the range of options available to consumers. Child devoted ten pages of *The Efficient Kitchen* to a discussion of the six types of cooking appliances then on the market. As we have seen, she considered electricity still too costly, but that left five other fuels: wood, coal, kerosene, denatured alcohol, and gas. Wood was "still in general use in farming communities where each family has a wood lot," she reported, and she considered wood stoves easier to manage than coal ranges. But wood did not "furnish sustained heat," which made "any long process like baking . . . very troublesome." Child preferred the "modern coal range with water-back connection." As long as coal was reasonably priced and families could afford a servant to tend the appliance, the coal range had "held its own" and was "undoubtedly still a valuable resource." The "best types" had oven thermometers, and some were even outfitted with pipes that connected the grate directly to an ash can in the cellar. But, Child concluded, the "common, coal range" filled the kitchen with "dust and dirt" and was "ruinously wasteful of both fuel and time."[61]

Child liked kerosene and alcohol stoves better; the former, in particular, were "a great resource" in locations without gas service. But for families who had access to an appropriate fuel supply, she considered gas the best choice. "Where the cost is a dollar a thousand [cubic feet] or less, it is more economical than coal for the kitchen," she argued, "because its use can be more easily regulated." Moreover, gas stoves were infinitely cleaner than coal ranges and required less care. They were ready for use at the touch of a match, could be turned off when no longer needed, were easy to operate, and produced uniformly good results, "even when used with only mediocre intelligence." They were also available in all price ranges, from a $7 "three-burner Junior . . . stove with oven" up to the $100 "latest type of gas range with insulated oven."[62]

As Child's remarks suggest, alternatives to wood and coal cookstoves were becoming more common in the United States, even in rural areas where gas and electric service was rare. In 1895, Montgomery Ward offered a gas range, a "grand oil cook stove," and three gasoline stoves in its mail-order catalog, together with twelve wood and coal models. Seven years later, the Sears Roebuck catalog advertised the Reliance Oil Stove, three versions of the "High Grade Acme Wickless Blue Flame Kerosene Oil Stove," and two sizes of the Acme Process Gasoline Stove, in addition to twelve wood and coal cookstoves.[63]

In urban areas, utility companies eager to enlarge their customer base competed to make alternatives to wood and coal stoves attractive. In Kansas City, for example, the establishment of the community's second gas company in 1895 induced competitor Kansas City Gas, Light & Coke to sell gas below cost for $.50 per thousand cubic feet. The company also offered new domestic customers a free gas stove, with installation included, and hired a Miss Andrews to give public lectures on how to cook with gas. Meanwhile, in Denver, the manager of the local gas and electric company instructed sales representatives to "specialize" in gas stove sales and gave cash awards to those compiling the "greatest number of points" per month. "Borrow a kitchen equipped with a gas stove," salesmen were told, "[and] invite in all the neighbors who have no stoves." The company also offered free cooking demonstrations in local churches.[64] Another popular way to boost the sale of gas stoves was for gas companies to manufacture their own models; the industry's trade association even subsidized firms interested in developing improved stoves, furnaces, and hot-water heaters.[65]

These efforts to increase gas stove usage would not have been successful unless consumers were convinced the new appliances were superior to those they replaced. On this point, they received abundant reassurance from a host of domestic advisors. In 1891, Ada Chester Bond told readers of the *Ladies' Home Journal* to replace their old stoves with "one of those wonderfully perfected gas-stoves on which any woman of average intelligence can fry, roast, broil and bake to entire satisfaction." Such a stove, she explained, "is more economical than a coal fire, makes no dust and conveys no heat to any part of the house outside the kitchen."[66] Two years later, *Scientific American* reiterated these advantages, pointing out in addition that, unlike wood or coal, gas did not have to be delivered and stored, thereby "saving the rent of a cellar and loss of money from market fluctuations."[67]

The author of *The Housewife's Library* (1892) agreed that gas cookstoves were the preferred choice. Conceding that there had been "strong prejudice" against early models because of the expense of operation and "the difficulty of burning . . . so as to avoid smoking and dirt," he went on to say that "within the last few years, . . . the construction of stoves has been . . . improved." He especially liked the model depicted in illustration 9.5 because "by means of the outlet pipe, a complete carrying away of the products of combustion is secured." He also highlighted other advantages of cooking with gas, emphasizing its "comfort and convenience . . . , especially during the summer months," as well as the nearly infinite heat adjustments it made possible. Now, he explained, "[we have] the cook controlling the fire instead of the fire controlling the cook." Also, "The lighting and extinguishing of gas is an instantaneous operation, neither entailing the drudgery, waste of fuel, of time, or of patience belonging to other methods." Compared to coal ranges, gas stoves saved both time and money. In a test that compared the performance of a "standard" coal range and a "standard" gas stove, the latter saved $1^{78}/_{100}$ cents in fuel, $33^{11}/_{16}$ cents in "shrinkage of articles cooked," and fifty minutes, primarily in fire management.[68]

Seven years later, similar experiments conducted by Boston's School of Housekeeping confirmed many of these findings. In six days, the coal range required a total of five hours and twenty-six minutes for upkeep: twenty minutes for sifting coal, twenty-four minutes for laying fires, an hour and forty-eight minutes for tending fires, thirty minutes for emptying ashes, fifteen minutes for carrying coal, and two hours and nine minutes for blacking. In contrast, the gas stove required only an hour and thirty minutes for cleaning and a mere ten minutes for tending the fire.[69] Sarah Tyson Rorer, culinary editor of the *Ladies' Home Journal* and founder of the Philadelphia Cooking School, achieved comparable results.

9.5. "Gas Cooking-Stove with Outlet Pipe." In *The Housewife's Library* (n.p.: n.p., 1892), 265.

In 1898, she told readers of *Mrs. Rorer's New Cook Book* that "gas is the cheapest and most easily managed of all fuels. . . . A good gas stove well managed will, counting in the time for care and lack of dust, cost one-third less than coal."[70]

The prospect of saving both time and money on cooking was understandably attractive. In the late nineteenth and early twentieth centuries, increasing numbers of American women were exploring activities outside the traditional domestic sphere, some by entering the paid labor force and others by joining women's clubs or volunteering for temperance, suffrage, or social service organizations.[71] Many of them also faced the challenge of doing their housework without the aid of live-in domestic help.[72]

Appliance manufacturers were aware of these trends and promised to make women's lives easier. In 1916, for example, the Western Electric Company depicted the housewife blessed with electrical appliances as a goddess of liberty (illus. 9.6). "Electricity," the company explained, "comes to free the modern woman. . . . It reduces the necessary hours of labor and lightens the nature of the work itself, adding hours to the leisure, recreation, and broader interests that claim modern woman's attention." An iron, a toaster, and a washing machine, together with electric light and a telephone, would help make these miracles possible, but the electric range was "the greatest boon of all."[73]

Manufacturers also had an answer for women who, for whatever reason, were not quite ready to abandon familiar technologies. The October 1916 issue of *Good Housekeeping* carried an advertisement for the Duplex Alcazar stove. "Here at last," the company proclaimed, "is a kitchen range that is really modern. It is made in two types, one burning coal or wood and gas, the other using coal, wood and oil separately or at the same time."[74] Hybrid cookstoves such as this remained popular for some years. In July 1931, *Electricity on the Farm,* a magazine that targeted "the progressive rural family," advertised a "combination fuel-electric" stove that had an electric oven, surface burners, and a "hard coal and wood firebox for kitchen heating and surface cooking." A woman fortunate enough to own such a stove had the best of everything. She could cook with old or new fuels, keep her kitchen warm or cool as the seasons changed, and appreciate her stove, with its "beautiful all-enamel" finish (available in white, "Nile-green," or "Ivory-Tan"), as a work of art.[75]

By 1930, the wood and coal cookstove, although still in use in many of the nation's homes, had been superseded by new technologies, especially gas.[76] The cumbersome, dirty cookstove, hailed in its day as a marvel of comfort and convenience, was no longer an important symbol of American domesticity. It looked out of place in the sleek, sanitary linoleum-and-tile kitchens where women who

9.6. "The New Enlightenment," Western Electric Company advertisement, *Good Housekeeping* (Oct. 1916), 149.

were trained in home economics turned out nutritious, vitamin-enriched meals with businesslike efficiency. As the Standard Gas Equipment Corporation of New York explained in a 1926 promotional brochure, the "old-fashioned kitchen range," with its "corners and crevices [and] its perched-on-high oven," "just didn't belong" anymore. The "new trend toward kitchen smartness" had made it obsolete.[77] Beginning in the 1970s, however, an oil crisis and emerging concern about the environment were to reawaken interest in the cast-iron cookstove.

10

"Rediscovering the Woodburning Cookstove"

BETWEEN 1930 AND 1970, cast-iron cookstoves largely vanished from the American scene. Although some remained in use and a few were converted into mailboxes, storage cabinets, and planters, most were discarded as junk.[1] Sleeker, faster gas and electric stoves became the norm, with ease of use the key factor in their selection. Cooking convenience, critics charged, had become more important than creativity. "The prebaked biscuit, the frozen fillet, the 'mix,' the bottled dressing, the all but predigested dinner have turned the . . . stove into something like . . . a Bunsen burner" and the woman who used it from an "artist" into a "minor technician," complained Russell Lynes in *The Domesticated Americans* (1957). The "magic of cookery" had disappeared from the nation's kitchens.[2]

In an era of cheap fuel, few Americans were willing to give up gas and electric stoves for the old-fashioned, time- and labor-intensive "magic of cookery." In the 1970s, however, shortages and high prices of Middle Eastern oil, as well as growing concern about the environment, led some people to reconsider. Since then, a small but growing number of enthusiasts has celebrated the joys of cooking with wood stoves. Their efforts were seconded in the late 1990s by entrepreneurs touting the wood-burning cookstove as a sensible investment in family security and independence in anticipation of Y2K.

Renewed interest in the cookstove emerged as increasing numbers of Americans were beginning to weigh the costs of their consumption-oriented lifestyle. In 1977, Wendell Berry reminded readers of *The Unsettling of America* that human beings cannot create energy; "they can only refine or convert it." He contended that "The energy that is made available to us by living things [such as trees]" had been managed better by "'primitive' peasants" than by "scientific experts." In the whole of the country, Berry maintained, only the Amish were "true masters of technology" because they held themselves "aloof from the ambitions of a machine-based society" and thereby escaped "the mainstream American life of distraction, haste, aimlessness, violence, and disintegration."[3]

Arguments such as Berry's, as well as rising utility bills, rekindled interest in wood stoves, especially in the northern states. In January 1978, *Newsweek* reported that 75 percent of Maine residents were using wood for heating. Jotul stoves, imported from Norway, were a popular choice, with more than 25,000 models sold in the state the previous year.[4] In November 1978, *Forbes* called stove production the nation's "newest growth industry," noting that the number of manufacturers had risen from 164 in 1975 to more than 500. Dealers anticipated selling more than 750,000 stoves that year, up from only 100,000 in 1974.[5] By 1980, 6 million Americans were heating with wood.[6] Truly, a "wood-heating revolution" was under way.[7]

Interest in cooking with wood was also redeveloping. Wood cookstoves were no longer "grand artifacts of a bygone era," reported Robert Bobrowski in *Rediscovering the Woodburning Cookstove* (1976). "They are being produced again," he noted, "and the original old models are being reclaimed by the thousands. . . . As I went about the countryside, . . . I discovered a world of people still believing . . . in the superiority of the wood cookstove, though many had converted to gas or oil over the last few decades." But, he found, "many were . . . converting back to wood." Bobrowski recounted as typical the story of Lyndon and Annie Rooks of Wellington, Maine. In 1958, they had replaced the wood grates in their Vernoise cookstove with kerosene wicks so both of them could work outside the home without worrying about periodic stove tending "to keep their pipes from freezing." But the high cost of kerosene in the mid-1970s sent the couple searching for new wood grates and linings, items they finally found at the Portland Stove Foundry outlet in Brewer, fifty miles away.[8]

Bobrowski's hand-lettered text, personalized recipes, and painstaking drawings of everything from stove lid lifters to decorative scrollwork affectionately celebrate the wood cookstove as a revitalized symbol of lost traditions. He was bowled over by the stoves he examined, calling one model "handy and efficient," "beautifully decorative," and "a lovely symbol of plenitude," and applauding another for its "elegance" and "functional ruggedness." Of a Canadian cookstove, he exclaimed, "I was almost knocked off my feet when I first saw it. Its entire surface is nickled, except for the black cook-top and the splash wall, which is covered with hand-painted enamel tiles. The background of the tile design is of the deepest midnight blue and the flowers are in yellows, reds and white. The contrast of the deep blue to the nickel plate is simply exquisite," he marveled.[9]

Bobrowski's praise of cookstoves was also based on personal experience in using them as well as drawing them. In addition to recipes and drawings, he also devoted several pages of his "unorthodox sketchbook of images and information" to instructions about stove operation and maintenance. But he was more concerned with conveying a sense of "the wonderfully solid presence of a wood cookstove, the feeling of social warmth it exudes and the companionable crackle of its fire."[10] His publisher, Chatham Press of Old Greenwich, Connecticut, applauded the appliance's "distinctly dependable and trustworthy aura," "solid bulk," and "reassuring beauty," as well as the "lingering smell of woodsmoke . . . and the warming glow which defrosted toes and dried snowy mittens."[11]

The year after Bobrowski's book appeared, Garden Way Publishing of Charlotte, Vermont, produced Jane Cooper's *Woodstove Cookery: At Home on the Range,* directed at people who believed that "a stove should do more than cook food." Although more instruction manual than sketchbook, this volume, like Bobrowski's, emphasizes the psychological benefits of cooking with a woodstove. "In the past century," Cooper explained in her introduction, "technology has accelerated at a dizzying rate. Scores of machines have replaced the working and thinking of people—and do them better. But some tasks, though they take more effort, offer greater rewards when done in the old-fashioned way. That's how an increasing number of cooks view the wood cookstove." Cooper acknowledged that "compared to the operation of its successors, . . . wood stove cooking is primitive, demanding much more skill and sensitivity from [the] operator." But "many agree there is greater satisfaction in distinguishing between different woods and the kind of fire each produces, rather than which button needs to be pushed for what."[12]

A wood cookstove, Cooper explained, was not a "slave" like modern stoves "programmed to de-frost, simmer, broil, and bake"; it was a "partner." Even better, "as well as fulfilling a functional role, a wood cookstove also appeals to the senses. Well-polished and clean, it is a pleasure to behold. The feel of its heat is soothing and steady, and the expanding metal ticks with contentment." "A kitchen range may not be for everyone," Cooper admitted. "It requires more work, time, attention, and patience than a 'turn-on' stove." But for those "willing to accept the demands of wood cookstoves," she insisted, "the versatility, delicious meals, warmth and beauty more than compensate."[13]

The illustrations in Cooper's book reinforce this message. In sharp contrast to nineteenth-century descriptions, Sherry Streeter's drawings of stove set-up (illus. 10.1) and cleaning (illus. 10.2) suggest that these straightforward and easy tasks promote family togetherness. Once they are completed, the man of the house can sit warming his feet and reading in front of the stove (illus. 10.3) while the family dog sleeps peacefully nearby. His wife, who apparently has little time for such relaxation, enjoys the stove in a different way. She is depicted judiciously tasting a work in progress (illus. 10.4), perhaps a "home-grown tomato soup" or a hearty "Captain's fish chowder."[14]

To fans such as Bobrowski and Cooper, the fact that wood stoves are cumbersome, dirty, and often difficult to manage matters less than their power to evoke

10.1. Drawing of cookstove set-up, by Sherry Streeter. In Jane Cooper, *Woodstove Cookery: At Home on the Range* (Charlotte, Vt.: Garden Way, 1977), 22. Copyright © by Storey Communications, Inc. Reprinted by permission of Storey Books, Pownal, Vt.

10.2. Drawing of a family cleaning a cookstove, by Sherry Streeter. In Jane Cooper, *Woodstove Cookery: At Home on the Range* (Charlotte, Vt.: Garden Way, 1977), 42. Copyright © by Storey Communications, Inc. Reprinted by permission of Storey Books, Pownal, Vt.

(and possibly create) an idyllic domestic environment. Because they already have the cachet of age, antique stoves do this even better than new models, despite the work involved in their restoration. According to Chris Casson Madden, author of *The Kitchen Book* (1993), old stoves have a "timeless quality" that, coupled with their "unique beauty and high-quality workmanship," can make them the "focal point" of any kitchen. Jack Santoro, president of the 500-member Old Appliance Club headquartered in Ventura, California, concurs, noting that old

10.3. Drawing of a man relaxing in front of a cookstove, by Sherry Streeter. In Jane Cooper, *Woodstove Cookery: At Home on the Range* (Charlotte, Vt.: Garden Way, 1977), 58. Copyright © by Storey Communications, Inc. Reprinted by permission of Storey Books, Pownal, Vt.

10.4. Drawing of a woman cooking on a wood stove, by Sherry Streeter. In Jane Cooper, *Woodstove Cookery: At Home on the Range* (Charlotte, Vt.: Garden Way, 1977), 64. Copyright © by Storey Communications, Inc. Reprinted by permission of Storey Books, Pownal, Vt.

cookstoves "are sturdier than newer models—as well as looking so attractive." Clifford Boram, founder of the 500-member Antique Stove Association headquartered in Monticello, Indiana, agrees that old stoves have a special appeal; "the spectacle is the thing," he explains.[15]

There are, of course, risks in buying an old stove. "Steer away from stoves that have been painted," warned Mary Lenore Presper in *The Joys of Woodstoves and Fireplaces* (1980); "that's a sure sign that something is very wrong." Place a lit flashlight inside the firebox to help identify cracks, she advised. Be sure all doors swing smoothly and close tightly. Check the operation of drafts and dampers. What is the condition of the firebox liner? Can the ash drawer be easily accessed? If there is a water reservoir, look for rust or leaks. "Before deciding [on an old stove]," she concluded, "check to see if there is a similar . . . new stove available. You might be better off."[16]

Consumers apparently have not been persuaded to buy new stoves by Presper's reservations about the poor condition of many antique stoves. In 1996, Santoro reported receiving "some 200 letters a week" from individuals interested in acquiring old stoves.[17] Stove restoration experts have built solid businesses across the country, from Thorndike, Maine, to Portland, Oregon. Some adventurous stove lovers have even taken on the daunting task of restoration themselves. In 1976, Anita Craw of Craws' Wood Stoves in Orofino, Idaho, explained the steps involved in choosing and repairing an old stove. Try to look past the "rust, dirt and grease," she suggested. Make sure no parts are missing or, if they are, that they can be replaced. Check for holes in the oven and for cracked or warped plates. Even a stove in poor condition can be fixed, she assured readers of *Wood Stove Cooking Adventures,* but she went on to warn them that "it will take time and lots of work, hard work." She followed this injunction with nine pages of exhaustive instructions on how to disassemble, clean, repair, reassemble, and paint an old stove—concluding with, "DONE??? GOOD! Now sit back and look at your finished work. . . . Isn't it about the prettiest thing you've seen?"[18]

Poet John Engels shares Craw's enthusiasm for stove restoration. In 1997, he recounted his experience with a seventy-year-old cookstove for readers of *Shenandoah.* Despite its poor condition, he was entranced by its promise and willingly spent hours removing a three-inch accumulation of soot. "Once it's clean," he promised himself, "it will be one goddamned glorious / beauty of a stove."[19]

Ironically, contemporary stove enthusiasts such as Engels extol the stoves of the 1880–1930 period in terms strikingly similar to those nineteenth-century stove critics employed in praising the open hearth. In 1988, for example, P. K. Thomajan called the era's stoves "silent, sturdy custodians of . . . family well-being." Ranges, he asserted, had "made Mama feel like queen of the roost," and parlor stoves had encouraged family members to gather "in a way that intensified feelings of togetherness." Such stoves, Thomajan concluded, created "a radiant reality, a happy haven on earth."[20]

According to some stove restorers, this homelike atmosphere can be reproduced even if purchasers of an antique stove do not intend to use it. In 1982, for example, the Bangor, Maine, firm Kitchens by Design advertised reconditioned turn-of-the-century cookstoves by appealing more to sentiment than practicality (illus. 10.5). "Start a Tradition," the headline announced. "Relive an experience your grandparents cherish. Select a beautiful cookstove like the 1896 'Our Clarion,' . . . meticulously restored to its original beauty."[21] The advertisement failed to mention the work involved in using such a stove, presenting it instead as an art object, tastefully accented by roses, decorative ears of corn, a statue of a chicken, and a basket of apples. This stove radiates quaintness; if the items littering its top are not enough, it is surrounded by other symbols of "tradition": an antique clock, a rifle, an earthenware jug, a braided rug, a colorful drawing, and a wreath.

Keokuk Antique Stoves in Hamilton, Illinois, employs a similar sales strategy. According to the firm's home page, antique stoves, those "jewels of yesterday," are a threatened but "integral experience of our heritage." "Enjoy a magnificent piece of history in your office, business, or home," the pitch reads; "live with an antique which will . . . become the focal point of any room." Although the firm promised that all its stoves were "in excellent working condition," function was unimportant. The stoves were "for aesthetic purposes only" and so could be "installed anywhere . . . to simulate the warmth and glow of a hearth of generations ago."[22] Thus, in an inversion of the artifact's original function, a nonworking stove can magically, albeit artificially, evoke the open fireplace.

Whether simulated or real, the "glow" of antique stoves is far from cheap, especially when compared to new electric stoves retailing for $300 to $650.[23] In May 1999, for example, Ed Semmelroth of Tekonsha, Michigan, advertised restored "grand old stoves" ranging in price from $1,850 to $5,000.[24] The same year, the Good Time Stove Company in Goshen, Massachusetts, charged between $2,850 and $7,650 for restored cast-iron and enamel ranges.[25]

Although they are marketed as much for use as for show, new cookstoves designed to resemble antiques are nearly as pricey. Consumers seeking to combine the appearance of early-twentieth-century stoves with modern fuels can find what they are looking for at the Elmira Stove Works in Waterloo, Ontario. "Only the look is old," the company home page announced in 1999. Since the mid-1970s, the firm has been manufacturing "antique styled appliances for

10.5. "Start a Tradition," advertisement for Kitchens by Design, *Maine Life* (May 1982), 7. Courtesy of Kitchens by Design, Bangor, Maine.

kitchens across North America." Seven models were offered in what was cheerfully called the Cook's Delight line, two "all electric," two "all gas," two with gas tops and electric ovens, and one with a combined gas/electric top and an electric oven. The "1850" all-electric model with "cast burners" sold for $3,345; with a "glass smoothtop," it went for $3,745. Several ornamental options were available as well: a "nickelled front skirt" for $100, "nickelled front legs" for $100, and a "nickelled warming shelf" for $50. Buyers interested in a cobalt blue or hunter green "country motif" paid $250 extra. Such a stove satisfies the growing demand "for a modern appliance with the aesthetics of a woodburning range," asserted company founder Tom Hendrick. Nor did the company neglect the needs of consumers who wanted to sustain "antique style" throughout their kitchens; it also offered "matching dishwasher and refrigerator panel kits" as well as a $569 microwave with an "antique styled door."[26]

Heartland Appliances of Kitchener, Ontario, has targeted much the same market. With more than 600 dealers worldwide, the company described itself in 1999 as "North America's leading maker of traditional cooking equipment and the largest manufacturer of woodburning cookstoves on the international scene." Designed to facilitate "the special magic that happens in the kitchen," Heartland's "classic" stoves were available in a wide array of models, fueled by electricity, gas, propane, or wood and enhanced by "lustrous nickel plated trim." Customers had a choice of colors as well, including "modern white," "vibrant red," and "dramatic black," and could pay $300 extra for a Williamsburg Motif splashback. In 1998, base retail prices ranged from $2,795 for a Sweetheart woodburning stove without a water reservoir to $4,895 for a forty-eight-inch gas "self-clean" model.[27]

Heartland entered the stove business in 1925, manufacturing Oval cookstoves still in production. The firm's link to old technologies is a strong selling point. "Heartland continues the woodburning cookstove tradition," company advertising literature announced, "warming hands, stomachs and hearts." "In this age when nothing seems to last, Heartland stands as a charming exception." Both the Oval model, with the "largest oven available on any woodburning stove," and the Sweetheart, with its "4 square feet of cast iron cooking surface," uphold "time-honored traditions . . . of a bygone era." Such a stove, company advertising implied, can strengthen families. One couple who received an Oval cookstove as a wedding present in the 1940s marked their fiftieth anniversary by buying another. Their experience is celebrated as "undeniable proof that a Heartland in the kitchen is a marriage made in heaven."[28]

Syndicated columnist Linda Weltner of Marblehead, Massachusetts, has also discovered that a woodstove can reinforce the bond between wives and husbands. "I love all the rituals we've established around that big black firebox," she explained in 1987, "from collecting shingles for kindling from new houses under construction to keeping the pot on top of the stove filled with water. I love the ease with which I've learned to start a fire, and the whoosh of the bellows in my hand." The stove helped forge a new cooperative relationship between Weltner and her "lumberjack" husband; while he chopped wood and hauled it inside, she started the fire, kept the kindling box full, and emptied the ashes. They derived even more benefit from the stove after the work was over. "The wood stove is our talisman against the winter," she asserted, "a series of small inexplicable miracles." "Sometimes, when my husband and I watch the embers glowing . . . late at night, I think a philosopher might find proof for the existence of God in our woodstove," she concluded.[29]

According to "Stove Black" Richardson, owner of the Good Time Stove Company, the typical buyer of a restored stove is fairly well-to-do, interested in antiques, and plans to use the stove as a supplemental appliance, often in a second home.[30] Acquiring an "antique-styled" stove has become chic in some circles. Actors Dan Aykroyd and Michael Douglas reportedly own Heartland models; race car driver Al Unser and Jerry Junkins, president and chairman of the board of Texas Instruments, have bought restored stoves.[31]

In 1985, actor Keith Carradine explained the attraction of his antique Eureka wood cookstove. It was the "first step in realizing a dream" he had had since childhood: "I had a longing for a simpler time [and entertained] fantasies of tranquil, rural domestic bliss complete with early American furniture, patchwork quilts and . . . homemade bread from the wood stove." When he ran across the Eureka in an antique store in Orem, Utah, he "had no choice" but to buy it. Once set up, he and his wife struggled to learn to operate it, burning many loaves of bread in the process. But, with practice, they collaborated in "a wonderful concert of wood-chopping, flour-mixing, dough-kneading, fire-stoking precision." Carradine philosophized, "I . . . find it reaffirming that in order to bake bread I must first chop wood."[32]

To enthusiasts such as Carradine, the demands of stove use and care pale in comparison to the benefits they receive. Laurie and Craig Samuel of Michigan, proud owners of Baby, an eighty-year-old wood cookstove manufactured by the Copper Clad Malleable Manufacturing Company, conceded that antique stoves are "extremely heavy, and have lots of parts that have to be handled carefully." Moreover, Baby's oven takes at least an hour to heat up to baking temperature, and on cold or windy days the stove tends to smoke. But cooking on Baby is "easy and enjoyable," they reported, "just different, with a little slower rhythm." To others thinking of getting an antique cookstove, they concluded encouragingly, "We . . . know you will enjoy your new friend as much as we do our 'Baby.'"[33]

Dave Ashenbrenner, who uses a Monarch cookstove manufactured in Beaver Dam, Wisconsin, likewise admitted that "a person brought up on electric or gas stoves will run into many problems when first trying a wood cookstove." "There is the ever present danger of fire," he observed, and smoke is a perennial difficulty, even for "veteran stove users." No matter what precautions one takes, he continued, "wood is dirty," and maintaining an even cooking temperature is "almost impossible." In addition, "you have to be near your stove all the time and constantly check the heat." "In spite of all these problems," Ashenbrenner asserted, "I still like the wood cookstove." He enjoys using a "renewable resource" for fuel and notes that the stove minimizes the need for other heating in winter. Even better, "you are . . . your own boss and not at the whim of some oil or electric company." A cookstove, he concluded, "just seems to add character to your kitchen."[34]

The Samuels and Ashenbrenner shared their experiences with readers of the *Countryside and Small Stock Journal,* evidence that the wood cookstove revival is strongest in rural America. In 1993, *Atlanta Journal and Constitution* staff writer Don O'Briant encountered similar devotion to the appliance in a small town in South Carolina. When the firebox of his mother's forty-year-old wood cookstove "disintegrated," his sister called to ask his help in finding a new one. "Now maybe she'll use the electric stove," O'Briant replied. "No," his sister said, "she wants . . . another [wood] stove." O'Briant visited the Crabapple General Store in Roswell, Georgia, but thought prices for new Heartland stoves too steep. He took the bad news to his mother and reflected on her apparently unreasonable insistence on an outdated technology. But as he sat with her around the battered old stove, recalling the "baby chicks tucked behind [it] in cardboard boxes, [the] puppies huddled beside the woodbin, [and the] city visitors . . . drawn to the warmth like moths," he finally understood. "It was not so foolish for my mother to want another antiquated stove," he decided. "In a small town that . . . is . . . becoming homogenized with fast-food franchises, video-rental parlors and Wal-Marts, it was comforting to hang on to a link to a time when the family gathered around the stove instead of the television." The next day, O'Briant's brother-in-law called to report that he had tracked down an antique cookstove costing only $300.[35]

If they were willing to buy new stoves, cookstove devotees like O'Briant's mother had a widening array of options. In 1999, Lehman's Hardware in Kidron, Ohio—established in 1955 to serve "our Amish friends and others seeking a simpler and more self-sufficient lifestyle"—carried "good," "better," and "best" models. The least expensive, the Baker's Choice produced by "Amish tinkerer and machinist Mark Stoll," went for $850 without a reservoir. Customers could also choose from several other basic models: a Mealmaster for $869, a Pioneer Maid for $1,450, an Enterprise King for $1,795, an Enterprise Savoy for $1,895, or a Waterford Stanley for $1,945. Lehman's also offered the Heartland Sweetheart for $2,750 and the Heartland Oval for $3,450. Adding optional shelves, warming closets, reservoirs, or hot-water fixtures increased the cost by several hundred dollars.[36]

Business has evidently been good. "Darrell M" of Granton, Wisconsin, reported that he and his family are "100% pleased" with their Enterprise cookstove, and Melvin Sowards of Greenwich, Ohio, considered his family's Stanley "gorgeous." "A cookstove was something I had always wanted," he continued, "and I have not been at all disappointed." "Kerrie H and Merle D" of Brookport, Illinois, were equally pleased with the cookstove they bought from Lehman's. "We're thrilled," they told the company. "Not only is it beautiful, but it fires great!" Lee and Susan Duff of Maine were just as delighted with their Enterprise Monarch model: "In addition to its utility it is aesthetically pleasing, reminding us of the value of the simple life. Everyone who comes into our house is impressed with its beauty and warmth."[37]

The threat of the Y2K computer "bug" also heightened consumer interest in such stoves. In March 1999, the Louisville, Kentucky, *Courier-Journal* reported that wood cookstoves "are making their first big comeback since the days before rural electrification." When Chris Adams, an employee at Farmer's S&T Hardware in Hyden (population 300), called in an order for more Mealmaster models, he was told that it was the last one on which the manufacturer could guarantee delivery before the end of the year. "People are stocking up," the news account explained, "just in case Y2K creates a need to revive the old ways."[38]

Mike Miller of Buffalo Cove, North Carolina, whose company markets the Todd wood cookstove, reported equally brisk business. "Attention Dealers," his home page announced in May 1999. "These stoves are moving *FAST!!* Better hurry if you want stoves this year." "Dealers throughout the USA and Canada are ordering this product in a frenzy,"[39] Miller stated, but efforts to pin him down about sales figures proved unsuccessful. "We have assigned dealerships in almost every state [but] due to dealer confidentiality we are not at liberty to discuss detailed information of quantity," Miller explained. "Sales are great."[40]

Whether fueled by fear of a Y2K-induced technological calamity or by nostalgic affection for "tranquil, rural domestic bliss," today's cookstove owners experience many of the same struggles as their nineteenth-century predecessors. "I learned the hard way," reported a rural Michigan woman to the Christian Self

Reliance List. "You can't set it at 350° and walk away," she said of her new Enterprise King stove. "The biggest challenge is keeping the oven heat even," she continued, a problem she addressed by turning baking items 180 degrees "halfway through the baking time." "Stay in the kitchen when there is cooking to be done," she warned. "Everything needs to be watched carefully."[41]

Authors of contemporary domestic advice books have given similar guidance to novice cookstove users. "You must watch it like you would a baby," insisted Craw in 1976. "It will demand your attention or the fire will go out."[42] "Your woodstove has its own personality," counseled Andrew Addkison in his 1980 book *Cooking on a Woodburning Stove*. "You cook by instinct, and let the stove have its way."[43] Understanding the characteristics of different types of wood is one of the first things to be mastered. "Different dishes require different intensities of heat," Addkison explained. Ash burns a long time, whereas maple burns more quickly. Black and yellow birch work better than their white and gray cousins.[44] Margaret Byrd Adams was even more specific, providing readers of *American Wood Heat Cookery* (1984) with a table listing BTU and smoke production for apple, ash, beech, yellow birch, cherry, dogwood, hickory, oak, and pecan.[45] According to Lynda Moultrie, author of *The Antique Kitchen Range Bible* (1984), ash and hickory are best for baking, but birch and maple do better for frying or broiling.[46]

Cookstove users also have to learn how to light and maintain fires during the day, bank them overnight, adjust dampers and drafts for efficient heat production, and pinpoint the location of their particular stove's hot and "cool" spots. "Cooking on a wood stove is as much art as science," observed Tom Lippert and Laurel Hilde Lippert in *The Woodstove Cookery Book* (1980), "since we can't simply turn a knob and instantly attain a desired temperature."[47] As was the case in the nineteenth century, baking is the most difficult challenge. According to Addkison, stove-top cooking "will come easily . . . after a few weeks, but working the oven may take more time." "You have to learn to juggle drafts and dampers, doors and lids," he noted, and come to trust your own "good cooking instinct" instead of a timer.[48] Moultrie agreed that baking in a cookstove can be tricky. "You must learn the [oven's] hot spots," she advised. "Most generally the side of the oven closest to the firebox is the hottest." Door-mounted thermometers are not much help because they "only [tell] you how hot the door is, not how hot the oven is." She, too, recommended turning items during baking.[49]

Determining the proper heat for any cooking process is difficult. Addkison recommended time-honored "hand and paper" tests for assessing oven temperature. If a piece of white paper turns "very dark brown," the oven is "right for biscuits;" "if it is dark but not quite brown, you can bake bread and cookies," and if it is "light yellow after 3 to 5 minutes," the oven is safe for "delicate pastries." "The hand test," he went on, "consists of opening the oven door and waving your hand about." If you can stand the heat for twenty seconds, the oven is "hot" (between 400° and 500°); thirty seconds means "moderate" (325° to 375°); and a minute equates to "low" (250° to 350°).[50] Susan Restino suggested a similar technique for evaluating stove-top temperature in *Mrs. Restino's Country Kitchen* (1996). If a piece of bread "burns before toasting," the cook can "sauté, fry, make pancakes, or boil a big pot of water fast." If the bread "toasts nicely," the temperature is right for "simmering, stewing, and steaming," and "if it takes forever and dries out," the heat is only sufficient to keep things warm.[51]

Making temperature adjustments is equally tricky. "Every wood stove has its own idiosyncratic differences," acknowledged the Lipperts. Precise instructions are therefore impossible. "If you want a very hot stove," they explained, "open the damper and draft and maybe even toss a couple pieces of kindling into the firebox. For a slower heat, close the damper and cut off the supply of combustion air by stopping down the draft control. After some experimentation," they concluded, "you will be able to adjust the heat to your liking by fiddling around with your stove's controls and fuel."[52] Phyllis Benham gave similar advice to readers of *Woodstove Cookery* (1981). If the stove surface gets too hot, "close down the draft until the desired temperature is reached," she directed. If the temperature drops too much, "open the draft or add wood, whichever is needed," but beware of a "rip-snorting fire." "Keep your fires under control at all times," she warned. Her technique depended on the use of a "wood stove thermometer, made with a magnet to hold it in place"; such a device, she asserted confidently, "takes any guesswork out of cooking times."[53] Regulating oven temperature is even harder. The door can be opened, but that poses a risk to delicate baked goods exposed to a sudden current of cooler air. Presper suggested adding damp wood to the firebox to cool off an oven, or placing bricks on the oven floor to absorb excess heat.[54]

Contemporary cookstove owners must also deal with the demands of stove maintenance. Ashes should be emptied every week or two, Craw advised, and soot buildup around the oven removed every two to four weeks. For the last task, which so often confounded nineteenth-century stove users, Craw gave directions for making a homemade soot scraper and explained that it had to be used "gently" so that the soot "doesn't fly so much."[55] Presper described a much fuller array of supplies: a hanging worklight or "strong-beamed" flashlight, a "bayonet-handled" wire brush, a soot scraper, an ash shovel, a metal bucket, a vacuum cleaner with a crevice attachment, "lots" of old newspapers, a hammer, a screwdriver, an adjustable wrench, and a can of furnace cement.[56]

To eliminate the need for "blacking," Moultrie recommended painting cookstoves with three to six coats of heat resistant paint. But she went on to point out that vegetable oil should be applied to the stove periodically "to keep it shiny," and she suggested cleaning nickel ornament with metal polish and an old toothbrush, and using a vacuum cleaner to remove ashes and soot from "hard to get at places." "You will be amazed," she concluded cheerfully. "This whole . . . process only takes . . . about half an hour to 45 minutes, and it only needs to be done occasionally. It is not as bad as the horrible oven cleaning in the modern range," she contended, overlooking the increasing availability of stoves with "self-cleaning" ovens. Moultrie also had no objection to the clutter of auxiliary tools cookstoves require, recommending at least two pairs of "heavy mitten [potholders] that go up your arms" ("as they will burn through with use"), plus a lid lifter, soot scraper, grate bolt crank (for shaking down ashes and clinkers), ash pan, coal shovel, fire extinguisher, wood box or coal hod, ash bucket, kindling basket, and perhaps a "little chopping block and a hatchet" for splitting kindling.[57]

Domestic advisors such as Moultrie have argued that cookstove owners are amply compensated for the burdens of stove care. "Why would anyone . . . go back to cooking on a wood . . . stove?" asked Craw. "You have to chop the wood, carry it in, and then carry out the ashes and soot. . . . It is not for all of us," she conceded. But cutting and chopping wood is good exercise, she observed, "as long as we don't overdo it." Cookstove-prepared food also tastes better because the heat surrounds pots more completely and food is cooked "more slowly and evenly." Plus, there are the attractions of additional heat and lower utility bills in winter. "It will take time to learn how to cook and bake on your wood stove," Craw concluded, "but it is really worth it, to learn this art!"[58]

Addkison presented a similar rationale for returning to the cookstove. "You can cut your utility bills in half," he promised. The cookstove will also add "character" and "old-fashioned beauty" to the home, and in winter "there is nothing that can beat the psychological plus of the heat from a wood stove." Moreover, "food tastes better because it cooks for a long time, allowing the ingredients to mingle." He did acknowledge that "Wood cookstoves require some patience and attention, but a little more time and attention to what you are doing might . . . be good for you. Try and think about job pressures while tending a wood stove," he challenged readers; "you can't."[59]

Moultrie likewise admitted that using a cookstove is "not as convenient as pressing buttons," but she insisted that it is "much more rewarding." A cookstove, she asserted, "brings a whole new atmosphere into the home . . . a togetherness that many people lack today." Family members and friends gather around it to review the day's events, while the dog snoozes on a rug in front and the cat curls up underneath. "The world outside goes by at its hustle-bustle pace," Moultrie concluded, "while we are all secure and warm." A cookstove, she maintained, creates "a real feeling of contentment and achievement," and promised, "In no time at all this big black cast iron 'Monster' will become one of your best friends, and actually turn itself into part of the family. As it radiates warmth, comfort, atmosphere, aromas of good things to eat, it has a way of turning a house into a home. Your kitchen range just about comes to life," Moultrie exulted, "and if you have any . . . imagination . . . you can almost picture its four little legs . . . doing a little dance upon the hearth."[60]

In 1997, experienced cookstove user Anne S. Warner aptly summarized the benefits and challenges of cooking with a wood stove for *Country Journal* readers. A cookstove is "like a relative," she explained; "it has a voracious appetite and the ability to perform magnificently, but does pretty much what it damn well pleases. It can make you glow with warmth and affection, scare the stuffing out of you when it really gets going, and make you mad enough to swear and kick." Cooking on a woodstove is, she noted, "an adventure—you [talk] nicely to it, [keep] your fingers crossed and your wits about you." Echoing late-nineteenth-century promoters of the cookstove as a symbol of feminine achievement, Warner contended that "a woman who [reaches] true harmony with her stove [can] turn out the most incredible food ever eaten by man." Such a woman needs "wily ways" to bake successfully in cold or windy weather and to master the trick of "judicious feeding of wood and delicate adjustments of damper and draft to maintain the status quo" in the oven, but her struggle pays handsome dividends. In marked contrast to nineteenth-century stove critics, Warner concluded that stoves bring family members together. The cookstove "demands that all the comfortable chairs face it instead of the television set," she insisted; "it dotes on conversation, popcorn and lingering cups of coffee. . . . You don't have one yet? Well, what are you waiting for?"[61]

Americans contemplating an affirmative response to Warner's question would do well to consider the verdict of the elderly cookstove users interviewed in rural Georgia for *Foxfire's Book of Woodstove Cookery* in the early 1980s. The consensus was that "food is better when it's slow-cooked on a wood stove,"[62] but few of the people consulted were willing to give up modern stoves. Gladys Nichols explained: "Today's way of cookin' . . . is better. . . . I like the electric best 'cause it's so much easier. I'd hate to have to go back to cooking on this wood stove all the time. . . . I couldn't do it. The heat would be a problem."[63] Blanche Harkins pointed out another drawback: "I wouldn't want to have to cook on a wood stove now," she opined. "That wood is messy,"[64] and Lucy York agreed: "I don't believe I'd go back to cooking on a wood stove. I hope that the time won't come when we have to do without electricity. . . . I don't . . . want to go back to those old times because it's a little more convenient to cook this other way. . . . You . . . had to keep watching," she explained. "It wasn't hard but I couldn't get out."[65]

The fact that the cookstove's "rediscovery" has been minimal is due in large part to the constant supervision it requires, a serious inconvenience at a time when more and more women are working outside the home. Even cookstove enthusiasts admit that the appliance demands hard work, unfailing attention, and skills that most Americans no longer possess. Like their nineteenth-century predecessors, many of these enthusiasts do not rely entirely on their woodstoves for cooking. Tracy and Robyn Renner of Lincoln County, Kentucky, for example, use an antique cookstove in the winter, largely because, Robyn explained, "it's . . . a sentimental thing. . . . My grandma used to cook on one." In summer, however, the family resorts to a "modern electric range."[66] Susan Restino has made a similar compromise. Although she considers her Enterprise cookstove "the heart and soul of our existence," she also uses an electric oven. This concession is, however, the only one she has made to modern cooking technology. Microwave ovens, she asserted disdainfully, "are no good for real cooking."[67]

It is probably not coincidental that the "rediscovery" of the cookstove occurred as Americans were coming to terms with the microwave, the ultimate triumph of culinary convenience over creativity. In 1978, fewer than 10 percent of the nation's households had a microwave; in 1995, 87 percent had at least one.[68] In its "heyday," from 1987 to 1990, cookbook authors and food companies deluged consumers with microwave recipes and products. But it turned out that cooking in a microwave was significantly different from cooking with a gas or electric stove. "You have to worry about the dielectric properties of . . . sauces," explained Jim Watkins, president of the company that makes Healthy Choice and other microwave products; "the angles and shapes have to be just right. Food cooks better in a round container than in a square one. No one really knows why. The microwave oven," he concluded, "is still a little bit of a black box." Originally hailed as a "revolutionary cooking tool," the microwave has become instead "primarily a reheating device."[69]

Someday, presumably, the microwave will be improved, then superseded, and finally relegated to antique stores and museums. Contemporary Americans' simultaneous reliance on and frustration with microwaves, as well as their continuing love of the open fireplace and the woodstove, recall the process by which nineteenth-century Americans adjusted to the cast-iron cookstove. At first, the appliance symbolized the beneficent power of technology to improve the quality of life, but it was soon seen in some quarters as evidence of the intrusion of the marketplace into the home. By the end of the nineteenth century, the cookstove was competing with gas, oil, and electric models, and on its way to becoming quaint. At the end of the twentieth century, it reemerged as an emblem of self-reliance and creativity. As the story of the shift from fireplace to cookstove demonstrates, adapting to technological change in the home has never been easy.

Notes

Bibliography

Index

Notes

Abbreviations

    AAS American Antiquarian Society, Worcester, Mass.
    HDL Historic Deerfield Library, Deerfield, Mass.
  NMAH National Museum of American History, Washington, D.C.
  NYHS New York Historical Society, New York, N.Y.
    OSV Old Sturbridge Village, Sturbridge, Mass.

Preface

1. The mechanization of the American home is treated in detail in the following: Ruth Schwartz Cowan, *More Work for Mother: The Ironies of Household Technologies from the Open Hearth to the Microwave* (New York: Basic, 1983); Siegfried Giedion, *Mechanization Takes Command: A Contribution to Anonymous History* (1948; reprint, New York: W. W. Norton, 1969); Mark H. Rose, *Cities of Light and Heat: Domesticating Gas and Electricity in Urban America* (University Park: Pennsylvania State Univ. Press, 1995); and Susan Strasser, *Never Done: A History of American Housework* (New York: Pantheon, 1982).

2. Giedion, 528.

3. Ruth Schwartz Cowan, *A Social History of American Technology* (New York: Oxford Univ. Press, 1997), 194.

4. Cowan, *More Work,* 54.

5. Mary Stranahan Pattison, *Principles of Domestic Engineering* (New York: Trow, 1915), 114.

6. The following works are the only ones I have discovered that deal in a direct and substantive way with this topic: Ruth Schwartz Cowan, "The Consumption Junction: A Proposal for Research Strategies in the Sociology of Technology," in *The Social Construction of Technological Systems,* ed. Wiebe E. Bijker et al. (Cambridge, Mass.: MIT Press, 1987), 261–80; Samuel Y. Edgerton Jr., "Heating Stoves in Eighteenth Century Philadelphia," *Bulletin of the Association for Preservation Technology* 3 (1971): 15–103; Tammis Kane Groft, *Cast with Style: Nineteenth Century Cast-Iron Stoves from the Albany Area* (Albany, N.Y.: Albany Institute of History and Art, 1981); Edwin Jackson, "New England Stoves," *Old Time New England* 26 (1935): 55–64; William J. Keep, "Early American Cooking Stoves," *Old Time New England* 22 (1931): 71–75; Josephine H. Peirce, *Fire on the Hearth: The Evolution and Romance of the Heating Stove* (Springfield, Mass.: Pond-Ekberg, 1951); John G. Waite and Diana S. Waite, "Stove-

makers of Troy, New York," *Antiques* 103 (1973): 136–44; Frank G. White, "Cookstoves: A Cure for Smoking Houses and Scolding Wives," *Early American Life* 26 (Apr. 1995), on-line, Lexis-Nexis, 21 Jan. 1999; Frank G. White, "Stoves in Nineteenth-Century New England," *Antiques* 116 (1979): 592–99; and Lawrence Wright, *Home Fires Burning: The History of Domestic Heating and Cooking* (London: Routledge and Kegan Paul, 1964).

7. Cowan, "Consumption Junction," 279.

1. "Good Living for Those That Love Good Fires"

1. William Cronon, *Changes in the Land: Indians, Colonists, and the Ecology of New England* (New York: Hill and Wang, 1983), 120.

2. John R. Stilgoe, *Common Landscape of America, 1580 to 1845* (New Haven: Yale Univ. Press, 1982), 299.

3. This is the central argument in James Deetz, *In Small Things Forgotten: The Archeology of Early American Life* (Garden City, N.Y.: Anchor, Doubleday, 1977).

4. Richard Hakluyt, "A Discourse Concerning Western Planting," in *Settlements to Society: A Documentary History of Colonial America,* ed. Jack P. Greene (New York: W. W. Norton, 1975), 6.

5. Quoted by David Cressy, *Coming Over: Migration and Communication Between England and New England in the Seventeenth Century* (New York: Cambridge Univ. Press, 1987), 41–42.

6. Lawrence Wright, 63.

7. Charles F. Carroll, *The Timber Economy of Puritan New England* (Providence, R.I.: Brown Univ. Press, 1973), 11; Thomas R. Cox et al., *This Well-Wooded Land: Americans and Their Forests from Colonial Times to the Present* (Lincoln: Univ. of Nebraska Press, 1985), 26.

8. Sumner Chilton Powell, *Puritan Village: The Formation of a New England Town* (Middletown, Conn.: Wesleyan Univ. Press, 1963), 55–56.

9. Quoted by Cressy, 2.

10. Kenneth Silverman, ed., *Colonial American Poetry* (New York: Hafner, 1968), 20.

11. Everett Emerson, ed., *Letters from New England* (Amherst: Univ. of Massachusetts Press, 1976), 21 and 35–36.

12. Karen Ordahl Kupperman, "Climate and Mastery of the Wilderness in Seventeenth-Century New England," in *Seventeenth-Century New England,* ed. David D. Hall and David Grayson Allen (Boston: Colonial Society of Massachusetts, 1984), 3 and 10.

13. Emerson, ed., 215.

14. Emerson, ed., 116.

15. John Winthrop, *History of New England,* 2 vols. (New York: Scribner's, 1908), 2:54.

16. William Wood, *New England's Prospect* (1634; reprint, New York: Da Capo, 1968), 4–5.

17. Michael Wigglesworth, "God's Controversy with New-England," in Silverman, ed., 70.

18. Mather Byles, "To Pictorio, on the Sight of His Pictures," in Silverman, ed., 235.

19. Cressy, 14.

20. Kupperman, 19.

21. John Smith, *Advertisements for the Planters of New-England* (1631; reprint, New York: Da Capo, 1971), 27.

22. Kupperman, 21–24.

23. Kupperman, 25.

24. Kupperman, 30.

25. Cotton Mather, *Diary of Cotton Mather,* 2 vols. (New York: Frederick Ungar, 1957), 1:216.

26. Gary B. Nash, *Red, White, and Black: The Peoples of Early America,* 3rd ed. (Englewood Cliffs, N.J.: Prentice Hall, 1992), 122.

27. Jean Longon and Raymond Cazelles, eds. *Très Riches Heures of Jean, Duke of Berry* (New York: George Braziller, 1989), Pl. 91.

28. Thomas Shepard, *The Works of Thomas Shepard, First Pastor of the First Church, Cambridge, Mass.,* 3 vols. (1853; reprint, New York: AMS, 1967), 1:43.

29. Jonathan Edwards, *Jonathan Edwards: Basic Writings,* ed. Ola E. Winslow (New York: NAL, 1966), 153.

30. Alexander Young, ed. *Chronicles of the First Planters of the Colony of Massachusetts Bay, 1623–1636* (1846; reprint, New York: Da Capo, 1970), 338.

31. Alexander Young, ed., 339.

32. Mather, 1:282–83. For an account of a similar accident, see Elizabeth Drinker, *The Diary of Elizabeth Drinker,* 3 vols., ed. Elaine Forman Crane (Boston: Northeastern Univ. Press), 1991), 1:623.

33. Anne Bradstreet, "The Foure Elements," in *The Complete Works of Anne Bradstreet,* ed. Joseph R. McElrath and Allan P. Robb (Boston: Twayne, 1981), 8–11.

34. Quoted by Lawrence Stone, *The Family, Sex, and Marriage in England, 1500–1800* (New York: Harper and Row, 1977), 221.

35. Stone, 232.

36. This is one of the central arguments in Witold Rybczynski, *Home: A Short History of an Idea* (New York: Viking Penguin, 1986).

37. See, for example, the early-fifteenth-century depiction of the "Holy Family at Supper" in John Plummer, *The Book of Hours of Catherine of Cleves* (New York: Pierpont Morgan Library, 1964), 12.

38. Carra Ferguson O'Meara, "'In the Hearth of the Virginal Womb': The Iconography of the Holocaust in Late Medieval Art," *Art Bulletin* 63, no. 1 (1981), 76.

39. Anne Bradstreet, "The Foure Seasons of the Yeare," in *Complete Works,* 52.

40. Daniel Russell, "An Almanack of Coelestiall Motions For the Year of the Christian Aera," in Silverman, ed., 119.

41. Mather, 1:381.

42. Silverman, ed., 177.

43. Donald E. Stanford, ed., *The Poems of Edward Taylor* (New Haven: Yale Univ. Press, 1960), 89.

44. Emerson, ed., 68.

45. Carole Shammas, "The Domestic Environment in Early Modern England and America," *Journal of Social History* 14, no. 1 (1980), 6–7.

46. Abbott Lowell Cummings, *The Framed Houses of Massachusetts Bay, 1625–1725* (Cambridge, Mass.: Harvard Univ. Press, 1979), 6, 24–25, and 119–21.

47. John P. Demos, *A Little Commonwealth: Family Life in Plymouth Colony* (New York: Oxford Univ. Press, 1970), 64–68; Robert V. Wells, *Revolutions in Americans' Lives: A Demographic Perspective on the History of Americans, Their Families, and Their Society* (Westport, Conn.: Greenwood, 1982), 51.

48. This figure excludes entries, closets, dairies, butteries, cellars, and garrets. Cummings, *Framed Houses,* 216–32.

49. Cummings, *Framed Houses,* 216–32.

50. Abbott Lowell Cummings, ed., *Rural Household Inventories* (Boston: Society for the Preservation of New England Antiquities, 1964), passim.

51. Cummings, ed., *Rural Household Inventories,* 30–31. The median estate value for this period was approximately £480.

52. Cressy, 116–17.

53. Cowan, *More Work,* 21.

54. Childe's inventory does not include a "slice" or "peel" (a long-handled paddle used to place items in and remove them from brick ovens), so it is unlikely his kitchen had a bake oven.

55. Cummings, ed., *Rural Household Inventories,* 8–9.

56. Cummings, ed., *Rural Household Inventories,* 54–57.

57. Even during the eighteenth century, the parlor remained the most common location for a family's best bed. Kevin M. Sweeney, "Furniture and the Domestic Environment in Wethersfield, Connecticut, 1639–1800," in *Material Life in America, 1600–1800,* ed. Robert Blair St. George (Boston: Northeastern Univ. Press, 1988), 276 and 281–82.

58. According to Cummings, by the late seventeenth century "the location of the kitchen was fixed as the large middle room of the lean-to" built onto the back of many New England homes. Cummings, *Framed Houses,* 31.

59. Roasting jacks were rare in New England homes in the colonial period. Only 19 of the 109 room-by-room probate inventories in Cummings, ed., *Rural Household Inventories,* specifically mention jacks. Jack owners were more affluent than average, with a median estate of £1,510 compared to £856 for the whole sample.

60. Diarists in the colonial and early national periods regularly recorded injuries or deaths involving young children who had been scalded by boiling water. See, for example, Abner Sanger, *Very Poor and of a Lo Make: The Journal of Abner Sanger,* ed. Lois K. Stabler (Portsmouth, N.H.: Peter E. Randall, 1986), 396, and Drinker, 2:1271.

2. "So Much of the Comfort of Our Lives Depends on Fire"

1. Richard Hofstadter, *America at 1750: A Social Portrait* (New York: Vintage, Random House, 1971), 5–9.

2. Jack P. Greene, *Pursuits of Happiness: The Social Development of Early Modern British Colonies and the Formation of American Culture* (Chapel Hill: Univ. of North Carolina Press, 1988), 180–82; James Henretta, *The Evolution of American Society, 1700–1815: An Interdisciplinary Analysis* (Lexington, Mass.: D. C. Heath, 1973), 41.

3. J. Hector St. John de Crèvecoeur, *Letters from an American Farmer* (1782; reprint, New York: Dutton, 1957), 40 and 53.

4. Greene, 195.

5. Rybczynski, 20–22.

6. Benjamin Franklin, *An Account of the New Invented Pennsylvania Fire-Places* (1744; reprint, New York: G. K. Hall, 1973), 5–6.

7. Franklin, *Account,* 6.

8. Peirce, *Fire,* 7.

9. Peirce, *Fire,* 12; Edgerton, 16.

10. Franklin, *Account,* 11.

11. Fernand Braudel, *The Structures of Everyday Life: Civilization and Capitalism 15th–18th Century* (New York: Harper and Row, 1981), 299.

12. Franklin, *Account,* 5.

13. Henry J. Kauffman, *The American Fireplace* (Nashville, Tenn.: Thos. Nelson, 1972), 152.

14. Cummings, *Framed Houses,* 122. The fireplace in the "Great Hall" of the Buttolph-Williams House, built in 1692 in Wethersfield, Connecticut, is an early example of the use of a smoke channel. Kauffman, *Fireplace,* 42–43.

15. Henry C. Mercer, *The Bible in Iron: Pictured Stoves and Stoveplates of the Pennsylvania Germans* (Doylestown, Penn.: Bucks County Historical Society, 1961), 89–91. Two of the 109 room-by-room household inventories recorded in rural Suffolk County, Massachusetts, between 1675 and 1775 list firebacks; in both cases, they appear in kitchens. Cummings, ed., *Rural Household Inventories,* 74–75 and 127–29.

16. Cummings, *Framed Houses,* 121; Paul R. Ladd, *Early American Fireplaces* (New York: Hastings House, 1977), 23–24; Frances Phipps, *Colonial Kitchens, Their Furnishings, and Their Gardens* (New York: Hawthorn, 1972), 94.

17. Mary Earle Gould, *The Early American House* (Rutland, Vt.: Charles E. Tuttle, 1965), 67.

18. Cummings, ed., *Rural Household Inventories,* passim.

19. Kauffman, *Fireplace,* 52 and 68. Photographs of mid-eighteenth-century American fireplaces with splayed sides are included in Kauffman, *Fireplace,* 83, 95, 96, 101, 103, 104, 107, 114, 116, and 117.

20. Franklin, *Account,* 6.

21. Kauffman, *Fireplace,* 49–50; Cummings, *Framed Houses,* 178–82 and 188–89.

22. Cummings, ed., *Rural Household Inventories,* passim.

23. Cummings, ed., *Rural Household Inventories,* 257–60. The designation "principal room" includes all spaces described as "rooms" or "chambers," plus halls, parlors, studies, and kitchens. It excludes cellars, dairies, butteries, garrets, shops, closets, and entries.

24. Peirce, *Fire,* 31.

25. Quoted by Georges Duby, ed., *A History of Private Life: Revelations of the Medieval World* (Cambridge, Mass.: Harvard Univ. Press, 1988), 499–500.

26. Quoted by Braudel, 301.

27. Norman J. G. Pounds, *Hearth and Home: A History of Material Culture* (Bloomington: Indiana Univ. Press, 1989), 197–98.

28. Johann Amos Comenius, *Orbis Sensualium Pictus* (1658; reprint, Detroit: Singing Tree, 1968), 89.

29. Fynes Moryson, *An Itinerary* (1617; reprint, New York: Da Capo, 1971), part 3, 77.

30. Peter Mundy, *The Travels of Peter Mundy in Europe and Asia, 1608–1667,* 4 vols., ed. Richard C. Temple (London: Hakluyt Society, 1907–25), 4:110.

31. Moryson, 3:77.

32. Mundy, 4:110–11.

33. Lawrence Wright, 135–36.

34. Quoted by Edgerton, 16.

35. John Winthrop, *Papers,* 5 vols. (Boston: Massachusetts Historical Society, 1929–1947), 5:140.

36. Peirce, *Fire,* 33.

37. Samuel Sewall, *The Diary of Samuel Sewall*, 2 vols., ed. M. Halsey Thomas (New York: Farrar, Straus and Giroux, 1973), 2:460–61 and 2:560.

38. Mercer, 30.

39. Cummings, ed., *Rural Household Inventories*, 114–20. The median value for the inventories recorded between 1720 and 1740 was £1,308.8.0. Cummings, ed., *Rural Household Inventories*, 99–125.

40. Cummings, ed., *Rural Household Inventories*, 124–25.

41. Mercer, 47.

42. Peirce, *Fire*, 33–38. A stove may have been installed as early as 1730 in the meetinghouse in Hadley, Massachusetts, but the evidence is inconclusive. Sylvester Judd, *History of Hadley, Including the Early History of Hatfield, South Hadley, Amherst, and Granby, Massachusetts* (Springfield, Mass.: H. R. Huntting, 1905), 315.

43. Peirce, *Fire*, 32.

44. Quoted by Peirce, *Fire*, 91.

45. John F. Watson, *Annals of Philadelphia and Pennsylvania in the Olden Time*, 2 vols. (Philadelphia: Elijah Thomas, 1857), 2:34.

46. Peter Kalm, *Peter Kalm's Travels in North America*, 2 vols., trans. and ed. Adolph B. Benson (New York: Dover, 1966), 2:416–20.

47. Kalm, 2:420.

48. Mercer, 28–31; Arthur C. Bining, *Pennsylvania Iron Manufacture in the Eighteenth Century* (Harrisburg: Pennsylvania Historical and Museum Commission, 1979), 23 and 39–40.

49. Franklin, *Account*, 11–13.

50. Kalm, 2:652–53.

51. Gunther Moltmann, ed., *Germans to America: 300 Years of Immigration, 1683–1983* (Stuttgart, Germany: Institute for Foreign Cultural Relations, 1982), 9.

52. Quoted in Benjamin Franklin, *The Papers of Benjamin Franklin*, 27 vols., edited by Leonard W. Labaree and William B. Willcox. New Haven: Yale Univ. Press, 1959–88), 4:120.

53. Franklin, *Papers*, 4:120–21, 4:234, and 4:485.

54. Johann David Schoepf, *Travels in the Confederation*, 2 vols., trans. and ed. Alfred J. Morrison (New York: Bergman, 1968), 1:103–4.

55. Schoepf, 1:36–37.

56. Schoepf, 1:221.

57. Kalm, 1:239.

58. Schoepf, 1:132.

59. Cronon, 120–21; Howard S. Russell, *A Long, Deep Furrow: Three Centuries of Farming in New England* (Hanover, N.H: Univ. Press of New England, 1982), 97.

60. Kalm, 1:239.

61. Schoepf, 1:38.

62. Michael Williams, *Americans and Their Forests: A Historical Geography* (Cambridge, England: Cambridge Univ. Press, 1989), 78.

63. Howard S. Russell, 93–94.

64. Franklin, *Account*, 1.

65. Quoted by Cronon, 113.

66. Quoted by Gary B. Nash, *The Urban Crucible: Social Change, Political Consciousness, and the Origins of the American Revolution* (Cambridge, Mass.: Harvard Univ. Press, 1979), 448.

67. Franklin, *Account,* 1.

68. Kalm, 1:50–51 and 2:656.

69. Franklin, *Account,* title page and 2.

70. Schoepf, 1:60.

71. Franklin, *Papers,* 2:420.

72. Franklin, *Account,* 13–26.

73. Schoepf, 1:61.

74. Franklin, *Account,* 27.

75. Franklin, *Account,* 27.

76. Kalm, 2:654.

77. Quoted by Franklin, *Papers,* 2:419.

78. Franklin, *Papers,* 2:419.

79. Franklin, *Papers,* 2:419–20.

80. Edgerton, 22.

81. Franklin, *Papers,* 2:420.

82. Kalm, 2:654.

83. Peirce, *Fire,* 40–41.

84. Edgerton, 22.

85. Hugh Roberts, letter to Benjamin Franklin, 27 Nov. 1765, in Franklin, *Papers,* 12: 386–87.

86. Kalm, 2:654.

87. Billy G. Smith, *The "Lower Sort": Philadelphia's Laboring People, 1750–1800* (Ithaca, N.Y.: Cornell Univ. Press, 1990), 101 and 104–5.

88. Nash, *Urban Crucible,* 251.

89. *Pennsylvania Gazette,* 1 Jan. 1760, 2.

90. Billy G. Smith, 106.

91. Bining, 139–44; J. Lawrence Pool, *America's Valley Forges and Furnaces* (Dalton, Mass.: Studley, 1982), 65.

92. W. David Lewis, *Iron and Steel in America* (Greenville, Del.: Hagley Museum, 1976), 16.

93. Bining, 67–68 and 83–84.

94. Stilgoe, 293; Bining, 63–64.

95. Mercer, 86.

96. Mercer, 44–47.

97. Peirce, *Fire,* 94.

98. Mercer, 86.

99. Keep, "Early American Cooking Stoves," 71–75.

100. Edgerton, 69.

101. The ledger of the Elizabeth Furnace for 1771–72 notes that six-plate stoves weighed between 249 and 448 pounds; the smallest ten-plate stove weighed 560 pounds, and the largest 626 pounds. Edgerton, 68.

102. Peirce, *Fire,* 38.

103. Joan M. Jensen, *Loosening the Bonds: Mid-Atlantic Farm Women, 1750–1850* (New Haven: Yale Univ. Press, 1986), 218.

104. *The Arts and Crafts in New York, 1726–1776* (New York: New York Historical Society, 1938), 213–14.

105. *Pennsylvania Gazette,* 11 June 1761, 4.

106. *Pennsylvania Gazette,* 22 Nov. 1780, 4.

107. Peirce, *Fire,* 38.

108. *Arts and Crafts in New York, 1726–1776,* 204 and 213–14.

109. Peirce, *Fire,* 143–47; Edgerton, 27.

110. *Pennsylvania Gazette,* 1 Nov. 1764, 3.

111. Edgerton, 26 and 82.

112. Edgerton, 68.

113. Josephine H. Peirce, "Stoves in the Henry Ford Museum and Greenfield Village, Dearborn, Michigan," typescript (Leicester, Mass., 1955), AAS, 4.

114. Billy G. Smith estimated that "laborers" in Philadelphia earned 3.8s per day in 1762, and Paul F. Paskoff found that unskilled woodcutters at Pennsylvania ironworks earned 6.7s per day in 1773. Billy G. Smith, 233; Paul F. Paskoff, *Industrial Evolution: Organization, Structure, and Growth of the Pennsylvania Iron Industry, 1750–1860* (Baltimore: Johns Hopkins Univ. Press, 1983), 13.

115. Alice Hanson Jones, *American Colonial Wealth: Documents and Methods* (New York: Arno, 1977), passim. Inventories not listing household furnishings are excluded.

116. The median net worth of Pennsylvania stove owners was £286; of non-stove owners, it was £212. One-third of decedents residing in Philadelphia County and 27.6 percent of those living in Northampton and Westmoreland Counties owned stoves. Alice Hanson Jones, passim.

117. Alice Hanson Jones, 165–68.

118. By comparison, his table was worth only 5s and his chairs 2s each. Alice Hanson Jones, 73–74.

119. Alice Hanson Jones, 190–98.

120. Alice Hanson Jones, passim. Inventories not listing household furnishings are excluded.

121. Evangeline W. Andrews, ed., *Journal of a Lady of Quality* (New Haven: Yale Univ. Press, 1923), 144–45.

122. Drinker, 1:251–53.

123. Schoepf, 1:60.

3. "The Art of Economizing Fuel"

1. This is one of the central arguments in Nathan O. Hatch, *The Sacred Cause of Liberty: Republican Thought and the Millennium in Revolutionary New England* (New Haven: Yale Univ. Press, 1977), and in Ernest Lee Tuveson, *Redeemer Nation: The Idea of America's Millennial Role* (Chicago: Univ. of Chicago Press, 1968).

2. Henretta, 189–90.

3. Schoepf, 2:99.

4. Timothy Dwight, "Greenfield Hill," in *The Major Poems of Timothy Dwight,* ed. William J. McTaggart and William K. Bottorff (Gainesville, Fla.: Scholars' Facsimiles, 1969), 520–21.

5. Edgerton, 15.

6. Tench Coxe, *A View of the United States* (1794; reprint, New York: Augustus M. Kelley, 1965), 10.

7. Dwight, *Major Poems,* 487–88.

8. Quoted by Cronon, 114.

9. Billy G. Smith, 101.

10. Thomas Cooper, *Some Information Respecting America* (1794; reprint, New York: Augustus M. Kelley, 1969), 50. On 3 Oct. 1794, Elizabeth Drinker of Philadelphia noted in her journal that she had paid £1.2.6 for half a cord of hickory, the equivalent of $7.34 per cord. Drinker, 1:601.

11. Charles William Janson, *The Stranger in America, 1793–1806* (1807; reprint, New York: Burt Franklin, 1971), vi and 61.

12. Thomas P. Cope, *Philadelphia Merchant: The Diary of Thomas P. Cope, 1800–1851,* ed. Eliza Cope Harrison (South Bend, Ind.: Gateway, 1978), 175.

13. Thomas Robbins, *Diary of Thomas Robbins, D.D., 1796–1854,* 2 vols., ed. Increase N. Tarbox (Boston: Beacon Press, 1886–87), 1:385.

14. Cope, 304.

15. *Transactions of the American Philosophical Society* 4 (1799), v. Quoted by Edgerton, 87.

16. *A List of Patents Granted by the United States from April 10, 1790 to December 31, 1836* (Washington, D.C.: Government Printing Office, 1872), passim. Thirty-two of these fifty-eight patents (55.2 percent) were granted to residents of New York or New England.

17. In 1794, Thomas Cooper noted that "remote from the great towns," hickory sold for just $1.50 a cord. Cooper, 50.

18. Henri L. Bourdin et al., eds., *Sketches of Eighteenth Century America: More "Letters from an American Farmer"* (New Haven: Yale Univ. Press, 1925), 144.

19. Louis C. Jones, ed., *Growing Up in the Cooper Country: Boyhood Recollections of the New York Frontier* (Syracuse, N.Y.: Syracuse Univ. Press, 1965), 44; Schoepf, 1:198.

20. Richard Beeman, *The Evolution of the Southern Backcountry: A Case Study of Lunenburg County, Virginia, 1746–1832* (Philadelphia: Univ. of Pennsylvania Press, 1984), 40.

21. Sanger, 335–95.

22. Sanger, 337.

23. Sanger's entry for 8 Feb. 1781 reads in part, "I have a jag, about one-half cord, to carry home at night." Sanger, 41.

24. Sanger, 339 and 343.

25. Sanger, 337, 368, and 390.

26. Sanger, 345, 354, 375, and 387.

27. Janson, 61.

28. A. William Hoglund, "Forest Conservation and Stove Inventors, 1789–1850," *Forest History* 5 (1962), 5.

29. Benjamin Franklin, letter to James Bowdoin, 2 Dec. 1758, in Franklin, *Papers,* 8:194–96.

30. Franklin, letter to Sir Alexander Dick, 21 Jan. 1762, in Franklin, *Papers,* 10:14–16.

31. National Park Service, *Benjamin Franklin's "Good House"* (Washington, D.C.: Government Printing Office, 1981), 23–26.

32. Franklin, letter to Deborah Franklin, 4 June 1765, in Franklin, *Papers,* 12:167.

33. C. W. Peale and Raphaelle Peale, "Description of Some Improvements in the Common Fire-Place" (17 Mar. 1797), in *The Selected Papers and Letters of Charles Willson Peale and His Family,* 2 vols., ed. Lillian B. Miller (New Haven: Yale Univ. Press, 1988), 2:192; C. W. Peale, letter, *Weekly Magazine* (Mar. 1798), in Lillian B. Miller, ed., 2:209.

34. C. W. Peale, letter, in Lillian B. Miller, ed., 2:209–10.

35. C. W. Peale and Raphaelle Peale, "Description of Some Improvements," in Lillian B. Miller, ed., passim; C. W. Peale, letter, *Weekly Magazine* (Mar. 1798), in Lillian B. Miller, ed., 2:192–96 and 211; Edgerton, 86.

36. C. W. Peale, letter, *Weekly Magazine,* in Lillian B. Miller, ed., 2:212–13.

37. C. W. Peale, letter, *Weekly Magazine,* in Lillian B. Miller, ed., 2:214.

38. Lawrence Wright, 113–14; Rybczynski, 131; Edgerton, 95.

39. Benjamin Thompson (Count Rumford), "On the Construction of Kitchen Fireplaces and Kitchen Utensils" (1799–1800), in *The Complete Works of Count Rumford,* 4 vols. (Boston: American Academy of Arts and Sciences, 1875), 3:177. For illustrations of Rumford kitchen installations in Europe, see Thompson, 3:203, 3:213, 3:216, and 3:219.

40. C. W. Peale, letter to Thomas Jefferson, 3 Mar. 1801, in Lillian B. Miller, ed., 2:300–302.

41. C. W. Peale, letter to Jefferson, in Lillian B. Miller, ed., 2:302.

42. C. W. Peale, letter to Raphaelle Peale, 7 Sept. 1805, in Lillian B. Miller, ed., 2:885; Pennsylvania Hospital Testimonial, 23 Nov. 1805, in Lillian B. Miller, ed., 2:912.

43. Edwin Morris Betts, ed., *Thomas Jefferson's Farm Book* (Charlottesville: Univ. Press of Virginia, 1976), 84.

44. Sarah Anna Emery, *Reminiscences of a Nonagenarian* (Newburyport, Mass.: William H. Huse, 1879), 108.

45. Probate inventory of Jonathan Jackson, Suffolk County, Massachusetts, 1810, no. 23493 (microfilm, OSV).

46. Wright & Barkman, bills to Judith Riddell, 6 Feb.–20 Mar. 1810, J. Hall Pleasants Papers, Maryland Historical Society. Quoted by Robert L. Alexander, "The Riddell-Carroll House in Baltimore," *Winterthur Portfolio* 28 (1993), 130–31.

47. Jane C. Nylander, *Our Own Snug Fireside: Images of the New England Home, 1760–1860* (New York: Knopf, 1993), 218.

48. Asher Benjamin, *The American Builder's Companion* (1827; reprint, New York: Dover, 1969), 112.

49. C. W. Peale, letter to Jefferson, in Lillian B. Miller, ed., 2:302.

50. Nylander, *Snug Fireside,* 218.

51. Quoted by Elisabeth Donaghy Garrett, *At Home: The American Family, 1750–1870* (New York: Harry N. Abrams, 1990), 101.

52. C. W. Peale, letter to Jefferson, in Lillian B. Miller, ed., 2:302. This observation is also based on my own experience using Rumford-style set kettles in the kitchen of the 1830 Brick Dwelling at Hancock Shaker Village, Pittsfield, Mass.

53. *List of Patents,* passim.

54. *The Arts and Crafts in New York, 1777–1799* (New York: New York Historical Society, 1954), 261.

55. *The Arts and Crafts in New York, 1800–1804* (New York: New York Historical Society, 1965), 418–19.

56. Quoted by Edgerton, 82.

57. John Adams, letter to Abigail Adams, 7 Feb. 1777, in *Adams Family Correspondence,* ed. L. H. Butterfield (Cambridge, Mass.: Harvard Univ. Press, 1963), 2:155.

58. Nancy Shippen, *Nancy Shippen: Her Journal Book,* ed. Ethel Armes (Philadelphia: J. B. Lippincott, 1935), 176.

59. C. W. Peale, letter, *Weekly Magazine,* in Lillian B. Miller, ed., 2:211.

60. According to Samuel Edgerton, the "Rittenhouse stove" was developed by either David Rittenhouse, the well-known scientist, or his brother Benjamin. Edgerton, 25.

61. Moreau de St. Mery, *Moreau de St. Mery's American Journey,* trans. and ed. Kenneth Roberts and Anna M. Roberts (Garden City, N.Y.: Doubleday, 1947), 326.

62. George Washington, letters to Clement Biddle, 21 Aug. and 15 Oct. 1797, in *The Writings of George Washington,* 39 vols., ed. John C. Fitzpatrick (Washington, D.C.: Government Printing Office, 1941), 36:15–16 and 36:47.

63. Betts, ed., 84.

64. Henry Vanderlyn, Diary (Oxford, N.Y.), 1827–1857, 3 Oct. 1829, NYHS.

65. Franklin, "Notes on Colds," in Franklin, *Papers,* 20:533.

66. Edgerton, 85.

67. Franklin, letter to Jacques Barbeu-Dubourg, 22 Jan. 1773, in Franklin, *Papers,* 20:25–26.

68. Edgerton, 85.

69. C. W. Peale, "The Improved Brick Stoves at Peale's Museum," *Aurora* (26 Jan. 1796), in Lillian B. Miller, ed., 2:140–41; C. W. Peale, letter, *Weekly Magazine* (Mar. 1798), in Lillian B. Miller, ed., 2:213.

70. C. W. Peale, "Description of a Stove," *Weekly Magazine* (21 July 1798), in Lillian B. Miller, ed., 2:218–20; C. W. Peale, letter to Rembrandt and Rubens Peale, 12 Dec. 1802, in Lillian B. Miller, ed., 2:472.

71. John D. Tyler, "Technological Development: Agent of Change in Style and Form of Domestic Iron Castings," in *Technological Innovation and the Decorative Arts,* ed. Ian M. G. Quimby and Polly Anne Earl (Charlottesville: Univ. Press of Virginia, 1973), 158–61; George Schuhmann, "Iron and Steel," *The Pilot* (1906), reprinted in "Iron and Steel," Society for Industrial Archeology Data Sheet No. 4 (Washington, D.C.: National Museum of American History, 1984), 1; Edgerton, 67–68; Kauffman, *Early American Ironware* (Rutland, Vt.: Charles E. Tuttle, 1966), 37–38.

72. *Arts and Crafts in New York, 1800–1804,* 234–35.

73. Edgerton, 63.

74. "Observations on the Effect of Close and Open Fire Places," *The Diary; or Loudon Register* (10 Oct. 1792), in *Arts and Crafts in New York, 1777–1799,* 187.

75. Dwight, *Major Poems,* 485, 398, and 379–80.

76. Edgerton, 44.

77. Peirce, "Stoves," 4.

78. Advertisement for Pyramidal Stoves, 7 Nov. 1801, in *Arts and Crafts in New York, 1800–1804,* 234–35; George Worrall, advertisement for Improved Patent Stoves, *Pennsylvania Gazette,* 6 Oct. 1813, 4.

79. Edgerton, 82.

80. Milo M. Naeve, *John Lewis Krimmel: An Artist in Federal America* (Newark: Univ. of Delaware Press, 1987), 74.

81. Louis C. Jones, ed., 29.

82. "Domestic Journal of Important Occurrences" (New Lebanon, N.Y., 1780–1860), 21 Dec. 1793, Shaker Collection, Western Reserve Historical Society, Cleveland, Ohio, V B 60.

83. William Bentley, *The Diary of William Bentley,* 4 vols. (1905; reprint, Gloucester, Mass.: Peter Smith, 1962), 2:150–51.

84. Tennie Gaskill Toussaint, "Danville—and Its Two Centuries," *Vermont History* 23 (1955), 207.

85. Silas Farmer, *History of Detroit and Wayne County and Early Michigan* (1890; reprint, Detroit: Gale, 1969), 470.

86. Bentley, 4:499.

87. Edgerton, 64.

88. Edgerton, 80.

89. Quoted by Peirce, *Fire,* 174.

90. Bentley, 3:494 and 4:499.

91. *History of Worcester County, Massachusetts,* 2 vols. (Boston: C. F. Jewett, 1879), 2:337.

92. Samuel G. Goodrich, *Recollections of a Lifetime,* 2 vols. (New York: Miller, Orton and Mulligan, 1857), 1:134–36. The story of the stove opponent who complained about the heat from a new meetinghouse stove only to find that no fire had been lit became part of New England folklore. Similar tales are repeated in Frank Smith, *A History of Dover, Massachusetts, as a Precinct, Parish, District, and Town* (Dover, Mass.: by the town, 1897), 69, and in Josiah H. Temple, *History of the Town of Whately, Mass., Including a Narrative of the Leading Events from the First Planting of Hatfield, 1660–1871* (Boston: T. R. Marvin and Son, 1872), 304. Robert Cray reports that the same story appears in histories of Litchfield and Greenwich, Connecticut, and Newburyport, Massachusetts. Cray, "Heating the Meeting: Pro-Stove and Anti-Stove Dynamic in Church Polity, 1783–1830," *Mid-America* 76 (1994), 105–6.

93. Thomas Robbins, 1:879 and 1:882. Robbins recorded his contribution to the meeting-house stoves on 6 Jan. 1826, 2:1.

94. Dennis Donovan and Jacob A. Woodward, *The History of the Town of Lyndeborough, New Hampshire, 1735–1905,* 2 vols. (Lyndeborough, N.H.: by the town, 1906), 1:295–96. Quoted by Cray, 102.

95. Cray, 107.

96. Levi Woodbury, "Levi Woodbury's Week in Vermont, May 1819," *Vermont History* 34 (1966), 52. Quoted by Nylander, "Toward Comfort and Uniformity in New England Meeting Houses, 1750–1850," in *New England Meeting House and Church: 1630–1850,* ed. Peter Benes (Boston: Boston Univ., 1979), 88.

97. Betts, ed., 83.

98. Probate inventory of Martha Saunders Salisbury, 12 Dec. 1792, Salisbury Family Papers, AAS.

99. Probate inventories for Hampshire and Worcester Counties, Massachusetts, for 1810 are available on microfilm at the Rockefeller Library, Brown University, Providence, R.I.

100. Probate inventories for Suffolk County, Massachusetts, for 1810 are available on microfilm at OSV; probate inventories for Providence County, Rhode Island, for 1810 are in the City Archives, City Hall, Providence, R.I.

101. Jensen, 220.

102. Margaret Bayard Smith, letter to Jane Bayard Kirkpatrick, 6 Dec. 1805, in Gaillard Hunt, ed., *The First Forty Years of Washington Society in the Family Letters of Margaret Bayard Smith* (1906; reprint, New York: Frederick Ungar, 1965), 48.

103. "An Essay on Warming Rooms" (1796), quoted by Bining, 86.

4. "A Great Variety of Stoves Just Received"

1. Stuart Bruchey, *The Roots of American Economic Growth, 1607–1861* (New York: Harper and Row, 1968), 74–75.

2. Edward Pessen, *Jacksonian America: Society, Personality, and Politics* (Urbana: Univ. of Illinois Press, 1985), 102.

3. Charles Sellers, *The Market Revolution: Jacksonian America, 1815–1846* (New York: Oxford Univ. Press, 1991), 41–44.

4. Cowan, "Consumption Junction," 263.

5. Jean V. Matthews, *Toward a New Society: American Thought and Culture, 1800–1830* (Boston: Twayne, 1991), 125.

6. John F. Kasson, *Civilizing the Machine: Technology and Republican Values in America, 1776–1900* (New York: Penguin, 1977), 41. For a similar argument, see Jennifer Clark, "The American Image of Technology from the Revolution to 1840," *American Quarterly* 39 (1987), 446.

7. Timothy Walker, "Defence of Mechanical Philosophy," *North American Review* 31 (1831), in *The Philosophy of Manufactures: Early Debates over Industrialization in the United States,* ed. Michael Brewster Folsom and Steven D. Lubar (Cambridge, Mass.: MIT Press, 1982), 298.

8. Ralph Waldo Emerson, *The Journals and Miscellaneous Notebooks of Ralph Waldo Emerson,* 14 vols., edited by William H. Gilman et al. (Cambridge, Mass.: Harvard Univ. Press, 1960–82), 4:65.

9. Goodrich, *Recollections,* 2:533.

10. *List of Patents,* passim; M. D. Leggett, comp., *Subject Matter Index of Patents for Inventions Issued by the United States Patent Office from 1790 to 1873, Inclusive,* 3 vols. (Washington, D.C.: Government Printing Office, 1874), 3:1459–86.

11. *Report of the Commissioner of Patents* (Washington, D.C.: Government Printing Office, 1845), 514.

12. *List of Patents,* passim; Leggett, comp., 3:1459–86.

13. John Pintard, letter to Eliza Pintard Davidson, 4 Feb. 1832, in *Letters from John Pintard to His Daughter,* 4 vols. (New York: New York Historical Society, 1941), 4:12–13.

14. *Historical Statistics of the United States: Colonial Times to 1957* (Washington, D.C.: Government Printing Office, 1960), 115–16.

15. *Niles' Weekly Register* 13 (30 Sept. 1817), 75.

16. Frances Trollope, *The Domestic Manners of the Americans* (1832; reprint, London: Century, 1984), 121.

17. *Memoirs of the Philadelphia Society for Promoting Agriculture* (Philadelphia, 1814), 3:141. Quoted by Frederick Moore Binder, *Coal Age Empire: Pennsylvania Coal and Its Utilization to 1860* (Harrisburg: Pennsylvania Historical and Museum Commission, 1974), 7.

18. H. Benjamin Powell, *Philadelphia's First Fuel Crisis: Jacob Cist and the Developing Market for Pennsylvania Anthracite* (University Park: Pennsylvania State Univ. Press, 1978), 60.

19. Pintard, letter to Eliza Pintard Davidson, 17 Feb. 1831, in *Letters,* 3:223.

20. *Historical Statistics,* 124.

21. *Niles' Weekly Register* 29 (22 Oct. 1825), 117.

22. J. Griscom, "Remarks upon the Coal Formation of the Susquehannah and Lackawannock," *New England Farmer* 3 (4 Feb. 1825), 220.

23. Benjamin Silliman, "Anthracite Coal of Pennsylvania, &c. Remarks upon Its Properties and Economical Uses," *American Journal of Science and Arts* 10 (1826), 331, 338, and 343–44.

24. Robert Roberts, *The House Servant's Directory* (1827; reprint, Waltham, Mass.: Gore Place Society, 1977), 161–62.

25. Denison Olmsted, "Observations on the Use of Anthracite Coal," in *The American Almanac and Repository of Useful Knowledge for the Year 1837* (Boston: Chas. Bowen, 1837), 61.

26. *Journal of the Franklin Institute,* n.s., 15 (Jan. 1835), 28.

27. *Journal of the Franklin Institute,* n.s., 8 (Dec. 1831), 2–3.

28. Leggett, comp., 3:1459–86.

29. Cox et al., 64.

30. A. F. M. Willich, *The Domestic Encyclopedia; Or, A Dictionary of Facts and Useful Knowledge Chiefly Applicable to Rural and Domestic Economy,* 3 vols. (Philadelphia: Abraham Small, 1821), 3:284.

31. Lydia Maria Child, letter to Convers Francis, 22 Dec. 1838, in *Lydia Maria Child: Selected Letters, 1817–1880,* ed. Milton Meltzer and Patricia G. Holland (Amherst: Univ. of Massachusetts Press, 1982), 102.

32. *New Genesee Farmer, and Gardener's Journal* 3 (Nov. 1842), 173.

33. Mrs. A. F. M. Annan, "Mr. Chancy's Cooking Stove," *Godey's Lady's Book* 24 (Feb. 1842): 99–102.

34. Annan, 102–4.

35. *Journal of the Franklin Institute,* n.s., 10 (Nov. 1832), 324.

36. *Journal of the Franklin Institute,* n.s., 15 (Feb. 1835), 105.

37. *Report of the Commissioner of Patents* (1845), 514.

38. Keep, "Early American Cooking Stoves," 78.

39. James Wilson, letter to Morse & Son, 6 Apr. 1839, Misc. Mss. Wilson, James, NYHS.

40. *Argus Spectator,* 28 Jan. 1837. Quoted by Nylander, *Snug Fireside,* 215–16.

41. *Journal of the Franklin Institute,* n.s., 6 (Aug. 1830), 75.

42. See advertisement for Hervey Sadd's cookstove, *Connecticut Courant,* 26 Oct. 1819, 3; description of William Naylor's "alterable" stove, *Journal of the Franklin Institute,* n.s., 4 (Sept. 1829), 180–81; description of Peter Sanburn's Fireplace Furnace, *Journal of the Franklin Institute,* n.s., 4 (Sept. 1829), 186; description of Thomas Woolson's combination fireplace/cookstove, *Journal of the Franklin Institute,* n.s., 9 (Jan. 1832), 47; advertisement for H. B. Smith's Franklin cookstove, *Hartford Times,* 17 Aug. 1835, 4; and advertisement for Douglas' Patent Stove, *New England Farmer* 14 (10 Feb. 1836), 243.

43. *Providence Journal,* 1 Dec. 1829, 3.

44. *Journal of the Franklin Institute,* n.s., 4 (Dec. 1829), 400.

45. See J. & S. Pierce, advertisement, *Greenfield Gazette and Franklin Herald,* 18 Nov. 1834, 4.

46. Sophie E. Eastman, *In Old South Hadley* (Chicago: Blakely, 1912), 173.

47. *Journal of the Franklin Institute,* 3rd ser., 1 (Feb. 1841), 100–101.

48. *New Hampshire Patriot and Gazette,* 12 Oct. 1819. Quoted by Nylander, *Snug Fireside,* 214.

49. *Providence Journal,* 30 Nov. 1833, 4.

50. *Providence Journal,* 29 Oct. 1838, 1.

51. Francis H. Underwood, *Quabbin: The Story of a Small Town with Outlooks upon Puritan Life* (1893; reprint, Boston: Northeastern Univ. Press, 1986), 90.

52. Williams, 138.

53. *Journal of the Franklin Institute,* n.s., 11 (May 1833), 304.

54. Weller, Haynes & Co., Norwich, N.Y., advertising broadside for J. Cross Elevated Oven Cooking Stove, 1840, AAS.

55. Jane Nylander reports that early-nineteenth-century cooking vessels weighed as much as sixty-five pounds. Nylander, *Snug Fireside,* 62.

56. Keep, "Early American Cooking Stoves," 77.

57. Frank G. White, "Cookstoves," 40.

58. *Journal of the Franklin Institute,* n.s., 13 (Apr. 1834), 256.

59. *Journal of the Franklin Institute,* n.s., 15 (Jan. 1835), 27–28; *Journal of the Franklin Institute,* n.s., 4 (Sept. 1829), 174.

60. *Journal of the Franklin Institute,* n.s., 13 (June 1834), 390.

61. *Journal of the Franklin Institute,* n.s., 14 (Oct. 1834), 266–68; *Journal of the Franklin Institute,* n.s., 16 (Oct. 1835), 245.

62. *Journal of the Franklin Institute,* n.s., 11 (June 1833), 381.

63. M. N. Stanley & Co., *Remarks and Directions for Using Stanley's Patented Rotary Cooking Stove* (New York: G. F. Bunce, 1835), 1 and 4.

64. M. N. Stanley & Co., 4–6.

65. M. N. Stanley & Co., 8–10.

66. J. Leander Bishop, *A History of American Manufactures from 1608 to 1860,* 3 vols. (Philadelphia: Edward Young, 1866), 2:547.

67. Daniel J. Walkowitz, *Worker City, Company Town: Iron and Cotton-Worker Protest in Troy and Cohoes, New York, 1855–84* (Urbana: Univ. of Illinois Press, 1978), 20–23.

68. Victor S. Clark, *History of Manufactures in the United States, 1607–1860* (1929; reprint, New York: Peter Smith, 1949), 347 and 377.

69. *Franklin Herald,* 7 Jan. 1812, 3.

70. *Connecticut Courant,* 10 Jan. 1815, 4.

71. *Connecticut Courant,* 18 Oct. 1815, 3.

72. *Connecticut Courant,* 17 Sept. 1816, 3.

73. *Rhode Island American,* 20 Nov. 1818, 3; *Providence Annual Advertiser* (Providence, R.I.: n.p., 1832), 142. Retailers in Keene, New Hampshire, were equally cautious. A. & T. Hall, whose "chief business was that of druggists," introduced cookstoves to the community in 1817. Three years later, a local bookseller added "an improved pattern" of cookstove to his stock. Some years later, a "general merchant" named Daniel Hough and a tinplate worker named John P. Barber also began to carry stoves. S. G. Griffin, *A History of the Town of Keene from 1732, When the Township was Granted by Massachusetts, to 1874, when it Became a City* (Keene, N.H.: Sentinel, 1904), 381.

74. Insurance inventory of Henry M. Miller, Worcester, Mass., Aug. 1837, Salisbury Family Papers, AAS.

75. *Massachusetts Spy,* 2 Nov. 1825, 4.

76. *Providence Directory* (Providence, R.I.: n.p., 1824), passim.

77. *Providence Directory* (Providence, R.I.: n.p., 1832), passim.

78. *Providence Almanac and Business Directory* (Providence, R.I.: Benjamin F. Moore, 1843), 46 and 50.

79. *Greenfield Gazette and Franklin Herald,* 18 Nov. 1834, 4.

80. J. Mayhew & Co., advertising broadside, Buffalo, N.Y., c. 1834, AAS.

81. S. B. Ludlow, letter to Robbins W. Douglas, 12 Apr. 1836, Misc. Mss. Ludlow, S. B., NYHS.

82. Lucius Hoyt, letter to Eliza Hoyt, 1 Sept. 1833, Hoyt-Meacham Family Papers, NYHS.

83. *Rhode Island American,* 20 Nov. 1818, 3.

84. *New-York Annual Advertiser* (New York: n.p., 1820), 17.

85. *Franklin Herald,* 7 Jan. 1812, 3.

86. John Adams Paxton, *Paxton's Annual Philadelphia Directory and Register* (Philadelphia: John A. Paxton, 1819), unpaginated.

87. *Massachusetts Spy,* 9 Oct. 1822, 4.

88. Frank G. White, "Cookstoves," 40.

89. Samuel Pierce & Son, Account Book (Greenfield, Mass., 1821–1826), passim, HDL. As was customary, these prices included the cost of stovepipe, protective sheet iron for the floor, and any accompanying "furniture," such as tea kettles and water boilers.

90. Samuel Pierce Jr., Account Book (Greenfield, Mass., 1834–1835), passim, HDL. The Hartford, Connecticut, firm of Ward, Bartholomew & Brainard had begun renting stoves to customers at least by 1818. *Connecticut Courant,* 15 Dec. 1818, 1.

91. See advertisements for Edward S. Sheldon, *Rhode Island American,* 7 Oct. 1825, 3; James Eames & Co., *Providence Journal,* 29 Dec. 1831, 4, and Peter Grinnell & Sons, *Providence Journal,* 8 Dec. 1835, 4.

92. Probate inventories of Asa Bates and Benjamin Scott, Hampshire County, Mass., 1810 (microfilm, Rockefeller Library, Brown University, Providence, R.I.). For the purpose of this analysis, cooking equipment includes fireplace tools (andirons, cranes, trammels, pot hooks, tongs, shovels); cooking vessels (pots, kettles, basins, skillets, spiders, bake pans); and cooking tools (gridirons, peels, slices, reflector ovens, toasting irons).

93. Probate inventories of James Murry and Stephen Goff, Suffolk County Massachusetts, 1810, nos. 23429 and 23343 (microfilm, OSV).

94. Goodrich, *Recollections,* 1:68.

95. Margaret Hindle Hazen and Robert M. Hazen, *Keepers of the Flame: The Role of Fire in American Culture* (Princeton, N.J.: Princeton Univ. Press, 1992), 170. These remarks are also based on my own experience cooking in historic kitchens at Hancock Shaker Village, Pittsfield, Mass., and at Slater Mill Historic Site, Pawtucket, R.I.

96. Eliza Woodson Farnham, *Life in Prairie Land* (1846; reprint, Urbana: Univ. of Illinois Press, 1988), 35–36.

97. Caroline M. Kirkland, *A New Home, Who'll Follow? Or, Glimpses of Western Life* (1839; reprint, New Brunswick, N.J.: Rutgers Univ. Press, 1990), 48–49.

98. Robert Roberts, 158.

99. Harriet Beecher Stowe, *Oldtown Folks* (Boston: Fields, Osgood, 1869), 1 and 274–75.

100. Mary Palmer Tyler, *Grandmother Tyler's Book: The Recollections of Mary Palmer Tyler, 1775–1866,* ed. Frederick Tupper and Helen Tyler Brown (New York: G. P. Putnam's Sons, 1925), 319–20.

101. Mary Palmer Tyler, Diary (Guilford, Vt.), 28 Apr. 1822 and 5 Nov. 1824, excerpted in *Vermont History* 20 (1952): 21–24.

102. Ruth Henshaw Bascom, Diary (Leicester, Phillipston, and Ashby, Mass., 1789–1846), 6 Mar. 1819, AAS. The Bascoms' annual expenses for 1819 are recorded after the last entry for that year.

103. On the issue of bias in probate inventories, see Gloria L. Main, "Probate Records as a Source for Early American History," and Daniel Scott Smith, "Underregistration and Bias in Probate Records: An Analysis of Data from Eighteenth-Century Hingham, Massachusetts," *William and Mary Quarterly*, 3rd ser., 32 (1975), 96–98 and 104–6. Main and Smith agree that only about 40 percent of estates were probated in the late eighteenth and early nineteenth centuries.

104. Carole Shammas has estimated that probate records reflect consumption habits "a decade or so earlier than the dates listed." Shammas, 5.

105. Suffolk County, Mass., Probate Records, 1820, passim (microfilm, OSV). Here and throughout this analysis, only those probate inventories listing cooking equipment were considered.

106. Probate inventories of Thomas Emmons (no. 27606), Suffolk County, Mass., 1825, and of John Heard (no. 26031), Suffolk County, Mass., 1820 (microfilm, OSV).

107. The median estate value for probate inventories recorded in Boston in 1820 and 1825 was $1,584.42; the median value of the estates of the eight people who owned cookstoves was $4,918.38.

108. Probate inventory of Moses Atwood (no. 26307), Suffolk County, Mass., 1820 (microfilm, OSV). Atwood owned no real estate, and his personal estate was valued at $101.63. The 1820 census for his household lists only three people, yet the inventory includes six beds, suggesting that nonfamily members were often in residence.

109. Probate inventory of Jonathan Lawrence (no. 27755), Suffolk County, Mass., 1825 (microfilm, OSV). By 1830, Boston probate assessors had generally ceased listing kitchen furnishings separately, perhaps a sign that cookstoves were becoming so common they were no longer worthy of special mention.

110. Providence County Probate Records, 1820–35, passim, City Archives, Providence, R.I. The median value of the estates of the cookstove owners was $395.96; the median for the 1830 and 1835 samples was $512.52. No one with an estate worth less than $100 owned a cookstove, nor did anyone with an estate worth more than $5,000.

111. Probate inventories of Nathan W. Jackson, James Harris, David Borden, and James Young, Providence County Probate Records, 1830; probate inventories of Nicholas Sheldon, James Johnson, Power Knowles, and Russell Proctor, Providence County Probate Records, 1835.

112. Barnstable County, Mass., Probate Records, vols. 43 and 45 (1820 and 1825), passim, Barnstable County Courthouse, Barnstable, Mass. William Sandford's inventory is in 43:102.

113. Barnstable County, Mass., Probate Records, vols. 52 and 56 (1830 and 1835), passim. The median estate value for the cookstove owners was $2,610.51 compared to $858.39 for the group as a whole.

114. Probate inventory of Paron C. Cook (1830), Barnstable County, Mass., Probate Records, 56:212–15.

115. Worcester County, Mass., Probate Records, 1820 and 1830, passim (microfilm, OSV).

116. Probate inventory of Henry Ballard, Worcester County, Mass., 1830, 68:218–24 (microfilm, OSV). The median value of the estates probated in the county in 1830 was $496.68. Information about the composition of Ballard's household and the circumstances of his death is available in the 1830 census for Worcester County, 10:2 (microfilm, OSV), and in Henry S. Nourse, ed., *The Birth, Marriage, and Death Register, Church Records and Epitaphs of Lancaster, Massachusetts* (Lancaster, Mass.: W. J. Coulter, 1890), passim.

117. Samuel Pierce & Son, Account Book, passim. For the purpose of this analysis, stoves are considered cookstoves if they are specifically identified as such in the account book or if they sold for $25 or more.

118. Franklin County, Mass., Census, 1820, passim (microfilm, HDL). The 1820 census grouped as separate categories people age twenty-six to forty-four and those forty-five and older.

119. Samuel Pierce & Son, Account Book, 191; Mrs. Walter E. Burnham et al., *History and Tradition of Shelburne, Massachusetts* (Shelburne, Mass.: n.p., 1958), 176; Franklin County, Mass., Census, 1820, 39.

120. Burnham et al., 166; Samuel Pierce & Son, Account Book, 340.

121. Franklin County, Mass., Census, 1820, 37; Samuel Pierce & Son, Account Book, 3.

122. Samuel Pierce & Son, Account Book, 5; Franklin County, Mass., Census, 1820, 39.

123. Samuel Pierce & Son, Account Book, 6; Franklin County, Mass., Census, 1820, 37.

124. The average size of the 148 Shelburne households enumerated in 1820 was 6.9.

125. J. & S. Pierce, advertisement, *Greenfield Gazette and Franklin Herald,* 18 Nov. 1834, 4; Samuel Pierce Jr., Account Book, passim.

126. Samuel Pierce Jr., Account Book, 95, 96, 103, 139, and 157.

127. Samuel Pierce Jr., Account Book, 135, 141, 146, and 155.

128. Samuel Pierce, Jr., Account Book, 88, 90, and 175.

129. W. A. Arnold & Co., *Arnold's Patent Yankee Cooking Stove* (Northampton, Mass.: n.p., 1837), 2–3.

130. Hampshire County, Mass., Census, 1840, 6:390–410 (microfilm, OSV). In 1840, less than 23 percent of the town's population was comprised of men age thirty to forty-nine, yet ten of the twelve Northampton men who signed Arnold's testimonial were in this age group. The average household in Northampton in 1840 had 5.5 people; the average size of the twelve stove-owning households was 7.5.

131. Mary Janette Elmore, *Long Hill: South Windsor, Connecticut* (South Windsor, Conn.: South Windsor Historical Society, 1976), 24.

132. "Fifty Years Ago," c. 1880. Flanders Collection, Middlebury College, Middlebury, Vt. Recorded by Margaret MacArthur, *An Almanac of New England Farm Songs* (New Canaan: Green Linnet Records, 1982).

133. Susan Baker Blunt, *Childish Things: The Reminiscence of Susan Baker Blunt,* ed. Francis Mason (Grantham, N.H.: Tompson and Rutter, 1988), 33.

134. "Rules Necessary to Be Observed in Setting Stoves, &c.," *New England Farmer* 7 (13 Nov. 1829), 133.

135. W. A. Arnold & Co., 3.

136. Samuel Rodman, *The Diary of Samuel Rodman,* ed. Zephaniah Pease (New Bedford, Mass.: Reynolds Printing Co., 1927), 131.

137. Nylander, *Snug Fireside,* 213–14; Hazen and Hazen, 164.

138. *The American Housewife* (New York: Collins, Keese, 1839), 131.

139. Frances A. Breckenridge, *Recollections of a New England Town* (Meriden, Conn.: Journal, 1899), 142–44.

140. Tobias Walker, Diary (Kennebunk, Maine, 1828–1893), 27 Apr. 1840, Maine Historical Society, Portland, Maine. Quoted by Thomas C. Hubka, *Big House, Little House, Back House, Barn: The Connected Farm Buildings of New England* (Hanover, N.H.: Univ. Press of New

England, 1984), 172. Hubka notes that Walker's "portch" was actually an enclosed shed or workroom built off the kitchen.

141. Lucretia Warner Hall, Diary (Canaan, N.Y., 1838), 20 Mar. 1841, NYHS.

142. Olmsted, 68.

143. *Report of the Commissioner of Patents* (Washington, D.C.: Government Printing Office, 1846), 26.

144. Thomas G. Fessenden, *The Husbandman and Housewife* (Bellows Falls, Vt.: Bill Blake, 1820), 70.

145. Martha Coffin Wright, letter to Lucretia Mott, 7 Nov. 1841, Martha Coffin Wright Correspondence, 1825–1841, Garrison Family Papers, Sophia Smith Collection, Smith College, Northampton, Mass. Quoted by Jeanne Boydston, *Home and Work: Housework, Wages, and the Ideology of Labor in the Early Republic* (New York: Oxford Univ. Press, 1990), 107.

146. M. N. Stanley & Co., 7 and 9.

147. W. A. Arnold & Co., 4–5.

148. Sarah Josepha Hale, *The Good Housekeeper; Or, The Way to Live Well and to Be Well While We Live* (Boston: Weeks, Jordan, 1839), 28.

149. Breckenridge, 185.

150. Sophia Draper White, letter to James and Lucy Watson Draper, 6 Jan. 1839, Draper-Rice Family Papers, AAS.

151. Farnham, *Life,* 116–21.

152. Farnham, *Life,* 117.

153. Frank G. White, "Cookstoves," 40.

154. Sanger, 556.

155. Amanda Harris, "When This Old Stove Was New," *Country Life* (Jan. 1915), 68. Quoted by Nylander, *Snug Fireside,* 215.

156. Advertisement for "Stanley's Patent Rotary Cooking Stove," *Massachusetts Spy,* 7 Oct. 1835, 3.

157. Jane Eliza Johnson, *Newtown's History and Historian Ezra Levan Johnson* (Newtown, Conn.: n.p., 1917), 255.

158. Rodman, 170 and 203.

159. William Rice and Emeline Draper Rice, letter to Sophia Draper White, 13 Dec. 1838, Draper-Rice Family Papers, AAS.

160. Calista A. Draper, letter to Sophia Draper White, 21 Mar. 1839, Draper-Rice Family Papers, AAS.

161. Pintard, letter to Eliza Pintard Davidson, 10 Dec. 1827, in *Letters,* 2:380.

162. Asa Moore Janney and Werner L. Janney, eds., *John Jay Janney's Virginia: An American Farm Lad's Life in the Early 19th Century* (McLean, Va.: EPM, 1978), 22. Janney left Virginia for Ohio in 1831, so this stove must have been acquired before then.

163. Blunt, 33.

164. Faith Silliman Hubbard, letter to Benjamin and Harriet Silliman, 12 Aug. 1837, Silliman Family Papers, Yale University Library. Quoted by Garrett, 101.

165. Emeline Draper Rice, letter to Sophia Draper White, 4 May 1839, Draper-Rice Family Papers, AAS.

166. Lucy Watson Draper, letter to Sophia Draper White, 30 Jan. 1839, Draper-Rice Family Papers, AAS.

167. Alice J. Jones, *In Dover on the Charles* (Newport, R.I.: Milne, 1906), 43.

168. Anne Langton, *A Gentlewoman in Upper Canada: The Journals of Anne Langton,* ed. H. H. Langton (Toronto: Clarke, Irwin, 1950), 70.

169. Johnson, 254.

170. Nancy Barnard Batchelder, "Growing Up in Peru (1815–1840)," *Vermont History* 21 (1953), 7.

171. Delia Hoyt, letter to Jonathan and Chloe Hoyt, 3 Nov. 1825, Hoyt-Meacham Family Papers, NYHS.

172. Margaret Bayard Smith, letter to Jane Bayard Kirkpatrick, 10 Feb. 1834, in Hunt, ed., 345–46.

173. Sarah Orne Jewett, *A Country Doctor* (Boston: Houghton Mifflin, 1884), 21.

174. Sarah Anna Emery, *My Generation* (Newburyport, Mass.: M. H. Sargent, 1893), 84.

175. Mary Wilkins Freeman, *Pembroke* (1894; reprint, New York: Harper and Bros., 1899), 101.

176. Jewett, 10 and 21.

177. Adeline D. T. Whitney, "When I Was a Little Girl," in *Homespun Yarns* (Boston: Houghton, Mifflin, 1887), 2.

5. "Near a Stove the Heart Builds No Altars"

1. Sellers, 372.

2. A number of scholars have examined the emergence of the "cult of domesticity" and the ideology of "separate spheres" in nineteenth-century America. Among the key works are: Nancy F. Cott, *The Bonds of Womanhood: "Woman's Sphere" in New England, 1780–1835* (New Haven: Yale Univ. Press, 1977); Kirk Jeffrey, "The Family as Utopian Retreat from the City: The Nineteenth-Century Contribution," *Soundings* 55 (1972): 21–41; Mary P. Ryan, *Cradle of the Middle Class: The Family in Oneida County, New York, 1790–1865* (Cambridge, England: Cambridge Univ. Press, 1981); and Barbara Welter, "The Cult of True Womanhood, 1820–1860," in *The American Family in Social-Historical Perspective,* 2d ed., ed. Michael Gordon (New York: St. Martin's, 1978), 313–33. The term "cult of domesticity" is from Aileen Kraditor's introduction to *Up from the Pedestal: Selected Writings in the History of American Feminism* (New York: Quadrangle, *New York Times,* 1968), 10.

3. George Lunt [pseud. Wesley Brooke], *Eastford; Or, Household Sketches* (Boston: Crocker and Brewster, 1855), 9–11.

4. Sidney George Fisher, *A Philadelphia Perspective: The Diary of Sidney George Fisher,* ed. Nicholas B. Wainwright (Philadelphia: Historical Society of Pennsylvania, 1967), 176–77.

5. "Stoves," *New England Farmer* 18 (20 Nov. 1839), 180.

6. Olmsted, 66.

7. Thomas Webster and Frances B. Parkes, *The American Family Encyclopedia* (New York: J. C. Derby, 1854), 99.

8. Elizabeth F. Ellet, *The Practical Housekeeper* (New York: Stringer and Townsend, 1857), 19.

9. Catharine E. Beecher, *A Treatise on Domestic Economy* (1841; reprint, New York: Schocken, 1977), 299–300.

10. Catharine E. Beecher, *Letters to the People on Health and Happiness* (New York: Harper, 1856), 62 and 91.

11. "Stoves," *New England Farmer* 21 (14 Dec. 1842), 190.

12. Frank Hastings Hamilton, "Hygiene," *New York Journal of Medicine,* n.s., 7 (July 1859), 66–67.

13. Dr. J. A. Kennicott, "Rough Notes on Horticulture from the West," *The Horticulturist* 4 (Apr. 1850), 452.

14. [Andrew Jackson Downing], "The Favorite Poison of America," *The Horticulturist* 5 (Nov. 1850), 202–3.

15. *Scientific American,* n.s., 2 (5 May 1860), 304.

16. Andrew Jackson Downing, *The Architecture of Country Houses* (1850; reprint, New York: Dover, 1969), 472.

17. [Downing], "Favorite Poison," 203.

18. Lewis F. Allen, *Rural Architecture* (New York: C. M. Saxton, 1852), 57–58 and 66.

19. Solon Robinson, *How to Live: Saving and Wasting; Or, Domestic Economy Illustrated* (New York: Fowler and Wells, 1860), 298.

20. Earle Stove Co., Worcester, Mass., advertising broadside, c. 1865, NMAH.

21. Dr. T. and Mrs. L. A. Hopkins, *Science in the Kitchen; Or, The Art of Cooking in Everyday Life with the Economical Air Distending Cooking Powders* (Malden, Mass.: n.p., 1863), 11.

22. "Have We a National Dish among Us?" *Harper's New Monthly Magazine* 8 (Dec. 1853), 270.

23. *Eighty Years of Progress in the United States* (New York: L. Stebbins, 1861), 253. In the eighteenth century, a *range* was a fireplace with an oven on one side and a row (or "range") of set kettles on the other. In the nineteenth century, the word *range* usually referred to a dual oven and cooking appliance built into brickwork, whereas a *cookstove* was free-standing (therefore portable) and had only one oven. By the middle of the century, however, the terms were beginning to be used interchangeably.

24. Solon Robinson, address, American Institute of the City of New York, in *Transactions of the American Institute of the City of New York for the Years 1859–60* (Albany, N.Y.: C. Van Benthuysen, 1860), 281–82.

25. [Downing], "Favorite Poison," 203.

26. Henry W. Cleaveland et al., *Village and Farm Cottages* (1856; reprint, Watkins Glen, N.Y.: American Life Foundation, 1982), 140–41.

27. George Canning Hill, *Dovecote; Or, The Heart of the Homestead* (Boston: John P. Jewett, 1854), 76.

28. Anna Bache, *Scenes at Home: Or, The Adventures of a Fire Screen* (Philadelphia: Gihon, 1852), 11–13.

29. Harvey Green, *Fit for America: Health, Fitness, Sport, and American Society* (New York: Pantheon, 1986), 77–79.

30. Rybczynski, 132–36.

31. Nylander, *Snug Fireside,* 3–6.

32. Joel Pfister, "A Garden in the Machine: Reading a Mid-19th-Century, Two-Cylinder Parlor Stove as Cultural Text," *Technology and Society* 13 (1991), 339.

33. Hazen and Hazen, 59–64.

34. Katherine Anne Roberts, "Hearth and Soul: The Fireplace in American Culture" (Ph.D. diss., Univ. of Minnesota, 1990), 36.

35. Ebenezer Bailey, ed., *The Young Ladies' Class Book: A Selection of Lessons for Reading in Prose and Verse* (Boston: n.p., 1831), 166. Quoted by Welter, 320.

36. Samuel G. Goodrich, *Fireside Education* (London: William Smith, 1839), 16.

37. Katherine Anne Roberts, 43.

38. Hicks, a Pennsylvania folk artist born in 1780, painted approximately fifty-five versions of the "peaceable kingdom" between 1825 and 1849. His primary inspiration was the prophecy in the Old Testament book of Isaiah about the lion lying down with the lamb. For a discussion of these paintings and examples, see Mary Black and Jean Lipman, *American Folk Painting* (1966; reprint, New York: Bramhall House, 1987), 174–75 and 187–88.

39. "A New England Fireside," *Ballou's Pictorial* 8 (10 Mar. 1855), 145.

40. Hill, *Dovecote*, 36–39.

41. Ellen Sturgis Hooper, "The Wood-Fire," *The Dial* 1 (Oct. 1840), 193.

42. Nathaniel Hawthorne, letter to Maria Louisa Hawthorne, 25 Nov. 1842, in *The Letters, 1813–1843*, ed. Thomas Woodson et al., vol. 15 of *The Centenary Edition of the Works of Nathaniel Hawthorne* (Columbus: Ohio State Univ. Press, 1972), 658.

43. Nathaniel Hawthorne, *The American Notebooks*, ed. Claude M. Simpson, vol. 8 of *The Centenary Edition of the Works of Nathaniel Hawthorne* (Columbus: Ohio State Univ. Press, 1972), 364.

44. Hawthorne, "Fire Worship," in *Nathaniel Hawthorne: Selected Tales and Sketches*, 3rd ed., ed. Hyatt H. Waggoner (New York: Holt, Rinehart and Winston, 1970), 493 and 498–99. This essay was originally published in the *Democratic Review* in Dec. 1843.

45. Hawthorne, "Fire Worship," 494–95 and 499–501.

46. David S. Reynolds, *Beneath the American Renaissance: The Subversive Imagination in the Age of Emerson and Melville* (New York: Knopf, 1988), 256.

47. Henry David Thoreau, *Walden: A Writer's Edition*, ed. Larzer Ziff (New York: Holt, Rinehart and Winston, 1961), 196.

48. Mary Bushnell Cheney, *Life and Letters of Horace Bushnell* (1880; reprint, New York: Arno, 1969), 22.

49. John Greenleaf Whittier, "Snow-Bound: A Winter Idyl," in *The Complete Poetical Works of Whittier*, ed. Horace E. Scudder (Boston: Houghton Mifflin, 1894), 399–401.

50. James Russell Lowell, "The Courtin'," in *The Biglow Papers, 2nd Series* (1866; reprint, New York: AMS, 1973), 91.

51. John F. W. Ware, *Home Life: What It Is, and What It Needs* (Boston: W. V. Spencer, 1864), 13–14.

52. George Canning Hill [pseud. Thomas Lackland], *Homespun; Or, Five and Twenty Years Ago* (New York: Hurd and Houghton, 1867), 16–20.

53. Susan Fenimore Cooper, *Rural Hours* (1850; reprint, Syracuse, N.Y.: Syracuse Univ. Press, 1968), 295–96.

54. Harriet Beecher Stowe [pseud. Christopher Crowfield], *House and Home Papers* (Boston: Ticknor and Fields, 1865), 7.

55. Susan Warner [pseud. Elizabeth Wetherell], *The Wide, Wide World* (1850; reprint, New York: Feminist, 1987), 99, 103, 106, and 244.

56. Susan Warner, *Queechy*, 2 vols. (New York: George P. Putnam, 1852), 1:237–38 and 1:251.

57. Harriet Beecher Stowe, *Uncle Tom's Cabin* (1852; reprint, New York: Dodd, Mead, 1952), 203–9.

58. Ann Sophia Stephens, *The Old Homestead* (Philadelphia: T. B. Peterson, 1855), 408.

59. Ann Sophia Stephens, *Fashion and Famine* (New York: Bunce, 1854), 128–31.

60. Mary Kelley, "The Sentimentalists: Promise and Betrayal in the Home," *Signs* 4 (1979), 437.

61. William A. Alcott, *The Young Wife; Or, Duties of Woman in the Marriage Relation* (1837; reprint, New York: Arno, 1972), 158–68.

62. William A. Alcott, *The Young Housekeeper* (Boston: George W. Light, 1838), 31–32.

63. *Cookery As It Should Be* (Philadelphia: Willis P. Hazard, 1853), 5–7.

64. Faye E. Dudden, *Serving Women: Household Service in Nineteenth-Century America* (Middletown, Conn.: Wesleyan Univ. Press, 1983), 44–47 and 60–71.

65. Dudden, 54, 107, and 119.

66. Hazen and Hazen, 178.

67. Dudden, 54; Daniel E. Sutherland, "'The Stranger in the Gates': Employer Reactions Toward Domestic Servants in America, 1825–1875" (Ph.D. diss., Michigan State Univ., 1969).

68. Karen Halttunen, *Confidence Men and Painted Women: A Study of Middle-Class Culture in America, 1830–1870* (New Haven, Yale Univ. Press, 1982), 104–9.

69. "Hiring a Cook," *American Ladies' Magazine* 6 (1833), 518.

70. Ellen Louise Chandler [Moulton], *This, That, and the Other* (Boston: Phillips, Sampson and Co., 1854), 281.

71. Mary J. Holmes, *'Lena Rivers* (1856; reprint, New York: Carleton, 1863), 110–11 and 130.

72. *Plain Talk and Friendly Advice to Domestics, with Counsel on Home Matters* (Boston: Phillips, Sampson, 1855), 57.

73. Sarah Josepha Hale, *Keeping House and Housekeeping* (New York: Harper, 1845), 88–89.

74. Timothy Shay Arthur, *Trials and Confessions of an American Housekeeper* (Philadelphia: J. W. Bradley, 1859), 21–25.

75. Timothy Shay Arthur, "Cooks," in *Leaves from the Book of Human Life* (Philadelphia: G. G. Evans, 1860), 43–44.

76. Timothy Shay Arthur, "Short of Fuel," in *Leaves,* 109–11.

77. Timothy Shay Arthur, *The Lady at Home: Or, Leaves from the Every-day Book of an American Woman* (New York: John Allen, 1844), 79–80 and 94–95.

78. Timothy Shay Arthur, *Tired of Housekeeping* (New York: D. Appleton, 1842), 17.

79. Stowe, *House,* 77–78.

80. Kathryn Kish Sklar, *Catharine Beecher: A Study in American Domesticity* (New York: W. W. Norton, 1976), 151–56.

81. Catharine E. Beecher, *Treatise,* 149–51, 379–84, and 346.

82. Mary H. Cornelius, *The Young Housekeeper's Friend* (Boston: Charles Tappan, 1846), 13.

83. *American Ladies' Memorial* (Boston: n.p., 1850), 85.

84. Ryan, *Cradle,* 61–65.

85. Cowan, *More Work,* 71–73; Giedion, 215–18; Jack Larkin, *The Reshaping of Everyday Life, 1790–1840* (New York: Harper and Row, 1988), 175–77; Edgar W. Martin, *The Standard of Living in 1860* (Chicago: Univ. of Chicago Press, 1942), 13–18; Strasser, *Never Done,* 16–21; Daniel E. Sutherland, *The Expansion of Everyday Life: 1860–1876* (New York: Harper and Row, 1989), 69–70.

86. Sylvester Graham, *A Treatise on Bread and Bread-Making* (Boston: Light and Stearns, 1837), 52.

87. Graham, 33–45 and 105–6.

88. Perrin Bliss, *The People's Manual* (Worcester, Mass.: Henry J. Howland, 1848), 47–48.

89. Cornelius, *Young Housekeeper's Friend* (1846), 8.

90. Advertisement for *The American System of Cookery* in *The Union Magazine of Literature and Art* 1 (Dec. 1847), 287.

91. *Cookery,* 8.

92. Robinson, *How to Live,* 324.

93. Ann H. Allen, *The Housekeeper's Assistant* (Boston: James Munroe, 1845), 2.

94. Sara P. W. Parton [pseud. Fanny Fern], *Fanny Fern's Family Cook Book* (Philadelphia: William Fleming, 1856), iv–v.

95. Catharine E. Beecher, *Treatise,* 70–84, 297–307, and 366–76. The reference to cookstoves is on 283.

96. Eliza Leslie, *The House Book; Or, A Manual of Domestic Economy* (Philadelphia: Carey and Hart, 1841), 127.

97. Leslie, 145 and 234.

98. *The American Matron; Or, Practical and Scientific Cookery* (Boston: Jas. Munroe, 1851), 31.

99. Cornelius, *Young Housekeeper's Friend* (1846), 19–20, 35–36, and 99–100. A "spider" is a frying pan that has legs so it can be used over coals directly on the hearth.

100. Mary H. Cornelius, *The Young Housekeeper's Friend* (Boston: Brown and Taggard, 1860), 21.

101. Ann H. Allen, 86.

102. Elizabeth E. Lea, *Domestic Cookery* (Baltimore: Cushing, 1846), 24–29.

103. Bliss, 50.

104. Sarah Josepha Hale, *Mrs. Hale's New Cook Book* (Philadelphia: T. B. Peterson, 1857), 422.

105. Ann Douglas, *The Feminization of American Culture* (New York: Avon, 1977), 199.

6. "We Have Got a Very Good Cooking Stove"

1. Reynolds, 337–38.

2. Douglas, 11–12.

3. See Edmonds's *Sparking* (1839), *The Organ Grinder* (c. 1848), *The Speculator* (1852), and *The New Bonnet* (1858) in H. Nichols B. Clark, *Francis W. Edmonds: American Master in the Dutch Tradition* (Washington, D.C.: Smithsonian Institution Press, 1988), 5, 10, 12, and 17.

4. Elizabeth Johns, *American Genre Painting: The Politics of Everyday Life* (New Haven: Yale Univ. Press, 1991), 164.

5. Johns, 163–65.

6. Alice B. Haven, *The Coopers; Or, Getting Under Way* (New York: D. Appleton, 1858), 79–80.

7. Eunice White Beecher, *From Dawn to Daylight; Or, The Simple Story of a Western Home* (New York: Derby and Jackson, 1859), iii and 76.

8. Catherine M. Sedgwick, *Married or Single?* 2 vols. (New York: Harper, 1857), 1:103.

9. Mary Andrews Denison, *Orange Leaves* (Philadelphia: Lippincott, 1856), 209–10.

10. Abraham Oakey Hall, *Old Whitey's Christmas Trot* (New York: Harper and Bros, 1857), 117–18.

11. Providence County Probate Records, 1840 and 1845, City Archives, Providence, R.I.

12. Providence County Probate Records, 1840 and 1845. Inventories of John Atwood, 18 Aug. 1840; Robey Barker, 28 June 1840; Caleb Williams, 21 Jan. 1840; Hiram Kelley, 22 Feb. 1840; Shubael Kelly, 18 Mar. 1840; Joseph Fenner, 21 Apr. 1840; James Wilson, 13 June 1840; James Vaughn, 30 June 1840; John Carlile, 25 Aug. 1840; Lydia Pettis, 25 Sept. 1840; Simeon Ingraham, 6 Oct. 1840; Elias Barstow, 14 Dec. 1840; Abigail Proud, 4 Feb. 1845; Esek Eddy, 12 Feb. 1845; Pardon Mason, 8 July 1845; and Thomas Sessions, 21 Nov. 1845.

13. Barnstable County Probate Records, vol. 62 (1840), vol. 71 (1845), and vol. 84 (1850), Barnstable County Courthouse, Barnstable, Mass. Both John Wharf, whose estate was valued at $53.45 (62:298–99), and Samuel Emery, whose estate was valued at $7,260.51 (84:39–41), owned cookstoves.

14. Barnstable County Probate Records. Inventories of Bangs Kelly, 62:215; Smith Knowles, 62:225–26; Henry Bickford, 62:229–30; Nathaniel Nickerson, 62:235; Nathaniel Snow, 62:275–77; Jonathan Kendrick, 62:292–93; Reuben Pierce, 71:46; Joshua Atkins, 71:48–49; Lemuel Newcomb, 71:52–53; Leonard Clark, 71:68–69; Lydia Snow, 71:75–76; Shebua Rich, 71:79–80; James Lombard, 71:83; Ephraim Baker, 71:84–85; Washington Nickerson, 71:90; Darius Loveland, 71:94; Prince Gifford, 71:98–99; Samuel Emery, 84:39–41; Franklin Hopkins, 84:63–65; and Robert Lavender Jr., 84:70–72.

15. Probate inventory of Joshua Loring, 1851, Barnstable County Probate Records, 84:97–98. The median value of the twenty-six estates probated in the county in 1850 was $1,171.19.

16. Albert S. Bolles, *Industrial History of the United States* (Norwich, Conn.: Henry Bill, 1879), 202–4; Victor S. Clark, 412–13; Robert B. Gordon, *American Iron, 1607–1900* (Baltimore: Johns Hopkins Univ. Press, 1996), 17; Lewis, 25–26.

17. Bishop, 2:498; Groft, 19; Schuhmann, 1; John D. Tyler, 153.

18. Leggett, comp., 3:1459–86.

19. Victor S. Clark, 503.

20. Bishop, 2:453–56.

21. *Providence Almanac and Business Directory* (Providence, R.I.: Benjamin F. Moore, 1843), 50; *Providence Almanac and Business Directory* (Providence, R.I.: John F. Moore, 1846), 79; *Providence Almanac and Business Directory* (Providence, R.I.: John F. Moore, 1850), 52; *Providence Directory* (Providence, R.I.: n.p. 1860), 189; *Providence Directory* (Providence, R.I.: n.p., 1861), 195.

22. *Gloucester Telegraph,* 1844. My thanks to Frank G. White for providing me with a copy of this advertisement.

23. John O. Burleigh, Account Book (Douglas, Mass., 1846–1848), AAS. See, especially, the entries for 22 Oct. 1846, 4 Feb. 1847, and Mar. 1847.

24. George Pierce, Account Book (Greenfield, Mass., 1852–1855), passim, HDL. These stove prices and subsequent ones include the cost of accessories: assembly materials (stovepipe, stovepipe elbows, dampers, caps, zinc for protecting floors); tinware and cooking vessels (dish pans, bread pans, tea kettles, pans); laundry equipment (wash boilers, flat irons); cleaning equipment (stove blacking, blacking brushes); as well as labor fees charged at the time of purchase. The entry regarding Wellington Barnard is dated 21 Nov. 1854, 358; the entry regarding John Arms is dated 14 Dec. 1854, 372.

25. Franklin County, Mass. Census, 1850, passim (microfilm, HDL). For information regarding the immigrants, see entries for "Mr. Summers (German)," Wendell Partenheimer, and

Richard Wilkinson in George Pierce, Account Book, 86, 298, and 331; Franklin County Census, 1850, 125 and 127. The average household size in the United States in 1860 was 5.3 persons, excluding slaves. Wells, 151.

26. Franklin County Census, 1850, passim; George Pierce, Account Book, passim. The entry regarding Solomon Wheeler is dated 27 Oct. 1852, 22; the entries regarding Charles Mirick are dated 17 Dec. 1853, 208, and 9 Nov. 1854, 350.

27. Barstow Stove Co., advertising broadside, 1854, NMAH.

28. S. Shepard, billhead, 1856, AAS.

29. *Journal of the Franklin Institute,* 3rd ser., 14 (Dec. 1847), 372.

30. "American Cooking Stoves Abroad," *Scientific American,* n.s., 3 (3 Nov. 1860), 293.

31. Jesse Hutchinson Jr., advertisement, 7 Dec. 1843, Lynn, Mass. My thanks to Frank G. White for providing me with a copy of this advertisement.

32. E. Ward & Co., advertisement, *Providence Journal,* 2 July 1860, 1; W. A. Currier, *Catalog of W. A. Currier's Kitchen, House Furnishing, and Stove Warehouse* (Haverhill, Mass.: Eben H. Safford, c. 1861), 26–27; Almy & Swain, advertising broadside, 1859, AAS; Munsell, Thompson & Munsell, advertising broadside, 1859, AAS; Billings & Stow, advertising broadside, c. 1860, AAS; and National Stove Works, advertising broadside, 1861, AAS.

33. Halttunen, *Confidence Men,* 104–7.

34. *Etiquette at Washington, and Complete Guide through the Metropolis and Its Environs* (Baltimore: Murphy, 1857), 47–48. Quoted by Halttunen, *Confidence Men,* 105.

35. Pfister, 338.

36. Groft, 34 and 50–51.

37. Hazen and Hazen, 180.

38. C. Foster & Co., advertisement, *Massachusetts Spy,* 30 Sept. 1846, 3.

39. William J. Keep, "History of Heating Apparatus" (1916), 123–27, Baker Library, Harvard Business School, Boston, Mass.

40. "The Manufacture of Stoves, Ranges, and Heaters," *Scientific American,* n.s., 42 (29 May 1880), 340.

41. Keep, "History," 123–27.

42. Kelly & Van Hagen, advertisement, *Providence Journal,* 1 Dec. 1845, 1.

43. Greenman & Northrup, *Stewart's Patent Summer and Winter Air-Tight Cooking Stoves* (Boston: n.p., 1844), 4–6.

44. Fuller, Warren & Co., *P.P. Stewart's Large Oven Air-Tight Summer and Winter Cooking Stove* (Troy, N.Y.: n.p., 1863), 1–3, 6, and 8.

45. Shear, Packard & Co., *The American Hot Air, Gas Burning Cooking Stove* (Albany, N.Y.: C. Van Benthuysen, 1863), 2–4, 12, and 19.

46. Shear, Packard & Co., 20–22.

47. *Eighty Years of Progress,* 253.

48. [Gardner Chilson], *Gardner Chilson, Inventor and Manufacturer of, and Dealer in, Heating, Cooking, and Ventilating Apparatus of Every Description* (Boston: Damrell and Moore, c. 1865), AAS, 47–48.

49. William Resor & Co., advertisement for Harrison's Patent Kitchener, in David Bigelow, *History of Prominent Mercantile and Manufacturing Firms in the United States* (Boston: n.p., 1857), 285.

50. Advertisement for Stimpson's Improved Range, *Providence Journal,* 4 July 1850, 4; Moses Pond & Co., advertising broadside for Improved Union Range, 1852, AAS.

51. Bill from John Westerfield to James W. Beekman, 20 Aug. 1844, Beekman Family Papers, box VII A, NYHS.

52. [Chilson], 40.

53. Mrs. B. K. Wyeth, letter to H. K. Curtis, 8 May 1846, Essex Company Papers, Museum of American Textile History, Lowell, Mass.

54. Mary Ann Waterman, letter to Lucretia C. C. Sibley, 31 Mar. 1852, Lucretia Cargill Sibley Correspondence, 1841–1876, AAS.

55. Catharine White Forbes, Diary (Westborough, Mass., 1846–1902), 25 Oct. 1852, AAS.

56. Susan E. P. Brown Forbes, Diary (Epsom, N.H.; Boston and Springfield, Mass.; 1841–1908), 1 and 8 Oct. 1852, AAS.

57. Susan E. P. Brown Forbes, 1 and 14–16 Sept. 1863, 24–25 and 27 Oct. 1864.

58. Elizabeth Cady Stanton, *Eighty Years and More (1815–1897)* (New York: European, 1898), 205–6.

59. Stanton, 206–8.

60. Stanton, 209–10.

61. American Medical Association, *First Report of the Committee on Public Hygiene of the American Medical Association* (Philadelphia: T. K. and P. G. Collins, 1849), 446, 452, 565–66, 585, 615, and 620.

62. Joseph B. Lyman and Laura E. Lyman, *The Philosophy of Housekeeping* (Hartford, Conn.: Goodwin and Betts, 1867), 115.

63. See, for example, the reminiscences of Mary Colbert and Jennie Kendricks of Georgia in *The American Slave: A Composite Autobiography,* ed. George P. Rawick, 18 vols. (1941; reprint, Westport, Conn.: Greenwood, 1972), 12, part 1, 74 and 217; 13, part 3, 3. See also the recollections of Sally Brown and Neal Upson of Georgia in *Slavery Time When I Was Chillun Down on Marster's Plantation,* ed. Ronald Killion and Charles Waller (Savannah: Beehive, 1973), 32 and 105.

64. Millard Fillmore, letter to Solomon G. Haven, 21 Dec. 1850, in *Millard Fillmore Papers,* 2 vols., ed. Frank H. Severance (Buffalo, N.Y.: Buffalo Historical Society, 1907), 2:306.

65. Bess Furman, *White House Profile* (Indianapolis: Bobbs-Merrill, 1951), 155; Lonnelle Aikman, *The Living White House* (Washington, D.C.: White House Historical Association, 1966), 120.

66. Hubka, 126–28.

67. Bernard L. Herman, *Architecture and Rural Life in Central Delaware, 1700–1900* (Knoxville: Univ. of Tennessee Press, 1987), 194–95.

68. Joyce K. Bibber, *A Home for Everyman: The Greek Revival and Maine Domestic Architecture* (Lanham, Md.: University Publishing Associates, American Association for State and Local History, 1989), 163–64.

69. Josiah H. Hammond, *The Farmer's and Mechanic's Practical Architect* (Boston: John P. Jewett, 1858), 112.

70. Henry Conklin, *Through "Poverty's Vale": A Hardscrabble Boyhood in Upstate New York, 1832–1862* (Syracuse, N.Y.: Syracuse Univ. Press, 1974), 62, 90–91, and 101–3.

71. Sophia Draper White, letter to Lucy Watson Draper, 1 Feb. 1847, Draper-Rice Family Papers, AAS.

72. Kenneth L. Holmes, ed., *Covered Wagon Women: Diaries and Letters from the Western Trails, 1840–1890,* 10 vols. (Glendale, Calif.: Arthur H. Clark, 1983), 2:231.

73. Ellen Spaulding Reed, letter to Stedman and Arterista Haven Spaulding, 19 Nov. 1854, and Ellen Spaulding Reed, letter to Arterista Haven Spaulding, 27 Oct. 1854, in Linda Otto Lipsett, *Pieced from Ellen's Quilt: Ellen Spaulding Reed's Letters and Story* (Dayton, Ohio: Halstead and Meadows, 1991), 48 and 45.

74. Hannah Anderson Ropes, *Six Months in Kansas, By a Lady* (Boston: John P. Jewett, 1856), 55.

75. Miriam Davis Colt, *Went to Kansas; Being a Thrilling Account of an Ill-Fated Expedition* (1862; reprint, Ann Arbor, Mich.: University Microfilms, 1966), 65.

76. Melissa Anderson Moore, *The Story of a Kansas Pioneer* (Mt. Vernon, Ohio: Manufacturing Printers, 1924), 33.

77. Samary S. Sherman, letter to Lucretia C. C. Sibley, 14 May 1864, Lucretia Cargill Sibley Correspondence, AAS.

78. Vesta Robbins, *No Coward Soul* (Ames: Iowa State Univ. Press, 1974), 37.

79. James Elder Armstrong, *Life of a Woman Pioneer As Illustrated in the Life of Elsie Strawn Armstrong, 1789–1871* (Chicago: John F. Higgins, 1931), 17 and 45.

80. Kirkland, 146.

81. Mollie Dorsey Sanford, *Mollie: The Journal of Mollie Dorsey Sanford in Nebraska and Colorado Territories, 1857–1866* (Lincoln: Univ. of Nebraska Press, 1959), 63.

82. Charlotte Haven, letters to her family, 3 and 22 Jan. 1843, in *Among the Mormons: Historical Accounts by Contemporary Observers,* ed. William Mulder and A. Russell Mortensen (New York: Knopf, 1958), 116–19.

83. Jane A. Gould Tourtillot, Diary (1862). Quoted by Lillian Schlissel, *Women's Diaries of the Westward Journey* (New York: Schocken, 1982), 219.

84. Colt, 49.

85. Ellen Pennock, "Incidents in My Life as a Pioneer," *Colorado Magazine* 30 (Apr. 1953), 126. Quoted by Sandra L. Myres, *Westering Women and the Frontier Experience, 1800–1915* (Albuquerque: Univ. of New Mexico Press, 1982), 147.

86. Kenneth L. Holmes, ed., 4:37.

87. Kenneth L. Holmes, ed., 3:165–66.

88. Kenneth L. Holmes, ed., 2:60–61.

89. Kenneth L. Holmes, ed., 2:60–61.

90. Kenneth L. Holmes, ed., 8:36–37.

91. Kenneth L. Holmes, ed., 3:184.

92. Kenneth L. Holmes, ed., 4:257–58.

93. Phoebe Newton Judson, *A Pioneer's Search for an Ideal Home* (Bellingham, Wash.: Union Printing, 1925), 74.

94. Luzena Stanley Wilson, *Luzena Stanley Wilson '49er* (Oakland, Calif.: Mills College, Eucalyptus, 1937), 19.

95. Sarah Bayliss Royce, *A Frontier Lady: Recollections of the Gold Rush and Early California* (New Haven: Yale Univ. Press, 1932), 90.

96. Robert Glass Cleland, ed., *Apron Full of Gold: The Letters of Mary Jane Megquier from San Francisco, 1849–1856* (San Marino, Calif.: Huntington Library, 1949), 63.

97. Mrs. Orsemus Bronson Boyd [Frances Anne Mullen Boyd], *Cavalry Life in Tent and Field* (1894; reprint, Lincoln: Univ. of Nebraska Press, 1982), 57.

98. Kenneth L. Holmes, ed., 2:162.

99. Wilson, 27.

100. Kenneth L. Holmes, ed., 3:282–83.

101. Sanford, 137–38.

102. "Stoves and Heating of Rooms," *Scientific American* 5 (27 Oct. 1849), 45.

103. "The Great State Fair," *Scientific American* 5 (14 Sept. 1850), 413.

104. "Stoves, Something Wanted," *Scientific American* 8 (29 Jan. 1853), 157.

105. Mrs. M. L. Varney, "A Housekeeper's Hints to Inventors," *Scientific American,* n.s., 1 (24 Dec. 1859), 411.

106. E. M. Richards, "Inventions for Women—Sensible Suggestions," *Scientific American,* n.s., 2 (26 May 1860), 338.

107. John Fruit, "Further Improvement in Stoves Demanded," *Scientific American,* n.s., 11 (1 Oct. 1864), 214.

108. Eliza Woodson Farnham, *In-Doors and Out; Or, We Farm, Mine, and Live in the Golden State* (New York: Dix, Edwards, 1856), 54–56.

109. "Directions for Using the Air Tight Stove," advertising broadside for an unnamed "manufacturer of cooking, parlor and office stoves," Nashua, N.H., 1840s, AAS.

110. Leslie, 216–17.

111. Esther A. Howland, *The American Economical Housekeeper* (Cincinnati: H. W. Derby, 1845), 75.

112. *Scientific American* 2 (3 Oct. 1846), 16.

113. Bill from Henry Earley to James W. Beekman, 12 Oct. 1842; bill from Benjamin Valentine to James W. Beekman, 2 Dec. 1842, Beekman Family Papers, box VII A, NYHS.

114. Stowe, letter to Calvin Stowe, Aug.–Sept. 1849, Harriet Beecher Stowe Center, Hartford, Conn.

115. Caroline Dustan, Diary, 9 Jan. 1861, New York Public Library, New York, N.Y. Quoted by Garrett, 101.

116. Webster and Parkes, 820.

117. Cornelius, *Young Housekeeper's Friend* (1860), 87–88.

118. Caroline Howard King, *When I Lived in Salem, 1822–1866* (Brattleboro, Vt.: Stephen Day, 1937), 24. Based on several years' experience cooking before an open fire in the Sylvanus Brown House at Slater Mill Historic Site in Pawtucket, R.I., I can confirm that turkey roasted in a tin-reflector oven is juicier and better tasting than turkey "roasted" in the oven of a modern gas or electric stove.

119. Sarah Brewer Bonebright, *The Reminiscences of Newcastle, Iowa, 1848: A History of Webster County, Iowa* (Des Moines: Historical Department of Iowa, 1921), 168.

120. Harriet Connor Brown, *Grandmother Brown's Hundred Years, 1827–1927* (Boston: Little, Brown, 1929), 57.

121. American Medical Association, 457 and 475.

122. "Lyman's Apparatus for Warming and Ventilating Rooms," *Scientific American* 9 (11 Mar. 1854), 204.

123. Elizabeth Sullivan Stuart, letter to Robert Stuart Jr., 26 Dec. 1850, in *Stuart Letters of Robert and Elizabeth Sullivan Stuart and Their Children, 1819–1864,* 2 vols. (n.p.: n.p, 1961), 1:168–69.

124. "The Life, from birth of a child of cultured parents of means." Memorandum of Elizabeth Babcock Leonard by her mother, 1841–1850, HDL. Quoted by Nylander, *Snug Fireside*, 100–101.

125. *Scientific American* 7 (14 Feb. 1852), 174.

126. J. G. Whitlock, "Management of Boilers and Kitchen Ranges," *Scientific American*, n.s., 1 (5 Nov. 1859), 299.

127. Elisabeth Hysing Koren, *The Diary of Elisabeth Koren*, trans. and ed. David T. Nelson (Northfield, Minn.: Norwegian-American Historical Association, 1955), 117–18.

128. Koren, 173 and 179.

129. Koren, 221–22 and 227.

130. Koren, 324.

131. Brown, 105–6 and 117.

132. Sanford, 62 and 150.

133. Henry Ward Beecher, "The Wear and Tear of Housekeeping," *The Household* 1 (1869), 16–18.

134. Hale, *Mrs. Hale's New Cook Book*, 112.

135. Cowan, *More Work*, 62.

136. Ryan, *Cradle*, 198.

137. Dr. J. H. Hanaford, "Woman's Servitude," *The Household* 1 (1868), 136.

138. Varney, "Housekeeper's Hints," 410–11.

139. Mrs. M. L. Varney, "A Woman Pleads for New Inventions," *Scientific American*, n.s., 2 (28 Apr. 1860), 279.

7. "This Necessary Evil — The Cooking Stove"

1. Eunice White Beecher, *Motherly Talks with Young Housekeepers* (New York: J. B. Ford, 1873), 198–206.

2. Oscar Wilde, "The Practical Application of the Principles of the Aesthetic Theory to Exterior and Interior House Decoration," in *The Essays of Oscar Wilde* (New York: Albert and Charles Boni, 1935), 486–87.

3. Eugene Field, "Stoves and Sunshine," *The Poems* (1922), online, LION, 22 Feb. 1999.

4. "Stove Bronzes and Tiles," *Scientific American*, n.s., 57 (24 Sept. 1887), 196.

5. Laura C. Holloway, *The Hearthstone; Or, Life at Home* (Chicago: L. P. Miller, 1887), 34–35.

6. "The Manufacture of Stoves, Ranges, and Heaters," *Scientific American*, n.s., 42 (29 May 1880), 340.

7. Maria Parloa, *Miss Parloa's New Cook Book and Marketing Guide* (Boston: Estes and Lauriat, 1880), 64.

8. Barstow Stove Co., *Fireside and Kitchen Ancient and Modern* (Providence, R.I.: n.p., 1885), unpaginated.

9. Horace Greeley et al., *The Great Industries of the United States* (Hartford, Conn.: J. R. Burr and Hyde, 1872), 443–44.

10. *The Housewife's Library* (n.p.: n.p., 1892), 255–56.

11. Pauline E. Hopkins, "Sappho," in *Invented Lives: Narratives of Black Women, 1860–1960*, ed. Mary Helen Washington (New York: Anchor, 1987), 111–12.

12. Willa Cather, *My Ántonia* (1918; reprint, Boston: Houghton Mifflin, 1954), 65.

13. Marietta Holley, *My Opinions and Betsy Bobbet's* (Hartford, Conn.: American, 1875), 430.

14. Dorothy Richardson, *The Long Day: The Story of a New York Working Girl* (1905; reprint, Charlottesville: Univ. Press of Virginia, 1990), 27–28.

15. Lucelia A. Clark, "To My Old Cookstove" (28 Mar. 1899). Manuscript in possession of Mrs. Clark's granddaughter, Mrs. Nina Taylor, Cranberry Lake, N.Y.

16. Quoted by H. Kenneth Dirlam, *Baxter's Banner Stoves* (Mansfield, Ohio: n.p., 1969), 27.

17. Jeremiah Dwyer, "Stoves and Heating Apparatus," in *One Hundred Years of American Commerce,* 2 vols., ed. Chauncey DePew (New York: D. O. Haynes, 1895), 2:361; *Scientific American,* n.s., 27 (26 Oct. 1872), 257.

18. Leggett, comp., 3:1459–86. The data for 1874–79 were obtained from the patent descriptions and subject indexes of the weekly *Official Gazette of the United States Patent Office.*

19. "An Improved Household Ash Sifter," *Scientific American,* n.s., 57 (15 Sept. 1887), 243.

20. Peirce, *Fire,* 136–38.

21. Double Reservoir Stove Co., advertising broadside, 1870, NMAH.

22. Swett, Quimby & Perry, *The New Empire Hot-Air, Gas, and Base-burning Cooking Stove, for Wood and Coal, with Hawks' Auxiliary Air-Chamber* (Troy, N.Y.: n.p., 1869), 1–6.

23. Pratt & Wentworth, *"Peerless," The Best Cooking Stove Ever Made* (Boston: Marvin and Son, 1866), 3.

24. This statistic was derived from Leggett, comp., 3:1459–86, and from indexes and patent descriptions published in the weekly *Official Gazette of the United States Patent Office* from 1874 through 1880.

25. S. W. Gibbs & Co., *Price List of Stoves, Summer Ranges, Furnaces, Heaters* (New York: J. W. Orr, 1868), unpaginated; Perry & Co., *Price List of the Oriental and American Stove Works* (Albany, N.Y.: Weed, Parsons, c. 1869), AAS, unpaginated.

26. "In the Kitchen," *The Household* 5 (1872), 132.

27. Littlefield Stove Manufacturing Co., *The Morning Glory Hot-Blast Cooking Stove* (Albany, N.Y.: n.p., 1874), 18–53. Numbers add up to more than 117 because many letter writers commented about more than one feature of the stove.

28. Pratt & Wentworth, 7–19.

29. Swett, Quimby & Perry, 10–27.

30. Swett, Quimby & Perry, 11 and 17.

31. Swett, Quimby & Perry, 15 and 17.

32. Swett, Quimby & Perry, 11 and 12.

33. Swett, Quimby & Perry, 21 and 27; Littlefield Stove Manufacturing Co., 38 and 43.

34. *The Household* 3 (1870), 12.

35. L. H. Bingham, "Stove Castings," *Scientific American,* n.s., 42 (5 June 1880), 353.

36. *The Household* 3 (1870), 12.

37. "Stove-Makers' Association," *New York Times,* 10 Feb. 1881, 3.

38. George H. Barbour, "Report to National Association of Stove Manufacturers," *Scientific American,* n.s., 61 (3 Aug. 1889), 70.

39. Dwyer, 361.

40. Edgar Wilson Nye, "The Modern Parlor Stove," in *Bill Nye and Boomerang; Or, The Tale of the Meek-Eyed Mule, and Some Other Literary Gems* (1881; reprint, St. Clair Shores, Mich.: Scholarly, 1971), 41–43.

41. "Shocking Calamity," *New York Times,* 1 Jan. 1866, 3.

42. *New York Times,* 18 Nov. 1875, 4.

43. "Explosion of a Kitchen Range," *New York Times,* 27 Dec. 1870, 2.

44. E. G. Patter, "Dangerous Stoves," *Scientific American,* n.s., 22 (9 Apr. 1870), 237.

45. "M," "Improved Stove Legs Wanted," *Scientific American,* n.s., 252 (2 Apr. 1870), 220.

46. Between 1865 and 1880, seventy-one stove-leg designs and fastening mechanisms were patented. This information was obtained from Leggett, comp. 3:1459–86 and from the patent descriptions and subject indexes of the weekly *Official Gazette of the United States Patent Office.*

47. *Official Gazette of the United States Patent Office* 9 (8 Feb. 1876), 283; *Gazette* 21 (14 Mar. 1882), 750; *Gazette* 20 (29 Nov. 1881), 1535; *Gazette* 11 (24 Apr. 1877), 703; *Gazette* 21 (3 Jan. 1882), 55. The information regarding patents for stovepipe and related items was obtained from Leggett, comp., 3:1459–86, and from the patent descriptions and subject indexes of the weekly *Official Gazette of the United States Patent Office.*

48. Quoted by Cathy Luchetti, *Home on the Range: A Culinary History of the American West* (New York: Villard, 1993), 150.

49. "Justice to Stoves," *New York Times,* 4 Nov. 1876, 4; "The Stove-Pipe Agony," *New York Times,* 21 Oct. 1877, 6.

50. Ben Logan, *The Land Remembers: The Story of a Farm and Its People* (1975; reprint, Minnetonka, Minn.: Northword, 1999), 180.

51. Marietta Holley, *Samantha among the Brethren* (New York: Funk and Wagnalls, 1892), 53.

52. The Grand Windsor Ranges advertised by Montgomery Ward in 1895 weighed between 360 and 635 pounds, and the Acme Regal Steel Ranges advertised by Sears, Roebuck seven years later weighed between 291 and 417 pounds. Montgomery Ward & Co., *Catalogue No. 57* (1895; reprint, New York: Dover, 1969), 418; Sears, Roebuck & Co., *Catalogue* (1902; reprint, New York: Dover, 1969), 813.

53. Samuel Clemens [pseud. Mark Twain], "Putting Up Stoves," *Scientific American,* n.s., 22 (1 Jan. 1870), 13.

54. Emily French, *Emily: The Diary of a Hard-Worked Woman,* ed. Janet Lecompte (Lincoln: Univ. of Nebraska Press, 1987), 96, 123, 34, 115, 21, 125, 23, and 24.

55. Susan E. P. Brown Forbes, 21, 22, and 29 Dec. 1871.

56. Anne Ellis, *The Life of an Ordinary Woman* (1929; reprint, Lincoln: Univ. of Nebraska Press, 1980), 78 and 208.

57. Carrie Young, *Nothing to Do But Stay* (New York: Dell, 1991), 77.

58. Barbara Brandt, "Washing Day," *The Household* 7 (1874), 228.

59. Black & Gerner, *Radiant Home Ranges, Stoves, Ovens, and Double Heaters* (Buffalo, N.Y.: Matthews-Northrup, 1895), 35.

60. Susan Warner, *What She Could* (New York: Williams, 1870), 245–46.

61. Louisa May Alcott, *Little Women* (1868; reprint, Boston: Little, Brown, 1926), 142.

62. Elizabeth S. Miller, *In the Kitchen* (Boston: Lee and Shepard, 1875), 24–25.

63. Quoted by Luchetti, 150–51.

64. Edgar A. Guest, "When Father Shook the Stove" (1916). Quoted by Peirce, *Fire,* 141–42.

65. Juliet Corson, *Family Living on $500 a Year* (New York: Harper, 1888), 267–69.

66. Eunice White Beecher, *All Around the House; Or, How to Make Homes Happy* (New York: D. Appleton, 1879), 370–71.

67. Adeline D. T. Whitney, *Just How: A Key to the Cook-Books* (Boston: Houghton, Osgood, 1880), 7.

68. "Managing a Coal Fire," *Ladies' Home Journal* 1 (Nov. 1884), 5.

69. Thomas K. Beecher, "Bread-Making," *Wood's Household Magazine* 9 (1871), 173.

70. Rosetta B. Hastings, "About Baking," *The Household* 5 (1872), 110.

71. Kathleen Ann Smallzreid, *The Everlasting Pleasure: Influences on America's Kitchens, Cooks, and Cookery, from 1565 to the Year 2000* (New York: Appleton-Century-Crofts, 1956), 229.

72. Mae Savell Croy, *Putnam's Household Handbook* (New York: G. P. Putnam's Sons, 1916), 118. Similar advice had long been a staple of American cookbooks and domestic advice manuals. See, for example, Lydia M. Child, *The American Frugal Housewife* (Boston: Carter, Hendee, 1832), 79.

73. Jerry L. Twedt, *Growing Up in the 40s: Rural Reminiscence* (Ames: Iowa State Univ. Press, 1996), 127 and 122.

74. S. D. Farrar, *The Homekeeper* (Boston: n.p., 1872), 10.

75. Eunice White Beecher, *All Around the House*, 307–8 and 338–39.

76. Eugene C. Gardner, *Homes, and How to Make Them* (Boston: James R. Osgood, 1874), 220.

77. Elizabeth Hale Gilman, "Kitchen Sketches," *Scribner's Magazine* 33 (May 1903), 577–80.

78. Catharine E. Beecher and Harriet Beecher Stowe, *The American Woman's Home* (1869; reprint, Hartford, Conn.: Stowe-Day Foundation, 1975), 66–73.

79. *Smiley's Cook Book and Universal Household Guide* (Chicago: Smiley, 1894), 760.

80. Strasser, *Never Done*, 203–4; Smallzreid, 176–81.

81. Quoted by Strasser, *Never Done*, 203.

82. Quoted by Strasser, *Never Done*, 203.

83. "The Kitchen and Its Labors," *The Household* 1 (1868), 8.

84. Juliet Corson, *Everyday Cookery, Table Talk, and Hints for the Laundry* (Chicago: Adams and Westlake Mfg. Co., 1884), 41.

85. James C. Fernald, *The New Womanhood* (Boston: D. Lothrop, 1891), 72–73.

86. Gardner, *Homes*, 210–11.

87. Mrs. N. Orr, *DeWitt's Connecticut Cook Book and Housekeeper's Assistant* (New York: Robert M. DeWitt, 1871), 11–12.

88. Isabella Alden [pseud. Pansy], *The Pocket Measure* (Boston: D. Lothrop, 1881), 308–13.

89. "Household Talk," *The Household* 2 (1869), 25.

90. Smallzreid, 100.

91. Ella Farman, *The Cooking Club of Tu-Whit Hollow* (Boston: D. Lothrop, 1886), unpaginated.

92. Susan Warner, *What She Could*, 276–78.

93. Stephen Crane, "The Stove," in *Whilomville Stories* (1900; reprint, New York: Garrett, 1969), 120–25.

94. Crane, "The Stove," 126 and 131.

95. Crane, "The Stove," 132–35.

96. Crane, "The Stove," 135–40.

97. Marietta Holley, *My Wayward Pardner; Or, My Trials with Josiah, America, the Widow Bump, and Et cet ery* (Hartford, Conn.: American, 1881), 406.

98. Ellis, 235.

99. "Making It Hot for A Sewing Machine Agent," *The Day's Doings* 15 (9 Oct. 1875), 14.

100. George Madden Martin, "Fire from Heaven," *American Magazine* 67 (Dec. 1908), 138–41.

8. "The Disappearing Kitchen Range"

1. Quoted by Elizabeth Hampsten, *Read This Only to Yourself: The Private Writings of Midwestern Women, 1880–1910* (Bloomington: Indiana Univ. Press, 1982), 193.

2. Judy Nolte Lensink, *"A Secret to Be Burried": The Diary and Life of Emily Hawley Gillespie, 1858–1888* (Iowa City: Univ. of Iowa Press, 1989), 258.

3. This statistic comes from Leggett, comp., 3:1459–86, as well as from the patent descriptions and subject indexes of the *Official Gazette of the United States Patent Office.*

4. *Official Gazette of the United States Patent Office* 21 (14 Mar. 1882), 719.

5. "A Woman's Idea of What a Kitchen Should Be," *The Household* 2 (1869), 75.

6. Gardner, *Homes,* 215 and 239.

7. Eunice White Beecher, *All Around the House,* 95 and 233.

8. Charlotte Perkins Gilman, *The Home: Its Work and Influence* (1903; reprint, New York: Source Book, 1976), 145.

9. Holloway, 389.

10. Katharine C. Budd, "Model Kitchens," *The Outlook* 83 (Aug. 25, 1906), 952.

11. Clifford E. Clark, "The Vision of the Dining Room: Plan Book Dreams and Middle-Class Realities," in *Dining in America, 1850–1900,* ed. Kathryn Grover (Amherst: Univ. of Massachusetts Press, 1987), 147–53.

12. Gardner, *Homes,* 209.

13. George F. Barber, *The Cottage Souvenir No. 2* (1891; reprint, Watkins Glen, N.Y.: American Life Foundation, 1982), passim.

14. Adeline D. T. Whitney, *We Girls: A Home Story* (Boston: James R. Osgood, 1871), 93–96.

15. Whitney, *We Girls,* 99–103 and 150.

16. Whitney, *We Girls,* 128 and 147–49.

17. M. H. Carter, "The Disappearing Kitchen Range," *Ladies' Home Journal* 38 (Apr. 1921), 96.

18. Carter, 96–100.

19. Clifford E. Clark, *The American Family Home, 1800–1960* (Chapel Hill: Univ. of North Carolina Press, 1986), 23–24 and 82; Strasser, *Never Done,* 53–56; Gwendolyn Wright, *Building the Dream: A Social History of Housing in America* (New York: Pantheon, 1981), 102.

20. David P. Handlin, *The American Home: Architecture and Society, 1815–1915* (Boston: Little, Brown, 1979), 479.

21. "The Open Fire," *The Household* 1 (1868), 19.

22. Frank R. and Marian Stockton, *The Home: Where It Should Be and What to Put in It* (New York: G. P. Putnam's, 1873), 91.

23. Eugene C. Gardner, *Home Interiors* (Boston: James R. Osgood, 1878), 185–86.

24. Gwendolyn Wright, *Moralism and the Model Home: Domestic Architecture and Cultural Conflict in Chicago, 1873–1913* (Chicago: Univ. of Chicago Press, 1980), 32.

25. Paul G. Huston, *Around an Old Homestead: A Book of Memories* (Cincinnati: Jennings and Graham, 1906), 68.

26. William T. Davis, *Plymouth Memories of an Octogenarian* (Plymouth, Mass.: Memorial, 1906), 482.

27. Hamlin Garland, *A Daughter of the Middle Border* (New York: Macmillan, 1923), 298–304.

28. Kenneth L. Ames, introduction to *The Colonial Revival in America,* ed. Alan Axelrod (New York: W. W. Norton, 1985), 10–14.

29. Alice Morse Earle, *Home Life in Colonial Days* (1898; reprint, Stockbridge, Mass.: Berkshire Traveller, 1974), 52.

30. Rodris Roth, "The New England, or 'Olde Tyme,' Kitchen Exhibit at Nineteenth-Century Fairs," in Axelrod, ed., 159–60.

31. Quoted by Roth, 162.

32. Roth, 173–81.

33. David R. Proper, "The Fireplace at Memorial Hall, Deerfield, Massachusetts: Picturesque Arrangements; Tender Associations," in *Foodways in the Northeast,* ed. Peter Benes (Boston: Boston Univ., 1984), 121–22; Melinda Young Faye, "The Beginnings of the Period Room in American Museums: Charles P. Wilcomb's Colonial Kitchens, 1896, 1906, 1910," in Axelrod, ed. 218–25.

34. Walter A. Dyer, *The Lure of the Antique* (New York: Century, 1910), 446. Quoted by Proper, 114.

35. Huston, 53.

36. Stowe, *Oldtown Folks,* 61 and 341.

37. "Grandmother's Houses," *The Household* 5 (1872), 116.

38. Emily R. Barnes, *Narratives, Traditions, and Personal Reminiscences Connected with the Early History of the Bellows Family and of the Village of Walpole, New Hampshire* (Boston: George H. Ellis, 1888), 43.

39. George F. Hoar, *A Boy Sixty Years Ago* (Boston: Perry Mason, 1898), 11–14.

40. Ellen H. Rollins [pseud. E. H. Arr], *New England Bygones* (1883; reprint, Stockbridge, Mass.: Berkshire Traveller, 1977), 63–64.

41. Rollins, 64–65.

42. Harriet Beecher Stowe, *The Minister's Wooing* (1859; reprint, Hartford, Conn.: Stowe-Day Foundation, 1978), 2–3.

43. Rollins, 67.

44. Conklin, 17–18.

45. Lucy Larcom, *A New England Girlhood* (Boston: Houghton, Mifflin, 1889), 21–23.

46. In 1983, Ruth Schwartz Cowan concluded that "the enclosed stove . . . was not greeted with complete enthusiasm," citing Bolles's comments as evidence. Bolles, she thought, "was probably expressing the sentiments of the dominant English part of the population." Cowan, *More Work,* 55.

47. Bolles, 276.

48. For another example, see Edward Lamson Henry's 1872 painting of the Bullards, reproduced in John Maass, *The Victorian Home in America* (New York: Hawthorn Books, 1972), 92.

49. Karen Halttunen, "From Parlor to Living Room: Domestic Space, Interior Decoration, and the Culture of Personality," in *Consuming Visions: Accumulation and Display of Goods in*

America, 1880–1920, ed. Simon J. Bronner (New York: W. W. Norton, 1989), 166–67; William Seale, *The Tasteful Interlude: American Interiors Through the Camera's Eye, 1860–1917,* 2d ed. (Nashville, Tenn.: American Association for State and Local History, 1981), 14, 100, 135, and 176.

50. Clarence Cook, "Beds and Tables, Stools and Candlesticks: II," *Scribner's Monthly* 11 (Jan. 1876), 349.

51. "Squatter Life in New York," *Harper's New Monthly Magazine* 61 (Sept. 1880), 569.

52. Stephen Crane, *Maggie: A Girl of the Streets* (1893; reprint, New York: Fawcett, 1960), 16–19.

53. J. B. Campbell, "How the Farmer Spent His Christmas," *World's Columbian Exposition Illustrated* (Dec. 1891): 19–31.

54. Susan Warner, *What She Could,* 103.

55. C. Van C. Mathews, "The Open Fireplace," *Harper's Bazaar* 37 (Aug. 1903), 769.

56. Lizzie Wilson of Brattleboro, Vermont, noted in her diary on Sept. 22, 1866, for example: "Have been baking brown bread beans pies cake &c. we have heated the brick oven and had good luck." Lizzie A. Wilson Goodenough, Diary (Brattleboro, Vt., 1865–1875), AAS.

57. Farrar, 240.

58. Ann Howe, *The American Kitchen Directory and Housewife* (Cincinnati: Howe's Subscription Book Concern, 1867), 64–65.

59. Elmore, 22–23.

60. Edward Everett Hale, *A New England Boyhood* (Boston: n.p., 1900) 58. Quoted by Peirce, *Fire,* 143.

61. Stowe, *Oldtown Folks,* 88.

62. Mary A. Livermore, *The Story of My Life* (Hartford, Conn.: A. D. Worthington, 1897), 46–47.

63. "The Art of Housekeeping," *The Household* 3 (1870), 10–11.

64. Stowe, *House,* 294.

65. Lyman and Lyman, 531–32.

66. "Cooking Stoves," *The Household* 2 (1869), 95.

67. Dorothy Canfield, "The End," *American Magazine* 66 (June 1908), 135.

68. Caroline Howard Gilman, *Recollections of a Housekeeper* (New York: Harper, 1834), 152–54.

69. Carl N. Degler, *At Odds: Women and the Family in America from the Revolution to the Present* (New York: Oxford Univ. Press, 1980), 393–94; Dolores Hayden, *The Grand Domestic Revolution* (Cambridge, Mass.: MIT Press, 1981), 72–73; Gwendolyn Wright, *Building the Dream,* 37–38.

70. "Shall We Board?" *The Household* 1 (1869), 172–73.

71. Eunice White Beecher, *All Around the House,* 167–69.

72. Quoted by Hayden, 60.

73. J. V. Sears, "Housekeeping Hereafter," *Atlantic Monthly* 48 (Sept. 1881), 334–37.

74. Hayden, 3.

75. Quoted by Hayden, 226.

76. Hayden, 209 and 346–55.

77. Hayden, 26, 214–15, 227, and 281.

78. Benjamin R. Andrews, foreword in Pattison, 18.

79. Christine M. Frederick, *The New Housekeeping: Efficiency Studies in Home Management* (Garden City, N.Y.: Doubleday, Page, 1913), 23–59, 84–87, 126–45, and 101.

80. Hayden, 285.

81. Frederick, 41 and 71–80.

82. Ruth Schwartz Cowan, "Ellen Swallow Richards: Technology and Women," in *Technology in America: A History of Individuals and Ideas,* ed. Carroll W. Pursell Jr. (Cambridge, Mass.: MIT Press, 1981), 149.

83. Hayden, 157–59.

84. Mabel Hyde Kittredge, *Practical Homemaking* (New York: Century Co., 1915), 10.

85. Quoted by Hayden, 124.

86. Quoted by Hayden, 159.

87. Charlotte Perkins Gilman, *The Home,* 128 and 95–96.

88. Strasser, *Never Done,* 38.

89. Charlotte Perkins Gilman, "To the Young Wife," in *In This Our World* (1893; reprint, Boston: Small, Maynard, 1914), 129–31.

90. Charlotte Perkins Gilman, "Six Hours a Day," in *In This Our World,* 136–37.

91. Charlotte Perkins Gilman, "The Holy Stove," in *In This Our World,* 158–60.

92. Elizabeth Akers Allen, "Madge Miller," in *The Triangular Society* (1886), on-line, LION, 22 Feb. 1999.

93. "Our Market for Ranges—and Our Competition," *Electrical Merchandising* 43 (May 1930), 38. Cited by Cowan, *More Work,* 91.

94. Eleanor Arnold, ed., *Voices of American Homemakers* (Bloomington: Indiana Univ. Press, 1985), 179–80.

95. Beulah Meier Pelton, *We Belong to the Land; Memories of a Midwesterner* (Ames: Iowa State Univ. Press, 1984), 41–42.

96. Pelton, 42–43.

97. Pelton, 40–45.

98. Mary E. A. Wager, "Kitchen Aids," *The Household* 4 (1871), 84.

99. James W. Van Cleave, "The Stove Trade," *Annals of the American Academy of Political and Social Sciences* 35 (July–Dec. 1909), 463.

100. U.S. Department of Agriculture, *Domestic Needs of Farm Women* (Washington, D.C.: Government Printing Office, 1915), 3–5 and 22–26.

101. U.S. Department of Agriculture, 27, 29, and 43.

102. U.S. Department of Agriculture, 44.

103. Pattison, 114–15 and 121.

104. Gene Stratton-Porter, *Michael O'Halloran* (Garden City, N.Y.: Doubleday, Page, 1915), 394–96.

105. Stratton-Porter, 496–97.

106. Leggett, comp., 3:1476.

9. "A Nice, Clean Fire Whenever Needed"

1. Loris S. Russell, *Handy Things to Have Around the House: Oldtime Domestic Appliances of Canada and the United States* (Toronto: McGraw-Hill Ryerson, 1979), 34–35; Strasser, *Never Done,* 68–69.

2. Leggett, comp., 3:1476 and 3:1484.

3. Editorial, *Scientific American* 5 (24 Aug. 1850), 389.

4. "Gas Stoves," *Scientific American* 8 (9 Oct. 1852), 32.

5. "Economy and Comfort Combined. Air and Vapor for Fuel!" Advertising brochure for "Morrill's Erovapor Cooking Stoves, Flat Irons, and Nurse Lamps" (Boston: E. L. Mitchell, 1858), unpaginated, AAS.

6. William F. Shaw, *Illustrated and Descriptive Catalogue of Gas Heating and Cooking Apparatus* (Boston: Damrell and Moore, c. 1860), 1–3 and 9, AAS.

7. Elizabeth Nicholson, *The Economical Cook and House Book* (Philadelphia: Willis P. Hazard, 1857), 3 and 83.

8. Nicholson, 83.

9. "Economy and Comfort Combined"; Nicholson, 83; Shaw, 9–23.

10. Susan E. P. Brown Forbes, 20–23 Aug., Sept., and 25–27 Oct. 1864.

11. "Gas Stoves," 32.

12. "The Gas Question," *Scientific American,* n.s., 16 (23 Mar. 1867), 188.

13. Rose, 19–20.

14. "Gas vs. Coal," *New York Times,* 17 June 1866, 5.

15. Shaw, 48.

16. Susan E. P. Brown Forbes, 23 Aug. 1864.

17. Smallzreid, 200.

18. Quoted by Smallzreid, 200.

19. Smallzreid, 200.

20. Susan E. P. Brown Forbes, 6 Jan. 1866.

21. Shaw, 47.

22. Henry Ward Beecher, *Eyes and Ears* (Boston: Ticknor and Fields, 1863), 358–61.

23. Henry Ward Beecher, *Eyes and Ears,* 361–63.

24. "Chemistry of a Charcoal Fire," *Leslie's New York Journal* (Aug. 1856), 91.

25. "The Heating of Buildings," *The Household* 3 (1870), 37.

26. Leggett, comp., 3:1476–80.

27. Florence Sewing Machine Co., *The Florence Oil Stoves for Cooking, Heating, and Illuminating* (Florence, Mass.: n.p., c. 1880), unpaginated, NMAH.

28. Adams & Westlake Manufacturing Co., *Adams & Westlake Improved Wire Gauze, Non-Explosive Oil Stove* (Chicago: n.p., 1881), unpaginated, NMAH.

29. Florence Sewing Machine Co., *Price List and Cooking Receipts for the Florence Oil Cooking and Heating Stoves* (Florence, Mass.: n.p., 1883), 11, NMAH.

30. *Housewife's Library,* 275–77.

31. "K. L. D.," letter to editor, *Ladies' Home Journal* 3 (Nov. 1886), 8.

32. Central Oil Gas Co., advertising broadside (Boston: n.p., c. 1895), NMAH.

33. Florence Sewing Machine Co., *Florence Oil Stoves.*

34. Eleanor Arnold, ed., *Party Lines, Pumps, and Privies* (n.p.: Indiana Extension Homemakers Association, 1984), 19.

35. "Gasoline Stoves and How to Use Them," *Scientific American* 58 (19 May 1888), 310.

36. Arnold, ed., *Party Lines,* 19.

37. "Gasoline Stoves," 310.

38. Quoted by Russell Lynes, *The Domesticated Americans* (New York: Harper and Row, 1957), 120.

39. "Serious Gasoline Explosion," *New York Times,* 21 Oct. 1877, 1.

40. Lynes, 120.

41. Arnold, ed., *Party Lines,* 19–20.

42. Quoted by Lynes, 120.

43. Arnold, ed., *Party Lines,* 20.

44. Cowan, *More Work,* 93.

45. Pattison, 116.

46. A. E. Kennelly, "Electricity in the Household," *Scribner's Magazine* 7 (Jan. 1890): 102–113.

47. William Wilson Primm, "The Electrical Department," *World's Columbian Exposition Illustrated* 2 (Oct. 1892), 174.

48. R. R. Bowker, "Electricity," *Harper's New Monthly Magazine* 93 (Oct. 1896), 722.

49. Katharine C. Budd, "Model Kitchens," *The Outlook* 83 (25 Aug. 1906), 953.

50. "Cooking by Electricity," *New York Times,* 22 May 1898, 14.

51. Smallzreid, 217.

52. Lynes, 121.

53. Smallzreid, 217; Cowan, *More Work,* 93–94.

54. Georgie Boynton Child, *The Efficient Kitchen* (New York: McBride, Nast, 1914), 93.

55. Helen Kinne and Anna M. Cooley, *Foods and Household Management* (New York: Macmillan, 1915), 33 and 51–52.

56. Georgie Boynton Child, 93–94. Child appears to have exaggerated the cost of electricity, at least. David E. Nye reports that "by 1909, improved efficiency in generating equipment and concentration of production in larger power plants had lowered the average rate to 2.5 [cents] per kilowatt hour." Nye, *Electrifying America: Social Meanings of a New Technology, 1880–1940* (Cambridge, Mass: MIT Press, 1990), 261.

57. Strasser, *Never Done,* 78–81.

58. David E. Nye, 268.

59. Robert S. and Helen Merrell Lynd, *Middletown: A Study in American Culture* (1929; reprint, New York: Harcourt, Brace, 1956), 98 and 172.

60. H. Bohle, "The Electrical Kitchen for Private Houses," *Electricity* 38 (July–Aug. 1924). Quoted by Giedion, 546.

61. Georgie Boynton Child, 88–91.

62. Georgie Boynton Child, 91–98.

63. Montgomery Ward & Co., 418–24; Sears, Roebuck & Co., 813–28.

64. Rose, 31 and 77–78.

65. Cowan, *More Work,* 90.

66. Ada Chester Bond, "To Keep the House Cool," *Ladies' Home Journal* 8 (July 1891), 4.

67. "Cooking By Gas," *Scientific American* 69 (28 Oct. 1893), 274.

68. *Housewife's Library,* 259–67.

69. Cited by Susan Strasser, "Never Done: The Ideology and Technology of Household Work, 1850–1930" (Ph.D. diss., State Univ. of New York at Stony Brook, 1977), 84.

70. Sarah Tyson Rorer, *Mrs. Rorer's New Cook Book* (1898; reprint, New York: Crown, 1970), 35.

71. Mary P. Ryan, *Womanhood in America from Colonial Times to the Present,* 2d ed. (New York: New Viewpoints, 1979), 118–50.

72. David M. Katzman, *Seven Days a Week: Women and Domestic Service in Industrializing America* (Urbana: Univ. of Illinois Press, 1981), 228; Daniel E. Sutherland, *Americans and Their Servants: Domestic Service in the United States from 1800 to 1920* (Baton Rouge: Louisiana State Univ. Press, 1981), 183.

73. "The New Enlightenment," Western Electric Co. advertisement, *Good Housekeeping* (Oct. 1916), 149.

74. "See the Duplex-Alcazar Before You Buy a Range," Alcazar Range & Heater Co. advertisement, *Good Housekeeping* (Oct. 1916), 197.

75. "The Popular Farm Electric Range," Malleable Iron Range Co. advertisement, *Electricity on the Farm* (July 1931), 5.

76. In 1930, nearly 14 million of the nation's households cooked with gas, compared to the 7.7 million still using wood and coal. An additional 6.4 million used oil, whereas only 875,000 had switched to electricity. Cowan, *More Work*, 91.

77. Standard Gas Equipment Co., *How to Plan the New Style Kitchen* (New York: n.p., 1926), 7–8.

10. "Rediscovering the Woodburning Cookstove"

1. Robert Bobrowski, *Rediscovering the Woodburning Cookstove* (Old Greenwich, Conn.: Chatham, 1976), 51.

2. Lynes, 115–16.

3. Wendell Berry, *The Unsettling of America: Culture and Agriculture* (New York: Avon, 1977), 81–85 and 95.

4. "They're Cookin' with Wood," *Newsweek* (2 Jan. 1978), 53.

5. "Look Who's Setting the World on Fire," *Forbes* (13 Nov. 1978), 97.

6. Margaret Byrd Adams, *American Wood Heat Cookery* (Seattle: Pacific Search, 1984), 10.

7. "The New Generation of Stoves," *Mother Earth News* 126 (Nov.–Dec. 1990), 43.

8. Bobrowski, 7 and 50.

9. Bobrowski, 44, 52, and 70.

10. Bobrowski, 95.

11. Bobrowski, back cover.

12. Jane Cooper, *Woodstove Cookery: At Home on the Range* (Charlotte, Vt.: Garden Way, 1977), back cover and 1–2.

13. Jane Cooper, 1–3.

14. In addition to advice on stove selection, operation, and maintenance, Cooper's book includes more than one hundred pages of recipes.

15. Madden, Santoro, and Boram quoted in Suzanne Curley, "Still Cooking: The Lure of Old Stoves," *Newsday* (13 June 1996), on-line, Lexis-Nexis, 20 Jan. 1999.

16. Mary Lenore Presper, *The Joys of Woodstoves and Fireplaces* (New York: Grosset and Dunlap, 1980), 33–34.

17. Quoted in Curley.

18. Anita Craw, *Wood Stove Cooking Adventures* (Orofino, Idaho: Craws Wood Stoves, 1976), 31–41.

19. John Engels, "Stove Cleaning," *Shenandoah* 47 (1997), 5.

20. P. K. Thomajan, "Ye Olde Stove: A Sentimental Rememoir," foreword to *Authentic Vic-*

torian Stoves, Heaters, Ranges, etc.: An Unabridged Reprint of the Illustrated Floyd, Wells & Co. Catalog, ca. 1898 (New York: Dover, 1988), vii–viii.

21. Kitchens by Design advertisement, *Maine Life* (May 1982), 7.

22. Home page for Keokuk Antique Stoves, Hamilton, Ill., www.keokukstoveworks.com, 13 May 1999.

23. Best Buy and Sears advertising inserts, *St. Petersburg Times,* 6 June 1999.

24. Home page for Antique Stoves, Tekonsha, Mich., www.antiquestoves.com, 13 May 1999.

25. Frances Ingraham, "New Stoves Come with Old Touches," *Arizona Republic,* 1 May 1999, on-line, Lexis-Nexis, 20 May 1999.

26. Home page for Elmira Stove Works, Waterloo, Ontario, www.elmirastoveworks.com, 13 May 1999.

27. Heartland Appliances, Kitchener, Ontario, "The Heartland Classic Collection," unpaginated advertising brochure (1996), sent to the author with price list, July 1998.

28. Heartland Appliances.

29. Linda Weltner, "Warm Thoughts for Cold Days," *Boston Globe,* 27 Mar. 1987, A-16.

30. Telephone interview with author, 12 Aug. 1998.

31. Mike Strathdee, "Canadian Cookstoves Hot Property in Hollywood," *Toronto Star,* 15 June 1992, on-line, Lexis-Nexis, 21 Jan. 1999; home page for Keokuk Antique Stoves.

32. Keith Carradine, "Personal Pleasures," *Los Angeles Times,* 24 Nov. 1985, on-line, Lexis-Nexis, 21 Jan. 1999.

33. Laurie Samuel and Craig Samuel, "The Joys of the Wood Cookstove," *Countryside and Small Stock Journal* (May 1994), on-line, Lexis-Nexis, 21 Jan. 1999.

34. Dave Ashenbrenner, "Tips on Woodstove Cookery," *Countryside and Small Stock Journal* (March 1993), on-line, Lexis-Nexis, 21 Jan. 1999.

35. Don O'Briant, "Wood Stoves: There's More to a Warm Kitchen Than the Modern Electric Range," *Atlanta Journal and Constitution* 7 Feb. 1993, on-line, Lexis-Nexis, 21 Jan. 1999.

36. Home page for Lehman's Hardware, Kidron, Ohio, www.lehmans.com, 3 June 1999.

37. Home page for Lehman's Hardware.

38. Judy Jones, "Year 2000 Problem Generates Alarm," *Courier-Journal,* 15 Mar. 1999, on-line, Lexis-Nexis, 7 May 1999.

39. Home page for Buffalo Import Co., Buffalo Cove, N.C., http://members.aol.com/buffaloimp, 7 May 1999.

40. Mike Miller, e-mail to the author, 7 May 1999.

41. "How to Cook with a Wood Stove," on-line, www.freetechsupport.com/csr/woodcook, 13 May 1999.

42. Craw, 42.

43. Andrew Roy Addkison, *Cooking on a Woodburning Stove* (Sacramento, Cal.: Jalmar, 1980), back cover.

44. Addkison, 6.

45. Adams, 236–37.

46. Lynda Moultrie, *The Antique Kitchen Range Bible* (Georgetown, Mass.: A.B.A., 1984), 55.

47. Tom Lippert and Laurel Hilde Lippert, *The Woodstove Cookery Book* (Truckee, Calif.: Tulip, 1980), 6.

48. Addkison, 14.

49. Moultrie, 66.

50. Addkison, 10.

51. Susan Restino, *Mrs. Restino's Country Kitchen* (Bolinas, Calif.: Shelter, 1996), 300.

52. Lippert and Lippert, 5.

53. Phyllis Benham, *Woodstove Cookery*, 5 vols. (n.p.: n.p., 1981), 1:6–7.

54. Presper, 84.

55. Craw, 27–28.

56. Presper, 50.

57. Moultrie, 11 and 70–73.

58. Craw, 6–7.

59. Addkison, 1.

60. Moultrie, 5 and 77.

61. Anne S. Warner, "Tribute to an Old Friend; the Wood-burning Kitchen Range, *Country Journal* (19 Sept. 1997), on-line, Lexis-Nexis, 21 Jan. 1999.

62. Effie Lord, interview, *Foxfire's Book of Wood Stove Cookery* (Rabun Gap, Ga.: Foxfire Fund, 1981), 9.

63. *Foxfire's*, 13.

64. *Foxfire's*, 17.

65. *Foxfire's*, 4.

66. Byron Crawford, "Home on the Range: Old Stove Cooks Up a Storm," *Courier-Journal*, 23 Nov. 1994, on-line, Lexis-Nexis, 21 Jan. 1999.

67. Restino, 291 and 295.

68. Strasser, *Never Done*, 277; Diane Goldner, "Microwaves Full of Overheated Promise," *St. Petersburg Times*, 15 June 1995, D-1 and D-3.

69. Goldner, D-3.

Bibliography

Archival Materials

American Antiquarian Society, Worcester, Mass.

Ruth Henshaw Bascom, Diary (Leicester, Phillipston, and Ashby, Mass.), 1789–1846.
John O. Burleigh, Account Book (Douglas, Mass.), 1846–48.
Draper-Rice Family Papers.
Catharine White Forbes, Diary (Westborough, Mass.), 1846–1902.
Susan E. P. Brown Forbes, Diary (Epsom, N.H.; Boston and Springfield, Mass.), 1841–1908.
Lizzie A. Wilson Goodenough, Diary (Brattleboro, Vt.), 1865–75.
Josephine H. Peirce. "Stoves in the Henry Ford Museum and Greenfield Village, Dearborn, Michigan" (typescript). Leicester, Mass., 1955.
Salisbury Family Papers.
Lucretia Cargill Sibley Correspondence, 1841–76.

Baker Library, Harvard Business School, Boston, Mass.

William J. Keep. "History of Heating Apparatus," 1916.

Barnstable County Courthouse, Barnstable, Mass.

Barnstable County Probate Inventories, 1820–50.

City Archives, Providence, R.I.

Providence County Probate Inventories, 1810–45.

Lucelia A. Clark. "To My Old Cookstove." 28 Mar. 1899

Manuscript in possession of Mrs. Clark's granddaughter, Mrs. Nina Taylor, Cranberry Lake, N.Y.

Harriet Beecher Stowe Center, Hartford, Conn.

Harriet Beecher Stowe Correspondence.

Historic Deerfield Library, Deerfield, Mass.

George Pierce, Account Book (Greenfield, Mass.), 1852–55.

Bibliography

Samuel Pierce & Son, Account Book (Greenfield, Mass.), 1821–26.
Samuel Pierce Jr., Account Book (Greenfield, Mass.), 1834–35.

Museum of American Textile History, Lowell, Mass.

Essex Company Papers.

National Museum of American History, Washington, D.C.

Warshaw Collection of Business Americana.

New York Historical Society, New York, N.Y.

Beekman Family Papers.
Lucretia Warner Hall, Diary (Canaan, N.Y.), 1838–41.
Hoyt-Meacham Family Papers.
S. B. Ludlow, letter to Robbins W. Douglas, 12 Apr. 1836 (Misc. Mss. Ludlow, S. B.).
Henry Vanderlyn, Diary (Oxford, N.Y.), 1827–57.
James Wilson, letter to Morse & Son, 6 Apr. 1839 (Misc. Mss. Wilson, James).

Western Reserve Historical Society, Cleveland, Ohio

Shaker Collection. "Domestic Journal of Important Occurrences" (New Lebanon, N.Y.), 1780–1860.

Books, Articles, and Pamphlets

Adams & Westlake Manufacturing Co. *Adams & Westlake Improved Wire Gauze, Non-Explosive Oil Stove.* Chicago: n.p., 1881.
Adams, Margaret Byrd. *American Wood Heat Cookery.* Seattle: Pacific Search, 1984.
Addkison, Andrew Roy. *Cooking on a Woodburning Stove.* Sacramento, Calif.: Jalmar, 1980.
Aikman, Lonelle. *The Living White House.* Washington, D.C.: White House Historical Association, 1966.
Alcott, Louisa May. *Little Women.* 1868. Reprint. Boston: Little, Brown, 1926.
Alcott, William A. *The Young Housekeeper.* Boston: George W. Light, 1838.
———. *The Young Wife; Or, Duties of Woman in the Marriage Relation.* 1837. Reprint. New York: Arno, 1972.
Alden, Isabella [pseud. Pansy]. *The Pocket Measure.* Boston: D. Lothrop, 1881.
Alexander, Robert L. "The Riddell-Carroll House in Baltimore." *Winterthur Portfolio* 28 (1993): 113–39.
Allen, Ann H. *The Housekeeper's Assistant.* Boston: James Munroe, 1845.
Allen, Elizabeth Akers. "Madge Miller." In *The Triangular Society* (1886). On-line. LION. 22 Feb. 1999.
Allen, Lewis F. *Rural Architecture.* New York: C. M. Saxton, 1852.
The American Housewife. New York: Collins, Keese, 1839.
American Ladies' Memorial. Boston: n.p., 1850.

The American Matron; Or, Practical and Scientific Cookery. Boston: Jas. Munroe and Co., 1851.

American Medical Association. *First Report of the Committee on Public Hygiene of the American Medical Association.* Philadelphia: T. K. and P. G. Collins, 1849.

Andrews, Evangeline W., ed. *Journal of a Lady of Quality.* New Haven: Yale Univ. Press, 1923.

Antique Stoves. Tekonsha, Mich. Home page. www.antiquestoves.com. 13 May 1999.

Armstrong, James Elder. *Life of a Woman Pioneer As Illustrated in the Life of Elsie Strawn Armstrong, 1789–1871.* Chicago: John F. Higgins, 1931.

Arnold, Eleanor, ed. *Party Lines, Pumps, and Privies.* N.p.: Indiana Extension Home-makers Association, 1984.

———, ed. *Voices of American Homemakers.* Bloomington: Indiana Univ. Press, 1985.

Arnold, W. A., & Co. *Arnold's Patent Yankee Cooking Stove.* Northampton, Mass.: n.p., 1837.

Arthur, Timothy Shay. *The Lady at Home; Or, Leaves from the Every-day Book of an American Woman.* New York: John Allen, 1844.

———. *Leaves from the Book of Human Life.* Philadelphia: G. G. Evans, 1860.

———. *Tired of Housekeeping.* New York: D. Appleton, 1842.

———. *Trials and Confessions of an American Housekeeper.* Philadelphia: J. W. Bradley, 1859.

The Arts and Crafts in New York, 1726–1776. New York: New York Historical Society, 1938.

The Arts and Crafts in New York, 1777–1799. New York: New York Historical Society, 1954.

The Arts and Crafts in New York, 1800–1804. New York: New York Historical Society, 1965.

Ashenbrenner, Dave. "Tips on Woodstove Cookery." *Countryside and Small Stock Journal* (March 1993). On-line. Lexis-Nexis. 21 Jan. 1999.

Authentic Victorian Stoves, Heaters, Ranges, etc.: An Unabridged Reprint of the Illustrated Floyd, Wells & Co. Catalog, ca. 1898. New York: Dover, 1988.

Axelrod, Alan, ed. *The Colonial Revival in America.* New York: W. W. Norton, 1985.

Bache, Anna. *Scenes at Home; Or, The Adventures of a Fire Screen.* Philadelphia: Gihon, 1852.

Barber, George F. *The Cottage Souvenir No. 2.* 1891. Reprint. Watkins Glen, N.Y.: American Life Foundation, 1982.

Barnes, Emily R. *Narratives, Traditions, and Personal Reminiscences Connected with the Early History of the Bellows Family and of the Village of Walpole, New Hampshire.* Boston: George H. Ellis, 1888.

Barstow Stove Co. *Fireside and Kitchen Ancient and Modern.* Providence, R.I.: n.p., 1885.

Batchelder, Nancy Barnard. "Growing Up in Peru (1815–1840)." *Vermont History* 21 (1953): 3–9.

Beecher, Catharine E. *Letters to the People on Health and Happiness.* New York: Harper, 1856.

Bibliography

————. *A Treatise on Domestic Economy.* 1841. Reprint. New York: Schocken, 1977.

Beecher, Catharine E., and Harriet Beecher Stowe. *The American Woman's Home.* 1869. Reprint. Hartford, Conn.: Stowe-Day Foundation, 1975.

Beecher, Eunice White. *All Around the House; Or, How to Make Homes Happy.* New York: D. Appleton, 1879.

————. *From Dawn to Daylight; Or, The Simple Story of a Western Home.* New York: Derby and Jackson, 1859.

————. *Motherly Talks with Young Housekeepers.* New York: J. B. Ford, 1873.

Beecher, Henry Ward. *Eyes and Ears.* Boston: Ticknor and Fields, 1863.

Beeman, Richard. *The Evolution of the Southern Backcountry: A Case Study of Lunenburg County, Virginia, 1746–1832.* Philadelphia: Univ. of Pennsylvania Press, 1984.

Benham, Phyllis. *Woodstove Cookery.* 5 vols. N.p.: n.p., 1981.

Benjamin, Asher. *The American Builder's Companion.* 1827. Reprint. New York: Dover, 1969.

Bentley, William. *The Diary of William Bentley.* 4 vols. 1905. Reprint. Gloucester, Mass.: Peter Smith, 1962.

Berry, Wendell. *The Unsettling of America: Culture and Agriculture.* New York: Avon, 1977.

Betts, Edwin Morris, ed. *Thomas Jefferson's Farm Book.* Charlottesville: Univ. Press of Virginia, 1976.

Bibber, Joyce K. *A Home for Everyman: The Greek Revival and Maine Domestic Architecture.* Lanham, Md.: University Publishing Associates, American Association for State and Local History, 1989.

Bigelow, David. *History of Prominent Mercantile and Manufacturing Firms in the United States.* Boston: n.p., 1857.

Binder, Frederick Moore. *Coal Age Empire: Pennsylvania Coal and Its Utilization to 1860.* Harrisburg: Pennsylvania Historical and Museum Commission, 1974.

Bining, Arthur C. *Pennsylvania Iron Manufacture in the Eighteenth Century.* Harrisburg: Pennsylvania Historical and Museum Commission, 1979.

Bishop, J. Leander. *A History of American Manufactures from 1608 to 1860.* 3 vols. Philadelphia: Edward Young, 1866.

Black & Gerner. *Radiant Home Ranges, Stoves, Ovens, and Double Heaters.* Buffalo, N.Y.: Matthews-Northrup, 1895.

Black, Mary, and Jean Lipman. *American Folk Painting.* 1966. Reprint. New York: Bramhall House, 1987.

Bliss, Perrin. *The People's Manual.* Worcester, Mass.: Henry J. Howland, 1848.

Blunt, Susan Baker. *Childish Things: The Reminiscence of Susan Baker Blunt.* Edited by Francis Mason. Grantham, N.H.: Tompson and Rutter, 1988.

Bobrowski, Robert. *Rediscovering the Woodburning Cookstove.* Old Greenwich, Conn.: Chatham, 1976.

Bolles, Albert S. *Industrial History of the United States.* Norwich, Conn.: Henry Bill, 1879.

Bonebright, Sarah Brewer. *The Reminiscences of Newcastle, Iowa, 1848: A History of Webster County, Iowa.* Des Moines: Historical Department of Iowa, 1921.

Bourdin, Henri L., et al., eds. *Sketches of Eighteenth Century America: More "Letters from an American Farmer."* New Haven: Yale Univ. Press, 1925.

Boyd, Mrs. Orsemus Bronson [Frances Anne Mullen Boyd]. *Cavalry Life in Tent and Field.* 1894. Reprint. Lincoln: Univ. of Nebraska Press, 1982.

Boydston, Jeanne. *Home and Work: Housework, Wages, and the Ideology of Labor in the Early Republic.* New York: Oxford Univ. Press, 1990.

Bradstreet, Anne. *The Complete Works of Anne Bradstreet.* Edited by Joseph R. McElrath and Allan P. Robb. Boston: Twayne, 1981.

Braudel, Fernand. *The Structures of Everyday Life: Civilization and Capitalism 15th–18th Century.* New York: Harper and Row, 1981.

Breckenridge, Frances A. *Recollections of a New England Town.* Meriden, Conn.: Journal, 1899.

Brown, Harriet Connor. *Grandmother Brown's Hundred Years, 1827–1927.* Boston: Little, Brown, 1929.

Bruchey, Stuart. *The Roots of American Economic Growth, 1607–1861.* New York: Harper and Row, 1968.

Buffalo Import Co. Buffalo Cove, N.C. Home page. www.members.aol.com/buffaloimp. 7 May 1999.

Burnham, Mrs. Walter E., et al. *History and Tradition of Shelburne, Massachusetts.* Shelburne, Mass.: n.p., 1958.

Butterfield, L. H., ed. *Adams Family Correspondence.* Cambridge, Mass.: Harvard Univ. Press, 1963.

Carradine, Keith. "Personal Pleasures." *Los Angeles Times,* 24 Nov. 1985. On-line. Lexis-Nexis. 21 Jan. 1999.

Carroll, Charles F. *The Timber Economy of Puritan New England.* Providence, R.I.: Brown Univ. Press, 1973.

Cather, Willa. *My Ántonia.* 1918. Reprint. Boston: Houghton Mifflin, 1954.

Cheney, Mary Bushnell. *Life and Letters of Horace Bushnell.* 1880. Reprint. New York: Arno, 1969.

Child, Georgie Boynton. *The Efficient Kitchen.* New York: McBride, Nast, 1914.

Child, Lydia M. *The American Frugal Housewife.* Boston: Carter, Hendee, 1832.

———. *Lydia Maria Child: Selected Letters, 1817–1880.* Edited by Milton Meltzer and Patricia G. Holland. Amherst: Univ. of Massachusetts Press, 1982.

[Chilson, Gardner]. *Gardner Chilson, Inventor and Manufacturer of, and Dealer in, Heating, Cooking, and Ventilating Apparatus of Every Description.* Boston: Damrell and Moore, c. 1865, AAS.

Clark, Clifford E. *The American Family Home, 1800–1960.* Chapel Hill: Univ. of North Carolina Press, 1986.

———. "The Vision of the Dining Room: Plan Book Dreams and Middle-Class Realities." In *Dining in America, 1850–1900,* edited by Kathryn Grover, 142–72. Amherst: Univ. of Massachusetts Press, 1987.

Clark, H. Nichols B. *Francis W. Edmonds: American Master in the Dutch Tradition.* Washington, D.C.: Smithsonian Institution Press, 1988.

Bibliography

Clark, Jennifer. "The American Image of Technology from the Revolution to 1840."
American Quarterly 39 (1987): 431–49.

Clark, Victor S. *History of Manufactures in the United States, 1607–1860.* 1929. Reprint.
New York: Peter Smith, 1949.

Cleaveland, Henry W., et al. *Village and Farm Cottages.* 1856. Reprint. Watkins Glen,
N.Y.: American Life Foundation, 1982.

Cleland, Robert Glass, ed. *Apron Full of Gold: The Letters of Mary Jane Megquier from
San Francisco, 1849–1856.* San Marino, Cal.: Huntington Library, 1949.

Colt, Miriam Davis. *Went to Kansas; Being a Thrilling Account of an Ill-Fated Expedition.*
1862. Reprint. Ann Arbor, Mich.: University Microfilms, 1966.

Comenius, Johann Amos. *Orbis Sensualium Pictus.* 1658. Reprint. Detroit: Singing Tree,
1968.

Conklin, Henry. *Through "Poverty's Vale": A Hardscrabble Boyhood in Upstate New York,
1832–1862.* Syracuse, N.Y.: Syracuse Univ. Press, 1974.

Cookery As It Should Be. Philadelphia: Willis P. Hazard, 1853.

Cooper, Jane. *Woodstove Cookery: At Home on the Range.* Charlotte, Vt.: Garden Way,
1977.

Cooper, Susan Fenimore. *Rural Hours.* 1850. Reprint. Syracuse, N.Y.: Syracuse Univ.
Press, 1968.

Cooper, Thomas. *Some Information Respecting America.* 1794. Reprint. New York:
Augustus M. Kelley, 1969.

Cope, Thomas P. *Philadelphia Merchant: The Diary of Thomas P. Cope, 1800–1851.* Edited
by Eliza Cope Harrison. South Bend, Ind.: Gateway, 1978.

Cornelius, Mary H. *The Young Housekeeper's Friend.* Boston: Charles Tappan, 1846.

———. *The Young Housekeeper's Friend.* Boston: Brown and Taggard, 1860.

Corson, Juliet. *Everyday Cookery, Table Talk, and Hints for the Laundry.* Chicago: Adams
& Westlake Mfg. Co., 1884.

———. *Family Living on $500 a Year.* New York: Harper, 1888.

Cott, Nancy F. *The Bonds of Womanhood: "Woman's Sphere" in New England, 1780–1835.*
New Haven: Yale Univ. Press, 1977.

Cowan, Ruth Schwartz. "The Consumption Junction: A Proposal for Research Strategies
in the Sociology of Technology." In *The Social Construction of Technological Systems,*
edited by Wiebe E. Bijker et al., 261–80. Cambridge, Mass.: MIT Press, 1987.

———. "Ellen Swallow Richards: Technology and Women." In *Technology in America:
A History of Individuals and Ideas,* edited by Carroll W. Pursell Jr., 142–50. Cambridge, Mass.: MIT Press, 1981.

———. *More Work for Mother: The Ironies of Household Technology from the Open
Hearth to the Microwave.* New York: Basic Books, 1983.

———. *A Social History of American Technology.* New York: Oxford Univ. Press, 1997.

Cox, Thomas R., et al. *This Well-Wooded Land: Americans and Their Forests from Colonial Times to the Present.* Lincoln: Univ. of Nebraska Press, 1985.

Coxe, Tench. *A View of the United States.* 1794. Reprint. New York: Augustus M. Kelley,
1965.

Crane, Stephen. *Maggie: A Girl of the Streets.* 1893. Reprint. New York: Fawcett, 1960.

———. "The Stove." In *Whilomville Stories,* 120–40. 1900. Reprint. New York: Garrett, 1969.

Craw, Anita. *Wood Stove Cooking Adventures.* Orofino, Id.: Craws Wood Stoves, 1976.

Crawford, Byron. "Home on the Range: Old Stove Cooks up a Storm." *Courier-Journal,* 23 Nov. 1994. On-line. Lexis-Nexis. 21 Jan. 1999.

Cray, Robert. "Heating the Meeting: Pro-Stove and Anti-Stove Dynamic in Church Polity, 1783–1830." *Mid-America* 76 (1994): 93–107.

Cressy, David. *Coming Over: Migration and Communication Between England and New England in the Seventeenth Century.* New York: Cambridge Univ. Press, 1987.

Crèvecoeur, J. Hector St. John de. *Letters from an American Farmer.* 1782. Reprint. New York: Dutton, 1957.

Cronon, William. *Changes in the Land: Indians, Colonists, and the Ecology of New England.* New York: Hill and Wang, 1983.

Croy, Mae Savell. *Putnam's Household Handbook.* New York: G. P. Putnam's Sons, 1916.

Cummings, Abbott Lowell. *The Framed Houses of Massachusetts Bay, 1625–1725.* Cambridge, Mass.: Harvard Univ. Press, 1979.

———, ed. *Rural Household Inventories.* Boston: Society for the Preservation of New England Antiquities, 1964.

Curley, Suzanne. "Still Cooking: The Lure of Old Stoves." *Newsday,* 13 June 1996. On-line. Lexis-Nexis. 20 Jan. 1999.

Currier, W. A. *Catalog of W. A. Currier's Kitchen, House Furnishing, & Stove Warehouse.* Haverhill, Mass.: Eben H. Safford, c. 1861, AAS.

Davis, William T. *Plymouth Memories of an Octogenarian.* Plymouth, Mass.: Memorial, 1906.

Deetz, James. *In Small Things Forgotten: The Archeology of Early American Life.* Garden City, N.J.: Anchor, Doubleday, 1977.

Degler, Carl N. *At Odds: Women and the Family in America from the Revolution to the Present.* New York: Oxford Univ. Press, 1980.

Demos, John P. *A Little Commonwealth: Family Life in Plymouth Colony.* New York: Oxford Univ. Press, 1970.

Denison, Mary Andrews. *Orange Leaves.* Philadelphia: Lippincott, 1856.

de St. Mery, Moreau. *Moreau de St. Mery's American Journey.* Translated and edited by Kenneth Roberts and Anna M. Roberts. Garden City, N.J.: Doubleday, 1947.

Dirlam, H. Kenneth. *Baxter's Banner Stoves.* Mansfield, Ohio: n.p., 1969.

Douglas, Ann. *The Feminization of American Culture.* New York: Avon, 1977.

Downing, Andrew Jackson. *The Architecture of Country Houses.* 1850. Reprint. New York: Dover, 1969.

Drinker, Elizabeth. *The Diary of Elizabeth Drinker.* 3 vols. Edited by Elaine Forman Crane. Boston: Northeastern Univ. Press, 1991.

Bibliography

Duby, Georges, ed. *A History of Private Life: Revelations of the Medieval World.* Cambridge, Mass.: Harvard Univ. Press, 1988.

Dudden, Faye E. *Serving Women: Household Service in Nineteenth-Century America.* Middletown, Conn.: Wesleyan Univ. Press, 1983.

Dwight, Timothy. *The Major Poems of Timothy Dwight.* Edited by William J. McTaggart and William K. Bottorff. Gainesville, Fla.: Scholars' Facsimiles, 1969.

Dwyer, Jeremiah. "Stoves and Heating Apparatus." In *One Hundred Years of American Commerce.* 2 vols. Edited by Chauncey DePew, 2:357–63. New York: D. O. Haynes, 1895.

Earle, Alice Morse. *Home Life in Colonial Days.* 1898. Reprint. Stockbridge, Mass.: Berkshire Traveller, 1974.

Eastman, Sophie E. *In Old South Hadley.* Chicago: Blakely, 1912.

Edgerton, Samuel Y., Jr. "Heating Stoves in Eighteenth Century Philadelphia." *Bulletin of the Association for Preservation Technology* 3 (1971): 15–103.

Edwards, Jonathan. *Jonathan Edwards: Basic Writings.* Edited by Ola E. Winslow. New York: NAL, 1966.

Eighty Years of Progress in the United States. New York: L. Stebbins, 1861.

Ellet, Elizabeth F. *The Practical Housekeeper.* New York: Stringer and Townsend, 1857.

Ellis, Anne. *The Life of an Ordinary Woman.* 1929. Reprint. Lincoln: Univ. of Nebraska Press, 1980.

Elmira Stove Works. Waterloo, Ontario. Home page. www.elmirastoveworks.com. 13 May 1999.

Elmore, Mary Janette. *Long Hill: South Windsor, Connecticut.* South Windsor, Conn.: South Windsor Historical Society, 1976.

Emerson, Everett, ed. *Letters from New England.* Amherst: Univ. of Massachusetts Press, 1976.

Emerson, Ralph Waldo. *The Journals and Miscellaneous Notebooks of Ralph Waldo Emerson.* 14 vols. Edited by William H. Gilman et al. Cambridge, Mass.: Harvard Univ. Press, 1960–82.

Emery, Sarah Anna. *My Generation.* Newburyport, Mass.: M. H. Sargent, 1893.

———. *Reminiscences of a Nonagenarian.* Newburyport, Mass.: William H. Huse, 1879.

Farman, Ella. *The Cooking Club of Tu-Whit Hollow.* Boston: D. Lothrop, 1886.

Farmer, Silas. *History of Detroit and Wayne County and Early Michigan.* 1890. Reprint. Detroit: Gale, 1969.

Farnham, Eliza Woodson. *In-Doors and Out; Or, We Farm, Mine, and Live in the Golden State.* New York: Dix, Edwards, 1856.

———. *Life in Prairie Land.* 1846. Reprint. Urbana: Univ. of Illinois Press, 1988.

Farrar, S. D. *The Homekeeper.* Boston: n.p., 1872.

Fernald, James C. *The New Womanhood.* Boston: D. Lothrop, 1891.

Fessenden, Thomas G. *The Husbandman and Housewife.* Bellows Falls, Vt.: Bill Blake, 1820.

Field, Eugene. "Stoves and Sunshine." In *The Poems* (1922). On-line. LION. 22 Feb. 1999.

Fillmore, Millard. *Millard Fillmore Papers.* 2 vols. Edited by Frank H. Severance. Buffalo: Buffalo Historical Society, 1907.

Fisher, Sidney George. *A Philadelphia Perspective: The Diary of Sidney George Fisher.* Edited by Nicholas B. Wainwright. Philadelphia: Historical Society of Pennsylvania, 1967.

Florence Sewing Machine Co. *The Florence Oil Stoves for Cooking, Heating and Illuminating.* Florence, Mass.: n.p., c. 1880.

———. *Price List and Cooking Receipts for the Florence Oil Cooking and Heating Stoves.* Florence, Mass.: n.p., 1883.

Folsom, Michael Brewster, and Steven D. Lubar, eds. *The Philosophy of Manufactures: Early Debates over Industrialization in the United States.* Cambridge, Mass.: MIT Press, 1982.

Foxfire's Book of Wood Stove Cookery. Rabun Gap, Ga.: Foxfire Fund, 1981.

Franklin, Benjamin. *An Account of the New Invented Pennsylvania Fire-Places.* 1744. Reprint. New York: G. K. Hall, 1973.

———. *The Papers of Benjamin Franklin.* 27 vols. Edited by Leonard W. Labaree and William B. Willcox. New Haven: Yale Univ. Press, 1959–1988.

Frederick, Christine M. *The New Housekeeping: Efficiency Studies in Home Management.* Garden City, N.Y.: Doubleday, Page, 1913.

Freeman, Mary Wilkins. *Pembroke.* 1894. Reprint. New York: Harper and Bros., 1899.

French, Emily. *Emily: The Diary of a Hard-Worked Woman.* Edited by Janet Lecompte. Lincoln: Univ. of Nebraska Press, 1987.

Fuller, Warren, & Co. *P. P. Stewart's Large Oven Air-Tight Summer and Winter Cooking Stove.* Troy, N.Y.: n.p., 1863.

Furman, Bess. *White House Profile.* Indianapolis: Bobbs-Merrill, 1951.

Gardner, Eugene C. *Home Interiors.* Boston: James R. Osgood, 1878.

———. *Homes, and How to Make Them.* Boston: James R. Osgood, 1874.

Garland, Hamlin. *A Daughter of the Middle Border.* New York: Macmillan, 1923.

Garrett, Elisabeth Donaghy. *At Home: The American Family, 1750–1870.* New York: Harry N. Abrams, 1990.

Gibbs, S. W., & Co. *Price List of Stoves, Summer Ranges, Furnaces, Heaters.* New York: J. W. Orr, 1868.

Giedion, Siegfried. *Mechanization Takes Command: A Contribution to Anonymous History.* 1948. Reprint. New York: W. W. Norton, 1969.

Gilman, Caroline Howard. *Recollections of a Housekeeper.* New York: Harper, 1834.

Gilman, Charlotte Perkins. *The Home: Its Work and Influence.* 1903. Reprint. New York: Source Book, 1976.

———. *In This Our World.* 1893. Reprint. Boston: Small, Maynard, 1914.

Goodrich, Samuel G. *Fireside Education.* London, England: William Smith, 1839.

———. *Recollections of a Lifetime.* 2 vols. New York: Miller, Orton, and Mulligan, 1857.

Gordon, Robert B. *American Iron, 1607–1900.* Baltimore: Johns Hopkins Univ. Press, 1996.

Gould, Mary Earle. *The Early American House.* Rutland, Vt.: Charles E. Tuttle, 1965.

Bibliography

Graham, Sylvester. *A Treatise on Bread and Bread-Making.* Boston: Light and Stearns, 1837.

Greeley, Horace, et al. *The Great Industries of the United States.* Hartford, Conn.: J. R. Burr and Hyde, 1872.

Green, Harvey. *Fit for America: Health, Fitness, Sport, and American Society.* New York: Pantheon, 1986.

Greene, Jack P. *Pursuits of Happiness: The Social Development of Early Modern British Colonies and the Formation of American Culture.* Chapel Hill: Univ. of North Carolina Press, 1988.

———, ed. *Settlements to Society: A Documentary History of Colonial America.* New York: W. W. Norton, 1975.

Greenman & Northrup. *Stewart's Patent Summer and Winter Air-Tight Cooking Stoves.* Boston: n.p., 1844.

Griffin, S. G. *A History of the Town of Keene from 1732, When the Township Was Granted by Massachusetts, to 1874, When It Became a City.* Keene, N.H.: Sentinel, 1904.

Groft, Tammis Kane. *Cast with Style: Nineteenth Century Cast-Iron Stoves from the Albany Area.* Albany, N.Y.: Albany Institute of History and Art, 1981.

Hale, Sarah Josepha. *The Good Housekeeper; Or, The Way to Live Well and to Be Well While We Live.* Boston: Weeks, Jordan, 1839.

———. *Keeping House and Housekeeping.* New York: Harper, 1845.

———. *Mrs. Hale's New Cook Book.* Philadelphia: T. B. Peterson, 1857.

Hall, Abraham Oakey. *Old Whitey's Christmas Trot.* New York: Harper and Bros., 1857.

Halttunen, Karen. *Confidence Men and Painted Women: A Study of Middle-Class Culture in America, 1830–1870.* New Haven: Yale Univ. Press, 1982.

———. "From Parlor to Living Room: Domestic Space, Interior Decoration, and the Culture of Personality." In *Consuming Visions: Accumulation and Display of Goods in America, 1880–1920,* edited by Simon J. Bronner, 157–89. New York: W. W. Norton, 1989.

Hammond, Josiah H. *The Farmer's and Mechanic's Practical Architect.* Boston: John P. Jewett, 1858.

Hampsten, Elizabeth. *Read This Only to Yourself: The Private Writings of Midwestern Women, 1880–1910.* Bloomington: Indiana Univ. Press, 1982.

Handlin, David P. *The American Home: Architecture and Society, 1815–1915.* Boston: Little, Brown, 1979.

Hatch, Nathan O. *The Sacred Cause of Liberty: Republican Thought and the Millennium in Revolutionary New England.* New Haven: Yale Univ. Press, 1977.

Haven, Alice B. *The Coopers; Or, Getting Under Way.* New York: D. Appleton, 1858.

Hawthorne, Nathaniel. *The American Notebooks.* Edited by Claude M. Simpson. Vol. 8 of *The Centenary Edition of the Works of Nathaniel Hawthorne.* Columbus: Ohio State Univ. Press, 1972.

———. *The Letters, 1813–1843.* Edited by Thomas Woodson et al. Vol. 15 of *The Centenary Edition of the Works of Nathaniel Hawthorne.* Columbus: Ohio State Univ. Press, 1972.

————. *Nathaniel Hawthorne: Selected Tales and Sketches.* 3rd ed. Edited by Hyatt H. Waggoner. New York: Holt, Rinehart and Winston, 1970.

Hayden, Dolores. *The Grand Domestic Revolution.* Cambridge, Mass.: MIT Press, 1981.

Hazen, Margaret Hindle, and Robert M. Hazen. *Keepers of the Flame: The Role of Fire in American Culture.* Princeton, N.J.: Princeton Univ. Press, 1992.

Heartland Appliances. Kitchener, Ontario. "The Heartland Classic Collection." Unpaginated advertising brochure (1996). Sent to the author with price list, July 1998.

Henretta, James. *The Evolution of American Society, 1700–1815: An Interdisciplinary Analysis.* Lexington, Mass.: D. C. Heath, 1973.

Herman, Bernard L. *Architecture and Rural Life in Central Delaware, 1700–1900.* Knoxville: Univ. of Tennessee Press, 1987.

Hill, George Canning. *Dovecote; Or, The Heart of the Homestead.* Boston: John P. Jewett, 1854.

———— [pseud. Thomas Lackland]. *Homespun; Or, Five and Twenty Years Ago.* New York: Hurd and Houghton, 1867.

Historical Statistics of the United States: Colonial Times to 1957. Washington, D.C.: Government Printing Office, 1960.

History of Worcester County, Massachusetts. 2 vols. Boston: C. F. Jewett, 1879.

Hoar, George F. *A Boy Sixty Years Ago.* Boston: Perry Mason, 1898.

Hofstadter, Richard. *America at 1750: A Social Portrait.* New York: Vintage, Random House, 1971.

Hoglund, A. William. "Forest Conservation and Stove Inventors, 1789–1850." *Forest History* 5 (1962): 2–8.

Holley, Marietta. *My Opinions and Betsy Bobbet's.* Hartford, Conn.: American, 1875.

————. *My Wayward Pardner; Or, My Trials with Josiah, America, the Widow Bump, and Et cet ery.* Hartford, Conn.: American, 1881.

————. *Samantha among the Brethren.* New York: Funk and Wagnalls, 1892.

Holloway, Laura C. *The Hearthstone; Or, Life at Home.* Chicago: L. P. Miller, 1887.

Holmes, Kenneth L., ed. *Covered Wagon Women: Diaries and Letters from the Western Trails, 1840–1890.* 10 vols. Glendale, Calif.: Arthur H. Clark, 1983.

Holmes, Mary J. *'Lena Rivers.* 1856. Reprint. New York: Carleton, 1863.

Hopkins, Pauline E. "Sappho." In *Invented Lives: Narratives of Black Women, 1860–1960,* edited by Mary Helen Washington, 109–29. New York: Anchor, 1987.

Hopkins, Dr. T. and Mrs. L. A. *Science in the Kitchen; Or, the Art of Cooking in Everyday Life with the Economical Air Distending Cooking Powders.* Malden, Mass.: n.p., 1863.

The Housewife's Library. N.p.: n.p., 1892.

"How to Cook with a Wood Stove." On-line. www.freetechsupport.com/csr/woodcook. 13 May 1999.

Howe, Ann. *The American Kitchen Directory and Housewife.* Cincinnati: Howe's Subscription Book Concern, 1867.

Howland, Esther A. *The American Economical Housekeeper.* Cincinnati: H. W. Derby, 1845.

Bibliography

Hubka, Thomas C. *Big House, Little House, Back House, Barn: The Connected Farm Buildings of New England.* Hanover, N.H.: Univ. Press of New England, 1984.

Hunt, Gaillard, ed. *The First Forty Years of Washington Society in the Family Letters of Margaret Bayard Smith.* 1906. Reprint. New York: Frederick Ungar, 1965.

Huston, Paul G. *Around an Old Homestead: A Book of Memories.* Cincinnati: Jennings and Graham, 1906.

Ingraham, Frances. "New Stoves Come with Old Touches." *Arizona Republic,* 1 May 1999. On-line. Lexis-Nexis. 20 May 1999.

"Iron and Steel." Society for Industrial Archeology Data Sheet No. 4. Washington, D.C.: National Museum of American History, 1984.

Jackson, Edwin. "New England Stoves." *Old Time New England* 26 (1935): 55–64.

Janney, Asa Moore, and Werner L. Janney, eds. *John Jay Janney's Virginia: An American Farm Lad's Life in the Early 19th Century.* McLean, Va.: EPM, 1978.

Janson, Charles William. *The Stranger in America, 1793–1806.* 1807. Reprint. New York: Burt Franklin, 1971.

Jeffrey, Kirk. "The Family as Utopian Retreat from the City: The Nineteenth-Century Contribution." *Soundings* 55 (1972): 21–41.

Jensen, Joan M. *Loosening the Bonds: Mid-Atlantic Farm Women, 1750–1850.* New Haven: Yale Univ. Press, 1986.

Jewett, Sarah Orne. *A Country Doctor.* Boston: Houghton Mifflin, 1884.

Johns, Elizabeth. *American Genre Painting: The Politics of Everyday Life.* New Haven: Yale Univ. Press, 1991.

Johnson, Jane Eliza. *Newtown's History and Historian Ezra Levan Johnson.* Newtown, Conn.: n.p., 1917.

Jones, Alice Hanson. *American Colonial Wealth: Documents and Methods.* New York: Arno, 1977.

Jones, Alice J. *In Dover on the Charles.* Newport, R.I.: Milne, 1906.

Jones, Judy. "Year 2000 Problem Generates Alarm." *Courier-Journal,* 15 Mar. 1999. On-line. Lexis-Nexis. 7 May 1999.

Jones, Louis C., ed. *Growing Up in the Cooper Country: Boyhood Recollections of the New York Frontier.* Syracuse, N.Y.: Syracuse Univ. Press, 1965.

Judd, Sylvester. *History of Hadley Including the Early History of Hatfield, South Hadley, Amherst, and Granby, Massachusetts.* Springfield, Mass.: H. R. Huntting, 1905.

Judson, Phoebe Newton. *A Pioneer's Search for an Ideal Home.* Bellingham, Wash.: Union, 1925.

Kalm, Peter. *Peter Kalm's Travels in North America.* 2 vols. Translated and edited by Adolph B. Benson. New York: Dover, 1966.

Kasson, John F. *Civilizing the Machine: Technology and Republican Values in America, 1776–1900.* New York: Penguin, 1977.

Katzman, David M. *Seven Days a Week: Women and Domestic Service in Industrializing America.* Urbana: Univ. of Illinois Press, 1981.

Kauffman, Henry J. *The American Fireplace.* Nashville, Tenn.: Thos. Nelson, 1972.

———. *Early American Ironware.* Rutland, Vt: Charles E. Tuttle, 1966.

Keep, William J. "Early American Cooking Stoves." *Old Time New England* 22 (1931): 70–87.

Kelley, Mary. "The Sentimentalists: Promise and Betrayal in the Home." *Signs* 4 (1979): 434–46.

Keokuk Antique Stoves. Hamilton, Ill. Home page. www.keokukstoveworks.com. 13 May 1999.

Killion, Ronald, and Charles Waller, eds. *Slavery Time When I Was Chillun Down on Marster's Plantation.* Savannah: Beehive, 1973.

King, Caroline Howard. *When I Lived in Salem, 1822–1866.* Brattleboro, Vt.: Stephen Day, 1937.

Kinne, Helen, and Anna M. Cooley. *Foods and Household Management.* New York: Macmillan, 1915.

Kirkland, Caroline M. *A New Home, Who'll Follow? Or, Glimpses of Western Life.* 1839. Reprint. New Brunswick, N.J.: Rutgers Univ. Press, 1990.

Kittredge, Mabel Hyde. *Practical Homemaking.* New York: Century Co., 1915.

Koren, Elisabeth Hysing. *The Diary of Elisabeth Koren.* Translated and edited by David T. Nelson. Northfield, Minn.: Norwegian-American Historical Association, 1955.

Kraditor, Aileen. *Up from the Pedestal: Selected Writings in the History of American Feminism.* New York: Quadrangle, *New York Times,* 1968.

Kupperman, Karen Ordahl. "Climate and Mastery of the Wilderness in Seventeenth-Century New England." In *Seventeenth-Century New England,* edited by David D. Hall and David Grayson Allen, 3–37. Boston: Colonial Society of Massachusetts, 1984.

Ladd, Paul R. *Early American Fireplaces.* New York: Hastings House, 1977.

Langton, Anne. *A Gentlewoman in Upper Canada: The Journals of Anne Langton.* Edited by H. H. Langton. Toronto: Clarke, Irwin, 1950.

Larcom, Lucy. *A New England Girlhood.* Boston: Houghton Mifflin, 1889.

Larkin, Jack. *The Reshaping of Everyday Life, 1790–1840.* New York: Harper and Row, 1988.

Lea, Elizabeth E. *Domestic Cookery.* Baltimore: Cushing, 1846.

Leggett, M. D., comp., *Subject Matter Index of Patents for Inventions Issued by the United States Patent Office from 1790 to 1873, Inclusive.* 3 vols. Washington, D.C.: Government Printing Office, 1874.

Lehman's Hardware. Kidron, Ohio. Home page. www.lehmans.com. 3 June 1999.

Lensink, Judy Nolte. *"A Secret to Be Burried": The Diary and Life of Emily Hawley Gillespie, 1858–1888.* Iowa City: Univ. of Iowa Press, 1989.

Leslie, Eliza. *The House Book; Or, A Manual of Domestic Economy.* Philadelphia: Carey and Hart, 1841.

Lewis, W. David. *Iron and Steel in America.* Greenville, Del.: Hagley Museum, 1976.

Lippert, Tom, and Laurel Hilde Lippert. *The Woodstove Cookery Book.* Truckee, Calif.: Tulip, 1980.

Lipsett, Linda Otto. *Pieced from Ellen's Quilt: Ellen Spaulding Reed's Letters and Story.* Dayton, Ohio: Halstead and Meadows, 1991.

Bibliography

A List of Patents Granted by the United States from April 10, 1790, to December 31, 1836. Washington, D.C.: Government Printing Office, 1872.

Littlefield Stove Manufacturing Co. *The Morning Glory Hot-Blast Cooking Stove.* Albany, N.Y.: n.p., 1874.

Livermore, Mary A. *The Story of My Life.* Hartford, Conn.: A. D. Worthington, 1897.

Logan, Ben. *The Land Remembers: The Story of a Farm and Its People.* 1975. Reprint. Minnetonka, Minn.: Northword, 1999.

Longon, Jean, and Raymond Cazelles, eds. *Très Riches Heures of Jean, Duke of Berry.* New York: George Braziller, 1989.

Lowell, James Russell. *The Biglow Papers, 2nd Series.* 1866. Reprint. New York: AMS, 1973.

Luchetti, Cathy. *Home on the Range: A Culinary History of the American West.* New York: Villard, 1993.

Lunt, George [pseud. Wesley Brooke]. *Eastford; Or, Household Sketches.* Boston: Crocker and Brewster, 1855.

Lyman, Joseph B., and Laura E. Lyman. *The Philosophy of Housekeeping.* Hartford, Conn.: Goodwin and Betts, 1867.

Lynd, Robert S., and Helen Merrell Lynd. *Middletown: A Study in American Culture.* 1929. Reprint. New York: Harcourt, Brace, 1956.

Lynes, Russell. *The Domesticated Americans.* New York: Harper and Row, 1957.

Maass, John. *The Victorian Home in America.* New York: Hawthorn Books, 1972.

MacArthur, Margaret. *An Almanac of New England Farm Songs.* New Canaan, Conn.: Green Linnet Records, 1982.

Main, Gloria L. "Probate Records as a Source for Early American History." *William and Mary Quarterly,* 3rd ser., 32 (1975): 89–99.

Martin, Edgar W. *The Standard of Living in 1860.* Chicago: Univ. of Chicago Press, 1942.

Mather, Cotton. *Diary of Cotton Mather.* 2 vols. New York: Frederick Ungar, 1957.

Matthews, Jean V. *Toward a New Society: American Thought and Culture, 1800–1830.* Boston: Twayne, 1991.

Mercer, Henry C., et al. *The Bible in Iron: Pictured Stoves and Stoveplates of the Pennsylvania Germans.* Doylestown, Penn.: Bucks County Historical Society, 1961.

Miller, Elizabeth S. *In the Kitchen.* Boston: Lee and Shepard, 1875.

Miller, Lillian B., ed. *The Selected Papers and Letters of Charles Willson Peale and His Family,* 2 vols. New Haven: Yale Univ. Press, 1988.

Miller, Mike. E-mail to the author. 7 May 1999.

Moltmann, Gunther, ed. *Germans to America: 300 Years of Immigration, 1683–1983.* Stuttgart, Germany: Institute for Foreign Cultural Relations, 1982.

Montgomery Ward & Co. *Catalogue No. 57.* 1895. Reprint. New York: Dover, 1969.

Moore, Melissa Anderson. *The Story of a Kansas Pioneer.* Mt. Vernon, Ohio: Manufacturing Printers, 1924.

Moryson, Fynes. *An Itinerary.* 1617. Reprint. New York: Da Capo, 1971.

[Moulton], Ellen Louise Chandler. *This, That, and the Other.* Boston: Phillips, Sampson and Co., 1854.

Moultrie, Lynda. *The Antique Kitchen Range Bible.* Georgetown, Mass.: A.B.A. Printing, 1984.

Mulder, William, and A. Russell Mortensen, eds. *Among the Mormons: Historical Accounts by Contemporary Observers.* New York: Knopf, 1958.

Mundy, Peter. *The Travels of Peter Mundy in Europe and Asia, 1608–1667.* 4 vols. Edited by Richard C. Temple. London: Hakluyt Society, 1907–1925.

Myres, Sandra L. *Westering Women and the Frontier Experience, 1800–1915.* Albuquerque: Univ. of New Mexico Press, 1982.

Naeve, Milo M. *John Lewis Krimmel: An Artist in Federal America.* Newark: Univ. of Delaware Press, 1987.

Nash, Gary B. *Red, White, and Black: The Peoples of Early America.* 3rd ed. Englewood Cliffs, N.J.: Prentice Hall, 1992.

———. *The Urban Crucible: Social Change, Political Consciousness, and the Origins of the American Revolution.* Cambridge, Mass.: Harvard Univ. Press, 1979.

National Park Service. *Benjamin Franklin's "Good House."* Washington, D.C.: Government Printing Office, 1981.

New-York Annual Advertiser. New York: n.p., 1820.

Nicholson, Elizabeth. *The Economical Cook and House Book.* Philadelphia: Willis P. Hazard, 1857.

Nourse, Henry S., ed. *The Birth, Marriage, and Death Register, Church Records and Epitaphs of Lancaster, Massachusetts.* Lancaster, Mass.: W. J. Coulter, 1890.

Nye, David E. *Electrifying America: Social Meanings of a New Technology, 1880–1940.* Cambridge, Mass.: MIT Press, 1990.

Nye, Edgar Wilson. *Bill Nye and Boomerang; Or, The Tale of the Meek-Eyed Mule, and Some Other Literary Gems.* 1881. Reprint. St. Clair Shores, Mich.: Scholarly, 1971.

Nylander, Jane C. *Our Own Snug Fireside: Images of the New England Home, 1760–1860.* New York: Knopf, 1993.

———. "Toward Comfort and Uniformity in New England Meeting Houses, 1750–1850." In *New England Meeting House and Church: 1630–1850,* edited by Peter Benes, 86–100. Boston: Boston Univ.: 1979.

O'Briant, Don. "Wood Stoves: There's More to a Warm Kitchen Than the Modern Electric Range." *Atlanta Journal and Constitution,* 7 Feb. 1993. On-line. Lexis-Nexis. 21 Jan. 1999.

Olmsted, Denison. "Observations on the Use of Anthracite Coal." In *The American Almanac and Repository of Useful Knowledge for the Year 1837,* 61–69. Boston: Chas. Bowen, 1837.

O'Meara, Carra Ferguson. "'In the Hearth of the Virginal Womb': The Iconography of the Holocaust in Late Medieval Art." *Art Bulletin* 63, no. 1 (1981): 75–87.

Orr, Mrs. N. *DeWitt's Connecticut Cook Book and Housekeeper's Assistant.* New York: Robert M. DeWitt, 1871.

Bibliography

Parloa, Maria. *Miss Parloa's New Cook Book and Marketing Guide.* Boston: Estes and Lauriat, 1880.

Parton, Sara P. W. [pseud. Fanny Fern]. *Fanny Fern's Family Cook Book.* Philadelphia: William Fleming, 1856.

Paskoff, Paul F. *Industrial Evolution: Organization, Structure, and Growth of the Pennsylvania Iron Industry, 1750–1860.* Baltimore: Johns Hopkins Univ. Press, 1983.

Pattison, Mary Stranahan. *Principles of Domestic Engineering.* New York: Trow, 1915.

Paxton, John Adams. *Paxton's Annual Philadelphia Directory and Register.* Philadelphia: John A. Paxton, 1819.

Peirce, Josephine H. *Fire on the Hearth: The Evolution and Romance of the Heating Stove.* Springfield, Mass.: Pond-Ekberg, 1951.

Pelton, Beulah Meier. *We Belong to the Land; Memories of a Midwesterner.* Ames: Iowa State Univ. Press, 1984.

Perry & Co. *Price List of the Oriental and American Stove Works.* Albany, N.Y.: Weed, Parsons & Co., c. 1869, AAS.

Pessen, Edward. *Jacksonian America: Society, Personality, and Politics.* Urbana: Univ. of Illinois Press, 1985.

Pfister, Joel. "A Garden in the Machine: Reading a Mid-19th-Century, Two-Cylinder Parlor Stove as Cultural Text." *Technology and Society* 13 (1991): 327–43.

Phipps, Frances. *Colonial Kitchens, Their Furnishings, and Their Gardens.* New York: Hawthorn, 1972.

Pintard, John. *Letters from John Pintard to His Daughter.* 4 vols. New York: New York Historical Society, 1941.

Plain Talk and Friendly Advice to Domestics, with Counsel on Home Matters. Boston: Phillips, Sampson, 1855.

Plummer, John. *The Book of Hours of Catherine of Cleves.* New York: Pierpont Morgan Library, 1964.

Pool, J. Lawrence. *America's Valley Forges and Furnaces.* Dalton, Mass.: Studley, 1982.

Pounds, Norman J. G. *Hearth and Home: A History of Material Culture.* Bloomington: Indiana Univ. Press, 1989.

Powell, H. Benjamin. *Philadelphia's First Fuel Crisis: Jacob Cist and the Developing Market for Pennsylvania Anthracite.* University Park: Pennsylvania State Univ. Press, 1978.

Powell, Sumner Chilton. *Puritan Village: The Formation of a New England Town.* Middletown, Conn.: Wesleyan Univ. Press, 1963.

Pratt & Wentworth. *"Peerless," The Best Cooking Stove Ever Made.* Boston: Marvin and Son, 1866.

Presper, Mary Lenore. *The Joys of Woodstoves and Fireplaces.* New York: Grosset and Dunlap, 1980.

Proper, David R. "The Fireplace at Memorial Hall, Deerfield, Massachusetts: Picturesque Arrangements; Tender Associations." In *Foodways in the Northeast,* edited by Peter Benes, 114–29. Boston: Boston Univ., 1984.

Providence Almanac and Business Directory. Providence, R.I.: Benjamin F. Moore, 1843.

———. Providence, R.I.: John F. Moore, 1846.

Providence Annual Advertiser. Providence, R.I.: n.p., 1832.

Providence Directory. Providence, R.I.: n.p., 1824.

———. Providence, R.I.: n.p., 1832.

———. Providence, R.I.: n.p., 1860.

———. Providence, R.I.: n.p., 1861.

Rawick, George P., ed. *The American Slave: A Composite Autobiography.* 18 vols. 1941. Reprint. Westport, Conn.: Greenwood, 1972.

Report of the Commissioner of Patents. Washington, D.C.: Government Printing Office, 1845.

———. Washington, D.C.: Government Printing Office, 1846.

Restino, Susan. *Mrs. Restino's Country Kitchen.* Bolinas, Calif.: Shelter, 1996.

Reynolds, David S. *Beneath the American Renaissance: The Subversive Imagination in the Age of Emerson and Melville.* New York: Knopf, 1988.

Richardson, Dorothy. *The Long Day: The Story of a New York Working Girl.* 1905. Reprint. Charlottesville: Univ. Press of Virginia, 1990.

Robbins, Thomas. *Diary of Thomas Robbins, D.D., 1796–1854.* 2 vols. Edited by Increase N. Tarbox. Boston: Beacon, 1886–87.

Robbins, Vesta. *No Coward Soul.* Ames: Iowa State Univ. Press, 1974.

Roberts, Katherine Anne. "Hearth and Soul: The Fireplace in American Culture." Ph.D. diss., Univ. of Minnesota, 1990.

Roberts, Robert. *The House Servant's Directory.* 1827. Reprint. Waltham, Mass.: Gore Place Society, 1977.

Robinson, Solon. Address, American Institute of the City of New York. In *Transactions of the American Institute of the City of New York for the Years 1859–60,* 281–82. Albany, N.Y.: C. Van Benthuysen, 1860.

———. *How to Live: Saving and Wasting; Or, Domestic Economy Illustrated.* New York: Fowler and Wells, 1860.

Rodman, Samuel. *The Diary of Samuel Rodman.* Edited by Zephaniah Pease. New Bedford, Mass.: Reynolds, 1927.

Rollins, Ellen H. [pseud. E. H. Arr]. *New England Bygones.* 1883. Reprint. Stockbridge, Mass.: Berkshire Traveller, 1977.

Ropes, Hannah Anderson. *Six Months in Kansas, By a Lady.* Boston: John P. Jewett, 1856.

Rorer, Sarah Tyson. *Mrs. Rorer's New Cook Book.* 1898. Reprint. New York: Crown, 1970.

Rose, Mark H. *Cities of Light and Heat: Domesticating Gas and Electricity in Urban America.* University Park: Pennsylvania State Univ. Press, 1995.

Royce, Sarah Bayliss. *A Frontier Lady: Recollections of the Gold Rush and Early California.* New Haven: Yale Univ. Press, 1932.

Russell, Howard S. *A Long, Deep Furrow: Three Centuries of Farming in New England.* Hanover, N.H.: Univ. Press of New England, 1982.

Russell, Loris S. *Handy Things to Have Around the House: Oldtime Domestic Appliances of Canada and the United States.* Toronto, Canada: McGraw-Hill Ryerson, 1979.

Ryan, Mary P. *Cradle of the Middle Class: The Family in Oneida County, New York, 1790–1865.* Cambridge, England: Cambridge Univ. Press, 1981.

Bibliography

————. *Womanhood in America from Colonial Times to the Present.* 2d ed. New York: New Viewpoints, 1979.

Rybczynski, Witold. *Home: A Short History of an Idea.* New York: Viking Penguin, 1986.

Samuel, Laurie, and Craig Samuel. "The Joys of the Wood Cookstove." *Countryside and Small Stock Journal* (May 1994). On-line. Lexis-Nexis. 21 Jan. 1999.

Sanford, Mollie Dorsey. *Mollie: The Journal of Mollie Dorsey Sanford in Nebraska and Colorado Territories, 1857–1866.* Lincoln: Univ. of Nebraska Press, 1959.

Sanger, Abner. *Very Poor and of a Lo Make: The Journal of Abner Sanger.* Edited by Lois K. Stabler. Portsmouth, N.H.: Peter E. Randall, 1986.

Schlissel, Lillian. *Women's Diaries of the Westward Journey.* New York: Schocken, 1982.

Schoepf, Johann David. *Travels in the Confederation.* 2 vols. Translated and edited by Alfred J. Morrison. New York: Bergman, 1968.

Seale, William. *The Tasteful Interlude: American Interiors Through the Camera's Eye, 1860–1917.* 2d ed. Nashville, Tenn.: American Association for State and Local History, 1981.

Sears, Roebuck & Co. *Catalogue.* 1902. Reprint. New York: Dover, 1969.

Sedgwick, Catherine M. *Married or Single?* 2 vols. New York: Harper, 1857.

Sellers, Charles. *The Market Revolution: Jacksonian America, 1815–1846.* New York: Oxford Univ. Press, 1991.

Sewall, Samuel. *The Diary of Samuel Sewall.* 2 vols. Edited by M. Halsey Thomas. New York: Farrar, Straus and Giroux, 1973.

Shammas, Carole. "The Domestic Environment in Early Modern England and America." *Journal of Social History* 14, no. 1 (1980): 3–24.

Shaw, William F. *Illustrated and Descriptive Catalogue of Gas Heating and Cooking Apparatus.* Boston: Damrell and Moore, c. 1860, AAS.

Shear, Packard & Co. *The American Hot Air, Gas Burning Cooking Stove.* Albany, N.Y.: C. Van Benthuysen, 1863.

Shepard, Thomas. *The Works of Thomas Shepard, First Pastor of the First Church, Cambridge, Mass..* 3 vols. 1853. Reprint. New York: AMS, 1967.

Shippen, Nancy. *Nancy Shippen: Her Journal Book.* Edited by Ethel Armes. Philadelphia: J. B. Lippincott, 1935.

Silverman, Kenneth, ed. *Colonial American Poetry.* New York: Hafner, 1968.

Sklar, Kathryn Kish. *Catharine Beecher: A Study in American Domesticity.* New York: W. W. Norton, 1976.

Smallzreid, Kathleen Ann. *The Everlasting Pleasure: Influences on America's Kitchens, Cooks, and Cookery, from 1565 to the Year 2000.* New York: Appleton-Century-Crofts, 1956.

Smiley's Cook Book and Universal Household Guide. Chicago: Smiley, 1894.

Smith, Billy G. *The "Lower Sort": Philadelphia's Laboring People, 1750–1800.* Ithaca, N.Y.: Cornell Univ. Press, 1990.

Smith, Daniel Scott. "Underregistration and Bias in Probate Records: An Analysis of Data from Eighteenth-Century Hingham, Massachusetts." *William and Mary Quarterly,* 3rd ser., 32 (1975): 100–110.

Smith, Frank. *A History of Dover, Massachusetts, as a Precinct, Parish, District, and Town.* Dover, Mass.: by the town, 1897.

Smith, John. *Advertisements for the Planters of New-England.* 1631. Reprint. New York: Da Capo, 1971.

Standard Gas Equipment Co. *How to Plan the New Style Kitchen.* New York: n.p., 1926.

Stanley, M. N., & Co. *Remarks and Directions for Using Stanley's Patented Rotary Cooking Stove.* New York: G. F. Bunce, 1835.

Stanton, Elizabeth Cady. *Eighty Years and More (1815–1897).* New York: European, 1898.

Stephens, Ann Sophia. *Fashion and Famine.* New York: Bunce, 1854.

———. *The Old Homestead.* Philadelphia: T. B. Peterson, 1855.

Stilgoe, John R. *Common Landscape of America, 1580 to 1845.* New Haven: Yale Univ. Press, 1982.

Stockton, Frank R., and Marian Stockton. *The Home: Where It Should Be and What to Put in It.* New York: G. P. Putnam's, 1873.

Stone, Lawrence. *The Family, Sex, and Marriage in England, 1500–1800.* New York: Harper and Row, 1977.

Stowe, Harriet Beecher [pseud. Christopher Crowfield]. *House and Home Papers.* Boston: Ticknor and Fields, 1865.

———. *The Minister's Wooing.* 1859. Reprint. Hartford, Conn.: Stowe-Day Foundation, 1978.

———. *Oldtown Folks.* Boston: Fields, Osgood, 1869.

———. *Uncle Tom's Cabin.* 1852. Reprint. New York: Dodd, Mead, 1952.

Strasser, Susan. *Never Done: A History of American Housework.* New York: Pantheon, 1982.

———. "Never Done: The Ideology and Technology of Household Work, 1850–1930." Ph.D. diss., State Univ. of New York at Stony Brook, 1977.

Strathdee, Mike. "Canadian Cookstoves Hot Property in Hollywood," *Toronto Star,* 15 June 1992. On-line. Lexis-Nexis. 21 Jan. 1999.

Stratton-Porter, Gene. *Michael O'Halloran.* Garden City, N.Y.: Doubleday, Page, 1915.

Stuart Letters of Robert and Elizabeth Sullivan Stuart and Their Children, 1819–1864. 2 vols. N.p.: n.p., 1961.

Sutherland, Daniel E. *Americans and Their Servants: Domestic Service in the United States from 1800 to 1920.* Baton Rouge: Louisiana State Univ. Press, 1981.

———. *The Expansion of Everyday Life: 1860–1876.* New York: Harper and Row, 1989.

———. "'The Stranger in the Gates': Employer Reactions Toward Domestic Servants in America, 1825–1875." Ph.D. diss., Michigan State Univ., 1969.

Sweeney, Kevin M. "Furniture and the Domestic Environment in Wethersfield, Connecticut, 1639–1800." In *Material Life in America, 1600–1800,* edited by Robert Blair St. George, 261–90. Boston: Northeastern Univ. Press, 1988.

Swett, Quimby & Perry. *The New Empire Hot-Air, Gas, and Base-burning Cooking Stove, for Wood and Coal, with Hawks' Auxiliary Air-Chamber.* Troy, N.Y.: n.p., 1869.

Taylor, Edward. *The Poems of Edward Taylor.* Edited by Donald E. Stanford. New Haven: Yale Univ. Press, 1960.

Bibliography

Temple, Josiah H. *History of the Town of Whately, Mass., Including a Narrative of the Leading Events from the First Planting of Hatfield, 1660–1871.* Boston: T. R. Marvin and Son, 1872.

Thompson, Benjamin (Count Rumford). *The Complete Works of Count Rumford.* 4 vols. Boston: American Academy of Arts and Sciences, 1875.

Thoreau, Henry David. *Walden: A Writer's Edition.* Edited by Larzer Ziff. New York: Holt, Rinehart and Winston, 1961.

Toussaint, Tennie Gaskill. "Danville—and Its Two Centuries." *Vermont History* 23 (1955): 204–15.

Trollope, Frances. *The Domestic Manners of the Americans.* 1832. Reprint. London: Century, 1984.

Tuveson, Ernest Lee. *Redeemer Nation: The Idea of America's Millennial Role.* Chicago: Univ. of Chicago Press, 1968.

Twedt, Jerry L. *Growing Up in the 40s: Rural Reminiscence.* Ames: Iowa State Univ. Press, 1996.

Tyler, John D. "Technological Development: Agent of Change in Style and Form of Domestic Iron Castings." In *Technological Innovation and the Decorative Arts,* edited by Ian M. G. Quimby and Polly Anne Earl, 141–65. Charlottesville: Univ. Press of Virginia, 1973.

Tyler, Mary Palmer. *Grandmother Tyler's Book: The Recollections of Mary Palmer Tyler, 1775–1866.* Edited by Frederick Tupper and Helen Tyler Brown. New York: G. P. Putnam's Sons, 1925.

Underwood, Francis H. *Quabbin: The Story of a Small Town with Outlooks upon Puritan Life.* 1893. Reprint. Boston: Northeastern Univ. Press, 1986.

U.S. Department of Agriculture. *Domestic Needs of Farm Women.* Washington, D.C.: Government Printing Office, 1915.

Waite, John G., and Diana S. Waite. "Stovemakers of Troy, New York." *Antiques* 103 (1973): 136–44.

Walkowitz, Daniel J. *Worker City, Company Town: Iron and Cotton-Worker Protest in Troy and Cohoes, New York, 1855–84.* Urbana: Univ. of Illinois Press, 1978.

Ware, John F. W. *Home Life: What It Is, and What It Needs.* Boston: W. V. Spencer, 1864.

Warner, Anne S. "Tribute to an Old Friend; the Wood-burning Kitchen Range." *Country Journal* (19 Sept. 1997). On-line. Lexis-Nexis. 21 Jan. 1999.

Warner, Susan. [pseud. Elizabeth Wetherell]. *Queechy.* 2 vols. New York: George P. Putnam, 1852.

———. *What She Could.* New York: Williams, 1870.

———. *The Wide, Wide World.* 1850. Reprint. New York: Feminist, 1987.

Washington, George. *The Writings of George Washington.* 39 vols. Edited by John C. Fitzpatrick. Washington, D.C.: Government Printing Office, 1941.

Watson, John F. *Annals of Philadelphia and Pennsylvania in the Olden Time.* 2 vols. Philadelphia: Elijah Thomas, 1857.

Webster, Thomas, and Frances B. Parkes. *The American Family Encyclopedia.* New York: J. C. Derby, 1854.

Wells, Robert V. *Revolutions in Americans' Lives: A Demographic Perspective on the History of Americans, Their Families, and Their Society.* Westport, Conn.: Greenwood, 1982.

Welter, Barbara. "The Cult of True Womanhood, 1820–1860." In *The American Family in Social-Historical Perspective,* 2d ed., edited by Michael Gordon, 313–33. New York: St. Martin's, 1978.

White, Frank G. "Cookstoves: A Cure for Smoking Houses and Scolding Wives." *Early American Life* 26 (Apr. 1995). On-line. Lexis-Nexis. 21 Jan. 1999.

———. "Stoves in Nineteenth-Century New England." *Antiques* 116 (1979): 592–99.

Whitney, Adeline D. T. *Homespun Yarns.* Boston: Houghton, Mifflin, 1887.

———. *Just How: A Key to the Cook-Books.* Boston: Houghton, Osgood, 1880.

———. *We Girls: A Home Story.* Boston: James R. Osgood, 1871.

Whittier, John Greenleaf. *The Complete Poetical Works of Whittier.* Edited by Horace E. Scudder. Boston: Houghton Mifflin, 1894.

Wilde, Oscar. "The Practical Application of the Principles of the Aesthetic Theory to Exterior and Interior House Decoration." In *The Essays of Oscar Wilde,* 485–96. New York: Albert and Charles Boni, 1935.

Williams, Michael. *Americans and Their Forests: A Historical Geography.* Cambridge, England: Cambridge Univ. Press, 1989.

Willich, A. F. M. *The Domestic Encyclopedia; Or, A Dictionary of Facts and Useful Knowledge Chiefly Applicable to Rural and Domestic Economy.* 3 vols. Philadelphia: Abraham Small, 1821.

Wilson, Luzena Stanley. *Luzena Stanley Wilson '49er.* Oakland, Calif.: Mills College, Eucalyptus, 1937.

Winthrop, John. *History of New England.* 2 vols. New York: Scribner's, 1908.

———. *Papers.* 5 vols. Boston: Massachusetts Historical Society, 1929–47.

Wood, William. *New England's Prospect.* 1634. Reprint. New York: Da Capo, 1968.

Wright, Gwendolyn. *Building the Dream: A Social History of Housing in America.* New York: Pantheon, 1981.

———. *Moralism and the Model Home: Domestic Architecture and Cultural Conflict in Chicago, 1873–1913.* Chicago: Univ. of Chicago Press, 1980.

Wright, Lawrence. *Home Fires Burning: The History of Domestic Heating and Cooking.* London: Routledge and Kegan Paul, 1964.

Young, Alexander, ed. *Chronicles of the First Planters of the Colony of Massachusetts Bay, 1623–1636.* 1846. Reprint, New York: Da Capo, 1970.

Young, Carrie. *Nothing to Do But Stay.* New York: Dell, 1991.

Newspapers and Periodicals

American Journal of Science and Arts
American Ladies' Magazine
American Magazine
Annals of the American Academy of Political and Social Sciences

Bibliography

Atlantic Monthly
Ballou's Pictorial
Boston Globe
Connecticut Courant
The Day's Doings
The Dial
Electricity on the Farm
Forbes
Franklin Herald
Godey's Lady's Book
Good Housekeeping
Greenfield Gazette and Franklin Herald
Harper's Bazaar
Harper's New Monthly Magazine
Hartford Times
The Horticulturalist
The Household
Journal of the Franklin Institute
Ladies' Home Journal
Leslie's New York Journal
Maine Life
Massachusetts Spy
Mother Earth News
New England Farmer
New Genesee Farmer, and Gardener's Journal
New York Journal of Medicine
New York Times
Newsweek
Niles' Weekly Register
The Outlook
Pennsylvania Gazette
Providence Journal
Rhode Island American
St. Petersburg Times
Scientific American
Scribner's Magazine
Scribner's Monthly
Shenandoah
Union Magazine of Literature and Art
Wood's Household Magazine
World's Columbian Exposition Illustrated

Index

Italic page number denotes illustration.

Index

Index

Index

Index

Index

Index

Index